P9-CIU-603

01733369

RC 531 .A637 1992
Anxiety : recent

173336

DATE DUE

MAR - 8	
MAR 2 2 1994	JAN 2 6 2001
APR 1 1 1994	JUN 2 6 2001
DEC _ 3 1994	NOV 2 0 2003
JAN 2 6 1995	
FEB 1 0 1995	
FEB 2 6 1995	
MAR - 9 1995	
APR 2 1 1995	
OCT 1 0 1995	
OCT 2 4 1995	
OCT 2 6 1995	
Nov 7/95	
OCT 1 7 1996	
FEB - 4 1997	
FEB 1 4 1997	
MAY 2 9 1997	
NOV 1 2 1997	
FEB - 3 1998	
MAR 1 6 2000	

BRODART   Cat. No. 23-221

ANXIETY

The Series in Health Psychology and Behavioral Medicine

Charles D. Spielberger, *Editor-in-Chief*

Byrne, Rosenman Anxiety and the Heart
Chesney, Rosenman Anger and Hostility in Cardiovascular and Behavioral
  Disorders
Elias, Marshall Cardiovascular Disease and Behavior
Forgays, Sosnowski, Wrzesniewski Anxiety: Recent Developments in Cognitive,
  Psychophysiological, and Health Research
Hackfort, Spielberger Anxiety in Sports: An International Perspective
Hobfoll The Ecology of Stress
Johnson, Gentry, Julius Personality, Elevated Blood Pressure, and Essential
  Hypertension
Lamal Behavioral Analysis of Societies and Cultural Practices
Lonetto, Templer Death Anxiety
Morgan, Goldston Exercise and Mental Health
Pancheri, Zichella Biorhythms and Stress in the Physiopathology
  of Reproduction
Sartorius et al. Anxiety: Psychobiological and Clinical Perspectives
Seligson, Peterson AIDS Prevention and Treatment: Hope, Humor, and Healing

IN PREPARATION

Elias, Robbins, Elias, Streeten, Anderson Behavioral Consequences of
  Antihypertensive Drugs
Gilbert Smoking, Personality, and Emotion

OKANAGAN UNIVERSITY COLLEGE
LIBRARY
BRITISH COLUMBIA

ANXIETY:
Recent Developments in Cognitive, Psychophysiological, and Health Research

Edited by
Donald G. Forgays
University of Vermont

Tytus Sosnowski
University of Warsaw

Kazimierz Wrzesniewski
Warsaw Medical Academy

⊙ **HEMISPHERE PUBLISHING CORPORATION**
A member of the Taylor & Francis Group

Washington   Philadelphia   London

USA	Publishing Office:	Taylor & Francis 1101 Vermont Avenue, N.W., Suite 200 Washington, DC 20005-3521 Tel: (202) 289-2174 Fax: (202) 289-3665
	Distribution Center:	Taylor & Francis 1900 Frost Road, Suite 101 Bristol, PA 19007-1598 Tel: (215) 785-5800 Fax: (215) 785-5515
UK		Taylor & Francis Ltd. 4 John Street London WC1N 2ET, UK Tel: 071 405 2237 Fax: 071 831 2035

ANXIETY: Recent Developments in Cognitive, Psychophysiological, and Health Research

Copyright © 1992 by Hemisphere Publishing Corporation. All rights reserved. Printed in the United States of America. Except as permitted under the United States Copyright Act of 1976, no part of this publication may be reproduced or distributed in any form or by any means, or stored in a data base or retrieval system, without the prior written permission of the publisher.

1 2 3 4 5 6 7 8 9 0   B R B R   9 8 7 6 5 4 3 2

This book was set in Times Roman by Hemisphere Publishing Corporation. The editors were Heather Jefferson and Radhika Rao Gupta; the production supervisor was Peggy M. Rote; and the typesetter was Phoebe Carter. Cover design by Michelle Fleitz.
Printing and binding by Braun-Brumfield, Inc.

A CIP catalog record for this book is available from the British Library.

⊗ The paper in this publication meets the requirements of the ANSI standard Z39.48-1984(Permanence of Paper).

Library of Congress Cataloging-in-Publication Data

Anxiety: recent developments in cognitive, psychophysiological, and
  health research / Donald G. Forgays, Tytus Sosnowski & Kazimierz
  Wrzesniewski (eds.).
     p.   cm.
  Includes bibliographical references and index.

    1. Anxiety—Physiological aspects—Congresses.   2. Cognitive-
psychology—Congresses.   I. Forgays, Donald G.
II. Sosnowski, Tytus.   III. Wrzesniewski, Kazimierz.
    [DNLM: 1. Anxiety—congresses.   2. Cognition—congresses.   3. Psychophysiology—
congresses.   WM 172 A63768]
  RC531.A637   1992
  616.85′223—dc20
  DNLM/DLC
for Library of Congress
                                                                                92-1458
                                                                                CIP

ISBN 1-56032-265-9

Contents

II
PSYCHOPHYSIOLOGICAL DEVELOPMENTS

      and Emotional Reactivity in Rats**   *Jan Matysiak, Pawel M. Ostaszewski,
      Wojciech Pisula, and Sniezyna Watras*   **167**

      Introduction   **167**
      Method   **168**
      Results   **170**
      Discussion   **172**
      References   **177**

                                        III
                             HEALTH DEVELOPMENTS

13   **Motivational Approach to Anxiety Disorders**   *Don C. Fowles*   **181**

      Gray's Theory   **181**
      Diagnostic Criteria of the Anxiety Disorders   **183**
      Barlow's Theory of Panic Disorder and Generalized Anxiety Disorder   **183**
      The Perception of Control   **187**
      Heart Rate and Anxiety   **188**
      Motivational Hypotheses and the Anxiety Disorders   **189**
      References   **190**

14   **Emotional Quality of Life After Mycocardial Infarction**
      Tadeusz M. Ostrowski   **193**

      Method   **194**
      Results   **195**
      Discussion   **197**
      References   **199**

15   **Emotional Responses to Illness Involving High or Low Risk of Life
      in Type A Patients**   *Kazimierz Wrzesniewski*   **201**

      Method   **202**
      Discussion   **208**
      References   **210**

16   **Test Anxiety Can Harm Your Health: Some Conclusions Based
      on a Student Typology**   *Eric Depreeuw and Hubert De Neve*   **211**

      Introduction   **211**
      The Achievement Process Model   **212**
      Design and Subjects   **213**
      Analyses and Results   **214**

Contributors

GABRIELLA BARTOLI, Department of Psychology, University of Bologna, Bologna, Italy

VALERIA BIASI, Department of Psychology, 1st University of Rome, "La Sapienza," Rome, Italy

MARINO BONAIUTO, Department of Social Developmental Psychology, 1st University of Rome, "La Sapienza," Rome, Italy

PAOLO BONAIUTO, Department of Psychology, 1st University of Rome, "La Sapienza," Rome, Italy

CHARLES S. CARVER, Department of Psychology, University of Miami, Coral Gables, Florida

ANNA LAURA COMUNIAN, Department Psychology, University of Padua, Padua, Italy

MARTIN V. COVINGTON, Department of Psychology, University of California, Berkeley, California

HUBERT DE NEVE, University Education Service, Catholic University of Leuven, Leuven, Belgium

ERIC DEPREEUW, Student CounselinG Service, University of Leuven, Leuven, Belgium

DEBORAH K. FORGAYS, Department of Psychology, University of Vermont, Burlington, Vermont

DONALD G. FORGAYS, Department of Psychology, University of Vermont, Burlington, Vermont

DON C. FOWLES, Department of Psychology, The University of Iowa, Iowa City, Iowa

ESTEVE FRIEXA I BAQUÉ, Laboratoire de Psychophysiologie, Universite de Lille I, Cedex, France

ANNA MARIA GIANNINI, Department of Psychology, 1st University of Rome, "La Sapienza," Rome, Italy

KNUT A. HAGTVET, Department of General Psychology, University of Bergen, Bergen, Norway

JAN MATYSIAK, Faculty of Psychology, University of Warsaw, Warsaw, Poland

YE REN MIN, Educational Research Institue, Shanghai Teachers University, Shanghai, People's Republic of China

JANICK NAVETEUR, Laboratoire de Psychophysiologie, University of Lille I, Cedex, France

CAROL L. OMELICH, Department of Psychology, University of California, Berkeley, California.

PAWEL M. OSTASZEWSKI, Faculty of Psychology, University of Warsaw, Warsaw, Poland

TADEUSZ M. OSTROWSKI, Department of Clinical Psychology, Jagiellonian University, Cracow, Poland

REINHARD PEKRUN, Department of Psychology, University of Munich, Munich, Germany

WOJCIECH PISULA, Faculty of Psychology, University of Warsaw, Warsaw, Poland

MICHAEL F. SCHEIER, Department of Psychology, Carnegie-Mellon University, Pittsbnrgh, Pennsylvania

WOLFGANG SCHONPFLUG, Department of Psychology, Free University Berlin, Berlin, Germany

EUGENY N. SOKOLOV, Department of Psychology, Moscow State University, Moscow, Russia

TYTUS SOSNOWSKI, Faculty of Psychology, University of Warsaw, Warsaw, Poland

JOHN A. STERN, Department of Psychology, Washington University, St. Louis, Missouri

JAN STRELAU, Faculty of Psychology, University of Warsaw, Warsaw, Poland

SNIEZYNA WATRAS, Faculty of Psychology, University of Warsaw, Warsaw, Poland

KAZIMIERZ WRZESNIEWSKI, Department of Clinical Psychology, Warsaw Medical Academy, Warsaw, Poland

Preface

In 1989, Professor Jan Strelau of the University of Warsaw, Poland, with the help of Professor Tytus Sosnowski and Kazimierz Wrzesniewski of that university, organized an international conference as a satellite of the Stress and Anxiety Research Society (STAR) annual meeting to be held in Berlin, Germany, in July 1990.

The focus of the satellite meeting was to examine the construct of anxiety from various points of view: cognitive, psychophysiological, and health, and to attempt to seek rapprochement in these views. This appeared to be a meaningful goal, as the state of anxiety research is one of disarray—in terms of definitional properties of the concept, research paradigms, and comparisons across approaches.

The meeting was held in Nieborow Castle, about 50 miles from Warsaw, from July 1–3, 1990. The setting was beautiful, comfortable, and isolated, and was selected to allow complete concentration on the theme. Because of housing limitations at the castle, only 24 people were invited to participate. They were all established researchers within the field of anxiety and, indeed, represented reasonably well the three approaches to this area listed above. Twenty-two accepted; they were from eight countries: six west and east European countries, the USSR, and the United States.

The conference opened with an address by Professor Strelau. During the following three days, presentations were made by all senior attendees, and discussions occurred at these times as well as more informally at meals and in the evenings.

When the conference ended, all presenters were invited to revise their presentations in light of conference events and to submit them to the three editors selected at the conference. Eighteen presenters were able to meet the time schedules mandated by the preparation of a book based on the conference, and they are the senior authors of the chapters that follow. Their editors thank them for their patience and diligence in respecting requests for copy, revisions, and so on.

The editing task has been interesting, and, at times, difficult, largely because of communication difficulties. Several of the authors are from Poland, and one is from the former Soviet Union. In addition, the senior editor exited the United States for a year's sabbatical leave in Rome. The publisher is located in Washington, D.C. This had led to a barrage of faxes, telephone calls, and a number of mailings made with fingers crossed. But all worked out well, and the product is in front of you. We hope that you find it as provocative as we who have been involved in its production do.

With respect to those involved in the production of this book, we thank Professor Charles D. Spielberger for his interest in the Nieborow Conference and in the book emanating from it. He has been fully supportive throughout and has made many suggestions during the book's development, always gently. This book would not have been developed were it not for his help. Also involved from conception to fruition has been Ron Wilder and Carolyn Baker of Hemisphere Publishing Corporation. Mr. Wilder saw the import of the appearance of this material, and Ms. Baker had the demanding tasks of keeping up with the faxes and uncertain mailings and sorting out the words and tribulations of three editors and many more authors. As psychologists, we are intrigued by their dedication.

In the early days of preparation, while Donald G. Forgays was still in Vermont, Samantha Austin of the Psychology Department, University of Vermont, provided herculean efforts to produce many of the chapters in expert form before the senior editor left that bucolic state. We thank her and wish her well. In Italy, Deborah K. Forgays, one of the authors and a close relative of the senior editor, filled the lacuna of a nonexisting secretarial pool in Italy, and produced on computers (which often functioned in a foreign manner), the remaining chapters and other materials for the book. We know the difficulty of her efforts and our thanks are hers.

The many facilities of the Department of Psychology of the University of Vermont, the First University of Rome, and the University of Warsaw, including computers, photocopy machines, and those precious fax units, were all importantly involved in this work. We warmly thank our academic colleagues for their support.

The Polish Ministry of Higher Education supported the conference held at Nieborow (grant RPBP.III.25/VI), as well as part of the editorial work on this book (grants RPBP.III.25/VI and BST 91/91). We are grateful to the Ministry for this financial support.

Donald G. Forgays
Tytus Sosnowski
Kazimierz Wrzesniewski

1

Introduction: Current Studies on Anxiety from the Perspective of Research Conducted During the Last Three Decades

Jan Strelau
University of Warsaw, Poland

Anxiety is one of the few concepts in psychology that, at first glance, seems to be understood even by laymen. On the basis of their own experience, everyone knows what anxiety is, especially when they are in stressful situations. Anxiety is one of the crucial emotions that affects behavior not only in humans but also in animals and, from the evolutionary point of view, has important adaptive functions. This explains why psychologists pay so much attention to this phenomenon. Anxiety became a substantial concept in the psychoanalytic approach introduced by Freud and in most neo–psychoanalytic-oriented conceptualizations. It also was studied by Pavlov, who experimentally produced a state of anxiety in dogs by exposing them to conflict caused by ambiguous stimuli during the conditioning procedure of differentiation.

When considering the concept of anxiety from a scientific perspective, it is clear that its definition is much more equivocal than it seems to be in everyday life. In the second half of our century, many approaches and trends have developed in the field of anxiety and they have been pursued by researchers with increasing interest. For example, Spielberger (1966) stated that during the period of 1950 to 1963 there appeared 3,500 monographs and papers in which anxiety was used as one of the key words. About 20 years later, from 1974 to 1982, the number of publications with *anxiety* as a key word recorded in 'Psychological Abstracts' (Psych-Lit records) had grown to 6,800. In the past 9 years (1983–1991), this rate of increase has continued and the number of publications has grown to 13,023. The aspects of anxiety that have gained the most popularity in recent decades refer to social and health problems. Much less research has been conducted with the aim of studying the psychological and physiological mechanisms underlying the development of anxiety or of advancing our knowledge of the nature of anxiety.

THREE DECADES OF RESEARCH ON ANXIETY

Looking at the psychological literature on anxiety from a perspective of the last three decades, different approaches and trends in this field of research can be

This introduction was written during my 1-year visit (1991–92) as a Humboldt Research Award Winner to the Faculty of Psychology, University of Bielefeld, Germany.

observed. The *drive-reflex-oriented concept of anxiety*, also known as the *conditioned reflex (CR) approach to anxiety*, was developed by the Iowa School in the 1950s (Spence, 1956; Spence & Taylor, 1951). Although it is still present in current research, it has lost its popularity. This is mainly because the mechanistic approach, represented by the learning theories of anxiety (see Krohne, 1980), did not take into account the psychic states of the individual or the interaction between the individual and the situation in generating anxiety.

Drive-oriented research on anxiety, based on the conditioned reflex paradigm of K. W. Spence and Janet A. Taylor (1951), has, however, given rise to new approaches to anxiety that have not been appreciated by most investigators in the field of anxiety. Several issues are worth mentioning here.

1. The fact that individuals differ in the speed of conditioning to aversive stimuli (regarded as the measure of anxiety), explained by differences in the strength of drive evoked by these stimuli, has given way to the individual differences approach to anxiety. This approach has gained much popularity in recent decades.

2. To select a large number of individuals who can be characterized as having high or low levels of anxiety and to have a validity measure for experimentally assessed anxiety, Taylor (1953) developed the Manifest Anxiety Scale (MAS). This scale, mainly based on items from the MMPI, was and still is used to diagnose anxiety as understood as a trait. MAS serves also as one of the principal validity criteria for other trait anxiety inventories.

3. Spence and Taylor (1951) were the first researchers simultaneously to use physiological and psychometric measures for assessing anxiety. It has been shown recently that when psychometric and physiological data are compared, not only are different measures of anxiety used but also different kinds of anxieties are being compared (see Strelau, 1991).

4. By comparing MAS measures with speed of conditioning of the eyelid reflex and by showing that efficiency and speed of conditioning to unconditioned stimuli of different intensities depend on the level of anxiety, Spence and Taylor (1951) accomplished the first experiments on the relationship between anxiety and level of performance. Studies in which the interrelationships between anxiety and level of performance and/or achievement are investigated are currently among the most popular ones.

It has been shown in personality research (Mischel, 1968, 1977) and also in studies on anxiety (Endler, 1975) that the trait approach explains only about one third of the variance of anxiety measured under threatening situations. These kinds of findings resulted in the development of at least two new approaches in anxiety research.

The interactional approach to anxiety was the first to gain popularity (Endler, 1975; Endler & Hunt, 1966). The interactional paradigm made researchers aware of the fact that not only trait anxiety but also the situation and, in particular, the interaction between the individual's anxiety trait and the situation contributes to the anxious behavior recorded in experimental and field studies. This kind of thinking about anxiety also has led to the development of situation-specific (S-R) types of inventories of anxiety (Endler, Hunt & Rosenstein, 1962; Endler & Okada, 1974). These latter measures, however, have not dominated the field of anxiety assessment because the amount of variance explained by such measures usually does not extend the variance explained by traditional anxiety inventories.

The fact that anxious behavior develops not only as a function of the tendency to react anxiously to aversive stimuli but also as a result of situation-specific conditions has led to the distinction between *trait anxiety* and *state anxiety* introduced by Cattell (Cattell & Scheier, 1958; Cattell, Shrader & Barton, 1974). This idea has been elaborated most fully by Spielberger (1966, 1972). According to him, trait anxiety refers to individual differences in anxiety proneness; the latter is regarded as a tendency to respond anxiously under stress. In turn, state anxiety consists of unpleasant feelings of tension and apprehension accompanied by arousal of the autonomic nervous system. The distinction between state anxiety and trait anxiety gained a good deal of popularity, especially after the State-Trait Anxiety Inventory (STAI) was developed by Spielberger, Gorsuch, and Lushene (1970). The STAI allows the separate measuring of anxiety as a state and of anxiety as a trait. Other inventories of this kind also have been developed (e.g., see Endler, Edwards, Vitelli & Parker, 1989).

Spielberger's definition of state anxiety emphasizes the *cognitive approach* to anxiety in distinction to the conditioning paradigm of anxiety. This line of research developed under the influence of cognitive psychology. The studies and conceptualizations of McReynolds (1962), Lazarus (1966), Epstein (1967), Morris and Liebert (1973), and others have shown the importance of internal states such as cognitive incongruity, uncertainty, appraisal of threat, unexpectancy, helplessness, cognitive dissonance, and so forth as determinants of anxiety and also as states that are affected by anxiety.

These studies not only demonstrated the importance of cognitive functioning in generating anxiety but also introduced a cognitive component to the structure of anxiety. Liebert and Morris (1967) and Morris and Liebert (1970) have shown that anxiety consists of two components: *arousal* (the physiological component; also called *emotionality*) and *worry* (the cognitive component of anxiety). Worry has been defined as a primarily cognitive concern about the consequences of failure and includes negative self-evaluation (lack of confidence) and concerns about poor performance.

This approach to anxiety, which developed in studies in which levels of anxiety were related mainly to academic performance, has led to the development of a new direction known as *test anxiety*. The popularity of this kind of research is attested to by the establishment of an international association of test anxiety, Society for Test Anxiety Research, and the availability of the book series *Advances in Test Anxiety Research* since 1982.

The studies conducted on test anxiety also have shown that physical threat and psychological threat are qualitatively different sources of anxiety and that they probably refer to different kinds of anxiety. Psychological threat (the kinds of internal states mentioned previously) generates the cognitive component of anxiety, worry, whereas physical threat activates the arousal component of anxiety, emotionality (see Rost & Schermer, 1987; Schwarzer, Jerusalem & Lange, 1982). The fact that level of anxiety under physical threat does not permit us to predict level of anxiety under psychological threat also has been found in studies on trait and state anxiety (see Glanzmann & Laux, 1978; Kendall, 1978; Lamb, 1978).

Of special importance to the cognitive approach to anxiety is the research on stress done by Lazarus and his co-workers (Lazarus, 1966; Lazarus & Averill,

1972). Lazarus has demonstrated that anxiety develops when an individual appraises a situation as threatening. To be more specific, anxiety emerges when unsuccessful coping mechanisms have been developed or when the individual fails to cope with stress. Such a conceptualization of anxiety has led to the study of the relationship between anxiety and stress, and coping with stress has been regarded as a strategy for reducing anxiety (i.e., the state of appraising a situation as threatening). This field of research gained a considerable following in clinical and health psychology (e.g., see Janisse, 1988). To demonstrate the popularity of the studies aimed at solving theoretical and applied issues, it is worth noting that, between 1975 and 1991, 13 volumes have been published under the title *Stress and Anxiety*, edited by C. D. Spielberger, I. G. Sarason, and others. These are the proceedings of international symposia that have been organized every few years under the same label.

Important for a better understanding of the nature and determinants of state and trait anxiety is research aimed at comprehending the biological mechanisms underlying this phenomenon. This line of inquiry is not represented by as large a number of publications as are the other areas presented above.

Probably most influential with respect to the biological approach to anxiety is the research conducted since the early 1970s by J. A. Gray, a leading representative of the learning theoretical approach to appetitive and aversive motivational systems. Neuropsychological and neuropharmacological experiments conducted on rats led Gray (1972, 1976, 1982) to describe the hypothetical mechanisms underlying anxiety. According to him, the orbital frontal cortex, medial septal area, and hippocampus should be considered as the anatomical centers of anxiety. They constitute the behavioral inhibition system (BIS), which became a subject of study by several researchers (e.g., see Fowles, 1983, 1987; Sosnowski, Nurzynska & Polec, in press). The BIS is activated by conditioned aversive stimuli (signals of punishment, frustrative nonreward, and novel stimuli). However, the question as to what extent this biological mechanism of anxiety is generalizable to human beings remains open (e.g., see 'Open Peer Commentary' in Gray, 1982). Wilson, Barrett, and Gray (1989) tried without success to transfer Gray's neuropsychological model of anxiety and impulsivity to human studies. The reason for failure may be because of this study's use of psychometric measures of behavioral characteristics as expressions of anxiety and impulsivity.

In the domain of biological bases of anxiety, the most common approach consists of examining the physiological correlates of anxiety, which are then used as direct measures of anxiety or as indicators of the arousal component (emotionality) of this state/trait. The electrodermal system, regulated by the autonomic nervous system, is especially sensitive to stimuli-generating emotions, most importantly anxiety. Electrodermal activity (EDA) has been used since the beginning of this century (Veraguth, 1909) as the most popular indicator or correlate of anxiety (state and trait). Fowles (1983) treats EDA as a measure of the activity of BIS. During the last three decades, dozens of studies have been designed to compare levels of EDA (tonic, spontaneous, and phasic) with independent measures of state and trait anxiety. The results summarized by Naveteur and Freixa i Baque (1987; Chapter 10) are rather pessimistic (see also Stern & Janes, 1973). They demonstrate that in normal persons no prediction of state or trait anxiety can be made on the basis of EDA scores.

The lack of consistency between the EDA scores of the arousal component of anxiety and independent measures of this phenomenon, mostly provided by psychometric measures, is not surprising. First, it has been found in many experiments that different measures of the level of arousal (tonic and phasic) do not even correlate with each other (see Lacey, 1950, 1967; Venables, 1984). Second, studies in the domain of arousal-oriented personality/temperament dimensions (extraversion, neuroticism or emotionality, anxiety, sensation seeking, and strength of excitation) have shown that there is almost no agreement between psychometric measures and physiological correlates of these traits (see Amelang & Ullwer, 1991; Fahrenberg, 1986, 1987; Kohn, Cowles & Lafreniere, 1987; Stelmack, 1990; Strelau, 1983). The lack of relationship is found especially when tonic states of the physiological correlates are taken into account. In a recent article (Strelau, 1991), I have argued that there seem to be no grounds for expecting congruence between psychometric and physiological measures of arousal-oriented personality/ temperament characteristics. Without going into detail, one may assume that on both levels (psychometric and physiological) different phenomena are not necessarily correlated with each other; this may also be true for anxiety.

In presenting the main trends in anxiety research done during the last three decades, I deliberately have avoided commenting on the findings concerned with clinical and health issues of anxiety, for at least two reasons. First, the number of publications in this area is extremely large, especially as regards anxiety in the context of neurotic disorders and therapeutic treatments; thus any presentation of this line of research in a brief introduction such as this would be impossible. Second, I am not familiar with the research in this area.

CURRENT RESEARCH ON ANXIETY
AS EXEMPLIFIED BY THE CONTRIBUTIONS
TO THIS VOLUME

I have described the state of affairs in anxiety research done in recent decades so as to provide a frame of reference for the chapters to be presented in this volume. Because of the enormous variety in current research on anxiety, these chapters tap only selected topics and issues. They have been organized into three sections: cognition, psychophysiology, and health. I will limit myself only to those issues of anxiety that seem to be of special interest while avoiding evaluative comment; the latter will be found in the last chapter of this book.

Cognitive Approach to Anxiety

The first section of the book is composed of six papers, all of which represent a cognitive approach to anxiety but which refer to different issues. All of them have a common denominator, which consists of the measurement of anxiety by means of test anxiety or state–trait anxiety inventories. These are the diagnostic tools preferred by cognitive-oriented anxiety researchers.

Carver and Scheier (Chapter 2) deal with the problem of how people respond to the experience of anxiety. Their chapter aims to show that such general expectancies as confidence and doubts may influence the individual's response to different kinds of experienced anxiety (test and speech anxiety). The authors show also that when the level of confidence is expressed in dispositional optimism versus pessimism, the relationship to anxiety is as expected. Pessimists show more signs of ineffective coping and experience greater distress.

Taking as a starting point a purely cognitive approach, Pekrun (Chapter 3) introduces an expectancy–value theory of anxiety. The aim of the theory is to integrate, systematize, and enlarge some of the assumptions of cognitive theories of anxiety. According to the author, anxiety is a function of multiplicative combinations of total expectancy and total valence. Negative expectancies and valences may be regarded as primary determinants of human anxiety. The author is aware that cognitive theories do not explain genetically based anxiety. Presenting data on the relationship between test anxiety and achievement, Pekrun demonstrates the reciprocal dependencies between anxiety and achievement.

The study presented by Comunian (Chapter 4) is based on a Gestalt approach, which describes the organizational unity of a person as a whole. Among the factors contributing to this unity, the self construct is of special importance. The author shows that different configurations of the subjective self (self beliefs, beliefs about the ideal self, and beliefs of how the self is perceived by others) are related differently to the two main components of test anxiety, worry, and emotionality. Perfect harmony between the selfs is related to the lowest scores of worry and emotionality.

Understanding anxiety as a trait operationalized by means of Spielberger's STAI, Schönpflug (Chapter 5) has experimentally studied the relationship between anxiety and cognitive performance. Considering performance as a regulatory process, the author has hypothesized that effort, understood as a top-down process of arousal designed to improve performance, is a component of self-regulation. Schönpflug found that low-anxious individuals execute more effective self-control and thus are superior in coping with emotional load. Low-anxious individuals who also happen to be highly competent are the only ones with improved performance under all study conditions.

The fact that level of performance in solving intellectual tasks depends on more than anxiety also has been shown by Hagtvet and Min (Chapter 6). Their chapter describes an integrated research model that combines anxiety, motivation, and ability as related to the process of solving intellectual tasks. The authors focus on the fact that task novelty seems to be an important factor in arousing state anxiety. The results of their study indicate that all three factors (ability, anxiety, and motivation) come into operation in school performance, but at different stages of problem solving.

The study by Bonaiuto, Biasi, Giannini, Bartoli, and Bonaiuto (Chapter 7) is the most complex of those presented in this volume because of the many variables it takes into account. The authors' experiments were aimed at studying cognitive performance, consisting of the projection of expectations and perceptions of cause-and-effect relationships, under experimentally evoked stress and relaxation. Part of their results indicate that the principal emotions generated under stress are anxiety and anger.

Psychophysiology of Anxiety

The second section of the book deals with the psychophysiological approach to anxiety. These five chapters illustrate the diversity rather than the commonality within this domain of research.

Stern (Chapter 8) reviews studies in which eye-blinking rates are used as measures of anxiety. No unequivocal conclusions can be drawn about the blink rate–anxiety relationship; however, most of the studies seem to suggest that state and trait anxiety are related to an increase in the eye-blink rate. Based on this review, the author asks about the effect of anxiety on the timing of blinks and blink closure duration. However, he has no answer to this question.

Taking Lacey's (1967) position as a starting point, Sosnowski (Chapter 9) argues that psychophysiological activity is a manifestation not only of the energetic dimension of behavior but also of the content-related attitude toward stimuli. He hypothesizes that the attitude of coping actively or passively with a given situation involves differently organized physiological processes. In three independent experiments using measures of electrodermal activity (EDA) as the index of activation of the Behavioral Inhibition System (BIS), and tonic heart rate changes as the index of activation of the behavioral approach system (BAS), Sosnowski is able to show that under certain conditions there exists an inverted relationship between the two psychophysiological variables. He finds that the activation of BIS, regarded as a physiological indicator of anxiety, results in an increase in EDA.

Naveteur and Freixa i Baque (Chapter 10), who also used EDA indices but in relation to psychometrically measured anxiety, obtained results opposite to those reported by Sosnowski. In Naveteur and Freixa i Baque's experiments, subjects with high trait anxiety demonstrated lower levels of EDA while performing aversive tasks as compared with low-anxiety individuals. The authors try to integrate their data within Gray's theory of anxiety.

Referring to his detector theory of perception, Sokolov (Chapter 11) presents a detector theory of emotion. The theory assumes that different emotional experiences depend on specific detector neurons. A given emotion arises when an excitation maximum occurs in an appropriate emotion detector. Although Sokolov does not refer to the specific emotion of anxiety, it can be assumed that a further elaboration of this theory will be profitable to research on anxiety.

The last chapter of this section deals not with psychophysiology but behavior genetics in animals. By rearing three different strains of rats under conditions varying in stimulative value, Matysiak, Ostaszewski, Pisula, and Watras (Chapter 12) have shown that the impact of genetic and environmental factors in determining individual differences in behavior depends on the degree of its complexity. Individual differences in emotional reactivity (anxiety), regarded as being expressed in more complex behavior, were shown to be affected by both environment and heredity.

Anxiety and Health

My earlier statement regarding the remarkable increase in research on anxiety holds especially true for health issues in relation to anxiety. The number of publications in this area has grown from 505 in 1974 to 1982 to 1,569 in 1983 to 1991; this is a threefold growth. The Anxiety and Health section of this book consists of six chapters that variously refer to anxiety as a risk factor, an expression of disorder, an outcome of illness, and a subject of therapeutic treatment.

Applied issues concerning anxiety as related to health can be dealt with most effectively if based on appropriate conceptualizations. Referring to Barlow's theory of panic and generalized anxiety disorders and to Gray's BIS and fight/flight system, Fowles (Chapter 13) developed a theoretical approach that applies motivational constructs to anxiety disorders. The usefulness of the motivational approach lies in considering panic a primitive alarm reaction, learned panic as based on conditioning, and in treating the aversive motivational system (similar to BIS) as the basis for all anxiety disorders.

An experiment conducted on over 5,000 students to assess the perceived costs and benefits of cigarette smoking is described by Covington and Omelich in Chapter 18. On the basis of this sophisticated study in which many variables were under control, a conclusion is drawn that seems to be of special importance with respect to the impact of anxiety on the perceived costs of smoking. The affective costs, associated with self-upset and other-upset as anxiety indices, are the most important components contributing to smoking or nonsmoking tendencies.

The assessment of the emotional quality of life as judged by people who have suffered myocardial infarction without complication (MI) and with complication (ventricular fibrillation, CMI), is the subject of study in Ostrowski's chapter (Chapter 14). His data shows that CMI patients display higher state and trait anxiety as compared with MI patients. These characteristics become even greater with an increase in the number of years after infarction.

The emotional consequences of somatic diseases are also reported in Wrzesniewski's chapter (Chapter 15). The aim of his study was to determine whether Type A and Type B patients differ in their emotional responses to illness that involves various degrees of risk to life. MI patients were regarded as representative of high risk to life whereas patients whose leg(s) had been amputated and those who suffered from rheumatic diseases were classified as representative of low risk to life. In general, he found that anxiety state did not play any role in distinguishing the three groups nor in distinguishing Type A and Type B subjects across and within groups.

The aim of Depreeuw and De Neve's study (Chapter 16) was to describe the needs and problems of students at the University of Leuven, with an emphasis on their well-being. On the basis of cluster analysis of psychometric data, seven student types were distinguished. Among these types, two anxiety types were identified: active test-anxious and passive test-anxious students. The authors found that test-anxious students score more poorly on most of the health criteria and that the most disadvantaged type as regards the parameters of well-being is the passive-anxious type.

Forgays and Forgays (Chapter 17) describe a series of laboratory studies in which changes in behavior are recorded under conditions of relaxation associated with the flotation technique. The authors used different psychometric tests to measure pretreatment and posttreatment emotions; the studies consisted of different numbers and durations of floats. Their results show that flotation, regarded as a relaxation technique, is associated with a decrease in anxiety. However, no long-lasting changes in the emotional sphere caused by means of flotation were observed.

FINAL REMARKS

The question of whether the theoretical conceptualizations and empirical results presented in this volume contribute to our knowledge of the varied issues of anxiety has to be answered by the reader. The intensive and extensive research in this area over many years suggests that there is a strong desire to understand the nature of anxiety and the role it plays in everyday life. When I read this volume, I felt that it constituted progress on the long road of inquiries about anxiety.

REFERENCES

Amelang, M., & Ullwer, U. (1991). Correlations between psychometric measures and psychophysiological as well as experimental variables in studies on extraversion and neuroticism. In J. Strelau & A. Angleitner (Eds.), *Explorations in temperament: International perspectives on theory and measurement* (pp. 287–315). New York: Plenum Press.

Cattell, R. B., & Scheier, I. H. (1958). The nature of anxiety: A review of 13 multivariate analyses comparing 814 variables. *Psychological Reports, 5*, 351–388.

Cattell, R. B., Shrader, R. R., & Barton, K. (1974). The definition of anxiety as a trait and a state in the 12- to 17-year range. *British Journal of Social and Clinical Psychology, 13*, 173–182.

Endler, N. S. (1975). A person-situation interaction model for anxiety. In C. D. Spielberger & I. G. Sarason (Eds.), *Stress and anxiety* (Vol. 1, pp. 145–164). New York: Hemisphere.

Endler, N. S., Edwards, J. M., Vitelli, R., & Parker, J. D. A. (1989). Assessment of state and trait anxiety: Endler Multidimensional Anxiety Scales. *Anxiety Research, 2*, 1–14.

Endler, N. S., & Hunt, J. McV. (1966). Sources of behavioral variance as measured by the S-R Inventory of Anxiousness. *Psychological Bulletin, 65*, 336–346.

Endler, N. S., Hunt, J. McV., & Rosenstein, A. J. (1962). An S-R Inventory of Anxiousness. *Psychological Monographs, 76*, 1–33.

Endler, N. S., & Okada, M. (1974). An S-R Inventory of General Trait Anxiousness. *Department of Psychology Reports, 1*, York University, Toronto.

Epstein, S. (1967). Toward a unified theory of anxiety. In B. A. Maher (Ed.), *Progress in experimental psychology research* (Vol. 2, pp. 2–90). New York: Academic Press.

Fahrenberg, J. (1986). Psychophysiological individuality: A pattern approach to personality research and psychosomatic medicine. *Advances in Behaviour Research and Therapy, 8*, 43–100.

Fahrenberg, J. (1987). Concepts of activation and arousal in the theory of emotionality (neuroticism): A multivariate conceptualization. In J. Strelau & H. J. Eysenck (Eds.), *Personality dimensions and arousal* (pp. 99–120). New York: Plenum Press.

Fowles, D. C. (1983). Motivational effects on heart rate and electrodermal activity: Implications for research on personality and psychopathology. *Journal of Research in Personality, 17*, 48–71.

Fowles, D. C. (1987). Applications of a behavioral theory of motivation to the concepts of anxiety and impulsivity. *Journal of Research in Personality, 21*, 417–435.

Glanzmann, P., & Laux, L. (1978). The effects of trait anxiety and two kinds of stressors on state anxiety and performance. In C. D. Spielberger & I. G. Sarason (Eds.), *Stress and anxiety* (Vol. 5). Washington: Hemisphere.

Gray, J. A. (1972). The structure of the emotions and the limbic system. In R. Porter & J. Knight (Eds.), *Physiology, emotion and psychosomatic illness* (pp. 87–130). Amsterdam: Associated Scientific Publishers.

Gray, J. A. (1976). The behavioural inhibition system: A possible substrate for anxiety. In M. P. Feldman & A. M. Broadhurst (Eds.), *Theoretical and experimental bases of behaviour modification* (pp. 3–41). London: Wiley.

Gray, J. A. (1982). Précis of the neuropsychology of anxiety: An enquiry into the functions of the septohippocampal system. *The Behavioral and Brain Sciences, 5*, 469–534.

Janisse, M. P. (Ed.). (1988). *Individual differences, stress, and health psychology*. New York: Springer.

Kendall, P. C. (1978). Anxiety: States, traits—situations? *Journal of Consulting and Clinical Psychology, 46*, 280–287.

Kohn, P. M., Cowles M. P., & Lafreniere, K. (1987). Relationships between psychometric and experimental measures of arousability. *Personality and Individual Differences, 8*, 225–231.

Krohne, H. W. (1980). Angsttheorie: Vom mechanistischen zum kognitiven Ansatz. (Theory of anxiety: From a mechanistic to a cognitive approach.) *Psychologische Rundschau, 31*, 12–29.

Lacey, J. I. (1950). Individual differences in somatic response patterns. *Journal of Comparative and Physiological Psychology, 43*, 338–350.

Lacey, J. I. (1967). Somatic response patterning and stress: Some revisions of activation theory. In

M. H. Appley & R. Trumbull (Eds.), *Psychological stress: Issues in research* (pp. 14–44). New York: Appleton-Century-Crofts.

Lamb, D. H. (1978). Anxiety. In H. London & J. E. Exner (Eds.), *Dimensions of personality* (pp. 37–83). New York: Wiley.

Lazarus, R. S. (1966). *Psychological stress and the coping process.* New York: McGraw-Hill.

Lazarus, R. S. & Averill, J. R. (1972). Emotion and cognition: With special reference to anxiety. In C. D. Spielberger (Ed.), *Anxiety: Current trends in theory and research* (Vol. 2, pp. 241–283). New York: Academic Press.

Liebert, R. M. & Morris, L. W. (1967). Cognitive and emotional components of test anxiety: A distinction and some initial data. *Psychological Reports, 20,* 975–978.

McReynolds, P. (1962). Exploratory behavior: A theoretical interpretation. *Psychological Reports, 11,* 311–318.

Mischel, W. (1968). *Personality and assessment.* New York: Wiley.

Mischel, W. (1977). On the future of personality measurement. *American Psychologist, 32,* 246–254.

Morris, L. W. & Liebert, R. M. (1970). Relationships of cognitive and emotional components of test anxiety to physiological arousal and academic performance. *Journal of Consulting and Clinical Psychology, 35,* 332–337.

Morris, L. W. & Liebert, R. M. (1973). Effects of negative feedback, threat of shock, and level of trait anxiety on the arousal of two components of anxiety. *Journal of Counseling Psychology, 20,* 321–326.

Naveteur, J. & Freixa i Baque, E. (1987). Individual differrences in electrodermal activity as a function of subjects' anxiety. *Personality and Individual Differences, 8,* 615–626.

Rost, D. H. & Schermer, F. J. (1987). Auf dem Weg zu einer differentiellen Diagnostik der Leistungsangst. (On the way to a differential diagnosis of test anxiety.) *Psychologische Rundschau, 38,* 14–36.

Schwarzer, R., Jerusalem, M., & Lange, B. (1982). A longitudinal study of worry and emotionality in German school children. In R. Scharzer, H. M. van der Ploeg, & C. D. Spielberger (Eds.), *Advances in test anxiety research* (Vol. 1, pp. 67–81). Lisse: Swets and Zeitlinger.

Sosnowski, T., Nurzynska, M., & Polec, M. (in press). Active-passive coping and skin conductance and heart rate changes. *Psychophysiology.*

Spence, K. W. (1956). *Behavior theory and conditioning.* New Haven: Yale University Press.

Spence, K. W. & Taylor, J. A. (1951). Anxiety and strength of the UCS as determiners of the amount of eyelid conditioning. *Journal of Experimental Psychology, 42,* 183–188.

Spielberger, C. D. (1966). Theory and research on anxiety. In C. D. Spielberger (Ed.), *Anxiety and behavior* (pp. 3–20). New York: Academic Press.

Spielberger, C. D. (1972). Anxiety as an emotional state. In C. D. Spielberger (Ed.), *Anxiety: Current trends in theory and research* (Vol. 1, 24–49). New York: Academic Press.

Spielberger, C. D., Gorsuch, R. L., & Lushene, R. B. (1970). *Manual for the State-Trait Anxiety Inventory.* Palo Alto: Consulting Psychologists Press.

Stelmack, R. M. (1990). Biological bases of extraversion: Psychophysiological evidence. *Journal of Personality, 58,* 293–311.

Stern, J. A. & Janes, C. L. (1973). Personality and psychopathology. In W. F. Prokasy & D. C. Raskin (Eds.), *Electrodermal activity in psychological research* (pp. 284–337). New York: Academic Press.

Strelau, J. (1983). *Temperament, personality, activity.* London: Academic Press.

Strelau, J. (1991). Are psychophysiological/psychophysical scores good candidates for diagnosing temperament/personality traits and for a demonstration of the construct validity of psychometrically measured traits? *European Journal of Personality, 5,* 323–342.

Taylor, J. A. (1953). A personality scale of manifest anxiety. *Journal of Abnormal and Social Psychology, 48,* 285–290.

Venables, P. H. (1984). Arousal: An examination of its status as a concept. In M. G. H. Coles, J. R. Jennings, & J. A. Stern (Eds.), *Psychophysiological perspectives. Festschrift for Beatrice and John Lacey* (pp. 134–142). New York: Van Nostrand/Reinhold.

Veraguth, O. (1909). *Das psychogalvanische Reflexphaenomen. (The psychogalvanic reflect phenomenon.)* Berlin: Karger Verlag.

Wilson, G. D., Barrett, P. T., & Gray, J. A. (1989). Human reaction to reward and punishment: A questionnaire examination of Gray's personality theory. *British Journal of Psychology, 80,* 509–515.

I

COGNITIVE DEVELOPMENTS

2

Confidence, Doubt, and Coping with Anxiety

Charles S. Carver
University of Miami, Florida

Michael F. Scheier
Carnegie-Mellon University, Pennsylvania

Four questions concerning anxiety seem important to us. First, what is the nature of the conditions that bring anxiety into being—what generates anxiety in the person who is experiencing it? Second, what are the physiological and neurological mechanisms by which anxiety occurs? Third, how do people respond when they experience anxiety? Fourth, how should dysfunctional responses to anxiety be dealt with clinically? Our work has emphasized most strongly the third of these questions, and this chapter focuses primarily on that question.

BASIC PRINCIPLES

Our approach to anxiety derives from a more general viewpoint on the self-regulation of behavior. The main points of the conceptual analysis are very straightforward. First, like many theorists today (e.g., Cantor & Kihlstrom, 1987; Elliott & Dweck, 1988; Emmons, 1986; Klinger, 1977, 1987; Little, 1983; Pervin, 1983, 1989), we assume that behavior is goal directed. People have long-term and short-term goals, narrow and broad goals, plans for their attainment, and strategies to use in implementing the plans. In this view, people's goals give form to their lives.

We believe that when people act in pursuit of their goals, their self-regulatory efforts take the form of feedback loops. People monitor their actions, periodically assess whether the actions are producing the intended results, and when necessary adjust the actions to remedy any discrepancy sensed between the two values (Carver & Scheier, 1981, 1982, 1990). In this way, behavior proceeds smoothly in the direction of the intention and the person's goals are realized in his or her actions. Sometimes, however, things do not go so smoothly. Sometimes people encounter difficulties in their efforts to move toward their goals. This difficulty can have any of several sources, either internal or external. External impediments can disrupt behavior and so can internal doubts or conflicts. Yet another source of difficulty is the perception that the effort to move toward one goal is creating an undesired discrepancy with respect to another important goal. Simon (1967) suggests that this is what happens when the attempt to execute a particular behavior

Preparation of this chapter was facilitated by NSF grants BNS90-11653 and BNS90-10425.

results in anxiety. Simon argues that emotions serve an important purpose in the human's internal information processing system. They serve the purpose of calling for a change in the prioritization of one's goals. Emotions do this by becoming intense enough to interrupt whatever it is the person is doing. In Simon's view, an emotion such as anxiety is an internal signal to the person that insufficient attention is being devoted to his or her personal well-being (an important goal) and that more attention ought to be devoted to it, perhaps quickly.

It is implicit in Simon's theory that progress toward various goals is monitored outside awareness, as the person concentrates on something else, until a discrepancy with respect to an important goal becomes evident. As the discrepancy increases, anxiety intrudes on the person's subjective experience. When the discrepancy is large enough and the emotion is intense enough, the person's behavior is interrupted and attention is drawn from the action that is now under way to the alternative goal. In the case of anxiety, the alternative goal may be the goal of personal safety or of making a good impression on someone (or avoiding the possibility of a bad impression) (cf. Higgins, 1987; see also Fowles, Chapter 13). It may even be a goal as broad as holistic personal integration (cf. Rogers, 1980) or the maintenance of one's world view (cf. Kelly, 1955).

Rising anxiety, then, is a sign of an impending problem. Anxiety also interrupts ongoing behavior (cf. Mandler, 1984; Mandler & Watson, 1966; Simon, 1967); that is, when anxiety becomes intense enough, the person stops whatever he or she is doing and assesses the likelihood of being able to complete the behavior. This usually is an implicit assessment and is not necessarily made in probabilistic terms. Indeed, when it takes place in vivo, the assessment may occur in dichotomous terms, as a general sense of confidence versus doubt.

We assume that what follows from this assessment process depends critically on this dimension of confidence versus doubt (see Figure 1). People who are sufficiently confident will continue to try to take steps in the direction of the goal they are trying to attain; however, people who are sufficiently doubtful will experience a conflicting impulse to withdraw.

This withdrawal or disengagement impulse can be expressed in several different ways. It can be expressed behaviorally, by leaving the field of action. It can be displayed as a reduction in effort at moving forward toward the goal. It can also be displayed less overtly, via off-task thinking or daydreaming. Because several of these manifestations of the withdrawal impulse have the additional effect of interfering with task performance, doubtful people who are experiencing anxiety often display performance impairments. Depending on the nature of the situation, the doubt may even generate additional distress as the person focuses on the anxiety and the inability to reduce it (see Figure 2). In other words, if the person is constrained in some fashion to remain in the anxiety-producing situation, he or she may enter a spiral of feeling anxious, assessing doubt, feeling the impulse to disengage, being unable to do so fully, being further reminded of his or her inadequacy or inability to deal with the situation, and so on.

These differential responses to the experience of anxiety represent a special case of what we take to be more general themes in behavior. People operating under stress or adversity continue to move forward in their actions as long as they remain sufficiently confident of being able to attain their goals. Anxiety is one of the conditions that potentially can interrupt goal-directed efforts, causing the person to reassess the likely outcome, but it is only one of several such conditions.

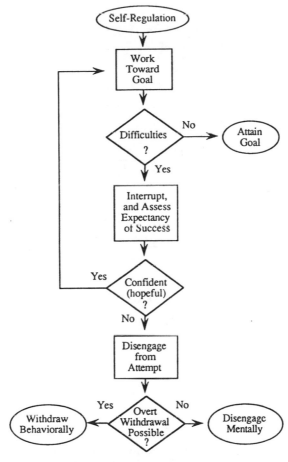

Figure 1 Flow diagram of three behavioral possibilities. Sometimes behavior proceeds unimpeded and uninterrupted, resulting in attainment of the desired goal. Sometimes difficulties of one sort or another cause behavior to be interrupted and the person to evaluate, explicitly or implicitly, the chances of successful goal attainment. Confidence leads to further effort; sufficient doubt leads to a tendency to disengage. Disengagement can mean behavioral withdrawal, if circumstances permit, or it can be expressed mentally.

One further point in considering the process of assessing expectancies: In general, we believe that this process relies as much, or more, on information taken from memory as it does on information inherent in the current situation. The tendency to give extra weight to information taken from memory would seem to be particularly strong at the extremes of the confidence distribution; that is, it is difficult to persuade people who are very confident that their fears are too strong to

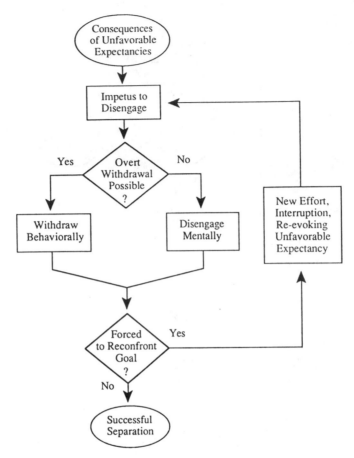

Figure 2   When unfavorable expectancies prompt an impulse to
disengage or give up, sometimes that impulse can be
expressed fully and sometimes not. If the person remains
committed to the goal, circumstances are likely to force the
person to confront the goal once again and attempt to move
toward it. If the situation remains unfavorable to forward
progress, however, the result is a cycle of sporadic effort and
withdrawal, which is accompanied by heightened distress.

overcome. It is hard to persuade people who are very doubtful that they can indeed
overcome their doubts.

CONSEQUENCES OF CONFIDENCE VERSUS DOUBT

The importance of confidence versus doubt is illustrated by evidence from
several different areas of our own research, although this research is certainly not
unique in making these points. We refer briefly to several of our studies that are
relevant here, as illustrations of the points made in the preceding section.

Test Anxiety

One area of work concerns test anxiety. Test anxiety is a person's tendency to become anxious before and during evaluative examinations, especially under highly evaluative conditions, with the result that the person's performance deteriorates. In some respects, test anxiety represents an ideal and easy-to-study example of the more general case of responding to anxiety.

It should be noted that test anxiety is a more complex phenomenon than this portrayal might indicate. For example, test anxiety appears to play a role in problems of studying and preparing for exams, as well as in problems of test taking. However, it is solely the area of test taking on which we are focusing. We are oversimplifying the picture here to make a point about the model with which we have been working.

There is evidence to suggest that the root problem in test anxiety is a sense of doubt about being able to cope effectively with the test situation or about being able to do well on the test. (An alternative though similar view is that the root problem is doubt about being able to perform well enough on the exam to gain or hold the esteem of significant others such as teachers or parents; cf. Wine, 1982.) Given enough doubt, the person is thrown into the spiral described earlier of debilitating self-talk, off-task thinking, impulse to disengage, and performance impairment. This line of reasoning is consistent with the repeated finding that the main contributor to the deficit of test anxiety is worry (i.e., cognitive preoccupation with failure) rather than emotional reactivity per se (e.g., Deffenbacher, 1986; Morris, Davis, & Hutchings, 1981; see also Sarason & Sarason, 1987). It is also consistent with the results of several experiments conducted by ourselves and others that examine the behavior of subjects who are high and low in test anxiety in various circumstances.

Some of this research was intended to examine test anxiety in interaction with self-focused attention, a variable that we otherwise disregard in this chapter. The prediction in these studies is that self-focus exaggerates both the task-focused efforts of people who are low in test anxiety and the impairment of people who are high in test anxiety. (For a broader statement see, e.g., Carver & Scheier, 1986.) Such interactive effects of test anxiety have been shown now in several studies (Carver, Peterson, Follansbee, & Scheier, 1983; Rich & Woolever, 1988).

In one such study (Carver et al., 1983, Experiment 1), subjects were asked to work on a set of anagrams, in a highly evaluative situation, and with a specific time limit for each item. An experimental manipulation caused self-focus to be either high or low during the task period. The measure of interest was the number of correct anagram solutions the subject was able to generate. This study yielded an interaction between self-focus and test anxiety such that subjects low in test anxiety solved more anagrams under conditions of high rather than low self-focus, whereas subjects high in test anxiety solved fewer anagrams under conditions of high rather than low self-focus. This interactive effect was quite consistent across two levels of item difficulty. Highly test-anxious subjects also reported a greater incidence of intrusion of task-irrelevant thoughts during the testing, and they reported having spent a lower percentage of time focusing on the concrete elements of the task under conditions of high self-focus. In contrast, but fully consistent with the effects on task performance and with theory, those lower in test anxiety reported the opposite pattern of contents of consciousness, with self-focus facilitating task focus.

This study demonstrated the expected performance difference and also the interactive role of self-focus in the difference. However, it did not provide any information on the disengagement impulse that we believe underlies the performance difference. Another study (Carver et al., 1983, Experiment 2) was aimed at obtaining evidence of such an impulse. In principle this is not easy to do because situational constraints usually cause the withdrawal tendency of test-anxious subjects to be restrained in testing situations; as a result it typically gains expression mentally rather than behaviorally.

We reasoned, however, that if a situation could be created in which a behavioral disengagement were sanctioned fully, the impulse might be expressed more openly. Accordingly, this is the sort of situation we set out to create. Subjects in this study were asked to work on a series of anagrams and to do so in a particular order. There was no mention of a time limit in the instructions, and the implication was that the subject could work as briefly or for as long on a particular item as he or she desired. Subjects were also told that the items could be attempted more than once, as long as they were attempted in the same order each time. If the subject wished to leave an item and go on, he or she was to simply place it face down on the desk. In reality, the first item of the set was impossible to solve, and the measure of interest was how persistent subjects were in attempting it. An interaction resulted that was similar in form to that of the other study: In conditions of high self-focus, the highly test-anxious subjects moved on to the next item more quickly than did those who were less anxious. Thus there appears to have been a disengagement impulse among the highly test-anxious subjects that was not present among the less test-anxious subjects.

The theoretical model we are using has also received support from several other studies in the literature of test anxiety. Galassi, Frierson, and Sharer (1981) conducted a study that is particularly supportive of our assumption that a disengagement impulse underlies the various manifestations of test anxiety in exam settings. Galassi et al. (1981) had people work on a real exam and report the thoughts that entered their minds during it. Among highly test-anxious subjects, the single most common thought reported was a wish to be somewhere else. Although Galassi et al. (1981) did not have our conceptual model in mind while conducting their research, this finding clearly reflects the disengagement impulse that we have assumed underlies the deficits of test anxiety.

Another important study was conducted by Rich and Woolever (1988). They experimentally manipulated subjects' expectancies of performing well on a test and then measured test performance as a function of high versus low self-focus. Subjects high in test anxiety were influenced by both these manipulations in a manner consistent with the effects described above: highly test-anxious students who were led to be doubtful about their performances were impaired by self-focus, whereas highly test-anxious students who were led to be confident about their performances were facilitated by self-focus. This finding is particularly striking in that both facilitation and impairment occurred among subjects who were high in test anxiety. Thus this finding seems clearly to indicate the importance of expectancies in determining people's reactions to anxiety.

Speech Anxiety

Another more recent study provides some more information about the subjective experience of being anxious, but does so in a different sort of sample. Subjects in this research (Baggett, Saab & Carver, 1991) were high versus low in their self-reports of speech anxiety. They came to an experiment in which they were told they would have 3 minutes to plan a speech and then would spend 3 minutes delivering it while being videotaped. The speech was to reflect the following situation: Subjects were asked to imagine they had been accused unfairly of stealing something in a store, and they had been taken to the store manager to whom they were now speaking in order to defend themselves.

Before starting to prepare for the speech, subjects made appraisal ratings regarding their view of the task they were facing. After the speech period, they reported on the sorts of mental activities they either had engaged in order to cope with the stress of the situation during the two task periods (preparation and presentation), or had experienced involuntarily during those periods. Throughout both task periods, heart rate (HR) was monitored continuously and blood pressure (BP) was recorded at intervals of several minutes.

Analysis of subjects' ratings revealed several differences between those who were high versus those who were low in speech anxiety. Highly speech-anxious subjects reported that they expected the task to be harder, they found it more threatening, and they expected to do more poorly at it. As might be expected, they later reported feeling more anxious during both phases of the task. After the task periods were over, they also reported they had felt more stressed and frustrated than had those who were lower in speech anxiety.

There were also differences between groups on the coping responses that subjects reported having used. During both the preparation and presentation phases, people low in speech anxiety reported making more positive self-statements than did those high in speech anxiety. High speech-anxious subjects reported focusing on the passage of time and trying to minimize the importance of the task. During the preparation but not the performance phase, they also reported experiencing greater feelings of giving up. The high-anxious people also reported having more of a tendency toward off-task thinking while making their speeches.

Interestingly enough, although HR and BP increased significantly in both groups during the task, there was no trace of a difference between the two groups. This finding is consistent with results of several earlier studies, which showed no difference in arousal among high test-anxious subjects as compared to low test-anxious subjects when in the test situation, despite the fact that the test clearly was arousing for both subject groups (Deffenbacher & Hazaleus, 1985; Hollandsworth, Glazeski, Kirkland, Jones & Van Norman, 1979; Holroyd, Westbrook, Wolf & Badhorn, 1978).

In sum, the cognitive experiences reported by subjects in the Baggett et al. (1991) study were generally consistent with the theoretical picture presented earlier in this chapter. Subjects high in self-reported speech anxiety had less favorable expectancies about how well they would do on the speech task. These subjects also displayed several of the characteristics we identified as being the consequences of these doubts: feelings of giving up, off-task thinking, less self-exhortation, and more focus on the passage of time, which would ultimately mark the end of their ordeal in the task.

OPTIMISM AND PESSIMISM

Our most recent research has moved in a somewhat different direction from the work described thus far in the chapter. We currently are involved in examining the effects of dispositional optimism versus pessimism, a general sense of confidence versus one of doubt about life's important outcomes (Scheier & Carver, 1985, 1987, 1992). This work has an important conceptual connection to everything we have described thus far, in that the theme underlying the work is how confidence versus doubt influences the manner in which people act, the way they feel, and the tactics they use to cope with whatever kinds of adversity they experience. Now, however, we are talking about generalized expectancies instead of task-specific or domain-specific expectancies. These generalized expectancies are measured with an instrument called the Life Orientation Test (LOT) (Scheier & Carver, 1985).

Given the structural similarity of the logic behind this work and the logic of the anxiety research already reviewed, the fundamental predictions are much the same as those discussed throughout the chapter. We expect optimists to display evidence of continued effort in the face of adversity. We expect pessimists to show more signs of ineffective coping and of giving up, and also to experience greater distress. One difference between this research and the research described thus far is that the research on optimism does not focus explicitly on anxiety-provoking situations. In many cases, however, it is quite reasonable to assume that subjects in the research are experiencing anxiety or other forms of distress, such as depression.

In this section, we describe a few examples of the optimism research to provide a sense of how this variable influences people's experiences and their behavior. The major point to be made here is that the effects of this variable take much the same form as the effects we have described thus far. Several studies have examined how optimists and pessimists cope and what tactics they deploy when they are under stress (Scheier, Weintraub & Carver, 1986). In one of these studies (Scheier et al., 1986, Study 2), subjects were presented with a series of hypothetical situations. They were asked to imagine themselves in these situations and to write down what they would do. These reports were coded on several dimensions and then correlated with optimism scores. Optimism in this sample was associated with a greater tendency toward problem-focused coping and also with a tendency to put other things aside in order to deal with the problem situation. Pessimism was associated with a greater tendency toward the venting of emotions and also with a tendency toward a disengagement from the goals that were being threatened in the hypothetical situation. Another study examined a further implication of the idea that pessimists are prone to disengage their efforts when things become too difficult (Strack, Carver & Blaney, 1987). This study also had applied implications in that the sample consisted of people who recently had completed a treatment program for alcoholism. They had just moved from the treatment center into an 'aftercare' facility where they were given free room and board for 3 months, provided that they looked for work and remained abstinent. This is a difficult period of transition for people in this situation because the temptation to drink is strong and they have little in the way of support from outsiders. Many who confront this situation find it hard to cope; many give up the effort to forward, and return to drinking. Of particular importance at present, this study found that the relapse rate was greater among pessimists than among optimists, which is consistent with our line of reasoning.

Yet another study examined the experiences of women in the last trimester of pregnancy (Carver & Gaines, 1987). It is well known that many women experience a period of postpartum blues or depression. The question under investigation was whether optimists might be more resistant to developing this depression than pessimists. In this study, scores were collected on a measure of depression, along with optimism scores, at about the beginning of the last trimester of pregnancy. Depression data were collected again shortly after the women had delivered their babies. After controlling for the initial depression levels, pessimism proved to be a reliable predictor of postpartum depression.

CONCLUDING COMMENT

The studies described in this chapter range from examinations of the dynamics of test anxiety, to a study of speech anxiety, to work on the dimension of optimism versus pessimism. These concepts, which are diverse in some ways, share an important theme: the idea that some people are more confident than others about the eventual outcomes of their efforts. We have argued further that this difference in confidence has an important effect on how people cope with adversity. The results of the several research projects reviewed are consistent with this position. How people respond to life's difficulties in general—and to anxiety in particular—appears to depend on their level of confidence. Confident people tend to disregard whatever symptoms of anxiety they experience, focusing instead on moving forward in their task-directed efforts. Doubtful people respond instead to the signals that bad things are about to happen to them and so pull away. These dynamics appear to be very pervasive in the human experience. Indeed, we suspect that they are fundamental to the nature of human responses to adversity.

REFERENCES

Baggett, H. L., Saab, P. G., & Carver, C. S. (1991). *Cardiovascular reactivity, appraisal, and coping during a speech task: Effects of individual differences in speech anxiety.* Unpublished manuscript, University of Miami, Coral Gables, FL.

Cantor, N., & Kihlstrom, J. F. (1987). *Personality and social intelligence.* Englewood Cliffs, NJ: Prentice-Hall.

Carver, C. S., & Gaines, J. G. (1987). Optimism, pessimism, and postpartum depression. *Cognitive Therapy and Research, 11,* 449–462.

Carver, C. S., Peterson, L. M., Follansbee, D. J., & Scheier, M. F. (1983). Effects of self-directed attention on performance and persistence among persons high and low in test anxiety. *Cognitive Therapy and Research, 7,* 333–354.

Carver, C. S., & Scheier, M. F. (1981). *Attention and self-regulation: A control-theory approach to human behavior.* New York: Springer-Verlag.

Carver, C. S., & Scheier, M. F. (1982). Control theory: A useful conceptual framework for personality–social, clinical, and health psychology. *Psychological Bulletin, 92,* 111–135.

Carver, C. S., & Scheier, M. F. (1986). Functional and dysfunctional responses to anxiety: The interaction between expectancies and self-focused attention. In R. Schwarzer (Ed.), *Self-related cognitions in anxiety and motivation* (pp. 111–141). Hillsdale, NJ: Erlbaum.

Carver, C. S., & Scheier, M. F. (1990). Principles of self-regulation: Action and emotion. In E. T. Higgins & R. M. Sorrentino (Eds.), *Handbook of motivation and cognition: Foundations of social behavior* (Vol. 2, pp. 3–52). New York: Guilford.

Deffenbacher, J. L. (1986). Cognitive and physiological components of test anxiety in real-life exams. *Cognitive Therapy and Research, 10,* 635–644.

Deffenbacher, J. L., & Hazaleus, S. L. (1985). Cognitive, emotional, and physiological components of test anxiety. *Cognitive Therapy and Research, 9,* 169–180.

Elliott, E. S., & Dweck, C. S. (1988). Goals: An approach to motivation and achievement. *Journal of Personality and Social Psychology, 54,* 5–12.

Emmons, R. A. (1986). Personal strivings: An approach to personality and subjective well-being. *Journal of Personality and Social Psychology, 51,* 1058–1068.

Galassi, J. P., Frierson, H. T., Jr., & Sharer, R. (1981). Behavior of high, moderate, and low test-anxious students during an actual test situation. *Journal of Consulting and Clinical Psychology, 49,* 51–62.

Higgins, E. T. (1987). Self discrepancy: A theory relating self and affect. *Psychological Review, 94,* 319–340.

Hollandsworth, J. G., Glazeski, R. C., Kirkland, K., Jones, G. E., & Van Norman, L. R. (1979). An analysis of the nature and effects of test anxiety: Cognitive, behavioral, and physiological components. *Cognitive Therapy and Research, 3,* 165–180.

Holroyd, K., Westbrook, T., Wolf, M., & Badhorn, E. (1978). Performance, cognition, and physiological responding in test anxiety. *Journal of Abnormal Psychology, 87,* 442–451.

Kelly, G. A. (1955). *The psychology of personal constructs.* New York: Norton.

Klinger, E. (1977). *Meaning and void.* Minneapolis: University of Minnesota Press.

Klinger, E. (1987). Current concerns and disengagement from incentives. In F. Halisch & J. Kuhl (Eds.), *Motivation, intention, and volition* (pp. 337–347). Berlin: Springer-Verlag.

Little, B. R. (1983). Personal projects: A rationale and methods for investigation. *Environment and Behavior, 15,* 273–309.

Mandler, G. (1984). *Mind and body: Psychology of emotion and stress.* New York: Norton.

Mandler. G., & Watson, D. L. (1966). Anxiety and the interruption of behavior. In C. D. Spielberger (Ed.), *Anxiety and behavior* (pp. 263–288). New York: Academic Press.

Morris, L. W., Davis, M. A., & Hutchings, C. H. (1981). Cognitive and emotional components of anxiety: Literature review and a revised worry–emotionality scale. *Journal of Educational Psychology, 73,* 541–555.

Pervin, L. A. (1983). The stasis and flow of behavior: Toward a theory of goals. In M. M. Page & R. Dienstbier (Eds.), *Nebraska symposium on motivation* (Vol. 31, pp. 1–53). Lincoln: University of Nebraska Press.

Pervin, L. A. (Ed.) (1989). *Goal concepts in personality and social psychology.* Hillsdale, NJ: Erlbaum.

Rich, A. R., & Woolever, D. K. (1988). Expectancy and self-focused attention: Experimental support for the self-regulation model of test anxiety. *Journal of Social and Clinical Psychology, 7,* 246–259.

Rogers, C. R. (1980). *A way of being.* Boston: Houghton Mifflin.

Sarason, I. G., & Sarason, B. R. (1987). Cognitive interference as a component of anxiety: Measurement of its state and trait aspects. In R. Schwarzer, H. van der Ploeg, & C. D. Spielberger (Eds.), *Advances in test anxiety research* (Vol. 5, pp. 3–14). Lisse, Netherlands: Swets & Zeitlinger.

Scheier, M. F., & Carver, C. S. (1985). Optimism, coping, and health: Assessment and implications of generalized outcome expectancies. *Health Psychology, 4,* 219–247.

Scheier, M. F., & Carver, C. S. (1987). Dispositional optimism and physical well-being: The influence of generalized outcome expectancies on health. *Journal of Personality, 55,* 169–210.

Scheier, M. F., & Carver, C. S. (1992). Effects of optimism on psychological and physical well-being: Theoretical overviews and empirical update. *Cognitive Therapy and Research,* in press.

Scheier, M. F., Weintraub, J. K., & Carver, C. S. (1986). Coping with stress: Divergent strategies of optimists and pessimists. *Journal of Personality and Social Psychology, 51,* 1257–1264.

Simon, H. A. (1967). Motivational and emotional controls of cognition. *Psychological Review, 74,* 29–39.

Strack, S., Carver, C. S., & Blaney, P. H. (1987). Predicting successful completion of an aftercare program following treatment for alcoholism: The role of dispositional optimism. *Journal of Personality and Social Psychology, 53,* 579–584.

Wine, J. D. (1982). Evaluation anxiety: A cognitive–attentional construct. In H. W. Krohne & L. C. Laux (Eds.), *Achievement, stress, and anxiety* (pp. 207–219). Washington, DC: Hemisphere.

3

Expectancy–Value Theory of Anxiety: Overview and Implications

Reinhard Pekrun
University of Regensburg, Germany

Many authors have assumed that anxiety is induced by the expectancy of threatening negative events (e.g., see Beck & Clark, 1988; Lazarus, 1966; Price, Barrell, & Barrell, 1985). Expectancies are cognitions relating to future events, and threat implies that something of importance is in danger. Thus any interpretation of anxiety relating to expectations and threat basically implies that anxiety depends on (a) expectancies of future events and (b) the subjective value of these events. The expectancy–value theory of anxiety (EVTA; Pekrun, 1984, 1985, 1988a) attempts to make the assumptions implied by such a formulation more precise. By integrating constructs used by different expectancy theories, it delineates which expectancies and valence cognitions may be of specific relevance for anxiety and presents formalized assumptions about their function. Furthermore, using expectancy and value constructs, it also allows us to integrate anxiety theory with expectancy–value approaches to motivation.

Without going into details of formalization (see Pekrun, 1984, 1988a), the first section of this chapter outlines basic assumptions of the theory. In the second and third parts, implications for anxiety/achievement relations and for social determinants of anxiety are discussed. Empirical examples are given that are based on a longitudinal study of affective–motivational personality development in students. The last section describes briefly some implications for prevention and therapy.

BASIC ASSUMPTIONS

Ways of Anxiety Formation

The expectancy–value theory of anxiety implies that cognitive mediation of anxiety is just one of several ways in which emotions can arise. Two other modes of anxiety formation are genetically based anxiety and habitualized anxiety. Both of them are triggered directly by perceptions (i.e., without further cognitive mediation).

Genetically Based Anxiety

It may be assumed that human beings are capable of experiencing anxiety very early in life (perhaps even before birth). Since cognitive development is only in its beginnings, then perceptually triggered anxiety may be more typical of early stages of life. Such anxiety may be induced, for example, by perceptions of physically dangerous situations (like perceptions of depth) or by perceptions of deprivation of basic physiological and socio-emotional needs. Even in adult life, this type of anxiety formation may be important in some situations (cf. Asendorpf, 1989).

Cognitively Mediated Anxiety

Anxiety mediated by cognitive appraisals is addressed by contemporary cognitive–psychological thinking about anxiety. Today this often seems to be the only type of anxiety that is acknowledged theoretically. Cognitive anxiety formation will be discussed in more detail below.

Habitualized Anxiety

Cognitive mediation of anxiety implies that situational perceptions do not trigger anxiety directly, but only after the situation has been appraised cognitively. In recurring situations, however, anxiety mediated by cognitive appraisals may be assumed to habitualize. The final stage of habitualization implies that appraisals are no longer necessary, which means that anxiety can be triggered directly by perceptions of the situation. For example, if an employee has experienced repeatedly that a supervisor's comments imply criticism and devaluation, an appraisal of the probability of negative consequences may no longer be necessary. After such a learning history, anxiety can be induced directly when the supervisor enters the room. Partly similar to the proceduralization of cognitive skills (cf. Anderson, 1987), habitualization of anxiety may involve three stages (Pekrun, 1988a): (a) automatization of declarative cognitive appraisals, (b) gradual shortening of the implied sequence of cognitions, and (c) final short-circuiting of perception and anxiety. Habitualized anxiety is sustained if the situation recurs without changes. However, if the situation changes, reappraisals may be enforced that eventually may break up habitualized situation–anxiety connections.

This implies that appraisals are important in habitualized anxiety, although they are not necessary in the final stage. Habitualized anxiety develops from cognitively mediated anxiety and it may be changed by reappraisals.

Expectancies, Valences, and Anxiety

Although acknowledging other types of anxiety formation, EVTA focuses on cognitively mediated anxiety. Attempting to integrate assumptions presented by Lazarus (1966), Bandura (1983), and Heckhausen (1977), future-related expectancy and valence cognitions are held to be proximal determinants of cognitively mediated anxiety. Other types of cognitions are assumed to contribute to anxiety by influencing expectancies and valences. For example, this is postulated for causal attributions. The theory implies that the following types of expectancy–value cognitions may be of specific importance.

Situation–Outcome Expectancies

Expectancies of this type imply that situational conditions will lead to negative events if no countermeasures are taken (cf. Heckhausen, 1977; see also Seligman, 1975, for a lucid analysis of anxiety). Examples may be expectations that an infectious disease will break out if there is no inoculation, that an examination may be failed if no effort is invested, or that loneliness will prevail if no friends are made, and so forth.

Action–Control Expectancies

Expectancies of this type imply that actions intended to prevent these negative events can be performed. Expectancies to be able to initiate and perform intended actions have variously been called self-efficacy expectations (Bandura, 1977), competence expectations (e.g., Krampen, 1988), or intent–action expectations (Pekrun, 1984). For two reasons, the term *action–control expectancy* is preferred here over the more popular term *self-efficacy expectation*. 'Self-efficacy' easily may be misunderstood as relating to the total efficacy of a person, including the efficacy to produce outcomes. Contrary to what the word suggests, however, it is designed to relate only to expectations of action performance and not to outcome expectations (Bandura, 1977). 'Action–control expectancy' refers directly to what such expectations are about (subjective control of actions), thus relating expectation terms to the volitional analysis of action control (cf. Kuhl, 1984).

Action–Outcome Expectancies

These are expectancies that the outcome of actions intended to prevent threatening negative events will in fact be preventive.

Intrinsic Valences of Outcomes

This construct refers to subjective values of the threatening events themselves. Examples would be the importance of academic failures or of social rejection, as such.

Extrinsic Valences of Outcomes

This construct refers to subjective values of threatening events stemming from appraisals of their consequences (like parents' and teachers' negative reactions to examination failures).

EVTA contains formalized assumptions about how these different types of cognitions may combine within the process of cognitive anxiety formation. Essentially, the following is postulated as a complete process of appraisals.

1. Situation–outcome, action–control, and action–outcome expectations are combined cognitively. This leads to an appraisal of the net probability of the threatening event, called the *total expectancy* of the event. Total expectancy is assumed to be high when the situation–outcome expectation of the event is high, but action–control and/or action–outcome expectations are low (i.e., when the event is probable, but its subjective controllability is low). Total expectancy is assumed to be low either when the situational probability of the event is low, or when both action–control and action–outcome expectations are high (i.e., when the event is subjectively improbable even if no countermeasures are taken, or when it is controllable).

2. Intrinsic and extrinsic valences are combined into an appraisal of what is termed the *total valence* of the threatening event.

3. *Anxiety* is a function of a basically multiplicative combination of total expectancy and total valence. This implies that anxiety is higher with high expectancy and high valence, but only if both components are above some minimum value. If

either expectancy or value is zero, cognitively mediated anxiety is not experienced even if the other component is high. For example, an earthquake destroying one's house would be a rather threatening event, but if one's house is located in a region where no earthquake has ever been registered, one need not be anxious. Conversely, if failure in an upcoming examination is highly probable, but one does not care about the outcome, no anxiety will be experienced. Finally, it is assumed that anxiety is a nonmonotonic function of expectancy x value, reaching its maximum with high event expectancy, but dropping off if the event becomes subjectively certain. In such cases, anxiety may rather be replaced by hopelessness (cf. Pekrun & Frese, 1992).

The temporal order of different expectancy and value appraisals is not regarded as fixed because it may differ according to situational and subjective conditions of cognitive activation. However, a typical sequence of appraisals may imply that some expectancy of a negative situational outcome is formed first, which leads to a more differentiated appraisal of the implied harm and to an evaluation of possible counteractions and their chances for success (see Figure 1).

Furthermore, it is assumed that processing all five of the above-mentioned types of expectancy–value cognitions may be the exception rather than the rule. In many situations it is not necessary to appraise situation–outcome probabilities because negative events are certain by default if nothing is done to prevent them. One example of this is when failure is certain because one did not attend an examination. Furthermore, for many simple actions, an appraisal of action–control competencies is not necessary because action performance is available in a proceduralized way. Similarly, for many anxiety-eliciting events, valences are innately available or have been learned over the years, thus making an elaborate processing of value information unnecessary. Generally, any extended processing of information may not be needed when appraisal processes have become habitualized to some degree.

Personality Determinants and Development of Anxiety

Personality

EVTA assumes that anxiety-eliciting expectancy and value cognitions are determined both by situation and by person variables, thus implying that anxiety depends on situation and personality (Figure 1). Concerning personality determinants, expectancies and values are assumed to be influenced by enduring expectancy and valence beliefs stored in memory. According to the above assumptions, situation–outcome, action–control, action–outcome, and intrinsic/extrinsic valence beliefs may be of primary relevance. Influencing momentary expectancy and value cognitions, such beliefs may be regarded as dispositional determinants of momentary state anxiety as well as of habitual trait anxiety, although other dispositions may also contribute to anxiety (e.g., physiological traits).

The influence of beliefs may be greater in ambiguous situations and smaller if clear and comprehensive situational information is available. Furthermore, for familiar situations there may be situation-specific, differentiated belief systems, whereas in new situations more generalized beliefs will be influential. Beliefs may be more or less generalized along two dimensions, among others: (a) the situational domains to which they pertain, and (b) the stages of situation–action pro-

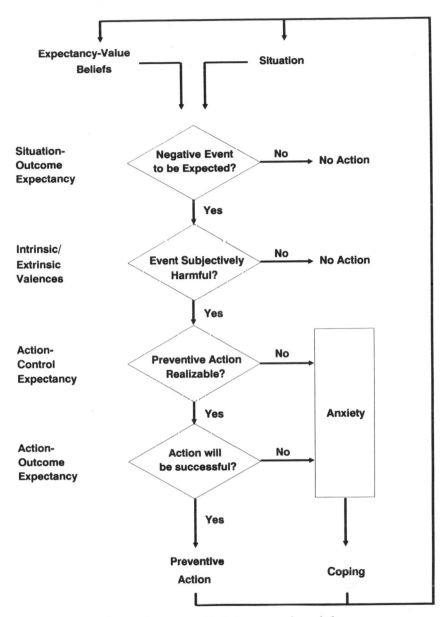

Figure 1 The cognitive anxiety process: Typical sequence of appraisals.

cesses to which they relate. For example, internal/external locus of control beliefs (cf. Rotter, 1966) relate to action–outcome versus situation–outcome expectancies, whereas general optimism/pessimism (see Carver and Scheier, Chapter 2) pertains to people's total event expectancy beliefs, thus implying a high degree of generalization over temporal stages of situation–action processes.

Development

Because expectancy–value beliefs may function as an enduring basis of anxiety experiences, the development of anxiety may be mediated largely by the acquisition or modification of relevant belief systems. This pertains not only to cognitively mediated anxiety, but also to its habitualized forms, because habitualized anxiety can be assumed to develop from cognitive mediation (see above). By implication, distal influences on anxiety development may be mediated by building up or changing expectancy–value belief systems.

Implications

Theoretical and practical implications of EVTA pertain to the relationship between anxiety and other future-related emotions (cf. Pekrun, 1988a; Pekrun & Frese, 1992), to anxiety and motivation (Pekrun, 1988b), to the relationship between anxiety and achievement (Pekrun, 1991a, 1991b), to the impact of educational and occupational environments (cf. Pekrun, 1985, 1991b; Pekrun & Frese, 1992), and to therapy for and prevention of anxiety (Pekrun, 1988a), among other things. Some of these implications will be discussed now.

ANXIETY AND ACHIEVEMENT

Previous Research

The relationship between anxiety and achievement has been one of the main topics of anxiety research during recent decades. Pioneered by Spence and Taylor's work (1951), many early studies analyzed the impact of general anxiety variables on learning and achievement. The bulk of research, however, followed the avenue opened by Mandler and Sarason's (1952) reintroduction of the concept of test anxiety (which had been discussed previously by psychoanalytic writers like Stengel [1936]). Therefore, relevant research largely concentrated on relations between achievement-specific anxiety and performance during the following decades.

So far, several hundred studies have analyzed the relationships between test anxiety and achievement (see Hembree, 1988; Schwarzer, Seipp, & Schwarzer, 1989). Two main findings arise from this research. First, experimental laboratory studies have demonstrated that anxiety impairs intellectual performance on complex or difficult tasks. Second, educational field research has shown consistently that habitual test anxiety and academic achievement tend to correlate negatively, although the strength of this relationship seems to be moderated by factors like grade level and classroom context (c.f., Helmke, 1988; Hembree, 1988).

Today most explanations of these findings refer to attentional mechanisms. A prototypical interpretation of this type may be the following: Anxiety occupies the capacity of the working memory. Therefore, the amount of capacity remaining for task performance is reduced and all kinds of performance using working memory resources are impaired (e.g., Eysenck, 1988; Wine, 1971).

Assumptions of this type have not only been used to interpret experimentally induced effects of anxiety, but also as an explanation of the correlations between anxiety and academic achievement. Therefore, anxiety–achievement relationships usually have been interpreted as being caused by the effects of anxiety on achievement (e.g., Hembree, 1988). Such an interpretation is congruent with the basic principles of contemporary educational and occupational research. Achievement is regarded as a dependent variable that should be optimized; other processes primarily are viewed as positive or negative determinants of achievement (e.g., see Walberg, 1990, for productivity models of educational achievement).

EVTA and the Anxiety-Achievement Relationship

What does the expectancy-value theory of anxiety tell us about anxiety-achievement relationships? EVTA is concerned primarily with the determinants of anxiety, implying that anxiety may be caused by expectancy and valence cognitions, and that any distal influences are mediated largely by expectancies and valences. The implications for anxiety-achievement relations are straightforward: From the perspective of EVTA, any correlates of anxiety need not be regarded as effects of anxiety, but instead or additionally often can be viewed as variables influencing anxiety. From such a perspective it can be assumed that negative achievements (failures) induce achievement-related anxiety in the first place, whereas positive achievement alleviates anxiety. Furthermore, EVTA implies that such effects are mediated by achievement-related expectancies and valences, which are built up by achievement feedback and which in turn trigger or reduce anxiety.

Therefore, an alternative interpretation of negative anxiety/achievement correlations is that failure induces anxiety, not that anxiety impairs achievement (for related views, see also Covington & Omelich, 1982; Meece, Wigfield, & Eccles, 1990). Specifically, seen from a developmental perspective, ontogenetic effects of cumulative failures on anxiety may be among the primary sources of anxiety in achievement-oriented societies. Such a mechanism would also explain why test anxiety tends to rise substantially during the elementary years (e.g., Hembree, 1988); it is because many students are experiencing cumulative failures during those years for the first time in their lives. Furthermore, if the development of test anxiety is a gradually growing reaction to cumulative failures, viewing anxiety as a dependent variable could also explain why anxiety-achievement correlations tend to become stronger over the first years of schooling (Hembree, 1988).

Of course, reality normally will also be characterized by reverse influences of anxiety on achievement. However, contrary to what is suggested by purely attentional interpretations, EVTA implies that the effects of anxiety on performance may probably be mediated not only by cognitive but also by motivational mechanisms (e.g., Pekrun, 1988b; see also Carver & Scheier, 1988; Schönpflug, Chapter 5). Above all, anxiety may reduce intrinsic task motivation and it may strengthen avoidance-related extrinsic task motivation. Therefore, motivational effects of anxiety on the whole may be either detrimental or beneficial. As a consequence, the net effect of anxiety on performance may be either negative or positive because it may depend on different, partly opposing cognitive and motivational mechanisms.

In most everyday situations, both directions of causal effects between achievement and anxiety will occur. This implies that anxiety-achievement relations are characterized by feedback loops. In case (positive) achievement reduces anxiety and anxiety reduces achievement, these will be positive feedback loops (causal effects of both directions bearing the same sign). If anxiety exerts beneficial overall effects on performance, such feedback loops are of a negative type (cf. Pekrun, 1988a, for implications).

Empirical Example: Test Anxiety and Academic Achievement

Feedback loops of achievement and anxiety have been investigated empirically using data from a longitudinal study on the personality development of students (Munich longitudinal study on student personality). This study analyzed students' development from grades 5 through 10, including four waves located in grades 5, 6, 8, and 10.

Samples consisted of approximately 800 students per wave. Students were recruited from the Bavarian variant of the German state school system, which is composed of different tracks segregated by achievement level. Up to grade 4 this system implies comprehensive schooling. In grades 5 and 6, there are lower-track 'Hauptschulen' and higher-track 'Gymnasien.' For grades 7 to 10, there are additional medium-track 'Realschulen' recruiting their students mainly from lower-track 'Hauptschulen.' Schooltime is finished by grade 9 for lower-track 'Hauptschulen' and goes on for the other tracks. This system of schooling implies differential transitions for all students from grade 4 to 5, and for some students after grade 6.

Variables included school-related test anxiety, achievement-related expectancies and values, and academic achievement, among other measures of students' personalities and of school and family environments. Anxiety and expectancy–value variables were measured by self-report scales constructed for this study (cf. Pekrun, 1991a; reliabilities for the scholastic test anxiety scale were between $\alpha = .87$ and $\alpha = .93$ for each wave). Academic achievement scores were measured by summing final yearly grades in the main subjects of German, English, and mathematics.

For all grade levels included and in line with the assumptions of EVTA, effort–control expectancy (i.e., task-specific action–control expectancy) correlated negatively with test anxiety, whereas expectancy of academic failures and the subjective valence of failures correlated positively (correlations between $r = .30$ and .55). Expectancies and valence themselves were nearly uncorrelated. This corroborates that they may contribute independently to the genesis of anxiety. Academic achievement correlated significantly negatively with both failure expectancy and test anxiety, which is consistent with the above mediational assumptions (for details, see Pekrun, 1991a, 1991b; cf. also Pekrun, 1984).

To test assumptions about feedback loops more directly, competitive causal models were constructed and analyzed by means of LISREL VI structural equations modeling (Jöreskog & Sörbom, 1984). As an example of results, Figure 2 shows a model relating to the time span from grades 5 to 8, also including grade 4 final achievement (see Pekrun, 1991a). The longitudinal sample used here consists of 365 students with complete data sets. Using manifest variables, the model assumes that achievement effects on anxiety are mediated by failure expectancies. Failure expectancy was included instead of other expectancy–value variables because it can be assumed to be influenced directly by achievement, unlike other types of expectancies or values. The basic time structure of the model conforms to the temporal structure of the Munich longitudinal study. All self-report variables

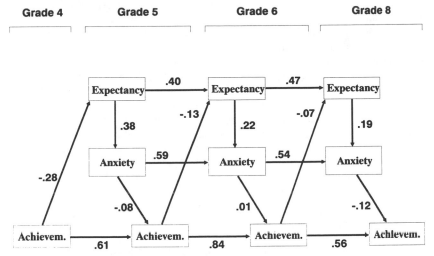

Figure 2 Academic achievement, failure expectancy, and test anxiety: Causal analysis (standardized solution).

were measured in the middle of the school year, whereas achievement relates to the final grades of each year.

The model is sufficiently fitted to the data (*GFI* = 0.96; $\chi^2(29)$ = 96.2). Furthermore, the structure of causal effects is largely in line with assumptions. For each time interval from one wave to the next, there is a negative effect of academic achievement on failure expectancy. This implies that positive achievement reduces anticipations of failure. Failure expectancy in turn exerts a positive (raising) effect on test anxiety. There are no direct effects of achievement on anxiety, thus corroborating the mediating role of expectancy. Finally, test anxiety exerts a weak negative effect on academic achievement. An exception is the near-zero effect of anxiety on achievement in grade 6. However, this may be because of the rather high stability of achievement from grade 5 to 6, which leaves little room for external influences. Generally, effects become gradually weaker across grade levels because influences at higher grade levels consist of incremental effects adding to earlier effects.

In sum, this pattern of findings corroborates that anxiety–achievement relations may be characterized both by anxiety effects on achievement and by influences of achievement on the development of anxiety. Therefore, such relations may be viewed best as implying feedback loops precluding any simplistic unidirectional interpretation. Furthermore, the findings of this causal analysis are in line with EVTA assumptions on the mediational role of achievement-related expectancies.

SOCIAL DETERMINANTS OF ANXIETY

Social-Cognitive Learning Conceptions

Social–cognitive learning views of human development have long assumed that social influences on experience and action are mediated by building up individual cognitive systems (e.g., Bandura, 1986; Mischel, 1973; Rotter, 1954). In line with such views, the impact of child-rearing behavior on the genesis of anxiety has been explained as being caused by inducing anxiety-related subjective competencies and expectancies. A recent example is Krohne's two-process model of child-rearing effects (Krohne, 1985, in press). This model assumes that anxiety is caused by negative competence expectations and negative consequence expectations (i.e., by negative action–control and outcome expectations according to EVTA terminology). Therefore, Krohne postulates that child-rearing behaviors that produce such negative expectations have to be regarded as social–educational determinants of anxiety, two domains of such behavior being restrictive control and negative feedback. Although scarce and largely cross-sectional to date, empirical evidence is in line with the assumption that such behaviors influence the development of children's anxiety (e.g., Helmke, 1983; Hembree, 1988; Kohlmann & Krohne, 1988).

Toward a Generalized Expectancy–Value Theory of the Social Determinants of Anxiety

EVTA differs from other theories of anxiety in simultaneously taking into account different kinds of anxiety-relevant expectancies and valences. Attempting to enlarge the scope of theoretical thinking about cognitive determinants of anxiety, EVTA implies that beyond action- and outcome-related expectations, anxiety may also depend on situation–outcome expectancies and on valence appraisals. The following may therefore be deduced.

First, in line with general social–cognitive thinking, it may be assumed that social influences on anxiety are mediated by building up or changing expectancies and valences related to negative events. This may apply not only to cognitively mediated anxiety, but also to habitualized anxiety developing from cognitive anxiety formation (see above). Short-term effects of this type may be based on direct induction of momentary expectancy–value cognitions by situational information (e.g., by information about an upcoming examination). More generalized long-term effects, however, should be mediated by enduring expectancy–value beliefs. For development, prevention, and therapy, environmental effects on belief systems therefore may be of primary importance.

Second, mediational assumptions may be used heuristically to search for external determinants of anxiety—any external factor influencing expectancies and values might by implication also exert an impact on anxiety. Some such variables may be the following.

Factors Influencing Situation–Outcome Expectancies

Generally, any social environment that delivers negative events to individuals is likely to foster anxiety. Specifically, this is the case when events are possible but not certain, thus producing negative situation–outcome expectancies that imply some degree of unpredictability. A second specific condition fostering anxiety may be that these events are not circumvented easily by the individual, which implies that high competencies are necessary for preventive actions and thus allow compensation of negative situational expectations only if there are high expectancies of event control.

Examples of such *dangerous environments* involving whole societies are times of war, economic crisis, or societal restructuring (as in unified Germany).

Examples in the work domain are labor markets with high degrees of unemployment or work places that deliver noxious effects (cf. Bowler & Schwarzer, 1991; Pekrun & Frese, 1992). In education, typical cases are school systems with differential nonpromotion of students, or parents who punish their children in noncontingent ways by withdrawing emotional security irrespective of the child's behavior.

Factors Influencing Action–Control and Action–Outcome Expectancies

Positive action–control and outcome–control expectancies may be fostered when action-related competencies are built up, when the situation permits the production and control of one's own actions, and when these actions are answered environmentally by positive outcomes. Therefore, crucial factors may be (a) that the environment helps in building up competencies (e.g., by instruction), (b) that it allows the trial, exercise, and performance of self-regulated behavior, and (c) that the behavior's outcomes are sufficiently and contingently positive. One further favorable condition may be (d) that competence and outcomes are evaluated externally as being positive. In other words, competence-related support, discretion level, positive environmental responsivity, and positive competence/outcome evaluations may be four general conditions that are favorable for positive action-related expectancies. Conversely, competence-related hindrance, lack of discretion, lack of positive responsivity to preventive actions, and competence/outcome-related negative evaluations may produce negative action-related expectations, thus contributing to anxiety. Examples for the work domain are given in Pekrun and Frese (1992); some educational implications will be discussed below.

Factors Influencing Valences

Some types of negative events can be assumed to be valued negatively on a genetic basis. This may apply, for example, to deprivation of physiological needs, to physical harm, and to lack of emotional support in early infancy. Other events may acquire negative subjective valences during the course of development. One primary mechanism might be that innately negative events are made contingent on other events by social environments. For example, academic examination failures may be followed by physical punishment or by withdrawal of parents' emotional support. From this perspective, one general mechanism as to how social environments produce negative subjective valences may be to deliver negative consequences following the respective event, that is, to deliver punishment. Another mechanism may be to inform the subject about the negative value of an event, that is, to give value information.

Of course, all these environmental factors need not be experienced directly to exert an impact on anxiety. It may often be sufficient to observe actions and outcomes of models, or to get symbolic expectancy–value information (see Bandura, 1986; Pekrun, 1985).

Example: Educational Environments and Students' Test Anxiety

From the above considerations, theoretical models of educational effects on the development of anxiety can be derived. One such model relates to family and school effects on test anxiety (Pekrun, 1985, 1988c). This model takes the mediating role of different expectancies and valences into account. It also incorporates feedback effects of students' test anxiety on parents, teachers, and peers, thus analyzing relationships between environment and student as feedback loops.

Among other things, the model attempts to account for the available empirical evidence on test anxiety's educational determinants. Relevant studies state that environmental pressure for achievement, competition in the classroom, and punishment by parents and teachers correlate positively with test anxiety. Correlations with social support, however, were less consistent and often near zero (Helmke, 1983; Hembree, 1988). The following assumptions of the model attempt to explain these findings.

1. Achievement pressure may raise students' test anxiety because it implies high achievement goals, which foster failure expectancies. It also implies that achievement is highly valued.

2. For the same reasons, competition between students may also raise test anxiety.

3. Failure-contingent punishment may produce test anxiety because it makes failures negatively valent.

4. Task-related social support may reduce test anxiety via the strengthening of positive effort–control and achievement expectancies. On the other hand, it might also be interpreted by the student as indicating pressure for achievement (cf. Helmke, 1983; Trudewind & Windel, 1991), thus making effects ambivalent. Furthermore, support may be provoked by students' anxiety and failures in the first place. This would imply a negative (reducing) effect of support on anxiety, but an enhancing effect of anxiety on support, thus providing for an overall zero correlation.

5. An additional assumption is that lack of structure in scholastic instruction may foster test anxiety by producing negative action–control expectancies as well as unpredictability of outcomes.

Parts of these assumptions have been tested using data from the Munich longitudinal study described above. Using self-report scales constructed for this study, environmental variables were measured as perceived by students. One reason was that students' perceptions can be assumed to be more proximal determinants of their development than other indicators. Table 1 shows the overall cross-sectional correlations between selected environmental variables and test anxiety (cf. Pekrun, 1991b). In addition to achievement-specific environmental factors, general positive emotional family cohesion was also included because of its possible buffering functions.

The results are basically in line with the above assumptions. Pressure for achievement, competition, and punishment correlate positively with test anxiety. Task-related support, however, shows only moderate correlations. Furthermore, these correlations tend to be positive instead of negative, which renders valid the notion of ambiguous or even detrimental effects of support. Family cohesion correlates negatively with test anxiety, which might indicate that it does in fact buffer academic anxiety. All five of these relationships remain essentially stable over grade levels. Interestingly, this does not apply to lack of instructional structure. Correlations for this variable go down from significantly positive to zero across

Table 1 Educational environments and test anxiety: correlations

	Grade level			
	5	6	8	10
Family				
Cohesion	−.23	−.18	−.16	−.17
Support	.16	.09	.06	.11
Punishment	.25	.27	.17	.21
Teacher				
Achievement pressure	.29	.36	.28	.32
Support	.12	.09	.01	.11
Punishment	.24	.21	.18	.21
Classmates				
Competition	.31	.33	.13	.23
Support	.08	.05	.02	.11
Punishment	.29	.27	.19	.25
Instruction				
Lack of structure	.36	.28	.17	.00

Note. Grade 5/6/8/10: N = 859/802/1109/702; $p < .01$ for $|r| >$ .09/.09/.07/.10.

grades. This might indicate that lack of structure in academic matters implies more threat for younger than for older students.

To investigate the relative contributions of different environmental variables as well as their longitudinal impact, correlational analysis was complemented by cross-sectional and longitudinal regression analysis. As may be seen from Table 2, these analyses corroborate the anxiety-producing impact of achievement pressure and punishment, as well as the alleviating role of a positive emotional family climate. However, results should be interpreted cautiously because most regression coefficients are weak and because feedback effects of students on their environments have not been included. Finally, the present data also have been used for

Table 2 Educational environments and test anxiety: regression analyses

	Cross-sectional analyses				Longitudinal analyses		
	Grade level				Interval[a]		
	5	6	8	10	5/6	6/8	8/10
Family							
Cohesion	−.15***	−.05	−.14***	−.13***	−.10**	−.03	−.12*
Punishment	.04	.07	.08*	.06	.08	.08	.03
Teacher							
Ach. pressure	.19***	.23***	.28***	.27***	.18***	.16**	.14**
Punishment	.09*	.03	.05	.09*	.09*	−.04	.13**
Classmates							
Competition	.14***	.15***	−.01	.08*	.04	.04	−.04
Punishment	.14***	.12**	.09**	.12**	.06	.14*	.11*
R	.46***	.43***	.28***	.44***	.34***	.27***	.27***
N	805.	761.	1082.	664.	649.	465.	468.

[a]Predictors grade 5/6/8; criterion (text anxiety) grade 6/8/10.
*$p < .05$; **$p < .01$; ***$p < .001$.

preliminary analyses of expectancy–value mediational assumptions. Findings imply that environmental effects on test anxiety may in fact be mediated largely by expectancy- and value-related cognitive structures of students (Pekrun, 1985).

IMPLICATIONS FOR PREVENTION AND THERAPY

By its very nature, human existence is fraught with danger. Therefore, some amount of anxiety seems to be an inevitable component of human life. However, if anxiety becomes excessively frequent and intense, it may be detrimental to psychological and physical well-being and to the individual and collective productivity of a society. Therefore, to be free of excessive anxiety may be seen as an important part of psychological health, and to reduce such anxiety may be seen as a goal of psychological intervention.

Expectancy–value theory implies that anxiety may be caused by proximal momentary and enduring expectancy–value appraisals, which may in turn depend on internal/external situations of the individual. Therefore, any intervention may basically focus either on situational variables, subjective appraisal systems, or both. In deciding which side to concentrate on, or on the relative veridicality of appraisals may be a crucial factor. In the event that subjective appraisals are more or less congruent to reality, any intervention based on changing appraisals may be in conflict with reality, thus being either ineffective or detrimental. An example would be to tell an unemployed person during an enduring economic crisis that individual unemployment is self-produced and can be changed simply by taking an optimistic perspective and actions. In the event that appraisals are more negative than would be necessary to cope with reality, however, intervention may well focus on appraisal systems.

The Importance of the Situation

In contemporary societies, anxiety seems to be produced no less often by situational factors than by excessive negative appraisals. EVTA implies that psychological intervention may concentrate on both the situational and the subjective side of human anxiety. From such a perspective, current anxiety-related intervention, which still focuses largely on individual determinants of anxiety (cf. Spielberger & Vagg, 1987), should be enlarged to include systematic attempts to change situations. For example, in the educational domain there is extensive motivation research that analyzes the possibility of restructuring schools in motivationally beneficial ways (Maehr, 1991). Few systematic analyses of this type that focus on student anxiety are available to date (see Fend, 1982; Hembree, 1988).

There is a second reason why EVTA implies that a contemporary psychology of anxiety should take situations more seriously. This is the assumption that negative situation–outcome expectancies may be crucial, necessary determinants of cognitively mediated as well as habitualized anxiety. Whereas action-related expectancies may be determined by information about the interplay of actions and situational conditions, situation–outcome expectancies relate exclusively to situational developments. The relevance of such expectancies for anxiety also implies that situational determinants may be of primary relevance for anxiety-related intervention.

Beyond pointing to the importance of situational factors and situation–outcome expectations, EVTA may also serve as a means of ordering methods of prevention and therapy according to the determinants of anxiety they may attempt to influence.

Prevention

Prevention of excessive anxiety implies that we shape situations in such a way that excessive negative expectancy–value appraisals do not arise. Specifically, one aim of prevention should be that negative expectancy–value beliefs do not develop. Other theoretical possibilities would be to change the individual genes that underlie physiological anxiety dispositions, or to induce enduring neurochemical changes that would reduce anxiety. However, the latter two methods are not viable today. Furthermore, genetic prevention may not be desirable because of its ethical implications.

Expectancy–value-oriented prevention implies a focus on external and internal conditions building up favorable expectancies and preventing negative valences. Some such conditions have already been discussed in the previous section on anxiety's social determinants.

Situation-Centered Prevention

First, prevention should provide for physically and psychologically safe environments, thus preventing negative situation–outcome expectancies. This implies that prevention should aim at reducing physical danger in today's world (e.g., danger stemming from environmental pollution; Bowler & Schwarzer, 1991). Furthermore, it should reduce the danger of psychologically negative situation outcomes. Examples would be to educate parents to give their children developmentally favorable amounts of emotional support, or to reduce excessive competition between students in an educational system by changing the system's goal structures.

Action-Centered Prevention

Second, prevention could try to optimize the individual's chances of coping even in aversive environments. This could prevent negative action–control and action–outcome expectations. According to the above considerations basic methods might involve (a) supporting the individual directly in building up competencies, (b) providing for sufficiently high discretion levels, (c) establishing environmental responsivity implying that actions lead to positive outcomes or prevention of negative outcomes, and (d) evaluating competencies and outcomes positively.

Valence-Centered Prevention

To the extent that negative valences are built up by learning, the development of such valences might be influenced by reducing contingent punishment and by devaluative information. For example, excessive negative valences of academic failures may be prevented by not delivering punishment after failure, by reducing negative career consequences as far as possible, and by value communications making realistic assessments of importance possible.

Therapy

Changing Reality

If anxiety is based on negative reality instead of unrealistic appraisals, reality has to be changed. Suitable methods generally may be equivalent to measures of prevention. Concerning modification of external situations, systems-oriented therapy has begun to design methods of changing social, family, and work environments (e.g., see Carter & McGoldrick, 1988). Beyond that, psychology might also contribute to changing more generalized structural features of environments by giving advice to administrators, company leaders, and politicians. For modifying competencies and action–outcome relations, skills training may be a viable method (e.g., skills-oriented study counseling in the therapy of test anxiety; cf. Spielberger & Vagg, 1987). Finally, changing the conditions that underlie negative valences may imply a change in the individual's social environments by reducing punishment-delivering structures.

Breaking Up Habitualized Anxiety

Excessive anxiety as in panic disorders and phobias seems often to be characterized by high degrees of habitualization. This implies that strong procedural schemata have been built up that link anxiety to perceptions, and that therefore trigger anxiety immediately upon schema-congruent perceptions. Any reduction of such anxiety may presuppose that these schemata are broken up. This may be achieved by linking situation perceptions to a state of not experiencing anxiety. Having achieved such a state, underlying negative expectancy and valence may be more accessible for modification (cf. Foa & Kozak, 1986). One prominent example that links nonanxiety to relevant perceptions is flooding, which seems to work by simple exhaustion of anxiety over time. Another example is relaxation training (e.g., in systematic desensitization), which links threat-related perception to subjective states that are incompatible with anxiety.

Changing Expectancies and Valences

To the extent that excessive anxiety is caused by unnecessarily high negative expectancies and valences, therapy has to concentrate on changing appraisals. Most contemporary methods of modifying anxiety may be included here. This seems to apply not only to cognitive–behavioral and rational–emotive therapy, but also to traditional behavioral methods. For example, besides breaking up habitualized anxiety, systematic desensitization leads to more realistic appraisals of situation–outcome contingencies.

Taking Side Effects and Feedback Loops into Account

EVTA assumptions imply that anxiety may act back on its determinants, and that anxiety is embedded in a wider network of emotional and motivational processes (Pekrun, 1988a, 1988b). For prevention and therapy, this means that it may be useful to account for feedback effects of anxiety and for side effects of intervention. For example, the expression of anxiety may be a mechanism for a patient to provoke support from other people. If this feedback effect of anxiety is not taken into account, therapy may fail because the patient resists attempts to deprive him or her of this mechanism. Another example may be therapy for academic anxiety that focuses on the reduction of achievement valences. Such therapy might reduce anxiety, but may at the same time be detrimental for academic motivation that also depends on valences. Taking such side effects into account, it may be wise to design and select methods that have a positive balance of beneficial main effects and detrimental side effects (e.g., by concentrating on expectancies rather than on values in the therapy of academic problems).

CONCLUSION

The assumptions of EVTA imply that negative expectancies and valences may be regarded as primary determinants of human anxiety. Among them may be competence- and outcome-related expectations as well as situational expectancies and subjective values. As a consequence, expectancy–value cognitions and beliefs are postulated to mediate the relationships between anxiety and achievement, the influences of social determinants on anxiety, and most methods of prevention and therapy. Some corroborating evidence is presented that refers to the specific case of test anxiety's relationship to academic achievement, and to its social-educational determinants. Parts of this evidence lend some credibility to EVTA's notion that expectancy–value appraisals, anxiety, and the effects of anxiety are typically linked by feedback loops.

The main theoretical aim of EVTA is to integrate, systematize, and enlarge some of the assumptions of cognitive theories of anxiety. By implication, however, EVTA may not only share the features that give such theories their strength, but may also share some of their limitations. Specifically, cognitive theories of anxiety may be assumed to explain only one type of anxiety formation, namely, cognitively mediated anxiety. Genetically based anxiety as well as habitualized anxiety fall outside the immediate range of validity of cognitive theories. Furthermore, cognitive theories themselves cannot account for the relationships between anxiety and peripheral expressive and physiological processes. To integrate cognitive theories of anxiety with perspectives on its basic evolutionary, expressive, and physiological principles should be one primary aim of future theoretical development.

REFERENCES

Anderson, J. R. (1987). Skill acquisition: Compilation of weak-method problem solutions. *Psychological Review, 94,* 192–210.

Asendorpf, J. (1989). Shyness as a final common pathway for two different kinds of inhibition. *Journal of Personality and Social Psychology, 57,* 481–492.

Bandura, A. (1977). Self-efficacy: Toward a unifying theory of behavioral change. *Psychological Review, 84,* 191–215.

Bandura, A. (1983). Self-efficacy determinants of anticipated fears and calamities. *Journal of Personality and Social Psychology, 45,* 464–469.

Bandura, A. (1986). *Social foundations of thought and action.* Englewood Cliffs, NJ: Prentice-Hall.

Beck, A. T., & Clark, D. A. (1988). Anxiety and depression: An information processing perspective. *Anxiety Research, 1,* 23–36.

Bowler, R., & Schwarzer, R. (1991, July). *Identifying anxiety in subjects exposed to environmental toxins.* Paper presented at the 12th conference of the Society for Test Anxiety Research, Budapest, Hungary.

Carter, B., & McGoldrick, M. (1988). *The changing family life cycle: A framework for family therapy.* New York: Gardner Press.

Carver, C. S., & Scheier, M. F. (1988). A control–process perspective on anxiety. *Anxiety Research, 1,* 17–22.

Covington, M. V., & Omelich, C. (1982). Achievement anxiety, performance and behavioral instruction: A cost/benefit analysis. In R. Schwarzer, H. M. van der Ploeg, and C. D. Spielberger (Eds.), *Advances in test anxiety research* (Vol. 1, pp. 139–154). Lisse, Netherlands/Hillsdale, NJ: Swets & Zeitlinger/Erlbaum.

Eysenck, M. W. (1988). Anxiety and attention. *Anxiety Research, 1*, 9–15.

Fend, H. (1982). *Gesamtschule im Vergleich* [Comparing comprehensive to traditional German schools]. Weinheim: Beltz.

Foa, E. B., & Kozak, M. J. (1986). Emotional processing of fear: Exposure to corrective information. *Psychological Bulletin, 99*, 20–35.

Heckhausen, H. (1977). Achievement motivation and its constructs: A cognitive model. *Motivation and Emotion, 1*, 283–329.

Helmke, A. (1983). *Schulische Leistungsangst* [Scholastic test anxiety]. Frankfurt a.M.: Lang.

Helmke, A. (1988). The role of classroom context factors for the achievement-impairing effect of test anxiety. *Anxiety Research, 1*, 37–52.

Hembree, R. (1988). Correlates, causes, effects, and treatment of test anxiety. *Review of Educational Research, 58*, 47–77.

Jöreskog, K. G., & Sörbom, D. (1984). *LISREL VI. Analysis of linear structural relationships by maximum likelihood, instrumental variables, and least squares methods.* Unpublished manuscript, University of Uppsala, Department of Statistics, Sweden.

Kohlmann, C.-W., & Krohne, H. W. (1988). Erziehungsstildeterminanten schulischer Leistung und Leistungsängstlichkeit. (Educational determinants of school achievement and test anxiety.) *Zeitschrift für Pädagogische Psychologie, 4*, 271–279.

Krampen, G. (1988). Toward an action–theoretical model of personality. *European Journal of Personality, 2*, 39–55.

Krohne, H. W. (1985). Entwicklungsbedingungen von Ängstlichkeit und Angstbewältigung (Developmental conditions of trait anxiety and coping with anxiety). In H. W. Krohne (Ed.), *Angstbewältigung in Leistungssituationen* (Coping with anxiety in achievement situations; pp. 136–160). Weinheim: Edition Psychologie.

Krohne, H. W. (in press). Developmental conditions of anxiety and coping: A two-process model of child-rearing effects. In K. A. Hagtvet (Ed.), *Advances in test anxiety research* (Vol. 7). Lisse, Netherlands: Swets & Zeitlinger.

Kuhl, J. (1984). Volitional aspects of achievement motivation and learned helplessness: Toward a comprehensive theory of action control. In B. A. Maher (Ed.), *Progress in experimental personality research* (Vol. 13, pp. 99–171). New York: Academic Press.

Lazarus, R. S. (1966). *Psychological stress and the coping process.* New York: McGraw-Hill.

Maehr, M. (1991, April). *Changing the school.* Paper presented at the annual meeting of the American Educational Research Association, Chicago, IL.

Mandler, G., & Sarason, S. B. (1952). A study of anxiety and learning. *Journal of Abnormal and Social Psychology, 47*, 166–173.

Meece, J. L., Wigfield, A., & Eccles, J. S. (1990). Predictors of math anxiety and its influence on young adolescents' course enrollment intentions and performance in mathematics. *Journal of Educational Psychology, 82*, 60–70.

Mischel, W. (1973). Toward a cognitive social learning reconceptualization of personality. *Psychological Review, 80*, 252–283.

Pekrun, R. (1984). An expectancy–value model of anxiety. In H. M. van der Ploeg, R. Schwarzer, and C. D. Spielberger (Eds.), *Advances in test anxiety research* (Vol. 3, pp. 63–72). Lisse, Netherlands/Hillsdale, NJ: Swets & Zeitlinger/Erlbaum.

Pekrun, R. (1985). Classroom climate and test anxiety: Developmental validity of expectancy–value theory of anxiety. In H. M. van der Ploeg, R. Schwarzer, and C. D. Spielberger (Eds.), *Advances in test anxiety research* (Vol. 4, pp. 147–158). Lisse, Netherlands: Swets & Zeitlinger.

Pekrun, R. (1988a). *Emotion, Motivation und Persönlichkeit* (Emotion, motivation, and personality). München: Psychologie Verlags Union.

Pekrun, R. (1988b). Anxiety and motivation in achievement settings: Towards a systems–theoretical approach. *International Journal of Educational Research, 12*, 307–323.

Pekrun, R. (1988c, July). *Family correlates of students' test anxiety: Theory and evidence.* Paper presented at the 9th conference of the Society for Test Anxiety Research, Padua, Italy.

Pekrun, R. (1991a). Prüfungsangst und Schulleistung: Eine Längsschnittanalyse (Test anxiety and academic achievement). *Zeitschrift für Pädagogische Psychologie, 5*, 99–109.

Pekrun, R. (1991b). Schulleistung, Entwicklungsumwelten und Prüfungsangst (Academic achievement, educational environments, and test anxiety). In R. Pekrun & H. Fend (Eds.), *Schule und Persönlichkeitsentwicklung* (Schools and personality development, pp. 164–180). Stuttgart: Enke.

Pekrun, R., & Frese, M. (1992). Emotions in work and achievement. In C. L. Cooper & I. T. Robertson (Eds.), *International Review of Industrial and Organizational Psychology, (Vol. 7, pp. 153–200)*. Chichester, UK: Wiley.

Price, D. D., Barrell, J. E., & Barrell, J. J. (1985). A quantitative–experiental analysis of human emotions. *Motivation and Emotion, 9*, 19–38.

Rotter, J. B. (1954). *Social learning and clinical psychology.* Englewood Cliffs, NJ: Prentice–Hall.

Rotter, J. B. (1966). Generalized expectancies for internal versus external control of reinforcement. *Psychological Monographs, 80* (1, Whole No. 609).

Schwarzer, R., Seipp, B., & Schwarzer, C. (1989). Mathematics performance and anxiety: A meta-analysis. In R. Schwarzer, H. R. van der Ploeg, and C. D. Spielberger (Eds.), *Advances in Test Anxiety Research* (Vol. 6, pp. 105–119). Lisse, Netherlands: Swets & Zeitlinger.

Seligman, M. E. P. (1975). *Helplessness: On depression, development and death.* San Francisco: Freeman.

Spence, K. W., & Taylor, J. A. (1951). Anxiety and strength of UCS as determiner of amount of eyelid conditioning. *Journal of Experimental Psychology, 42*, 183–188.

Spielberger, C. D., & Vagg, P. R. (1987). The treatment of test anxiety: A transactional process model. In R. Schwarzer, H. M. van der Ploeg, & C. D. Spielberger (Eds.), *Advances in test anxiety research* (Vol. 5, pp. 179 186). Lisse, Netherlands: Swets & Zeitlinger.

Stengel, E. (1936). Prüfungsangst und Prüfungsneurose (Test anxiety and examination neurosis). *Zeitschrift für psychoanalytische Pädagogik, 10*, 300–320.

Trudewind, C., & Windel, A. (1991). Elterneffekte auf die kindliche Kompetenzentwicklung (Parental effects on the development of children's competencies). In R. Pekrun & H. Fend (Eds.), *Schule und Persönlichkeitsentwicklung* (Schools and personality development) (pp. 131–148). Stuttgart: Enke.

Walberg, H. J. (1990). A theory of educational productivity: Fundamental substance and method. In P. Vedder (Ed.), *Fundamental studies on educational research* (pp. 19–34). Lisse: Swets & Zeitlinger.

Wine, J. D. (1971). Test anxiety and direction of attention. *Psychological Bulletin, 76*, 92–104.

4

Self-Organization, Self-Disorganization, and Anxiety

Anna Laura Comunian
Department of Psychology, University of Padua, Italy

Lewin (1935) describes the organizational unity of a person as a whole. Such organizational unity is a function of a number of contributing factors; there are important differences among individuals in terms of organizational and disorganizational unity.

When one experiences an anxiety-producing situation, the result is an increase in general tension. Thus this tension can be expected to influence the organizational unity of the person, at times resulting in disorganizational changes. We use the term *organizational unity* comprehensively to cover the entire field of authentic and more or less nonauthentic cognitive processes (presentation of self, personality traits, personal control, self-esteem, social approval, motivational variables, abilities, attitudes, emotion, etc.). We actively construct our reality by selecting, transforming, encoding, storing, and retrieving information (Kelly, 1955).

Anxiety has been a difficult construct to define and assess. Each conceptualization of anxiety is associated frequently with a different measurement approach. With respect to the relationship between self-organization and anxiety, anxiety has been conceptualized variously as a drive, a trait, a motive, and an emotion. It is very difficult to define the precise nature of the interaction of self-organization/ self-disorganization and stimulus-induced anxiety; once anxious, the person develops an organized or disorganized scheme. Disorganization is undefined and therefore uncontrollable. Consequently, cognitive factors are viewed as necessary but not sufficient to the production of the organizational unity of a person as a whole. Unfortunately, there is no current generally accepted theory within the cognitive–clinical perspective.

In the present study, we will focus on the experience of anxiety and the experience of the self, including beliefs about the self, beliefs held by others about the self, and beliefs about the self in everyday life. All these aspects of the self contribute equally to the organizational unity of the whole person. When an individual experiences anxiety, even a few beliefs about the self seem sufficiently strong enough to suppress other contrasting beliefs that may not be acceptable to the self. In this event, some disorganization of the unity of the individual may be expected.

A rather different type of unity of the person occurs while experiencing anxiety, when several beliefs about the self are organized on a relatively equal footing with little contrast. It is possible that happier, more easygoing people who experience anxiety demonstrate this type of organizational unity in self-belief systems.

These relationships are suggested generally by Lewin's field theory (1935) in its treatment of the concept of the whole and the organizational unity of a person. Lewin (1936) proposed that the increase in differentiation of a person's central needs during development may well lead to a decrease in the organizational unity of that person. However, if developmental differentiation results in one emotional need predominating over the others and it is then demoted to a lower position because of strong anxiety experiences, the degree of unity of the whole is increased, as is the degree of hierarchical organization. However, this type of integration is quite different from that of the happy person.

The degree of organizational unity, however, may decrease to some degree if the 'tool region' of the person becomes less fluid. This could well be the result of high levels of general tension, or if the tools are under the simultaneous influence of conflicting forces (Lewin, 1935). This is the focus of the present study of the relationship of anxiety to the organization and disorganization of the individual. We hope to provide evidence concerning organizational unity as it relates to a variety of basic forms of anxiety. Considerable empirical evidence exists to suggest that anxiety is a pervasive, cross-cultural phenomenon (McReynolds, 1975). More specifically, we will assess with several self-rating measures of personality the relationship of anxiety to self-beliefs, to beliefs held by others about the self, and to beliefs held by the self in everyday life, in a sample of young Italian adults.

METHOD

Subjects

Subjects were 30 males whose mean age was 19 years and 3 months, and 30 females whose mean age was 18 years and 8 months. All participants were Italian students enrolled in their last year of high school. Data collection was arranged to be part of an initial assessment procedure that took place shortly before these students took their final high school examinations.

Measures

We used the Test Anxiety Inventory (TAI) (Spielberger, 1989) as our measure of anxiety. The TAI is an empirically developed 20-item self-report index of anxiety. Each item is responded to on four-point scales of frequency and intensity. These values are summed to yield two subscales called *worry* and *emotionality.* Each subscale reflects both cognitive concern over one's performance (worry) and also physiological arousal (emotionality). Worry is defined as the cognitive component concerned with the consequences of failure. Emotionality is defined in terms of the reactions of the autonomic nervous system elicited by a situation that is evaluated by an individual as being stressful. Worry and emotionality may also be thought of as major components of anxiety reactions that occur in test situations, including tension, apprehension, nervousness, and arousal of the autonomic nervous system.

To measure important aspects of the self, we employed the Intrapersonal and Interpersonal Matrix of Group Processes (MIPG) method (Abraham, 1978). Abraham developed this technique as a means of investigating the subjective self. This measure includes subjective estimates of self beliefs, beliefs about how the self is perceived by others, beliefs about the ideal self, and, importantly, provides an index of the defense mechanisms that maintain the unity of the self, whether consciously or unconsciously.

The MIPG makes use of the Q-sort technique developed by Stephenson. Using this method, the subject describes himself using 22 items on the matrix and indicates different personality traits. The subject sorts the items three times. In the first sort, the subject describes himself as he really is (self for self, indicated by the symbol $|S|$). In the second sort, the subject describes himself as he would wish to be (ideal self, indicated by the symbol $|I|$). In the third and final sort, the subject describes how he believes himself to be perceived by others (self for others, indicated by the symbol $|O|$).

Five configurations are developed that provide measures of self-belief systems. Each configuration consists of a set of agreements and disagreements relative to the relationships among the terms S, I, and O, which are dependent on their qualitative differences or equivalences. The five configurations are provided below:

1. The first configuration is the fear of being unmasked ($S \neq I, S = O$). In this category, the individual sees himself $|S|$ as different from what he would like to be $|I|$ and he believes that others $|O|$ see him as closer to his ideal than he himself does. Anxiety that the truth can be discovered is fundamental to this configuration mechanism.

2. The second configuration is the rejection of others ($S \neq I, S \neq O$). Here there is a disagreement between the self $|S|$ and the ideal self $|I|$, but in this case $|O|$ is further from the ideal $|I|$ than is the self $|S|$. 'I'm not as I should be, but others see me as even worse than I am.'

3. The third configuration is an openness–dependence measure ($S \neq I, S = O$). 'I'm not as I would like to be, but others see me just as I am.'

4. The fourth configuration involves accusing others ($S = I, S \neq O$). In this case, the individual considers himself to be exactly as he wishes to be and there is agreement between S and I, but others see him as different ('other than he is').

5. The fifth configuration is concerned with the absence of conflict and the appearance of perfect harmony ($S = I, S = O$). 'I'm just as I wish to be and others see me as I am.' Here there is complete agreement among the three aspects of self and this is reflected in the absence of any intrapersonal and interpersonal tension. There is no anxiety in the traits characterizing this configuration, but rather self-satisfaction and a feeling of wholeness.

The five configurations are provided schematically in Table 1. Minimal presence of these configurations indicates a higher level of integration of the self. Finding many traits would indicate that these configurations are maintained to avoid anxiety. Scoring the three aspects of the self through these five configurations provides a description of the personal dimensions of the organizational unity of self experience.

Statistical Analysis

To identify organization and disorganization of the self in anxiety situations, we first cluster-analyzed the MIPG scores. A hierarchical clustering procedure similar to that described by Bradley, Prokop, Margolis, and Gentry (1978) was employed.

Table 1 The five configurations of the MIPG

Configuration	S^a	I^b	O^c		
1	2	4	4		
	1	5	2		SI > OI
	3	4	5	Fear of being unmasked	SI = OI
2	4	5	2		
	2	3	1		
	2	5	1	Total rejection	SI < OI
3	4	3	4		
	5	4	5		S = O
	2	1	2	Openness–dependence	S ≠ I
4	2	2	4		
	3	3	2		S = I
	4	4	5	Accusing others	S ≠ O
5	5	5	5		
	2	2	2		
	3	3	3	Perfect harmony	S = I = O

^{a}S = |self|. ^{b}I = |ideal|. ^{c}O = |others|.

Specifically, this procedure forms clusters by minimizing within-group variance while maximizing between-group variance. The clusters present in the data are determined by selecting set clusters that yield the smallest ratio of within-group to between-group variance. When these cluster analyses were completed, their results were used to assign subjects to profile groups. Classification was done separately for males and females. Finally, within each of the gender groups, multivariate analyses of variance were performed on the TAI subscale scores. Profile group configurations were the classificatory variables for these analyses.

RESULTS

Mean scores for the two TAI scales and the five configurations for all 60 subjects are given in Table 2. As can be seen there, the highest values are for configuration 1 (fear of being unmasked) and for configuration 3 (openness–dependence); the lowest values are for configuration 2 (total rejection).

Table 2 Descriptive statistics for the TAI and MIPG scales for all 60 subjects

	M	SD	Min	Max
TAI				
Worry	13.33	2.70	11	22.15
Emotionality	19.6	3.40	8	25.00
MIPG				
Configuration 1	27.27	8.14	16.05	50.00
Configuration 2	13.63	3.40	4.59	15.31
Configuration 3	24.24	8.00	11.72	45.00
Configuration 4	18.93	7.20	10.09	30.00
Configuration 5	15.91	6.10	9.00	25.00

Mean scores and standard deviations of the MIPG variables for the three profile groups, self, ideal, and other, are given in Table 3. Cluster analysis revealed the presence of three trait–profile groups. The profile of group |S| (self as I am) was characterized by high scores (at or above the T score of 70) on the following items: need of approval, self-confidence, sociability, and free group expression. The profile for group |I| (the ideal self) includes high values for all these variables in addition to group confidence and group support. The trait profile for group |O|

Table 3 Mean MIPG scale *t* scores for S, I, and O profiles

MIPG item	S	I	O
1. Timidity	53.36	51.16	62.33
	(6.31)	(10.13)	(12.52)
2. Competition	55.14	61.50	52.66
	(4.85)	(8.76)	(7.39)
3. Understanding	81.93	90.66	60.00
	(6.04)	(7.52)	(6.40)
4. Self-restraint	48.74	48.17	52.52
	(9.15)	(7.56)	(7.25)
5. Rationality	66.17	67.63	67.00
	(6.82)	(8.16)	(5.15)
6. Self-criticism	54.78	55.26	50.10
	(10.77)	(8.70)	(9.15)
7. Self need of approval	73.31	63.93	67.36
	(7.39)	(7.51)	(8.10)
8. Dependency	61.36	52.35	96.63
	(7.15)	(8.73)	(7.80)
9. Inferiority	54.68	56.29	62.17
	(9.13)	(6.97)	(10.00)
10. Conformity	59.12	58.57	58.61
	(9.36)	(9.44)	(6.34)
11. Feeling expression	71.53	83.43	66.78
	(9.49)	(13.20)	(7.53)
12. Self-confidence	86.73	90.36	70.71
	(9.80)	(10.10)	(9.10)
13. Self-perception	90.20	91.14	67.12
	(10.10)	(11.30)	(9.67)
14. Sociability	87.50	84.30	69.00
	(11.00)	(9.50)	(10.11)
15. Aggressivity	61.13	64.10	65.11
	(8.50)	(7.00)	(9.03)
16. Self-acceptance	80.01	90.50	65.06
	(9.10)	(10.00)	(9.50)
17. Rebellion	63.36	68.09	71.09
	(7.70)	(8.82)	(10.00)
18. Group confidence	76.29	89.57	68.09
	(10.03)	(12.80)	(7.22)
19. Free group expression	73.77	79.80	60.17
	(6.97)	(9.85)	(8.33)
20. Attention to others	71.53	73.36	68.43
	(7.75)	(7.70)	(5.05)
21. Group support	65.05	80.71	60.64
	(5.30)	(8.33)	(11.30)
22. Free role choice	52.47	58.57	50.83
	(7.97)	(9.44)	(7.00)

Note. Standard deviations are given in parentheses.

(the self perceived by others) did not have any high scores at or above the T score of 70, but did present relatively high scores on the rebellion and self-confidence variables. The profile groups found here correspond very closely to those found by Abraham (1978).

The TAI scale scores were analyzed next to determine if there were anxiety differences between these three profile groups. Mean scores and standard deviations for the Worry and Emotionality scales for each of the five configurations for the entire sample of 60 are given in Table 4. Employing Wilk's criterion, the results of the one-way MANOVAs on the two-scale scores of TAI yielded a significant F ratio for profile group (p = < .001). The profile group configuration 5 accounted for 73% of the variance in the dependent variable set. Univariate analyses yielded significant F ratios for worry (p = < .001) and for emotionality (p = < .01), indicating that these were the major dimensions along which the configurations differed. Post-hoc analysis, using Tukey's HSD test, revealed that configurations 1 and 3 had higher mean scores for the emotionality scale than did configuration 5 (p = < .01). In addition, configurations 2 and 4 also had significantly higher worry scores than did configuration 5 (p = < .05).

To determine if the findings reported above would hold for both male and female subjects, univariate MANOVAs were performed by gender. No significant differences were found between the respective configuration profile groups for the gender groups of this study.

DISCUSSION

The results of the cluster analysis performed here revealed five distinct subgroups based on the MIPG profiles, and these profiles were similar for the male and female groups of subjects. A major aim of this study was to determine whether there were characteristic differences in anxiety scores associated with these configuration groups. The results of the TAI analyses suggest that these associations exist. Although configurations 1 and 3 had distinctly different profiles, they were similar in their anxiety scores. These configurations were associated with the emotionality aspect of anxiety more frequently than configurations 2 and 4 were. These latter two configurations had similar scores on the worry aspect of anxiety.

Table 4 Mean scores for the "worry" and "emotionality" scales (N = 60)

MIPG configurations	Worry	Emotionality
1	20.39	24.46
	(8.59)	(4.70)
2	20.50	16.22
	(6.16)	(4.99)
3	22.63	26.25
	(4.60)	(4.65)
4	21.31	17.29
	(3.75)	(3.12)
5	12.45	13.15
	(5.57)	(4.49)

Note. Standard deviations are given in parentheses.

Some differences in the experience and expression of anxiety in the organizational unity of self beliefs were found between the TAI scales and the configuration profile subgroups for both males and females. These affective differences in anxiety suggest a different organizational unity of the MIPG profile. Further research is required to investigate characteristic subgroup differences employing other affective and behavioral measures.

One possible implication of the present findings is that unwanted self beliefs reflect a disorganization process rather than anxiety. It might be expected that relatively automatic processes would tend to be associated with vulnerability to disorganization in anxiety-provoking situations whereas more controlled processes would tend to reflect correctly situations that stimulate an anxious mood. There are a number of reasons why attempts to investigate cognitive factors empirically may be particularly difficult. First, the private, subjective nature of the organizational unity of a person as a whole results in a considerable degree of interference with the dependent variables used to assess cognitive constructs. Second, we believe that any faulty cognitive functioning will be transient, situationally specific, and rather secondary in nature.

To understand these processes better than we now do, a two-stage approach seems to be necessary. The first stage would involve the accumulation of sufficient evidence to permit an accurate description of the differences in organizational unity between individuals with varying anxiety levels. The second stage would involve the assessment of the functional significance of such differences so that we can better understand the dynamics of anxiety. Future studies should employ a multifaceted assessment approach in which a number of constructs that represent various theoretical domains are measured.

REFERENCES

Abraham, A. (1978). *Modèle multi-dimensionnel pour l'étude du soi et du soi collectif.* [Multidimensional model for the study of the self and of the collective self.] Issy-les-Moulineaux: Editions Scientifiques et Psychologiques.

Bradley, L. A., Prokop, C. K., Margolis, R., & Gentry, W. D. (1978). Multivariate analyses of the MMPI profiles of low back pain patients. *Journal of Behavioral Medicine, 1,* 253–272.

Kelly, G. A. (1955). *The psychology of personal constructs.* New York: Norton.

Lewin, K. (1935). *A dynamic theory of personality.* New York: McGraw-Hill.

Lewin, K. (1936). *Principles of topological psychology.* New York: McGraw-Hill.

McReynolds, P. (1975). *Changing conceptions of anxiety: A historical review and a proposed integration.* Washington, DC: Hemisphere.

Spielberger, C. D. (1989). *Text anxiety inventory manual.* Florence, Italy: Organizzazioni Speciali.

5

Anxiety and Effort

Wolfgang Schönpflug
Department of Psychology, Free University of Berlin

In this chapter, I will look at two old topics from a new point of view. The first topic to be treated is the relationship between anxiety and arousal. There is some evidence in the literature that anxious individuals show higher arousal in achievement situations (Eysenck, 1979; Wieland-Eckelmann, 1986). This effect can be conceptualized in two ways: as a result of a bottom-up or a top-down process.

Typically, studies on the behavior of anxious individuals induce arousal by environmental agents such as task demands or physical stimulation. Anxious people who exhibit more arousal under external stimulation can be interpreted as having higher sensitivity or higher reactivity. From this perspective, arousal is conceptualized as a neurophysiological bottom-up process. Such a process has been proposed and described by Freeman (1948), Duffy (1962), and Lindsley (1952). In contrast, a more recent theoretical approach regards arousal as a top-down process. Individuals are seen as initiating and regulating their own state of arousal according to their own intentions. Such regulatory processes originate from the central nervous system and extend to peripheral structures, such as the muscles. The intentional arousal that originates from the central nervous system may follow a purpose, and an obvious purpose may be to tune the organism for better performance (Öhman, 1986; Ursin, 1986).

The neurophysiological description of arousal as a top-down process corresponds well to the subjective experience of effort. Effort can be characterized equally as an arousing process, originating within a person and being initiated and regulated by a central agent such as a hypothetical self. Effort as a subjective experience may be distinguished from top-down arousal as a neurophysiological concept. But when the subjective experience of the effort is interpreted as being an indicator of an underlying physiological arousal process, the term *effort* might as well be used to designate it (Kahneman, 1973). In light of more recent theorizing, the use of the term effort for top-down arousal emphasizes its intentional and self-regulatory nature, which is also why it is used in this chapter.

Keeping this concept of effort in mind the question can be raised whether the arousal of the anxious is also a top-down rather than just a bottom-up process, and to what extent this arousal is centrally initiated, self-controlled, and intentional rather than reactive. In particular, it can be suggested that anxious people in achievement situations perceive more task demands, or more specific task demands, and consequently increase their arousal to meet these demands. Again, the term effort can be substituted for the term *top-down arousal*. The question of whether the anxious are more aroused can be rephrased to: Do the anxious spend more effort? Evidence pertaining to this issue is rare; however, Dornic (1977) has presented behavioral and subjective data that has led him to the conclusion that the anxious do indeed expend more effort.

In terms of performance the anxious frequently are described as being high achievers on easy tasks and low achievers on difficult tasks (cf. Heinrich & Spielberger, 1982). However, achievement should not be described loosely because quite a few performance characteristics contribute to achievement in specific ways. Thus at least four such performance characteristics should be distinguished:

1. Speed: the number of tasks processed per unit of time.
2. Accuracy: the proportion of correct solutions.
3. Difficulty: the proportion of difficult tasks, when respondents are given the option to choose between easy and difficult tasks.
4. Self-control during performance (defined in this study as a concern for task-related feedback).

Given these four performance characteristics, a variety of patterns can arise, for example, an emphasis on accuracy and difficulty at the expense of speed and self-control.

The problem of performance characteristics can be linked to the problem of effort described above. Regulating one's effort may be associated with the modification of specific performance characteristics (Schönpflug, 1986). A frequently reported pattern is the speed/accuracy trade-off (Nährer, 1986). This trade-off also has been described as typical for work that involves effort. When making an effort, individuals have been found to increase speed at the expense of accuracy (Schneider & Kreuz, 1979). However, other trade-offs can also be hypothesized as resulting from effort expenditure. For example, it can be assumed that effort sometimes results in raising the difficulty level rather than increasing speed. Thus effort may be a kind of arousal that is regulated to maximize some performance characteristics, possibly at the expense of others.

However, effort regulation need not always result in trade-offs, or in gains of some performance characteristics at the expense of others. On the contrary, effort could operate against trade-offs. At least in some task situations, any sort of trade-off may reduce efficiency; for example, in some achievement situations, both speed and accuracy are required, or a gain in accuracy is only sought when the difficulty level is appropriately high. In such situations, effort should lead to simultaneous gains in different aspects of performance in order to enhance efficiency. Thus high effort should promote speed and accuracy, the choice of difficult tasks, and the involvement in self-control, all at the same time.

A simultaneous improvement in various aspects of efficiency can be conceptualized if effort is regarded as mobilizing spare capacities. Trade-offs can be interpreted as evidence for common internal resource capacities on which the different performance characteristics are based. Thus maximizing different aspects of efficiency resembles maximizing performance in multiple tasks (cf. Navon & Gopher, 1979; Wickens, 1984). However, as has been elaborated by Kahneman (1973), effort may lead to an augmentation of internal resources, which then lowers the competition between multiple tasks or different performance characteristics. Consequently, effort should prevent trade-offs between efficiency characteristics.

It should be admitted that few empirical data are available from the literature to support these speculations; however, they certainly deserve empirical testing. To examine these issues further, an experiment was designed and carried out. The following features of the experiment are emphasized because they were derived from the previously mentioned theoretical presuppositions:

1. The subjects were instructed to regulate their level of effort deliberately. In one experimental condition, they were asked to expend high effort to improve performance; in another condition they were asked to conserve effort to maintain a relaxed state.

2. The subjects were given a pool of tasks. Under one condition, they were free to choose their tasks. As the pool contained easy as well as difficult tasks, they had the option of determining the difficulty level of their tasks.

3. Speed and accuracy requirements were well balanced. The subjects received credits and could enlarge their point score by working fast, but credit for a task was granted only if the solution of the task was correct.

4. As a measure of self-control, the search for feedback was introduced. Subjects had the option of asking about the correctness of their last solution and their total point score. Search for feedback was conceived of as an extra task requirement; it constituted an auxiliary activity in the sense of Tomaszewski (1967).

From the theoretical approach proposed above, consistent individual differences were also predicted. We expected two factors to discriminate between subjects. One was intelligence, the other anxiety. Intelligence was included because one theoretical presupposition assumed a more homogeneous improvement of performance characteristics, or fewer trade-offs, with effort when more internal resources were available. Evidently intelligence can be accepted as a measure of internal resources. The prediction then was that if the highly intelligent expend more effort, they will improve their performance more homogeneously (i.e., they will simultaneously increase speed, accuracy, difficulty, and self-control).

Anxiety was included as an important individual factor because of its hypothesized relation to effort. On the basis of the available empirical evidence, however, we could not make any definite predictions. We rather regarded the present work as a pilot study that would yield more substantial hypotheses for further investigations. Yet we hoped for evidence that would shed light on the anxiety factor, which was of central concern to us. More explicitly, we expected to find specific performance patterns for the anxious. We believed that if anxious individuals expended effort, they would exhibit a bias for accuracy and self-control. This hunch was based on speculations about anxious thinking (Schönpflug, 1989). Thus trade-offs could not be explained by bottom-up arousal that affects behavior in a generalized fashion, but rather by a top-down process that differentially and intentionally modifies the behavior pattern. Because of the theoretical relevance of the hypothesized relationship between effort and anxiety, these two variables are the focus of the present study.

EXPERIMENTAL METHOD

Forty students at the Free University of Berlin were hired for a full day from a local labor agency. Approximately as many females as males were recruited. Students from any field but psychology were admitted, and a high language proficiency in German was required. The subjects received an hourly fee according to local labor payment regulations.

The experiment was conducted in the psychophysiological laboratory of the Institute of Psychology of the Free University of Berlin. The subjects were seated at a workplace that was equipped with a keyboard and monitor, both linked to a DEC 11/27 laboratory computer. In the database of the computer a pool of 300 office tasks was available. Some of the tasks were rather simple, such as typing a list of addresses. Other tasks were fairly difficult, such as calculating a salary. Difficult tasks required a dialogue in order to obtain or verify data pertinent to the case in question (e.g., personal data of an employee; the subjects also had to find or check the regulations for salaries). The subjects received credits for correct solutions: one point for a group of easy tasks, and three points for one difficult task. Under some conditions, their total point score was converted into an extra premium that augmented their basic payment for the time spent in the laboratory.

In addition, a task *environment* was implemented in the system. Between tasks, the subjects had the option to engage in dialogues that conveyed feedback information. They could inquire whether the last solution was correct, how many credits they had collected, and how much money they had accumulated as an extra premium. The database containing the difficult tasks and the feedback system were designed and implemented by Wolfgang Battmann, and had been used in an earlier study (Battmann, 1988).

After the testing session, the subjects were familiarized carefully with the tasks, the equipment, and the experimental conditions. The main part of the experiment consisted of two further sessions. In one of these sessions the subjects were instructed to expend high effort in order to maximize their point score; in the other session they were instructed to work with low effort in a relaxed style. In the high-effort condition they earned an extra premium for each point, and in the low-effort condition no extra premium was paid.

The time available was critical for the interpretation of the expected impact of effort on work speed. Therefore, the time limitation was varied. Provision was also made to allow the behavior in both the easy and difficult tasks to be assessed. As a result, two conditions were compared in which the factors of time limitations and of choice of task difficulty were combined. In one condition, a fixed series of both easy and difficult tasks was assigned to the subjects, but the time permitted to solve these tasks was not limited. In the other condition, time was limited to 1 hour, but subjects were free to decide about the number of difficult and easy tasks on which to work. Clearly, time limitations played a salient role in the selection of speed strategies, and task assignment was a prerequisite for obtaining data for both high– and low–difficult tasks from all subjects. In addition, in the condition that permitted the free choice of tasks, the proportion of difficult tasks chosen served as a separate measure of behavior. Both combinations of time limitation and choice of tasks (i.e., fixed time with free choice of tasks and unlimited time for an obligatory set of tasks) were replicated. One replication took place under the condition of high effort, the other one under the condition of low effort.

The temporal sequence of effort and task condition was balanced in a 2 × 2 design. Half of the subjects started with low effort in the first session and had continued with high effort in the second session; for the other half, this sequence was reversed. The factor-of-effort sequence was crossed with the sequence of time limitation/choice of task condition. Half the subjects started with an hour of free-selected tasks and continued for an unlimited period of time with the tasks assigned to thcm; this sequence was reversed for the other half. Each of the four resulting sequences was introduced as a real-life occurrence in a separate cover story (e.g., the assignment or nonassignment of tasks was explained as being the result of the presence or absence of a supervisor).

The overall experimental design was as follows: Each subject underwent all the conditions of task difficulty, time limitation/choice of tasks, and effort expenditure. The sequences of these conditions varied between subjects. However, as an alternative to sequence effects, group differences in intelligence and anxiety could be considered as factors that varied between subjects (see Table 1).

The subjects' interactions with the computer system were recorded in a log file. At the beginning and end of each work period, subjective ratings of personal state (satisfaction, concentration, fatigue, etc.) were collected; the self-descriptions were also assessed in a computer dialogue. Heart rate was monitored continuously throughout the main experiment.

Before beginning these tasks, the subjects underwent a series of personality tests including the German version of the State-Trait-Anxiety Inventory (Laux, Glanzmann, Schaffner, & Spielberger, 1981) and three subtests from the Intelligence-Structure Test (Amthauer, 1971). Each subject received a score of trait anxiety and intelligence. High- and low-anxious individuals as well as high- and low-intelligent individuals were defined by splitting the respective distribution at the median. When the two personal factors with their two levels were crossed, four groups of subjects resulted, with 8 or 12 subjects in each group.

RESULTS

Figure 1 gives the performance data, separated by experimental conditions (for details see figure caption). Figure 2 shows the same data, separated by personality groups (for details see figure caption). It should also be remembered that ratings of subjective state were collected and heart rate was monitored.

Multivariate analyses of variance were conducted on these data. The results presented below stem from analyses where effort expenditure, time limitation/

Table 1 Experimental design. Task difficulty, assignment of tasks/time limitations, and effort expenditure were crossed with subjects. The effort demand sequence, intelligence, and anxiety were between subjects' comparisons

| Tasks | Assignment | Time | Effort demand sequence | |
			Session 1	Session 2
Easy	Free	Limited	Low effort High effort	High effort Low effort
	Obligatory	Free	Low effort High effort	High effort Low effort
Difficult	Free	Limited	Low effort High effort	High effort Low effort
	Obligatory	Free	Low effort High effort	High effort Low effort

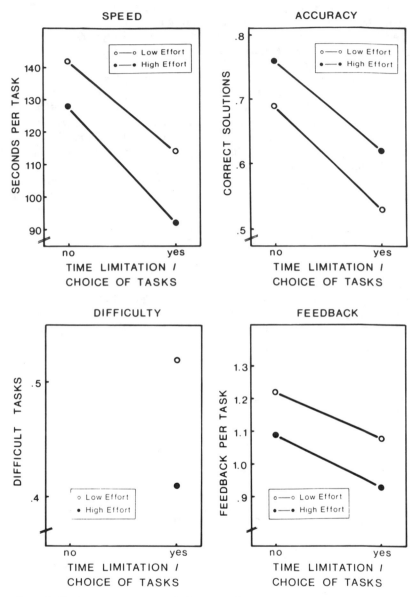

Figure 1 Performance scores: speed (time per task), accuracy (proportion of correct
tasks), choice of task difficulty (proportion of difficult tasks chosen),
requests for feedback (number of requests for feedback per task). The
scores are separated by effort expenditure, limitation of work time, and
choice of task difficulty. To vary effort expenditure, subjects were
instructed either to maximize performance (high effort) or to feel
comfortable at work (low effort). Furthermore, subjects had a free choice
of easy and difficult tasks within a limited time of 1 hour (time
limitation/choice of tasks), or they were assigned a series of both easy and
difficult tasks and were permitted unlimited time to finish the series (no
time limitation/no choice of tasks).

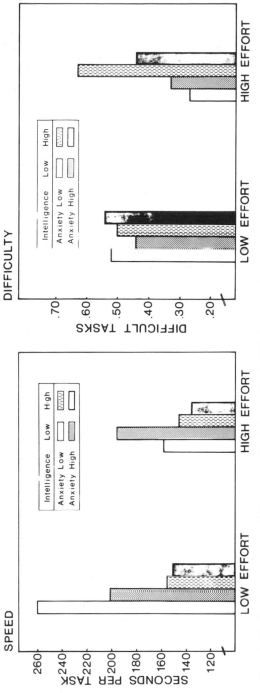

Figure 2 Performance scores: speed (time per task) and choice of task difficulty (proportion of difficult tasks chosen). The scores are separated by effort expenditure, intelligence, and anxiety. To vary effort expenditure, subjects were instructed either to maximize performance (high effort) or to feel comfortable at work (low effort). Groups were split at the median of both their intelligence and anxiety scores.

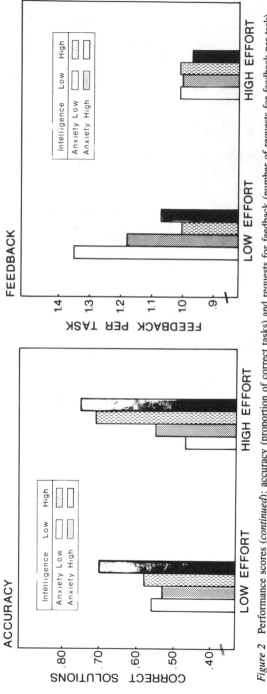

Figure 2 Performance scores (*continued*): accuracy (proportion of correct tasks) and requests for feedback (number of requests for feedback per task). The scores are separated by effort expenditure, intelligence, and anxiety. To vary effort expenditure, subjects were instructed either to maximize performance (high effort) or to feel comfortable at work (low effort). Groups were split at the median of both their intelligence and anxiety scores.

choice of tasks, and difficulty served as within-subject factors, and intelligence and anxiety as between-subject factors. The following results are emphasized:

1. Under conditions of effort, subjects reported less concentration ($F(1,36)$ = 6.0; p = $<.02$) and more fatigue ($F(1,36)$ = 8.0; p = $<.01$). The high intelligent and low anxious stand out in their ratings of fatigue ($F(1,36)$ = 5.3; p = $<$ .03 for the intelligence-anxiety interaction).

2. Speed increases, or average time per task decreases, with effort, but the overall effect misses significance. Subjects worked faster in the condition that had a time limitation ($F(1,36)$ = 12.5; p = $<.01$). Clearly, the high intelligent are faster than the low intelligent ($F(1,36)$ = 16.5; p = $<.01$), and a substantial 30% saving of time on task with effort is observed in only one group, the low intelligent and low anxious. This group, however, stands out in time consumption if working in a relaxed manner ($F(1,36)$ = 5.4; p = $<.03$ for the interaction of intelligence, anxiety, effort, and difficulty).

3. Accuracy, defined as the proportion of correct solutions, mostly benefits from effort ($F(1,36)$ = 4.1; p = $<.05$), and accuracy is higher if time is unlimited ($F(1,36)$ = 13.2; p $<.01$). The high intelligent work more accurately than the low intelligent ($F(1,36)$ = 6.5; p = $<.02$), the high anxious more than the low anxious ($F(1,36)$ = 5.2; p = $<.03$). The low intelligent low anxious who exhibited spectacular time savings with effort are among the few who increased their error rate when working with effort on difficult tasks ($F(1,36)$ = 7.1; p = $<.01$ for the interaction of intelligence, anxiety, effort, and difficulty).

4. Under the conditions of free choice of tasks, the majority of subjects shifted toward easier tasks with increased effort. There was, however, a remarkable exception: The high intelligent and low anxious subjects increased their difficulty level with effort ($F(1,36)$ = 3.5; p = $<.07$ for the interaction of intelligence, anxiety, and effort).

5. There were fewer calls for feedback with increased effort ($F(1,36)$ = 5.7; p = $<.02$). The high intelligent and low anxious subjects were the only group that did not follow this general trend.

6. Measures of heart rate that have been analyzed to the present do not discriminate between experimental conditions or groups.

DISCUSSION

As expected, the variation of effort was associated with changes in the performance characteristics. In one group, composed of the high intelligent and low anxious, effort led to an improvement in all performance characteristics, whereas the other groups showed different kinds of performance patterns. Effort also had an impact on ratings of subjective state although not on physiological measures. The failure to discriminate between groups by physiological measures may be because of methodological problems, which will not be discussed here. This means that personal state will be evaluated only on the basis of the subjective ratings.

The finding that high intelligence is associated with a homogeneous improvement in all the performance characteristics assessed agrees with the theoretical expectations presented in the preceding discussion. However, it is low rather than high anxiety that leads to a homogeneous improvement, and this is not in line with theoretical expectations. Consequently, interpretation of the data calls for new explanations. A complementary approach not yet considered in our earlier theoretical introduction is that effort also imposes a load with which individuals have to cope in order to take advantage of the benefits of effort. A tentative interpretation can be reached if two kinds of load are distinguished: mental and emotional (Schulz, 1980).

Mental load is defined by the ratio of demands and capacity. The intention to work with higher effort should increase demands. Simultaneously, as stated earlier, effort may mobilize spare capacities. Thus effortful work may balance the demand–capacity ratio at a higher level. This upward shift of demands and capacities may induce an emotional load. Working with higher demands and a reduced capacity reserve may be associated with more uncertainty and frustration. Consequently, mobilizing more capacities and meeting higher demands tends to destabilize the psychophysiological system.

Following this line of reasoning, the process of effort affects individuals in different ways. The factor of mental load seems to discriminate between the low and high intelligent. It would seem likely that high intelligent individuals have a larger reserve capacity and thus have more internal resources to be mobilized. Therefore they are better disposed to cope with higher mental demands as induced by effort, and may possibly suffer fewer destabilization effects. The ability to cope with destabilizing tendencies may be reflected in measures of anxiety. The low anxious are better disposed to execute effective self-control, and therefore are superior in coping with emotional load.

This interpretation may explain why individuals who are both high intelligent and low anxious form the only group that improves performance on all four aspects of efficiency if they expend more effort. This group also stands out as far as ratings of fatigue are concerned. From these observations it can be concluded that this group followed a highly motivated approach that was maintained by a high outcome; the latter was monitored continuously by feedback.

The three other groups exhibited trade-offs between efficiency aspects. All but the high intelligent and low anxious showed a transition to easier tasks in order to gain speed and accuracy while expending effort. Further, it should be noted that high anxious individuals worked at approximately the same pace during low and high effort. To the same degree, all but the high intelligent and low anxious spend less time monitoring their outcome. It is not easy to understand the nature of these trade-offs, but it can be stated that groups with trade-offs do not cope equally well with the mental and emotional loads induced by high effort.

The factors that discriminate between the low anxious, high intelligent subjects and the other groups may be conceived of as related to the regulation of arousal (Schönpflug, 1986). The former group favors an energetic style, copes well with the destabilizing effects of high arousal, and, finally, tolerates a state of tiredness and energy depletion. In contrast, the other groups may limit their arousal in order to prevent internal destabilization, tiredness, and energy depletion. However, it should be noted that stability is observed only with the high intelligent, that is, those in whom high operating capacities can be assumed to exist. Thus arousal is initiated depending on capacity; only if high capacity is available does high arousal seem to pay off.

CONCLUSIONS

It has to be admitted that the initial hypotheses regarding anxiety have not been corroborated. There are no indications for higher arousal, a more active style, and a characteristic performance pattern in the anxious. On the contrary, low anxiety, if paired with high intelligence, benefits efficient behavior. The discrepancy between the initial hypothesis and the empirical findings may be because of limitations in the assessment of anxiety. It is possible that the specific trait measure used in this study reflects emotional stability, but fails to assess functional characteristics such as increased self-control as expressed in a concern for feedback (Battmann, 1988) and preference for accuracy over speed. Such characteristics, however, may be significant facets of the construct of anxiety (cf. Schönpflug, 1989). If measures at hand do not reflect these facets, it is most important that other appropriate measures be developed.

REFERENCES

Amthauer, R. (1971). Der Intelligenz-Strukt-Test IST 70. (Test of the intelligence profile IST 70.) Göttingen: Hogrefe.

Battmann, W. (1988). Feedback seeking as a means of self-assessment and affect optimization. Motivation and Emotion, 12, 57–74.

Dornic, S. (1977). Mental load, effort and individual differences. Reports from the Department of Psychology, University of Stockholm, No. 509.

Duffy, E. (1962). Activation and behavior. New York: Wiley.

Eysenck, M. W. (1979). Anxiety, learning, and memory: A reconceptualization. Journal of Research in Personality, 13, 363–385.

Freeman, G. L. (1948). The energetics of human behavior. Ithaca, NY: Cornell University Press.

Heinrich, D. L., & Spielberger, C. D. (1982). Anxiety and complex learning. In H. W. Krohne & L. Laux (Eds.), Achievement, stress and anxiety (pp. 145–166). Washington, DC: Hemisphere.

Kahneman, D. (1973). Attention and effort. Englewood Cliffs, NJ: Prentice Hall.

Laux, L., Glanzmann, P., Schaffner, P., & Spielberger, C. D. (1981). Das State-Trait-Angstinventar. (State-trait-anxiety inventory.) Weinheim: Beltz.

Lindsley, D. B. (1952). Psychological phenomena and the electroencephalogram. EEG and Clinical Neurophysiology, 4, 443–456.

Nährer, W. (1986). Schnelligkeit und Güte als Dimensionen kognitiver Leistung. Berlin: Springer.

Navon, D., & Gopher, D. (1979). On the economy of the human processing system. Psychological Review, 86, 214–255.

Öhman, A. (1986). Integrating energetic and information processing concepts: Emotion from a functional–evolutionary perspective. In G. R. J. Hockey, A. W. K. Gaillard, & M. G. H. Coles (Eds.), Energetics and human information processing (pp. 337–352). Dordrecht: Nijhoff.

Schneider, K., & Kreuz, A. (1979). Die Effekte unterschiedlicher Anstrengung auf die Mengen- und Güteleistung bei einer einfachen und schweren Zahlensymbolaufgabe. (The effects of effort on speed and accuracy when solving digit-symbol tasks of varying difficulty.) Psychologie und Praxis, 23, 34–42.

Schönpflug, W. (1986). Effort regulation and individual differences in effort expenditure. In G. R. J. Hockey, A. W. K. Gaillard, & M. G. H. Coles (Eds.), Energetics and human information processing (pp. 271–283). Dordrecht: Nijhoff.

Schönpflug, W. (1989). Anxiety, worry, prospective orientation, and prevention. In C. D. Spielberger, I. G. Sarason, & J. Strelau (Eds.), Stress and anxiety (Vol. 12, pp. 245–257). New York: Hemisphere.

Schulz, P. (1980). Regulation und Fehlregulation im Verhalten. V. Die wechselseitige Beeinflussung von mentaler und emotionaler Beanspruchung. (Regulation and dysregulation of behavior. V. The initial influence of mental and emotional load.) Psychologische Beiträge, 22, 633–656.

Tomaszewski, T. (1967). Aktywnosc czlowieka. (Human Behavior. Psychology as a behavioral science.) In M. Maruszewski, J. Reykowski, & T. Tomaszewski (Eds.), *Psychologia jako nauka o czlowieku* (pp. 115–164). Warszawa: Ksiazka i Wiedza.

Ursin, H. (1986). Energetics and the self regulation of activation. In G. R. J. Hockey, A. W. K. Gaillard, & M. G. H. Coles (Eds.), *Energetics and human information processing* (pp. 53–70). Dordrecht: Nijhoff.

Wickens, D. A. (1984). Processing resources in attention. In R. Parasuraman & R. Davies (Eds.), *Varieties of attention* (pp. 63–102). New York: Academic Press.

Wieland-Eckelmann, R. (1986). Regulation und Fehlregulation im Verhalten. XI. Zur Makro- und Mikrostruktur des Leistungshandelns. (Regulation and dysregulation of behavior. XI. Macro- and microregulation of performance.) *Psychologische Beiträge, 28,* 457–487.

6

Changing Impact of Ability, Motivation, and Anxiety in Cognitive Performance: A Process Analysis

Knut A. Hagtvet
Department of General Psychology, University of Bergen, Norway

Ye Ren Min
Educational Research Institute,
Shanghai Teachers University, People's Republic of China

One of the major purposes of test anxiety research has been to improve the understanding of the academic cognitive performance of students (Hagtvet, 1989). Nevertheless, recent meta-analyses suggest that test anxiety explains only a limited amount of variance in cognitive or school performance measures (Schwarzer, Scipp, & Schwarzer, 1989). On the other hand, simple bivariate correlations between an anxiety measure and a performance measure seem to have limited potential to support conceptual implications of how different constructs of anxiety may relate to different types of performance in different types of situations.

There is good reason to believe that single zero-order anxiety–performance relationships may hide interesting relationships. Mainstream studies on the anxiety–performance relationship have been based on a simple construct of performance operationalized in terms of a mean score or a total score across a number of items or tasks. However, performance viewed as an ongoing process over time seems to have been ignored largely in this research area. Such a process approach would appear to be closer to current thinking in anxiety and motivation. On conceptual grounds, one may expect that the relationship between anxiety and performance may vary as one is working across a number of tasks. Nevertheless, the weak relationships found by meta-analyses indicate that other variables may have to be taken into account if we wish to have a comprehensive understanding of the dynamics of anxiety and performance.

This chapter will present an integrated research model combining anxiety, motivation, and ability into a common conceptual unit. Interestingly enough, the conceptual plan is based on research on ability and problem solving. It will be shown that its common features are very relevant to basic conceptualizations in test anxiety and related constructs.

RELEVANCE OF TASK NOVELTY

Ability Research

In educational psychology it is a common observation that intelligence and cognitive performance, as revealed by scores on tests of mathematics, are correlated positively. Nevertheless, intelligence has been found to vary dramatically in its relationship to problem solving during a series of puzzles constituting a problem-solving process (Raaheim, 1984). This paradigm suggests a performance construct other than the one usually used in test anxiety research, that of performance as a process construct versus performance as a summary construct such as an average or a total score. These two concepts seem to have different relevance for anxiety research in its attempt to understand how anxiety and cognitive performance may be related.

A process paradigm for researching the relationship between intelligence and problem solving suggested by Raaheim (1961, 1984) seems relevant for research in anxiety and motivation as well. This chapter presents a brief outline of the model; for a more comprehensive presentation the reader is referred to Raaheim (1961, 1974, 1984, 1988). This model (Figure 1) assumes an inverted U function between the importance of the intelligent use of past experience and the novelty or familiarity of the actual problem situation. This assumption implies that intelligence is involved only if a sufficient degree of familiarity with the actual problem is established. If the problem represents a totally unknown or totally known situation, intelligence will not be involved. Intelligence will be optimally at work as

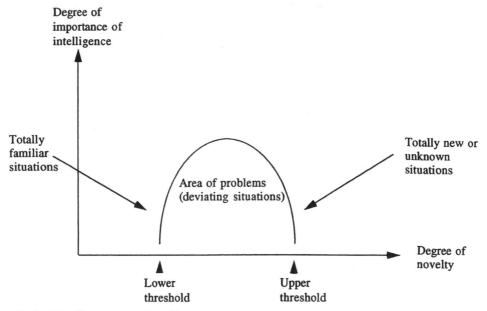

Figure 1   Problem solving and intelligence: intelligence and task novelty. Adapted from *Why Intelligence is Not Enough,* by K. Raaheim, 1984, Bergen, Norway: Sigma.

long as the problem represents a mixture of known and unknown elements relative to prior problem-solving experience. This property is based on the assumption that 'a problem situation S_n is a familiar situation that involves some deviation from otherwise similar situations S_1 . . . S_{n-1} experienced in the past' (Raaheim & Raaheim, 1986, p. 4).

The implicit concept of intelligence emphasizes the human capability to see various situations as being basically similar in spite of variations in external features. Thus it should be stressed that the importance of intelligence as a factor in problem solving will be optimal only for a limited amount of time provided that the novelty–familiarity feature is the only parameter that is varied.

The importance of task novelty as a condition for optimal intellectual functioning, provided the task is not totally novel, is also emphasized by Sternberg (1984) and Kaufmann (1990). The well-known distinction between fluid (Gf) and crystallized intelligence (Gc) also refers to task novelty. Snow and his associates (Snow, 1980, 1981; Snow, Kyllonen, & Marshalek, 1984; Snow & Lohman, 1984) have reviewed a response sampling view of the human cognitive system as 'a very large bank of cognitive processing skills and chunks of knowledge from which samples are drawn according to the demands of a particular cognitive task' (Snow & Lohman, 1984, p. 353). According to Snow (1981), crystallized intelligence represents prior assemblies of performance processes retrieved as a system and applied anew in later performance situations not unlike those experienced in the past. On the other hand, fluid intelligence represents new assemblies of performance processes needed for more extreme adaptations to novel situations. In Snow's terms: 'The distinction is between long-term assembly for transfer to familiar new situations vs. short-term assembly for transfer to unfamiliar new situations' (Snow, 1981, p. 360). With reference to the novelty–familiarity dimension in the Raaheim model, we may suggest that Gc represents response components called upon in handling problem-solving demands of more or less familiar or known situations. Fluid intelligence represents response components for handling demands in rather novel or unknown situations.

Anxiety and Motivation Research

The assumed importance attributed to task novelty in ability and problem-solving research may also be of importance in understanding how anxiety is related to performance. The dimension of task novelty can be related conceptually to critical parameters for arousing fear of failure and state anxiety in particular. According to both traditional and more recent achievement motivation theory (Atkinson, 1974, 1981), the motive to avoid failure (MaF) and the motive to approach success (MS) is aroused maximally if uncertainty about the outcome or probability of failure/success is maximized: that is, there is a 50-50 chance of being correct. It would seem reasonable to assume that if a situation is a rather novel one, an increase in uncertainty would be expected, and consequently an activation of the fear of failure motive would occur. However, as the situation becomes more familiar, the uncertainty about the outcome is reduced, which will weaken the situational conditions for activating the avoidance motive. Thus as one moves along the task novelty–familiarity dimension, a critical condition for activating the avoidance motive is varied.

The same task dimension also seems important in establishing the situational condition for arousing state anxiety (Spielberger, 1972). The perceived threat to one's self-concept is necessary to evoke state anxiety. A novel or familiar situation can be equally threatening, depending on its perceived content. However, as one moves along the task novelty–familiarity dimension, threat is believed to vary with experiences gained in the process of task solution and the associated perception of control. Repeated experiences of failure may make the task more familiar but it will continue to be threatening. This would cause activation of state anxiety, but deactivation of the motive to avoid failure. Assuming that the threat parameter will vary through the problem-solving process, the arousal of state anxiety will also vary.

By going through equivalent tasks that differ in terms of novelty as required by the problem-solving paradigm presented above, uncertainty about the outcome and threat to self-esteem associated with the task are very likely to change. Thus the conditions that call upon the motive to avoid failure and state anxiety will vary with task novelty. Therefore, it seems worthwhile to combine these parameters in the same design to explore their simultaneous influence on subsequent tasks in a problem-solving process.

Although we may easily predict that uncertainty and threat will change as the individual goes from one task to the next, the very challenge or hindrance to make more precise predictions seems to reflect the observation made by Rheingold (1985) in her penetrating analysis of the concepts of novelty and familiarity: 'The outside observer, the experimenter, is seldom if ever able to predict whether the individual will view a stimulus as novel or familiar, or how novel or how familiar' (1985, p. 4). However, when administering a sequence of equivalent cognitive tasks, we have the basis for stating that novelty will decrease or that familiarity will increase.

This reasoning, however, requires that problem solving not be operationalized only in terms of an overall score. If so, one is prevented largely from discovering the effects of anxiety and ability parameters that should differ with the novelty–familiarity status of the subsequent problems. Using an overall performance score may provide interesting information; however, its use seems to assume that parameters like uncertainty and threat are stable throughout the process. This assumption seems to be unwarranted.

Focusing on task novelty establishes a common conceptual basis for stating that ability, motivation, and anxiety are called upon by conditions that co-vary with this parameter. The present study was designed to examine how these crucial parameters will relate to different steps in an ongoing problem-solving process, which should lead to a better understanding of cognitive processes.

METHOD

Subjects and Procedure

Data were gathered over two periods of time. In the first phase, both a Chinese adaptation of the Norwegian Achievement Motives Scale (AMS) (Nygård & Gjesme, 1973) and the Raven Progressive Matrices, among other ability measures, were administered by the second author to 203 students (102 females and 101 males) of grades 10 and 11 (aged 16–18) in both Major and General High School in Shanghai. The AMS consists of two motivational subscales: the motive to approach success (MS) and the motive to avoid failure (MaF). The MS and the MaF subscales are conceptually relevant for the present research purpose. Special care has been taken to keep uncertainty about the outcome an embedded feature in all items throughout the scale (Rand, 1978). Thus the two scales of the AMS have been designed with the purpose of measuring 'failure avoidance' and not 'uncertainty avoidance' (cf. Shimkunas, 1970), and 'success approach' and not 'certainty approach.' Sample items of MaF and MS are 'I don't like working in situations where I am quite uncertain whether I will fail or not' and 'I like to try my hand on new, somewhat difficult tasks even when there is a risk that I will not succeed,' respectively. Those who score high on the MaF scale show a strong negative affective expectation under the condition of uncertainty. Those who score high on the MS scale show a strong positive affective expectation under uncertainty. High-scoring people on the MaF scale are characterized by a resistance to positive motivation, or by a 'negation tendency' (Atkinson, 1974, 1981). An equivalent interpretation also may be made in terms of disengagement (Carver & Sheier, 1984; Chapter 2). Both interpretations point to a state of no action. It is important to emphasize that it is uncertainty, not necessarily threat to self-esteem, that is the essential condition for scoring high on the present motivation scales.

During the second phase—1 month later—we administered five equivalent mental puzzles to two randomized groups with each type of school. The two corresponding conditions were labeled 'neutral' and 'stressed,' respectively, and were intended to vary the threat to self-esteem when working on a series of mental puzzles. The use of the five equivalent mental puzzles was derived from a problem-solving paradigm suggested by Raaheim (1961, 1974, 1984, 1988) as presented above. The formulation of each problem was inspired by the principle at work in the so-called water lilies problem previously found by Sternberg and Davidson (1982) to be a good predictor of intelligence.

These mental puzzles are assumed equivalent in the sense that they require the same or largely the same cognitive operations to be mastered or solved. It is a question of discovering a principle. By this procedure we hoped to vary only the novelty–familiarity parameter of the mental puzzles. The pupils were allowed to work on each problem for 3 minutes before the next was given.

Just after the subject finished the five mental problems, the first 10 items of the Cognitive Interference Questionnaire (CIQ) (Sarason & Sarason, 1987) and the state anxiety scale of the State Trait Anxiety Inventory (STAI) (Spielberger, 1983) were administered, both with reference to the series of five mental puzzles. Thus in the present study CIQ measured the amount of task-referenced irrelevant cognitions. Whereas the motivation scales referred to are linked to the uncertainty concept, the state anxiety concept is assumed to be sensitive for perceived threat to self-esteem.

DATA ANALYTIC APPROACH

Subgroup Structure

Besides the stress variable we inserted gender and school as fixed variables to take care of subgroup effects (Finn, 1974) in the data.

Prespecification of Ability and Personality Constructs

The five individual difference variables were prespecified in terms of latent variables. The MS and MaF constructs are prespecified by four arbitrarily defined indicators. Each indicator was formed as a sum of 3 or 4 items, respectively, based on the 15 items of each motive measure. The state anxiety factor was defined by 4 arbitrarily defined 5-item composites based on its 20 items. An arbitrary split of the 10 task-related items of the CIQ constituted the two indicators of the state worry construct. Only the total score of the Raven test was available. The variance of measurement errors was assumed to be .20; this is equivalent to a reliability coefficient of .80.

Estimating the Reliability of the Mental Puzzles

The problem of estimating the reliability of the mental puzzles was approached by assuming that all residuals of the five mental puzzles were equal. This assumption is equivalent to the one implicitly made in repeated measures ANOVA used to estimate internal consistency reliability (cf. Cronbach, Gleser, Nanda, & Rajaratnam, 1972). The reliability is estimated to be $1 - .27$ or .73 for each problem.

LISREL-7 Analysis

The presented model (Figure 2) consists of five latent variables besides the autoregressive process of problem solving and three fixed variables (gender, school, and stress). The program LISREL-7 (Jøreskog & Sørbom, 1988) here is used to simultaneously estimate factor loadings and relations among the latent and fixed variables in the model. The present input correlation matrix is created with variables of mixed scale types; the mental puzzles were scored dichotomously and considered of ordinal type, and the ability and anxiety variables were assumed to be interval. Ordinary product moment correlations are not recommended with mixed scale types (Jøreskog & Sørbom, 1984). Instead, we used the PRELIS program (Jøreskog & Sørbom, 1986) to estimate the suggested polychoric and polyserial correlations. The choice of these coefficients also was based on their potential to reduce problems caused by difficulty factors (Olsson, Drasgow, & Dorans, 1982). The weighted least-squares method would have been desirable for this input matrix (Jøreskog & Sørbom, 1988). However, because of the present sample size ($N = 203$) the input matrix was analyzed by the unweighted least-squares (ULS) method (Jøreskog & Sørbom, 1986). Even though we have reported chi-squares and probability values that are offered by the LISREL-7 program, the ULS solution should be considered primarily as a descriptive study with approximated standard errors (Jøreskog & Sørbom, 1988).

RESULTS

The observed mean values and standard deviations for the dichotomous subsequent puzzles are reported in Table 1. The observed mean values report that about 30% of the subjects solved puzzles 1 and 2, 20% solved puzzle 3, and about 42% solved puzzles 4 and 5. Standard deviations were all in the range between .40 and .50.

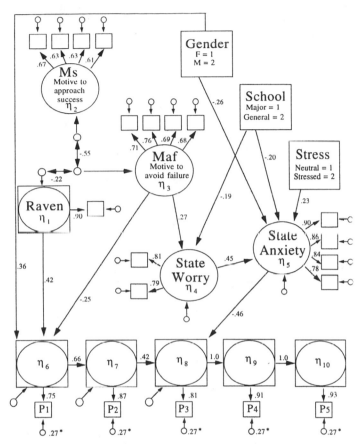

Figure 2 Autoregressive model. Standardized unweighted least squares solution. GFI = .956; RMR = .067; χ^2_{222} = 453.98. Squares indicate observed variables; circles indicate latent variables (cf. $\eta_2-\eta_5$); a circle inside a square indicates a latent variable with only one indicator where the amount of measurement errors are either prespecified (cf. η_1) or estimated under prespecified restrictions (cf. $\eta_6-\eta_{10}$). The one-sided arrows represent standardized regression coefficients in the structural part of the model and factor loadings for the measurement part of the model. The double-sided arrows represent correlations. Gender, school, and stress are treated as fixed variables. GFI = Goodness of fit index; RMR = Root mean squares residual (Jöreskog & Sörbom, 1988). *Fixed by equality constraints.

Table 1 Mean values and standard deviations of the mental puzzles

	P1	P2	P3	P4	P5
$\bar{X}$	.30	.32	.20	.43	.42
SD	.46	.47	.40	.50	.49

In examining to which mental puzzles in the problem-solving process the different ability, motivation, and anxiety parameters were related, an autoregressive model was applied. This model is portrayed in Figure 2. The results are summarized as follows:

1. The problem-solving process shows a dramatic change from the first phase consisting of P1 and P2 to the remaining part of P3 to P5; that is, relatively speaking, we found moderate stability or correspondence between P1 and P2, and between P2 and P3. After P3 the process is highly stable with respect to the rank order of individual subjects.

2. Gender (males scored higher than females), the Raven test, and the motive to avoid failure all affect the first problem in the series. Later in the process they display no direct effect on the puzzles. Surprisingly, the motive to approach success (MS) has no effects.

3. State anxiety is a mediating influence primarily from the state worry factor. The stress, school, and gender factors also influence state anxiety directly. The influence of MaF is mediated via state worry. Interestingly, although the motive to avoid failure affects the performance process even on the first problem, state anxiety does not affect the process until the third problem.

4. The relatively strong relationship between school membership and state anxiety is also interesting. Expressed in terms of standardized regression coefficients, its relation to state anxiety is comparable to the effect of the stress factor, which was actively manipulated: the major high school displaying higher state anxiety than the general high school. This strongly indicates the importance of including information about school membership or group membership in general in such analyses.

DISCUSSION

The present research problem, which was concerned with the network of effects in the conceptualized performance process, would seem to invite a structural modeling approach. It should be noted, however, that the present model is an end product of both exploratory and confirmatory aspects of the present structural modeling procedure. In the present study, the MaF variable was assumed to affect the worry construct, which in turn should affect state anxiety (Hagtvet, 1984, 1985). The stress factor was included to increase state anxiety. However, at which specific point in puzzle solution the Raven ability construct, the avoidance motivation, and state anxiety should come into play to affect the performance process remains to be investigated. These respective influences were assumed to co-vary with the task novelty parameter, which was operationalized only indirectly.

To interpret the present findings, close attention should be paid to the constructs of the present process in terms of the measures and the problem-solving design. Task novelty is assumed to vary by administering a sequence of equivalent mental puzzles. Logically, this procedure will lead to a decrease in novelty or an increase in familiarity with the puzzles. Thus uncertainty of outcome should be relatively high in the first puzzle and consequently lower as one is working through the sequence of problems.

The ability parameter measured by the Raven scale is assumed to be a proper measure of fluid intelligence (Snow, 1980). This implies that subjects scoring high on a fluid measure should more easily transform a rather novel situation into a more familiar one than those who are high on a crystallized measure (cf. Snow, 1981; Snow & Lohman, 1984). The present study did not allow us to compare the impact of the Raven measure with other ability measures. However, the obtained relationship between the Raven measure and the first puzzle supports the existence of a fluid intellectual capacity that is elicited easily in a new situation. When the effect of preceding problems is controlled, the Raven score is not related directly to puzzles beyond the first. The direct negative relationship between the motive to avoid failure and the first puzzle in the process closely agrees with assumptions linked to arousal of the negative motivation component. Later in the process, uncertainty is reduced and the arousal of MaF should therefore be weakened or should not occur. The present findings support this expectation.

The effect of state anxiety does not occur until the third puzzle. The underlying processes that account for the differentiated impacts of MaF and state anxiety appear to be related to the performance process. It seems reasonable to assume that state anxiety as applied to the present achievement-oriented performance process measures threat to self-esteem. The present findings suggest that threat to self-esteem occurs most strongly in the third puzzle. A reasonable assumption is that the student receives an autonomic feedback through perceived success or failure as familiarity with the tasks increases. A perceived failure feedback will increase threat to self-esteem whereas a positive feedback will support self-esteem. Because threat to self-esteem should affect the performance process after the student is exposed to one or two puzzles, it seems reasonable to suggest that students need some experience with the performance process before threat to self-esteem can operate. However, experimental studies are required to examine the nature of a feedback process that would produce such a threat to self-esteem.

Other things being equal, one would expect the mean values of the present mental puzzles to increase throughout the process. This seems to be supported except in the third puzzle, which has a drop in its mean value compared to the two preceding puzzles (Table 1). This drop may indicate a higher level of difficulty for this puzzle as well as a cumulative threat derived from familiarity with and experience of the preceding puzzles. However, we do not believe that this drop will affect severely the correlational relationship that is portrayed by the model because of the use of polychoric and polyserial correlations (cf. Olson, Drasgow, & Dorans, 1982).

The present latent autoregressive process analysis indicates that after the third puzzle the process is quite stable. Neither negative motivation nor state anxiety directly affects the process. The stability of the last part of the process may indicate that a state of learned helplessness has occurred for those who still experience failure (Abramson, Seligman, & Teasdale, 1978) but that a state of mastery has occurred for those who are now able to solve the problems.

This process analysis is similar in some respects to the one described by Schwarzer, Jerusalem, and Stiksrud (1984; see also Jerusalem, 1990; Schwarzer, 1986). It seems to differ, however, in the way in which uncertainty and threat to self-esteem are treated. In the analysis by Schwarzer et al. (1984), complete uncertainty about the outcome is combined with maximum level of threat. In the present analysis highest level of uncertainty is combined with an optimal level for eliciting the motive to avoid failure. The present findings suggest that maximum outcome uncertainty does not necessarily imply a strong threat to self-esteem, which in turn should activate state anxiety. It should be noted that the present measure of MaF or 'fear of failure' assesses the extent of dislike of involvement in an achievement-oriented activity. Its items do not refer to threat to self-esteem explicitly, which is the feature attached to the state anxiety scale used here.

The present results are in agreement with the prior findings of Hagtvet (1984, 1985) only in reproducing the paths between MaF and worry, and between worry and state anxiety. The new findings reported in this study have to be attributed to the present performance process approach. If one defines performance as an average score or a total score across a number of tasks, clear information about the uncertainty parameter cannot be provided. This design feature may be a reasonable explanation of why MaF did not correlate with the mathematical performance factor in the prior studies of Hagtvet (1984, 1985). Nevertheless, both the prior and present findings support the contention that MaF may also produce irrelevant worry cognitions. However, in the present study these cognitions affected performance via state anxiety somewhat later in the process. It seems most reasonable to interpret the direct effect of MaF in the first puzzle as a negative motivational effect or, in the terminology of Carver and Sheier (1984, Chapter 2), as a state of disengagement. This state of disengagement is very likely to be a function of high uncertainty. We may further assume a state of disengagement at the very end of the process, and this disengagement is very likely to be a function of learned helplessness.

A very interesting aspect of the present findings is that cognitive performance is not considered a function of ability only, anxiety only, or negative motivation only. Rather, all these parameters come into operation during the process, and they seem to be called upon at different stages of the process as a function of degree of task novelty. Furthermore, in the present approach the motive to avoid failure has been separated from state anxiety and state worry effects. As suggested in prior studies (Hagtvet, 1984, 1985), these parameters represent different foci of individual differences that are relevant for describing test-anxious students in achievement-oriented situations. The motive to avoid failure seems to have a component of disengagement or no-action as assumed in earlier writings of achievement motivation theory. Furthermore, this motive also seems to encompass a potential for affecting worry cognitions and state anxiety. Although MaF is part of a motivational arousal theory linked to the concept of uncertainty within a hedonistic tradition, state anxiety is part of a stress theory with an emphasis on the threat concept. The present approach and findings support the need for differentiating between uncertainty and threat in theoretical approaches to stress and anxiety.

REFERENCES

Abramson, L. Y., Seligman, M. E. P., & Teasdale, J. D. (1978). Learned helplessness in humans: Critique and reformulation. *Journal of Abnormal Psychology, 87*, 49–74.

Atkinson, J. W. (1974). The mainsprings of achievement-oriented activity. In J. W. Atkinson & J. O. Raynor (Eds.), *Motivation and achievement* (pp. 13–34). Washington, DC: Winston.

Atkinson, J. W. (1981). Thematic apperceptive measurement of motivation in 1950 and 1980. In G. D'Ydewalle & W. Lens (Eds.), *Cognition in human motivation and learning* (pp. 159–198). Leuven, Belgium: Leuven University Press.

Carver, C. S., & Sheier, M. F. (1984). Self-focused attention in test anxiety: A general theory applied to a specific phenomenon. In H. M. van der Ploeg, R. Schwarzer, & C. D. Spielberger (Eds.), *Advances in test anxiety research* (Vol. 3, pp. 3–20). Lisse, The Netherlands/Hillsdale, NJ: Swets and Zeitlinger/Erlbaum.

Cronbach, L. J., Gleser, G. C., Nanda, H., & Rajaratnam, N. (1972). *The dependability of behavioral measurements: Theory of generalizability for scores and profiles.* New York: Wiley.

Finn, J. D. (1974). *A general model for multivariate analysis.* New York: Holt, Rinehart, & Winston.

Hagtvet, K. A. (1984). Fear of failure, worry, and emotionality: Their suggestive causal relationships to mathematical performance and state anxiety. In H. M. van der Ploeg, R. Schwarzer, & C. D. Spielberger (Eds.), *Advances in test anxiety research* (Vol. 3, pp. 211–224). Lisse, The Netherlands: Swets & Zeitlinger.

Hagtvet, K. A. (1985). A three-dimensional test anxiety construct. In J. J. Sanchez-Sosa (Ed.), *Health and clinical psychology* (pp. 109–134). Amsterdam: North Holland.

Hagtvet, K. A. (1989). *The construct of test anxiety. Conceptual and methodological issues.* Bergen/London: Sigma Forlag/Jessica Kingsley Publishers.

Jerusalem, M. (1990). Temporal patterns of stress appraisals for high- and low-anxious individuals. *Anxiety Research, 3,* 113–129.

Jóreskog, K. G., & Sórbom, D. (1984). *LISREL VI analysis of linear structural relationships by maximum likelihood, instrumental variables, and least squares methods.* Mooresville, IN: Scientific Software.

Jóreskog, K. G., & Sórbom, D. (1986). *PRELIS. A preprocessor for LISREL.* Mooresville, IN: Scientific Software.

Jóreskog, K. G., & Sórbom, D. (1988). *LISREL 7. A guide to the program and applications.* Chicago, IL: SPSS.

Kaufmann, G. (1990). Imagery effects on problem solving. In P. J. Hampson & D. E. Marks (Eds.), *Imagery: current development* (pp. 169–196). London: Routledge.

Nygård, R., & Gjesme, T. (1973). Assessment of achievement motives: Comments and suggestions. *Scandinavian Journal of Educational Research, 17,* 39–46.

Olsson, U., Drasgow, F., & Dorans, N. J. (1982). The polyserial correlation coefficient. *Psychometrica, 47,* 337–347.

Raaheim, K. (1961). Problem solving: A new approach. *Acta Universitatis Bergensis. Series Humaniorum Litterarum, 5.*

Raaheim, K. (1974). *Problem solving and intelligence.* Bergen, Norway: Universitetsforlaget.

Raaheim, K. (1984). *Why intelligence is not enough.* Bergen, Norway: Sigma.

Raaheim, K. (1988). Intelligence and task novelty. In R. J. Sternberg (Ed.), *Advances in the psychology of human intelligence* (Vol. 4, pp. 73–97). Hillsdale, NJ: Erlbaum.

Raaheim, K., & Raaheim, A. (1986, April). *Intelligence and the solution of new tasks.* Paper presented at the AERA annual meeting, San Francisco, CA.

Rand, P. (1978). Some validation data for the Achievement Motive Scale (AMS). *Scandinavian Journal of Educational Research, 22,* 155–171.

Rheingold, H. L. (1985). Development as acquisition of familiarity. *Annual Review of Psychology, 36,* 1–17.

Sarason, I. G., & Sarason, B. R. (1987). Cognitive interference as a component of anxiety: Measurement of its state and trait aspects. In R. Schwarzer, H. M. van der Ploeg, & C. D. Spielberger (Eds.), *Advances in test anxiety research* (Vol. 5, pp. 3–14). Lisse, The Netherlands: Swets & Zeitlinger.

Schwarzer, R. (1986). Self-related cognitions in anxiety and motivation: An introduction. In R. Schwarzer (Ed.), *Self-related cognitions in anxiety and motivation* (pp. 1–17). Hillsdale, NJ: Erlbaum.

Schwarzer, R., Jerusalem, M., & Stiksrud, A. (1984). A developmental relationship between test anxiety and helplessness. In H. M. van der Ploeg, R. Schwarzer, & C. D. Spielberger (Eds.), *Advances in test anxiety research* (Vol. 3, pp. 73–79). Lisse, The Netherlands/Hillsdale, NJ: Swets & Zeitlinger/Erlbaum.

Schwarzer, R., Seipp, B., & Schwarzer, C. (1989). Mathematics performance and anxiety: A meta-analysis. In R. Schwarzer, H. M. van der Ploeg, & C. D. Spielberger (Eds.), *Advances in test anxiety research* (Vol. 6, pp. 105–119). Lisse, The Netherlands: Swets & Zeitlinger.

Shimkunas, A. M. (1970). Anxiety and expectancy change: The effects of failure and uncertainty. *Journal of Personality and Social Psychology, 15,* 34–42.

Snow, R. E. (1980). Aptitude processes. In R. E. Snow, P. A. Federico, & W. E. Montague (Eds.), *Aptitude, learning and instruction: Cognitive process analysis of aptitude* (Vol. 1, pp. 27–63). Hillsdale, NJ: Erlbaum.

Snow, R. E. (1981). Toward a theory of aptitude for learning: I. Fluid and crystallized abilities and their correlates. In M. P. Friedman, J. P. Das, & N. O'Connor (Eds.), *Intelligence and learning*. NATO Conference Series (Vol. 14). New York: Plenum.

Snow, R. E., Kyllonen, P. C., & Marshalek, B. (1984). The topography of ability and learning correlations. In R. J. Sternberg (Ed.), *Advances in the psychology of intelligence* (Vol. 2). Hillsdale, NJ: Erlbaum.

Snow, R. E., & Lohman, D. F. (1984). Toward a theory of cognitive aptitude for learning from instruction. *Journal of Educational Psychology, 76*, 347–376.

Spielberger, C. D. (1972). Anxiety as an emotional state. In C. D. Spielberger (Ed.), *Anxiety: Current trends in theory and research* (Vol. 1, pp. 481–493). New York: Academic Press.

Spielberger, C. D. (1983). *Manual for the State–Trait Anxiety Inventory* (STAI Form Y). Palo Alto, CA: Consulting Psychologists Press.

Sternberg, R. J. (1984). Toward a triarchic theory of human intelligence. *The Behavioral and Brain Sciences, 7*, 269–315.

Sternberg, R. J., & Davidson, J. E. (1982). The mind of the puzzler. *Psychology Today, 16 June*, 37–44.

7

Stress, Comfort, and Self-Appraisal: A Panoramic Investigation of the Dynamics of Cognitive Processes

Paolo Bonaiuto, Valeria Biasi, Anna Maria Giannini,
and Marino Bonaiuto
First University of Rome, Italy

Gabriella Bartoli
University of Bologna, Italy

INTRODUCTION

Psychologists study a large number of affective processes and anxiety, a particularly important and varied one, is but one of them. Anxiety can be seen as (a) an emotion, when it presents itself as a specific transitory emotional process that involves the total individual; (b) a motivating component, when it is perceived as a drive to act toward a positive target–object (such as the pleasure of adventure) or a negative object (such as panic); (c) a form of self-perception, when it is perceived as a quality of the self, an event, or an object within the area of the self; and (d) a distinctive characteristic of personality.

We are convinced that the study of emotions, motivations, perceptions, attitudes, and traits may be carried out more productively if different determining factors and intensity levels were compared, and opposite processes were studied. In the case of anxiety, for example, the processes of emotional relaxation, security, trust, and apathy should also be considered. Using opposites is useful in scientific demonstrations and it is also an effective didactic method (Bruner, 1966).

What we are suggesting is that we should study subjects who are very anxious, subjects who are averagely anxious, and subjects who are relaxed. We have known for some time that the conditions that determine anxiety are linked with emotional conflict, especially when it develops within partly unconscious desires (Freud, S.,

The authors wish to thank the university students in Rome who volunteered as subjects. Some faced, unknowingly and by lot, the 'experimental stress' treatment; those who were more fortunate faced the relaxation or control situations. Our various studies and the drafting of this chapter as well as conference attendance were supported partially by the *Consiglio Nazionale delle Ricerche* (National Research Council), grants No. 87.01107.10, 88.00958.08, and 00.00958.08; the *Ministero della Pubblica Istruzione* (Ministry of Education) and the *Ministero dell' Università e della Ricerca Scientifica e Tecnologica* (Ministry for University and for Scientific and Technological Research) of the Republic of Italy, the Universities of Rome ('*La Sapienza*'), and Bologna; and the *Istituto per lo Sviluppo e le Applicazioni della Psicologia Scientifica* (I.S.A.P.S.), Rome.

1901, 1923, 1926; Freud, A., 1946). Although it is useful to study the effects of more or less intense and durable emotional conflicts, it is also important to understand the responses to emotional harmony as occur in relaxation (Bonaiuto & Bartoli, 1968, 1970a, 1970b).

While developing this research area (Bonaiuto, Massironi, & Bartoli, 1975), we noticed that experimental or natural situations that lead to emotional conflict or to harmony can also promote emotional processes other than anxiety and relaxation; thus other emotions and other motivations are involved. As early as 1931, Dembo used typical conflict situations such as trying to solve impossible tasks to provoke and study the emergence of anger. Similar observations of aggressive and regressive reactions were described in Karsten's (1928) study of boring, conflicting duties, as cited by Koffka (1935). Observations of aggressive and regressive behavior, with various emotional variables, were also made in the well-known study by Barker, Dembo, and Lewin (1941) on children who could see, but were not allowed to touch, some very attractive toys. Experimental conditions of conflict such as those characterized by frustration, failure, and insults are also used currently in studies of aggressive behavior (Bandura, 1983; Berkowitz, 1983).

Since the publication of the works of Selye (1956), Lazarus (1966), and Zuckerman (1964), many authors have used psychic conflict to study the phenomenon of stress and its consequences (Appley & Trumbull, 1967, 1986; Goldberger & Breznitz, 1982). It seems clear that studies on stress have followed the ancient and solid path of research on psychic conflict, even when the word 'conflict' is not mentioned or is not listed in the analytic indices (as in the recent volume edited by Janisse, 1988). Stress strictly depends on conflict. A typical example of this is that of a person who in daily life must face unpleasant situations, such as a long and monotonous commute or a strong disagreement with other people, and cannot respond aggressively or escape: he or she thus must test his or her capacity to cope; in effect, he or she must test his or her 'hardiness' (Maddi & Kobasa, 1984).

We used phenomenological analysis and identified ourselves with the actors in situations of conflict and stress, and tried to understand the meaning of the emotional and cognitive consequences of placing oneself in such difficult or annoying situations and in the opposite kinds of situations. This exercise resulted in a specific research plan. Conflict and stress appear to activate different emotions such as anxiety, anger, and sadness, and also to mobilize various demands, some of which, like aggression or the need for avoidance, are well known. Other emotions such as the need for order, clarity, and congruence in cognition are less well known but they are experienced at times. Furthermore, conflict and stress are accompanied by typical perceptions of the self, the environment, and factors relating to them (threat, inadequacy, sense of inferiority, repulsion or attraction, a state of chaos or monotony, etc.). Other significant environmental features may be present simultaneously that can produce effects, including a continuous input of stimuli, excessive heterogeneity of experience, or, on the other hand, boredom, isolation, and confinement (Bonaiuto, 1969).

Thus it seemed worthwhile to study simultaneously anxiety and other parallel affective and cognitive components that are present in conflict and stress situations, and to paint a detailed picture of this set of phenomena. This rather 'panoramic' approach naturally involved problems and required the identification of appropriate research methods. In such cases, it is necessary to make a choice between using multiple measures with a single subject group and using limited measures with many subject groups.

Notwithstanding the difficulties, these broad, panoramic procedures seem to be necessary to (a) avoid attributing to anxiety characteristics caused by other processes of which anxiety is simply a side effect, (b) avoid not attributing to anxiety specific aspects that depend on it but are not brought to light because of limited instrumentation, and (c) delineate the interrelationship of the various antecedent and consequent processes.

For us the study of anxiety really requires the analysis of affective and cognitive processes of the individual under conditions of conflict and of stress and in conditions of emotional accord, comfort, and relaxation. One should also study how these processes are linked to other independent but relevant variables.

Figure 1 summarizes the overall theoretical pattern of the research to follow.

METHODS

Subjects

In all the experimental studies on which we will report the subjects were volunteer male and female university students of Rome's two state universities. They were between 18 and 39 years of age, were individually tested, and were not informed initially of the purpose and procedures of the study, except that they would be in a 'study of visual perception.' Assignment to specific subject groups was done randomly. No subject terminated participation because of feelings of malaise. However, 2% terminated because of scheduling difficulties and another 4% was terminated by the experimenters because they did not respond to the stress or relaxation paradigms.

Procedures

Treatments

Through a variety of experimental manipulations we attempted to create situations of stress, of relaxation, and of a condition in between. We administered simultaneous stressors to the subjects who were assigned to the experimental stress condition in a 15-minute session. First we had them attempting to solve some very difficult Raven Matrices (Raven, 1956; Figure 2), as other researchers have done (Meichenbaum, 1972; Tolkmitt & Scherer, 1986). We began with two relatively easy problems, followed by eight very difficult ones.[1]

In addition to the seated subject in the well-lighted test room, there were usually three experimenters, only one of whom spoke. The subject had been informed in general terms that this would be an 'experiment in visual perception;' he or she was told that this task was an 'intelligence test.' The experimenter emphasized that there was only one correct answer for each problem, that the subject should try to avoid making mistakes, and that his or her response time would be recorded.

---

[1]The succession of tables was as follows: B5, D1, D7, D9, D11, E1, E3, E5, E7, and E12.

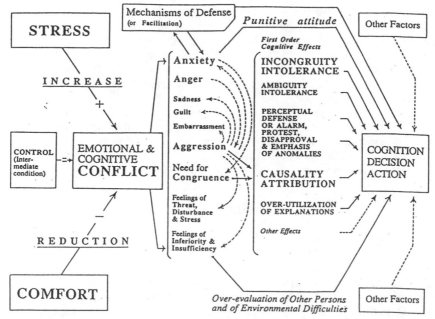

Figure 1   Graphic schema of the general theoretical reference model followed in our
experiments. Stress implies an overloading of conflict with an increase of its
emotional and motivational consequences. Within certain limits, in order to avoid
and/or reduce unpleasant features of such an affective activation, the subject may
consider as unpleasant other kinds of conflict, among which there are cognitive
incongruities and uncertainties. For these reasons, he or she increases the first
order cognitive effects, including perceptual intolerance of incongruity and
ambiguity, and consequently increases causality attributions, overutilization of
explanation, and similar processes. These effects may influence further levels of
behavior, fostering other attributions, such as responsibility, or certain decisions
and actions. Comfort and relaxation act in a rather opposite way. Other affective
processes may interfere, especially anxiety, because of defense mechanisms. For
example, stress may increase projections of aggression and consequently the
causality attribution when evaluating very energetic or aggressive actions, and may
foster wishes of punishment, and feelings of inferiority and insufficiency. We must
take into account these processes also if we are to understand and predict the final
effects on behavior. In the graphic schema, relationships among variables are
indicated by arrows, while word sizes are proportional to the theoretical
importance of the independent or dependent variables and to the intensity of the
effects, as found in our studies. Curved lines symbolize links between emotional
processes and phenomena as described in the general psychodynamic literature.

Regarding two randomly selected problems the subject was told, 'You have made a
mistake.' For two other problems, the experimenter said, 'Be careful. Avoid mistakes.' Nothing was said about the other six problems; thus erroneous or ambiguous feedback was part of the stress situation.

   To increase stress, the task was presented to the subject as important and urgent. In addition, during the test session, the experimenter made each of the
following statements in a worried tone: 'Make an effort . . . ,' 'You must find the
links between the elements . . . ,' 'Gather your best energies . . . ,' and 'There is

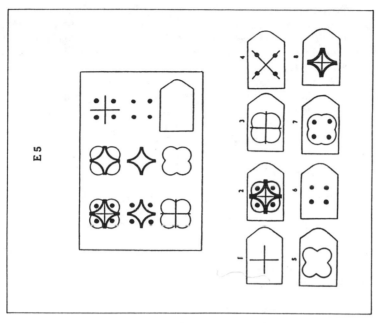

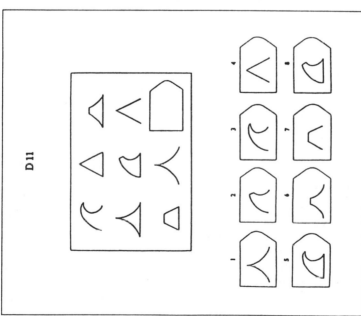

Figure 2 Reproductions of Raven's 1956 P.M. 38 tables (a) D11 and (b) E5.

no time . . .' Finally, an experimenter occasionally paced around the room behind the subject, or moved furniture noisily, or dropped a bunch of keys.[2]

In the experimental relaxation condition, the subject once again spent 15 minutes in the same room, which was now very quiet and semidark. The subject was seated in a relaxed position in a comfortable armchair with legs stretched out, palms of hands on highs, and eyes half or fully closed. Instructions were given in a soft voice, usually by a female experimenter who sat about 2 meters from the subject.

The subject was asked to relax body muscles progressively (Jacobson, 1929) and was told to visualize relaxing scenes, including a calm sea, a peaceful beach, a prairie caressed by a soft wind, and so on. When testing occurred later in the session, lighting was increased and decreased very gradually.

In some of our studies, we used an intermediate or control situation in which the subject sat in the same well-lighted room for 15 minutes. During part of this time, the experimenter asked him or her to answer easy questions. For the rest of the time the subject was allowed to browse through a travel magazine.

Self-Appraisal Scales of the Preemotional and Postemotional State

Measures of the influence of the stress, relaxation, and control procedures on the emotional, motivational, and self state of each subject in relation to the environment were taken immediately before and toward the end of treatment. As time was extremely limited, we developed seven-point scales whose polar terms were opposite adjectives or expressions (see Figure 3). Each scale consisted of about four of these items, and their order varied across subjects.

There were 8 scales for measuring emotion (anxiety vs. relaxation, anger vs. serenity, sadness vs. happiness, shame vs. pride, guilt vs. merit, embarrassment vs. self-confidence, pain vs. joy, and boredom vs. amusement), 10 scales to measure motivation (aggression; need achievement; need for cognitive congruity, clarity, and regularity; need for cognitive variety; need for activity; need for adventure; need to construct; sociability; sexuality; and nutrition), and 7 self scales that related to the environment (stress vs. comfort, frustration vs. gratification, monotony vs. excessive variety, threat vs. self-protection, self-insecurity vs. self-security, self-insufficiency vs. self-sufficiency, and self-inferiority and dependence vs. self-superiority and autonomy).

There were about 100 items in all, requiring about 9 minutes to complete. These paper-and-pencil surveys included written instructions and were presented to the seated subject immediately before treatment and again at about the 12th minute of the treatment period. After the subjects completed the scales, their 'treatment' was resumed for another 3 minutes. We have found that this interruption does not adversely affect subsequent results.

Although we wished to extend the test period to include other measures, this was not possible because of time considerations. However, as will be seen, even this short test period provided meaningful results. The test instrument itself was based on motivation research using the phenomenological method (Bonaiuto, 1967, 1969),

---

[2]For all treatments, the subject is not informed in advance of its duration. For the stress treatment, the subject is usually unable to complete all 10 tables of the P.M. 38 in 15 minutes. When the subject does complete them, the examiners continue with the tables of the final series. The post treatment data collection is done by interrupting the subject before he reaches a solution on the last table he tackles so as to ensure a distinctly conflictual situation.

Instruction: Take yourself and your situation into consideration as you feel right now. Focus on the feelings that you have at this moment, and only at this moment. Indicate your evaluations by placing a checkmark in one box only for each pair of opposite adjectives or opposite descriptive phrases. Do this spontaneously and rapidly.

I feel I am

	3	2	1	0	1	2	3	
TENSE								RELAXED
AGITATED								CALM
IN CONFLICT INTERNALLY								AT PEACE INTERNALLY
WORRIED								TRANQUIL
ANGRY								SERENE
IRRITATED								AGREEABLE
AGGRESSIVE								PEACEFUL
IMPATIENT								PATIENT
SAD								HAPPY
EMBITTERED								WELL-DISPOSED
DEPRESSED								EUPHORIC
MELANCHOLIC								JOYFUL

Figure 3 Examples of self-appraisal scales used for the study of emotional changes.

state anxiety scale development (Bonaiuto & Bartoli, 1968, 1970a, 1970b, 1971), and work on human desires in isolation and confinement experiments or, later, in psychodiagnostics (Bonaiuto, 1967; Bonaiuto, Giannini, & Biasi, 1987).

Cognitive Process Measurement

To evaluate the influence of treatment-linked changes in emotional status on the cognitive activity of the subject, in this first set of experiments we chose to measure the process of causal explanation of events and of the attribution of active and passive causal roles. Here, also, we made pretreatment and posttreatment measures. To understand our procedures better, refer to Figure 4. This figure is usually described as a left-handed athlete throwing a javelin. If the javelin was missing from the picture, the attitude of the man would seem strange and would require explanation; the explanation might not be plausible. If the man was missing but the javelin remained, the instrument would seem out of place. This example suggests the mobilization of the following cognitive operations:

1. Perception of incongruities or the anticipation of the possibility of perceptual incongruities and anomalies.
2. Activation of expectations of an explanation adequate to reduce or prevent these incongruities.
3. Evaluation of these incongruities as symptoms of actions, including the role of agent (the object that produces activity) or receiver (the element that undergoes an effect).
4. Identification of cause and effect. If either is not immediately given but is available, a search is made leading to the identification of the missing element, which is used as cause or effect in a complementary way.

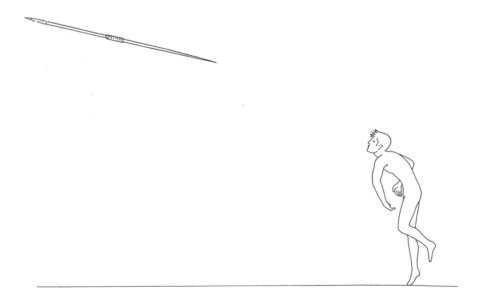

Figure 4

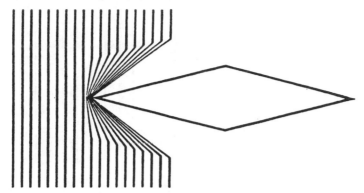

Figure 5 Illustration favoring visual perception of cause-and-effect
relationship (Massironi & Bonaiuto, 1965).

5. Integrating cause and effect into a cohesive whole that satisfies expectations, and attributing responsibility and efficiency to the cause and dependence and inevitability to the effect.

6. There are simultaneous influences of the successful causal explanation on the observer, including a reduction of the initial impression of anomaly and of the emotional tensions resulting from the first appearance of real or possible incongruities.

The above operations have been subjected to phenomenological analysis in the past (Bonaiuto, 1965, 1970), which goes beyond the analysis of Michotte (1946, 1957), who had linked the perception of causality by an observer only to the presentation of moving visual objects. This limitation was shared by later authors (Kanizsa & Metelli, 1961; Kanizsa & Vicario, 1965). In our research we have seen that even a simple static figure, such as shown in Figure 5, or one of analogous situations as in Figure 6, can provide strong impressions of causality that can be measured.[3]

Based on the analysis above, the general hypothesis of the research to follow can be stated as:

1. Perception of causality depends not only on the stimulus situation but also on the emotional state of the observer.

2. Causality expectations should be stronger after stress. Stress implies conflict and an increase in aggression and in other need systems, which themselves are opposed to other demands, are difficult to elaborate, and thus produce further conflicts. Such an overload of conflict should lead temporarily to a decrease in the ability to tolerate other conflicts and tensions, such as those linked to perceptual incongruity. If the subject in this situation can avoid or reduce incongruity by forming rapid cause-and-effect relationships, he or she will do so (cf. the paradigm presented in Figure 1).

---

[3]Metzger (1975) also supported this position: he accepted the proposed extension and included in the second edition of his book (p. 613) a modified version of the figure published by Massironi and Bonaiuto (1965), which demonstrated causality in illustrations.

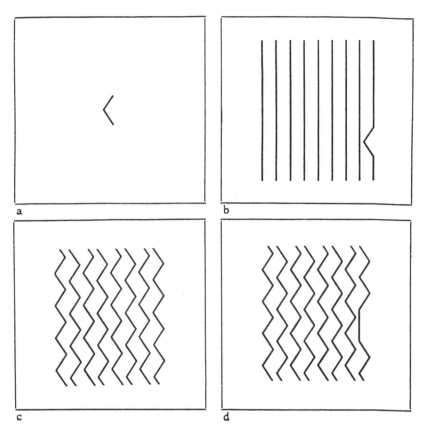

Figure 6 Anomaly with respect to the context (*b, d*) is a necessary condition for causality perception. Causality attribution appears more difficult or absent without context (*a*) or without anomaly (*c*) (Bonaiuto, 1970).

3. If the problem and solution are presented at different times, initial incongruities should be emphasized because of their contrast with expectations ('protest') and other factors.

4. In the preceding case, explanations given later to the subject to reduce incongruity should be accepted readily and will tend to be overused. In addition, the impression of causality and the attribution of responsibility should increase.

5. Once explanations have been presented and accepted, the resulting reduction of incongruity and tension should be heightened.

6. These phenomena can be heightened further through the 'projection' of aggression in the perceived causal relationships, especially if the stimuli are of a causal–aggressive type.[4]

[4]The influence of anger and of aggressive motivation on the perception of incongruities can be multifaceted, if one considers that incongruity is always based on contradiction and the overturning of schemata, operations which in themselves satisfy aggressiveness, as shown in studies conducted with works of art (Bonaiuto, 1983, 1985). Thus the very aggressive subject could have a drive to facilitate and emphasize anomalies, preferring not to avoid or reduce them, because they are satisfying.

7. However, if one experiences relaxation and 'comfort,' the tolerance of conflict, tension, anomalies, and incongruities should be increased, and aggressive 'projections' should be decreased. Perception of causality should be generally reduced.

8. Other factors, such as the relationship between self and the environment or attention oscillation, may influence these phenomena. Attention, for example, seems to be related to anxiety and stress in a curvilinear manner. Thus certain stress levels should increase attentional processes (Dirkin, 1983), but, further increases should operate as 'noise' and shift attention to bodily symptoms and decisional conflicts (Mandler, 1984). Thus lower stress levels may lead to more careful attention in a test situation but attention would be reduced in a relaxed situation or in a very stressful situation. If the test situation is measuring cause–effect relationships, attentional processes can make a contribution. However, variation in attention seems to be a more general and less specific mechanism with respect to conflict load and thus to tolerance of incongruity and potential aggressive projections. Fortunately we are able to distinguish and measure the relative importance of each of these mechanisms, as will be seen in the experiments and discussion below.

Specific Procedures

Experiment 1: Hallucinatory perception due to indices of cause-and-effect relationships, together with cues of figural concreteness. In the past our research group has been able to elicit hallucinatory perceptions ('illusory contours') using relatively simple graphics in which we portray groups of people acting or receiving action in a coordinated manner, without actually portraying the object involved in the action (Bonaiuto, Giannini, & Bonaiuto, 1988a, 1988b). At times this complementary object becomes a well-defined illusory (hallucinatory) form and emerges from the background. For example, most observers clearly see in Figure 7 not only the boys who are climbing over the wall but the wall itself, which is not delineated by any black contour. This hallucinated wall conforms to the cause-and-effect expectations of the subject induced by the position and shape of the boys in the drawing.

In our stress study, we intentionally used somewhat weaker, less coercive, and

Figure 7 A favorable situation for the formation of an hallucinatory visual object (the wall, limited by an 'illusory contour') in response to expectations of cause-and-effect relationships activated in the observer (Bonaiuto, Giannini, & Bonaiuto, 1988a).

more ambiguous drawings than those shown in Figure 7 or Figure 8 so as to encourage greater individual subject differences and differences linked to emotional change. Figure 9 is an example of this kind of drawing. In it 11 people appear to be interacting with a large globe-shaped object that is relatively irregular in shape. Some people are lifting the object, others are clinging to it or climbing down from it. Our dependent variable is the subjective clarity of the contour of the hallucinated object, measured on an 11-point scale (see Figure 10), ranging from 0 (no object seen) to 10 (maximum presence of object). To familiarize the subject with this procedure, he or she is trained with preliminary materials.

The test drawings, shown in Figure 9, are presented in two versions. In one we vary paper qualities (roughness) and lighting conditions (reflections on an opaque white surface) to enhance expectations of cause-and-effect relationships (a relatively ambiguous perceptual situation); in the other, we decrease these expectations (nonambiguous). In the first we expect higher subjective clarity scores, in the second lower scores.[5]

In this study, we also used four drawings (Figures 11-14) with classical illusory contours, based on the work of Ehrenstein (1941), Kanizsa (1974), Jastrow (1899), and Metzger (1975). In these materials the contours seen are not a result of causal expectations but rather of the tendency to structure the objects in three-dimensional space. Thus the illusory contours are generated because of the preference to see complete and superimposed figures (Figures 11 and 12) or even solid objects drawn with chiaroscuro (Figures 13 and 14) rather than irregular and fragmented elements (which should be flat and co-planary). Yet the anomalies that are avoided by organizing the figures are less likely with respect to the incongruities in the position and shape of the human actors and their 'motivational' impetus should be less intense. The results of this study are presented in the appropriate section later in this chapter.

Experiment 2: Perception of cause-and-effect relationships in concretely portrayed visual objects and events. For this study, we produced 10 drawings in which both the causal agent and the object of the action are portrayed concretely (Bonaiuto, Giannini, & Bonaiuto, 1990a, 1990b). The intensity of perceived cause-and-effect relationships is relatively weak in some of the drawings (Figures 15 and 16) and very strong in others (Figures 17 and 18). There are also two control drawings in which the phenomenon is almost absent, and two preliminary drawings in which the phenomenon is very clear. Drawings are presented one at a time

---

[5]The determinant role of the material upon which the drawing is printed, that is, the presence of credible indicators of figurative substance, was demonstrated in some of our studies in which situations similar to Figure 9 were printed on very smooth acetate, then on translucent paper, on normal paper, and, finally, on textured, very rough paper. In drawings on the first paper, the illusory contours are absent, whereas with the textured paper they are enormously emphasized. The influence of the roughness of the material is substantial. The illusory contours are also enhanced by the presence of surface color (lighting by reflection), whereas the contrary is true with the diaphanous colors (lighting by transparency). In practice, roughness and reflection, being more typical of figures rather than of backgrounds, produce an *ambiguity* in the qualities giving body to the area in the background of the drawing, that is, in the area where the hallucinatory object is going to appear. That ambiguity is necessary for obtaining a perceptual result that is coherent with expectations dictated by other factors (indices of cause-and-effect relationships and emotional states favoring causality). If ambiguity is lacking, information pertinent to the central area of the figure is too much out of tune with strong expectations of causality and the subject has the impression of an empty background (Bonaiuto, Giannini, & Bonaiuto, 1989a, 1989b, 1989c, 1989d, 1990a, 1990b).

Figure 8 A drawing by Bonaiuto, Giannini, & Bonaiuto
(1988b).

Figure 9 A less intense but still favorable situation for the formation
of a visual hallucinatory object, in response to expectations
of cause-and-effect relationships (Bonaiuto, Giannini, &
Bonaiuto, 1989a).

0	1	2	3	4	5	6	7	8	9	10

Figure 10   Reproduction of the evaluation scale for 'subjective clarity.'

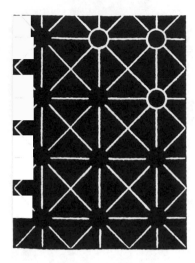

Figure 11   Figure adapted from Ehrenstein (1941).

at normal reading distance in a systematically varied order after the two prelimi-nary drawings, and perception of causality is measured on an 11-point scale, constructed as before. Levels of perceived activity and/or passivity and other attri-butional details are measured in a similar way. The results of this study are pre-sented later in this chapter.

Experiment 3: Impressions of cause-and-effect relationships and incongruity in

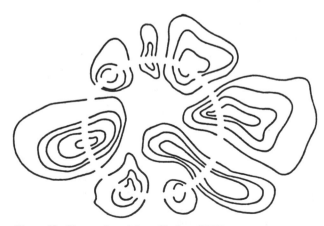

Figure 12   Figure adapted from Kanizsa (1974).

Figure 13   Figure adapted from Jastrow (1899).

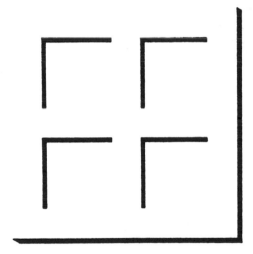

Figure 14   Figure adapted from Metzger (1975).

Figure 15   Example of a drawing used in the second experiment.

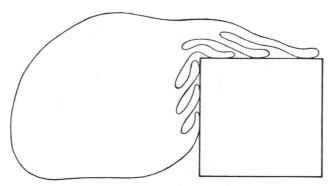

Figure 16 Example of a drawing used in the second experiment. Compared to the originals used in the study, all of the figures reproduced here are greatly reduced (1:2.2).

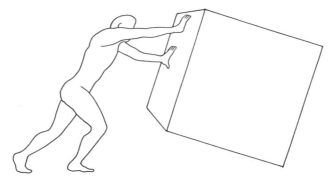

Figure 17 Example of a drawing used in the second experiment (Bonaiuto, Giannini, & Bonaiuto, 1990a).

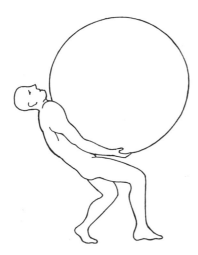

Figure 18 Example of a drawing used in the second experiment.

> Though there is no wind, a thin and very tall tree
> rustles; the branches move to the point that a few
> leaves and fruit pull off and fall.

Figure 19 Verbal description of an incongruous event used in the third experiment
(Bartoli, Biasi, Bonaiuto, Giannini, & Muccioli, 1990).

verbally described (written) events. In the past, we had found that the same principles apply to the use of incongruities and related phenomena by means of disparate 'media,' including paintings, advertising messages, film sequences, cartoons, and verbal passages (Bartoli, Biasi, & Bonaiuto, 1989a, 1989b, 1989c, 1989d; Bonaiuto, 1983, 1985). In the most recent studies, the level of incongruity was first measured on a seven-point scale and then a written appropriate explanation was provided, followed by a second measurement of incongruity. We typically found a diminished level of incongruity with the use of written explanations, that is, a reduction of conflict.

To examine if effects similar to those found with figures would occur with verbal material in the stress/relaxation situations, we developed 10 brief stories in which incongruous, bizarre situations requiring causal explanations are described verbally (Bartoli, Biasi, Bonaiuto, Giannini, & Muccioli, 1990). Here the subject is presented with a description similar to those in Figures 19 and 20, and having

> Ruggero has gone into a bank and towards a cashier.
> The cashier asks him what he needs and if he can
> help him... But this cashier is unable to finish
> his words; he suddenly stops, jerks and falls on
> the ground...

Figure 20 Verbal description of an incongruous event used in the third experiment.

A strong camper had taken hold of the base of the
thin trunk and he is shaking it energically.

Figure 21   Verbal description of the event complementary to a previous one (Figure 19)
and used as a causal explanation.

read it, fills out appropriate evaluation scales to indicate the degree of incongruity
and other impressions. After this the subject is presented with a card containing a
possible causal explanation (see Figures 21 and 22) and is asked to evaluate the
cause-and-effect relationship using the same 11-point scale. Then the subject again
evaluates the incongruity of the first event on the seven-point scale. In this way the
causal impression and the change in incongruity of the story after the causal explanation are both measured. With systematic rotation two different stories are provided each subject, one before and one after treatment. We also measure other
impressions similarly, including the anxiety-arousing power attributed to the event
and the emotional tension felt by the subject during the story reading. See Figure
23 for a summary of the experimental procedures.

Ruggero, despaired because he lost his job six
months before, has decided to rob the bank. When
he got to the cashier, he took out a big revolver
with a silencer and took off the safety-catch.
With this, he threatened the cashier, asking him
to give him the cash... In the emotion he
involuntariarly pressed the trigger and a bullet
wounded seriously the cashier.

Figure 22   Verbal description of the event complementary to a previous one (Figure 20)
and used as a causal explanation.

Procedural Components

1. **Pre-treatment measurement of cognitive processes.**
   Use of visual non verbal or verbal displays, fostering incongruity perceptions and/or other impressions, causality attributions, utilization of explanations, etc.

2. **Pre-treatment measurement of emotional processes.**
   Use of self-appraisal scales, for evaluating emotions, motivations, self-environment relationships.

3.

4. **Interruption at the 12th minute of treatment.**
   Administration of the second measurement of emotional processes (self-appraisal scales, for evaluating emotions, motivations, self-environment relationships).

5. **Return to treatment for 3 minutes.**

6. **Post-treatment measurement of cognitive processes.**
   Use of visual non verbal or verbal displays, fostering incongruous perceptions and/or other impressions, causality attibutions, utilization of explanations, etc.

7. **The subject is dismissed and initial processing of data occurs.**

Figure 23 Sequence of the standard experimental procedure.

RESULTS

General Findings Concerning Emotional Changes

Figure 24 shows a typical diagram of the pre- and post-changes in emotional scores and related statistics. In general, what were the effects of the manipulated stress, relaxation, and control conditions? What follows is a summary of the most important data collected. Under control conditions, that is, sitting peacefully in the room for 15 minutes, these subjects were slightly relaxed and elated. The impression of comfort increased slightly, anxiety lessened slightly, and the subject felt happier and more confident. Social and sexual tendencies were elevated slightly, but anger and aggression remained low.

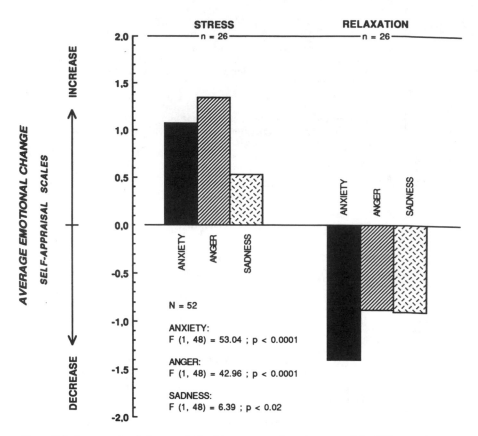

Figure 24 An example of changes obtained in some emotions, in terms of the differences in scores
obtained before and after the different treatments (averages derived from data obtained in
the third experiment; Bartoli, Biasi, Bonaiuto, Giannini, & Muccioli, 1990).

The stress situation, however, produced personal stress, frustration, feelings of
threat, insecurity, insufficiency, social inferiority, dependence, and an overload of
a variety of experience. Emotional reactions included anger, anxiety, and, to some
extent, sadness, guilt, and embarrassment. There was also an increase in aggressiveness. The cognitive tendency towards congruence, clarity, and regularity of
experience appeared slightly increased, whereas social and sexual tendencies were
slightly inhibited. The picture was one of a temporarily anxious, irritated, and
depressed subject who was a bit troubled and experienced conflict.

Subjects in the relaxation condition felt comfortable, gratified, and protected.
They often had a sense of superiority and autonomy, and of merit and self-
confidence. They did not feel inadequate but were somewhat bored. Anxiety was
strongly decreased, as was anger. Sadness was slightly decreased, and the mood
was happier. The cognitive requirement of congruence, clarity, and regularity was

slightly decreased, as were curiosity, self-affirmation, and the need for active movement. Sociability and sexuality were somewhat inhibited. The general picture here was of a subject who was self-oriented, much less available for energetic activity, had fewer problems and conflicts than subjects in the other two groups, and was more tolerant of incongruities in his or her evaluations.

Findings of the Three Experiments

Experiment 1

This study of stress and relaxation effects on perception of causality took place in 1989. Two groups of 16 students each (average age: 25.6 years) were used; there was no control condition. Results are shown in Table 1 and in Figure 25. With the relatively ambiguous presentations, the subjective clarity of the illusory contours was increased clearly in the stress condition and was decreased by a substantial amount under relaxation. Analysis of variance of these data reveals this difference to be significant ($F(1, 28) = 4.85$; $p = <.05$). This result supported our general hypothesis.

With the nonambiguous presentation technique, subjective clarity decreased after stress and increased after relaxation, which was our expectation in this case. This difference did not reach statistical significance; however, that between the two presentation methods did ($F(1, 28) = 5.87$; $p = <.05$).

There was no particular trend in the scores of subjective clarity generated by the classical figures; these three-dimensional perceptions were not influenced by our treatments and the subsequent changes in emotional state.

Experiment 2

This study was conducted in 1990 and used three groups of 12 subjects each (average age: 23.3 years). In addition to the stress and relaxation conditions, the intermediate (control) condition was also used. Results are shown in Table 2 and Figure 26.

The average score for the visual perception of cause-and-effect relationships was found to be increased distinctly after stress, distinctly decreased after relaxation, and increased slightly after the control condition. The control effect may be

Table 1 Statistics and average differences between pretreatment and posttreatment scores in Experiment 1

| | Changes of clarity scores | | | | | | |
| | Causality illusory contours (Fig. 7) | | Classical illusory contours | | | | |
Treatments	Ambiguous (favorable) situation	Unambiguous (unfavorable) situation	Fig. 9	Fig. 10	Fig. 11	Fig. 12	X̄
Stress ($n = 15$)	+1.06	−0.30	−0.30	−0.23	+0.30	+0.53	+0.08
Relaxation ($n = 15$)	−0.56	+0.61	+0.03	−0.73	+0.60	+0.33	+0.06
	$p < 0.05$	n.s.	n.s.	n.s.	n.s.	n.s.	n.s.
	$p < 0.05$						

Note. Analysis of variance was used to determine treatment effects.

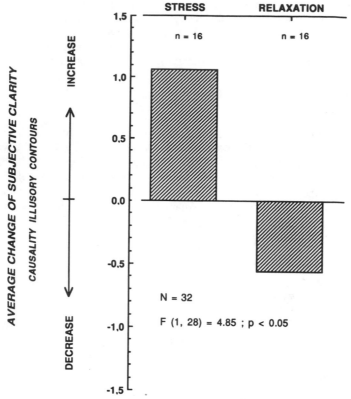

Figure 25 Graph of results of the first experiment in terms of the
differences between scores of subjective clarity of 'illusory
contours' before and after treatment (Bonaiuto, Giannini, &
Bonaiuto, 1989a).

Table 2 Average pretreatment and posttreatment scores, average pre- and post-changes and statistics
related to causality perception in Experiment 2

| | Average scores of the impression of cause–effect relationship (0/10) | | | |
| | Series of 10 test figures | | | Control figures |
Treatments	Pretreatment	Posttreatment	Change	Change
Stress ($n = 12$)	4.59	5.12	+0.54 a	−0.02
Intermediate condition ($n = 12$)	5.68	5.91	+0.23 a	+0.46
Relaxation ($n = 12$)	5.97	5.25	−0.72 b	−0.13
			$p < 0.02$	n.s.

Note. Analysis of variance was used to determine treatment effects. When Duncan's test was used,
significance is indicated by letters: mean values without comon letters are significantly different ($p < 0.05$).

due to some kind of learning or attitude change in these subjects. In some respects, we could subtract this change from the stress change or add it to the relaxation change to get a better understanding of the two extreme conditions. In this case, relaxation would be seen to have a particularly strong effect.

Analysis of variance of these data reveals overall significance among the three groups ($F(2, 23) = 5.30$; $p = <.02$); the difference between the two extreme groups is highly significant (Duncan's test: $p = <.01$).

Because the drawings were presented in random order it is possible to calculate the average effect of each drawing from immediately following treatment until about 20 minutes later. In the stress group, perception of causality diminishes gradually and almost disappears by the last drawing. This progressive, linear 'decay' is reasonable, is consistent with other psychological processes of a transitory, reversible nature (aftereffects), and reinforces our study techniques. Initially in the relaxation condition, perception of causality is low; halfway through the series it increases, and decreases later in the series. This effect appears to be because of a small amount of transitory stress in the relaxed subject caused by the early draw-

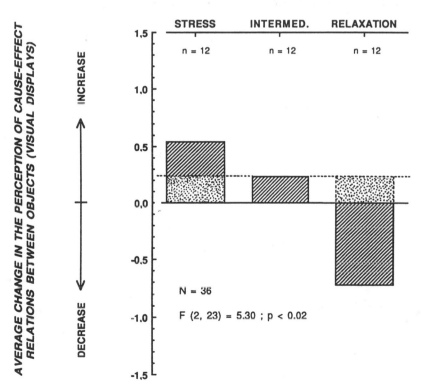

Figure 26   Graph of results of the second experiment in terms of the differences in the scores of causality obtained before and after treatment (Bonaiuto, Giannini, & Bonaiuto, 1990a).

ings, because they depict problem situations that require evaluation and responses. By the time the test is repeated the subject is used to the procedure, and the relaxation influence occurs again (see Figure 27).

We have obtained the greatest effects of stress and relaxation on causality perception with the most expressive drawings; those drawings that lack clear cause-and-effect relationships are least affected by our treatments. The two control drawings are extreme examples of the latter type; they lead to scores around zero and are unaffected by treatments.

Experiment 3

Causality attribution. This study was also done in 1990 and involved two groups of 26 subjects each (average age: 22.4 years) assigned to the two contrasting treatments described earlier. Here we used only verbally described (written) events.

Results are shown in Table 3 and in Figure 28. Analysis of variance of these data reveals highly significant differences between the two groups ($F(1, 48) = 8.43$; $p = <.01$). Examination of these results showed that the average score of cause-and-effect relationship between the first event (the apparently bizarre one) and the second event (the clarifying one) had increased remarkably after stress. This increase is higher than that obtained with the visual images in Experiment 2.

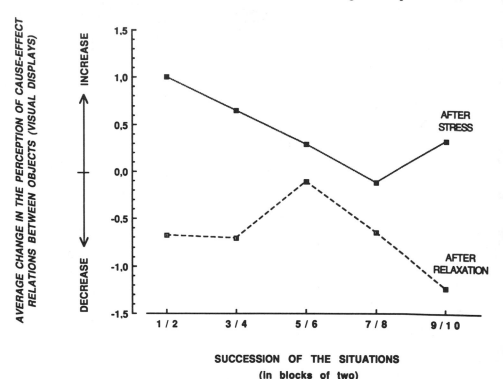

Figure 27   Graph of results of the second experiment (causality scores), taking into account the temporal distance from the end of each treatment (Bonaiuto, Giannini, & Bonaiuto, 1990a).

Table 3 Pretreatment and posttreatment average scores, average pre- and post-changes and statistics related to the evaluation of causality impression in Experiment 3

| Treatments | Average scores of the impression of cause-and-effect relationship (0/10) | | |
	Pretreatment	Posttreatment	Change
Stress (*n* = 26)	7.10	8.24	+1.14
Relaxation (*n* = 26)	7.80	6.66	−1.15
	n.s.	*p* < 0.01	*p* < 0.01

Note. Analysis of variance was used to determine treatment effects.

After relaxation there is a decrease that is strikingly similar in size to the increase just described.

Tolerance/intolerance of anomalies. Recall that in Experiment 3 we had a variety of measures obtained before and after treatment to evaluate degrees of incongruity of the story, anxiety-arousing power, and emotional tension. Pertinent

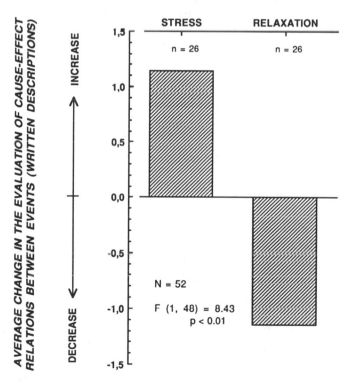

Figure 28 Graph of the results of the third experiment in terms of the differences in the scores of causality obtained before and after treatment (Bartoli, Biasi, Bonaiuto, Giannini, & Muccioli, 1990).

results are presented in Table 4 and Figure 29. Comparison of these pre- and post-measures indicates that immediately after stress the overall impression of anomaly and disturbance increases. Stressed subjects are more inclined to put anomalies in relief; in this sense they appear less tolerant of an incongruity such as that presented in the bizarre story.[6] Becoming more rigid about incongruities seems to be an effect of stress. Following stress treatment, the subject is more inclined to be tense when exposed to such bizarre stories.

Use of verbal explanation. Our general hypothesis suggested that providing an explanation of unusual events should lead to a reduction in the perceived anomaly of the story. If such incongruity is not reduced, it would appear that the explanation was not accepted. If, on the other hand, the incongruity is reduced to a high degree and in an exaggerated way, it may indicate overutilization of the explanation. We expected a marked reduction of the overall impression of anomaly and disturbance after the causal explanation where there was also a marked increase in the intensity of cause-and-effect relationships, as occurs in stressed subjects. In general, measures of causality and of reduction of the disturbing anomaly impression, after explanation, should be related.

Pertinent data are given in Table 5 and Figure 30, in which the verbal explanation appears to be overutilized after stress, and the overall impressions of anomaly and disturbance induced by the story are reduced more than in the other conditions after explanation. The correlation between the intensity of these decreases and the intensity of perceived causality tend to be positive.

DISCUSSION

The results of these studies can be summarized as follows:

1. Stress produced sizable increases in anxiety, anger, sadness, and aggressive motivation, and an increase in cognitive requirements for congruity, clarity,

[6]This type of incongruity intolerance is measured by the relief and the intensity of the impression of incongruity fostered by the bizarre situation when freely and clearly observed. Such an effect must be considered apparently opposed but substantially parallel to the effect of perceptual defense against incongruity during ambiguous observation, as in the case of tachistoscopic vision (Bonaiuto, Giannini, Bonaiuto, 1987, 1989e). Reviewing pertinent literature we have found that 25 years ago C. D. Smock (1955a, 1955b) was able to detect an increase of this last type of intolerance of visual incongruities after short-term experimental stress. We consider his results to be in agreement with our findings even though he has an alternative explanation.

Table 4 Average pretreatment and posttreatment scores related to the overall impression of anomaly and disturbance

	Pretreatment		Posttreatment	
Treatments	First impression: before the explanations	Second impression: after the explanations	First impression: before the explanations	Second impression: after the explanations
Stress (n = 26)	−0.24	+0.22	−0.44	+0.35
Relaxation (n = 26)	−0.28	+0.12	−0.17	+0.30

Note. Because of the seven-point scale (0 = ±3), the minus sign indicates the impression of anomaly and disturbance; the plus sign has the opposite meaning.

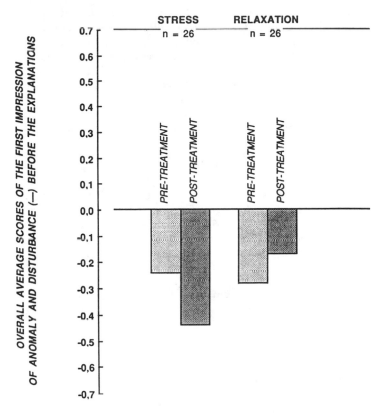

Figure 29   Graph of the results of the third experiment relative to the overall
impression of anomaly and disturbance when subjects are
evaluating the incongruous stories, before and after the
explanations for both pre- and post-treatment.

Table 5   Average pretreatment and posttreatment score changes related to the overall impression of
anomaly and disturbance in Experiment 3

Treatments	Pretreatment change due to the explanation	Posttreatment change due to the explanation	Change of the explanation utilization
Stress (*n* = 26)	+0.46	+0.79	+0.33
Relaxation (*n* = 26)	+0.40	+0.47	+0.07

Note. The plus (+) sign in the first two columns indicates the average change in the direciton of an
increase of congruence and normality, that is, of the utilization of the explanation in order to diminish
anomalies and disturbances. The plus (+) sign in the third column indicates that explanation utilization
has increased after the treatment.

and regularity. The emotional state created is likely to involve an overload of conflict with a resulting intolerance of anomalies and incongruities and a strong need for explanation, especially of cause-and-effect relationships.

2. Relaxation produced lowered anxiety, serenity, and happiness whereas aggression, the cognitive requirements for congruity, clarity, and regularity, self-affirmation, and the need for activity all decreased. This new emotional state must reflect a reduction in conflict, a greater tolerance for accepting anomalies and incongruities, and low expectations with respect to cause-and-effect relationships.

3. The control condition was linked with very little emotional change.

Cognitive performance corresponded to these emotional changes in the following manner:

1. With stress there was an increase in experimental hallucination ('illusory contours') fostered by the combination of strong pictorial cues of cause-and-effect relationships with sufficient cues of figural concreteness. This effect is reversed if the background appears to be very 'empty,' indicating that the demands for meaningful relationships also need the support of credible constitutive materials. Illu-

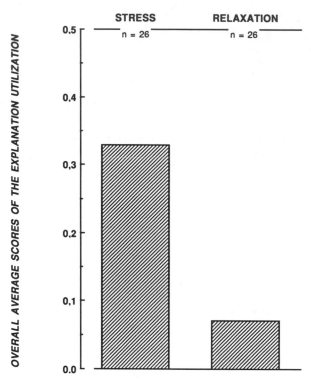

Figure 30   Graph of the results of the third experiment in terms
of the change of scores reflecting the overall
impression of anomaly and disturbance obtained before
and after treatment. This change expresses the degree
of utilization of the explanation.

sory contours elicited by three-dimensional pictorial images that require completion or constancy effects remain unchanged. Perceptual causality measures increase noticeably after stress when visual displays with clear cause-and-effect relationships are used, especially when the cues are strong and coercive. There is 'decay' in such measures as time passes after treatment. There is also an increase in measures of cause-and-effect relationships in accepting explanations—over two periods—of verbally described bizarre events. There is even an indication of initial emphasis of the degree of disturbing anomaly seen in such events, which is then followed by a 'hyperreduction' of this impression, which is a reflection of the overutilization of the explanations.

2. Relaxation, or comfort, leads to changes that are just the opposite of those of stress.

3. The intermediate, or control, condition was linked with minimal change in cognitive performance (as in emotions).

We feel these results confirm our general hypothesis, that is, that the perception of causality and the construction of causal links occurs in order to avoid an overburden of incongruities, perceptual anomalies, doubts, and mystery. This can occur in the perceiver if sufficient ambiguous images are used, as was shown in a crucial way by the first of our presentation methods. Otherwise, the subject responds to the strange elements by emphasizing them. The processes of causal attribution that lead to a large decrease in incongruity, anomaly, and uncertainty with verbal material operate in a similar manner. Conflict overload that results from stress amplifies all these phenomena.

We also found evidence for a role of the processes of 'projection' of aggressive drives and of other needs such as needs for affirmation, active movement, and of attitudes that included orientation towards external reality.

The possible role of modifications of visual attention in our results should be downplayed. Any potential influence of attention should have affected both causality cues and three-dimensional cues. However, in the first experiment we found no evidence of treatment influence with the classical figures based on three-dimensionality. We conclude, then, that our results are based specifically on the influence of stress or relaxation on the perception of causality.

FUTURE PROSPECTS

Future studies in this area will have to clarify further the proportional weight of many variables as they affect the phenomena we studied. Of particular importance is the determination of the specific roles of motivational 'projection' and of attentional processes. Additionally, better research tools should be developed to improve the direct measurement of the roles played by conflict, intolerance of incongruity, and their interaction with observation conditions.

An important investigation that needs to be done involves the study of people who have been stressed by means of more 'natural' laboratory conditions or as a result of the circumstances of daily life. Will they respond as our subjects did with respect to causality attributions? Also, do people with stable personality traits that are indicative of stressed or relaxed personality types respond in characteristic fashion as far as causality attributions are concerned?

In addition to these studies, we suggest the following questions also be investigated:

1. Do anxious managers who work under high-stress conditions overevaluate the consequences of certain actions or believe that vague causes are sufficient to produce specific effects? On the other hand, do very relaxed managers miss or underestimate the logical consequences of specific effective causes?

2. Could a police team or a court jury panel whose members are highly stressed accentuate attributions of responsibility in critical situations? Would relaxed people in similar circumstances be more lenient because they attribute less responsibility or intention? Panels evaluating merit to determine award assignments could be studied in the same way.

3. Do doctors, psychiatrists, psychoanalysts, and clinical psychologists who work under high stress provide rushed explanations to clients or make inappropriate links between symptoms and their potential causes? Under conditions of extreme relaxation, do these same individuals give insufficient attention to important cause-and-effect relationships?

4. Are clients who are exposed to very stressful verbal psychotherapy sessions more likely to accept and use certain causal explanations about incongruities in their behavior? Do clients who are provided relaxation training in their psychotherapy program tend to resist causal explanations of their behavior?

5. Do patients with more serious emotional disorders and with increased conflict and stress more readily develop delusional systems regarding cause-and-effect relationships? Providing relaxation interventions for such patients, especially paranoid patients, might be very useful therapeutically in weakening their dangerous attitudes about causality. We hope to provide answers to some of these important questions in studies we will undertake in the near future.

REFERENCES

Appley, M. H. & Trumbull, R. (Eds.). (1967). *Psychological stress: Issues in research,* New York: Appleton-Century-Crofts.

Appley, M. H. & Trumbull, R. (Eds.). (1986). *Dynamics of stress: Physiological, psychological and social perspectives.* New York: Plenum.

Bandura, A. (1983). Psychological mechanism of aggression. In R. G. Green & E. I. Donnerstein (Eds.), *Aggression: Theoretical and empirical reviews, Vol. l, Theoretical and methodological issues.* New York: Academic Press.

Barker, F., Dembo, T., & Lewin, K. (1941). Frustration and regression: An experiment with young children. *Studies in Child Welfare, University of Iowa, 18* (1), 1–315.

Bartoli, G., Biasi, V., & Bonaiuto, P. (1989a). *Experimental attribution of meaning and figures, objects and behaviors. The effects on conflict and anxiety scores.* Paper presented at the Tenth International Conference of STAR, Amsterdam.

Bartoli, G., Biasi, V., & Bonaiuto, P. (1989b). Effects of meaning attribution on conflict and incongruity. Paper presented at the First European Congress of Psychology, Amsterdam.

Bartoli, G., Biasi, V., & Bonaiuto, P. (1989c). Spiegazioni e attribuzioni di significaio che incidono sul conflitto e modificano l'incongruità percettiva. Paper presented at the Eighth Congresso Nazionale Divisione Ricerca di Base in Psicologia, S.I.P.s, Trieste, Italy.

Bartoli, G., Biasi, V., & Bonaiuto, P. (1989d). Manipulating conflict perception by meaning attribution. Paper presented at the Fourth Polish-Italian Conference in Psychology, Madralin, Poland.

Bartoli, G., Biasi, V., Bonaiuto, P., Giannini, A. M., & Muccioli, M. (1990). Stress and relaxation influences on the efficacy of explanation. Paper presented at the 11th International Conference of STAR, Berlin, Germany.

Berkowitz, L. (1983). The experience of anger as a parallel process in the display of impulsive, 'angry' aggression. In R. G. Green & E. I. Donnerstein (Eds.), *Aggression: Theoretical and empirical reviews, Vol. 1, Theoretical and methodological issues*. New York: Academic Press.

Bonaiuto, P. (1965). Tavola d'inquadramento e di previsione degli 'effetti di campo' e dinamica delle qualità fenomeniche. *Giornale di Psichiatria e Neuropatologia, 93*, (Suppl. 4), 1443-1685.

Bonaiuto, P. (1967). *L'inventario dei desideri 'B 66.'* Laboratorio di Psicologia, Università degli Studi di Salerno. Salerno, Italy.

Bonaiuto, P. (1967). *Le motivazioni dell'attività nell'età evolutiva. Analisi fenomenologica, riferimenti e indicazioni per la sperimentazione*. C.M.S.R.: Milano, Italy.

Bonaiuto, P. (1969). Sulle ricerche psicologiche europee in tema di monotonia percettiva e motoria ('Sensory deprivation') e simili. Il processo della saturazione di qualità fenomeniche. Paper presented at the International Symposium 'Man in Isolation and/or Enclosed Space,' Rome, Italy.

Bonaiuto, P. (1970). Creatività, produttività, percezione. In U. Apollonio, L. Caramel, & D. Mahlow (Eds.), *Ricerca e progettazione, Proposte per un'esposizione sperimentale*. Paper presented at the 35th Esposizione Biennale Internazionale d'Arte, Venice, Italy. Venice: Ente Autonomo La Biennale di Venezia. Rome: Kappa Publishers.

Bonaiuto, P. (1983). Processi cognitivi e significati nelle arti visive. Paper presented at the *Meeting 'Linguaggi visivi, Storia dell'Arte, Psicologia della percezione,'* Rome. Also published in L. Cassanelli (Ed.), *Linguaggi visivi, Storia dell'Arte, Psicologia della percezione*. Rome: Multigrafica, 1988 (pp. 47-79).

Bonaiuto, P. (1985). The usual, the ambiguous, and two forms of incongruity in the works of Maurits Cornelis Escher. Paper presented at the M. C. Escher Congress, Rome. In H. S. M. Coxeter, M. Emmer, R. Penrose, & M. Teuber (Eds.), *M. C. Escher Art and Science*, 1986 (pp. 359-368), Amsterdam: North Holland.

Bonaiuto, P. & Bartoli, G. (1968). *Influenza del livello basale d'ansietà, del tipo di 'feedback' e del trattamento psicofarmacologico (benzoctamina) su comportamenti e su vissuti durante conflitto sperimentale*. Laboratorio di Psicologia, Università degli Studi di Salerno, Salerno, Italy.

Bonaiuto, P. & Bartoli, G. (1970a). Experimental studies on social harmony and the relief of tension following psychopharmacological treatment with benzoctamine (Tacitin). Paper presented at the *International Symposium 'Anxiety and Tension: New Therapeutic Aspects,'* St. Moritz. In P. Kielhlotz (Ed.), *Anxiety and tension: New therapeutic aspects*. Basel: Ciba, 1970 (pp. 83-90).

Bonaiuto, P. & Bartoli, G. (1970b). Experiments on the psychopharmacological activation of social agreement in humans: Efficacy of some new measuring techniques. Paper presented at the Seventh Congress of the Collegium Internationale Neuro-Psychopharmacologicum, Prague. Published in *Il Lavoro Neuropsichiatrico*, 1970 (pp. 47, 143-161).

Bonaiuto, P. & Bartoli, G. (1971). Un esempio di studio dell'interazione fra variabili di personalità, trattamenti e variabili formali, nella sperimentazione con nuovi psicofarnaci in soggetti umani. Paper presented at the Fourth Riunione della Società Italiana di Neuropsicofarmacologia, Bologna, Italy.

Bonaiuto, P., Giannini, A. M., & Biasi, V. (1987). Human motivations, operator's personality, and visual design for human persuasion. Paper presented at the Third Italian-Polish Conference in Psychology, Cassino, Italy.

Bonaiuto, P., Giannini, A. M., & Bonaiuto, M. (1987). Piloting mental schemata on building images. Paper presented at the Third Italian-Polish Conference in Psychology, Cassino, Italy. Published in A. Fusco, F. Battisti, & R. Tomassoni (Eds.), *Recent experiences in general and social psychology in Italy and Poland*. Milan: Angeli, 1990 (pp. 85-130).

Bonaiuto, P., Giannini, A. M., & Bonaiuto, M. (1988a). Visual illusory production with or without amodal completion. Paper presented at the Workshop on 'New Issues on the Perception of Anomalous Surfaces and Subjective Contours,' 11th European Conference on Visual Perception, Bristol. Published also in *Perception*, 1991, 20 (in press).

Bonaiuto, P., Giannini, A. M., & Bonaiuto, M. (1988b). Illusory contours due to the pictorial representation of cause-effect relationship: A new procedure. *Rassegna di Psicologia, 5* (3), 73-79.

Bonaiuto, P., Giannini, A. M., & Bonaiuto, M. (1989a). Visual perception of cause-effect relationships producing 'illusory contours': The role of emotional and personality factors. Paper presented at the Tenth International Conference of STAR, Amsterdam, Holland.

Bonaiuto, P., Giannini, A. M., & Bonaiuto, M. (1989b). Visual illusory contours produced by pictorial representation of cause-effect relationships. Paper presented at the First European Congress of Psychology, Amsterdam, Holland.

Bonaiuto, P., Giannini, A. M., & Bonaiuto, M. (1989c). 'Illusory contours' e indizi pittorici di causalità: prove a favore dell'ipotesi di processi 'top down.' Paper presented at the Eighth Congresso Nazionale Divisione Ricerca di Base in Psicologia, S.I.P.s, Trieste, Italy.

Bonaiuto, P., Giannini, A. M., & Bonaiuto, M. (1989d). A new type of illusory contours. Emotional and personality factors. Paper presented at the Fourth Polish-Italian Conference of Psychology, Madralin, Poland.

Bonaiuto, P., Giannini, A. M., & Bonaiuto, M. (1989e). Maximizers, minimizers, acceptors, removers, and normals: Diagnostic tools and procedure. Rassegna di Psicologia, 6, (3), 100–107.

Bonaiuto, P., Giannini, A. M., & Bonaiuto, M. (1990a). Stress and relaxation influences on the perception of cause–effect relationships. Paper presented at the 11th International Conference of STAR, Berlin, Germany.

Bonaiuto, P., Giannini, A. M., & Bonaiuto, M. (1990b). Effetti contrapposti di stati emotivi (stress, rilassemento, etc.) sulla percezione di relazioni causa–effetto. Paper presented at the Ninth Congresso Nazionale Divisione Ricerca di Base in Psicologia, S.I.P.s, Bologna, Italy.

Bonaiuto, P., Massironi, M., & Bartoli, G. (1975). Atteggiamenti verso schemi di riferimento, utilizzazione di modelli, esigenze di libertà della persona. Paper presented at the meeting "Il bisogno della libertà," Roma. Published in Quadrangolo Rivista di psicoanalisi e scienze sociali, 1975, 2 (3/4, n.spec.mon.), 100–110. Reprint, Rome: Kappa Publishers.

Bruner, J. S. (1966). Toward a theory of instruction. Cambridge, MA: Harvard University Press.

Dembo, T. (1931). Der Arger als dynamisches Problem. Psychologische Forschung, 15, 1–144.

Dirkin, G. R. (1983). Cognitive tunnelling: Use of visual information under stress. Perceptual and Motor Skills, 56, (1), 191–198.

Ehrenstein, W. (1941). Über Abwandlungen der L. Hermannschen Helligkeitzerscheinung. Zeitschrift für Psychologie, 150, 83–91.

Freud, A. (1946). Das Ich und die Abwehrmeccanismen. Vienna (English translation: New York: International University Press).

Freud, S. (1901). Zur Psychopatologie des Alltagslebens Monatsschrift f. Psychiatr. u. Neurol., 10, (1), 1–32; (2), 95–143 (reprint, Leipzig: Internat. Psychoan. Ver., 1924).

Freud, S. (1923). Das Ich und das Es. Leipzig: Internat. Psychoan. Ver.

Freud, S. (1926). Hemmung, Symptoms und Angst. Leipzig: Internat. Psychoan. Ver.

Goldberger, L. & Breznitz, S. (Eds.). (1982). Handbook of stress: Theoretical and clinical aspects. New York: Free Press.

Jacobson, E. (1929). Progressive relaxation. Chicago: University of Chicago Press.

Janisse, M. P. (Ed.). (1988). Individual differences, stress, and health psychology. New York: Springer.

Jastrow, J. (1899). The mind's eye. Popular Science Monthly, 54, 299–312.

Kanizsa, G. (1974). Contours without gradients or cognitive contours? Italian Journal of Psychology, 1 (1), 93–112.

Kanizsa, G., & Metelli, F. (1961). Récherches expérimentales sur la perception visuelle d'attraction (Experimental research on the visual perception of attraction). Journal de Psychologie Normale et Pathologique, 385–420.

Kanizsa, G., & Vicario, G. (1965). Caratteri espressivi ed intenzionali dei movimenti. Paper presented at the 15th Congresso degli Psicologi Italiani, Turin, Italy.

Karsten, A. (1928). Psychische sattigung. Psychologische Forschung, 10, 254.

Koffka, K. (1935). Principles of Gestalt psychology. London: Routledge & Kegan.

Lazarus, R. S. (1966). Psychological stress and the coping process. New York: McGraw-Hill.

Maddi, S. R. & Kobasa, S. C. (1984). The hardy executive: Health under stress. Homewood, IL: Dow Jones-Irvin.

Mandler, G. (1984). Mind and body. Psychology of emotion and stress. New York: Norton.

Massironi, M. & Bonaiuto, P. (1965). Ricerche sull'espressività. Qualità funzionali, intenzionali e relazione di causalità in assenza di 'movimento reale.' Paper presented at the 14th Convegno Internazionale Artisti, Critici, Studiosi d'Arte, Rimini, Italy. Published also in Rassegna di Psicologia Generale e Clinica, 1966, 8, 1–42.

Meichenbaum, D. H. (1972). Cognitive modification of test-anxious college students. Journal of Consulting Clinical Psychology, 39 (3), 370–380.

Metzger, W. (1975). Gesetze des Sehens. Frankfurt: A. M. Kramer.

Michotte, A. (1946). La perception de la causalité. Edition 'Erasme'. Louvain: Université de Louvain, Belgium.

Michotte, A. (1957). La causalité phénoménale. Studium Generale,

Raven, J. C. (1956). Guide to use progressive matrices. London: Lewis.

Selye, H. (1956). *The stress of life.* New York: McGraw-Hill.

Smock, C. D. (1955a). The influence of psychological stress on the 'intolerance of ambiguity.' *Journal of Abnormal and Social Psychology, 50,* 177–182.

Smock, C. D. (1955b). The influence of stress on the perception of incongruity. *Journal of Abnormal and Social Psychology, 50,* 354–356.

Tolkmitt, F. J. & Scherer, K. R. (1986). Effect of experimentally induced stress on vocal parameters. *Journal of Experimental Psychology: Human Perception and Performance, 12* (3), 302–313.

Zuckerman, M. (1964). Perceptual isolation as a stress situation: A review. *Archives of General Psychiatry, 11,* 255–276.

II

PSYCHOPHYSIOLOGICAL DEVELOPMENTS

8

The Eye Blink: Affective and Cognitive Influences

John A. Stern
Washington University, St. Louis, Missouri

"Lust not after her beauty in thine heart; neither let her take thee with her eyelids." (Book of Proverbs 6:25)

INTRODUCTION

Why do we blink? According to most textbooks of physiology, we blink to maintain a protective coating of fluid over the cornea as well as to cleanse it. How often do we need to blink to maintain a film of tear fluid over the cornea?

Can the average blink rate for adults, reported to be between 15 and 30 blinks per minute, be used as the frequency necessary for this function? Two sets of data suggest this may not be the case. A number of studies, and we will use data reported by Ponder and Kennedy (1928) as the basis for our discussion, has demonstrated that manipulating humidity (a variable known to affect speed of evaporation of liquids from a surface) has little or no effect on blink rate in humans. Subjects observed in the hothouses of the University of Edinburgh Botanical Garden did not show differential blink rates when exposed to an arid, desertlike atmosphere or one like a humid tropical rainforest. If drying of the cornea is a major reason for blinking, one would expect a higher blink rate in an arid as compared with a humid environment. The second data set is based on studies of blink rates of infants. Newborn infants blink once or twice every 3 minutes, and the "normal" adult rate is not achieved fully until early adolescence. Both these observations should have warned scientists that factors other than the status of the fluid coating over the cornea affect blinking. Why then do adults blink so frequently? This chapter reviews a number of variables that affect blinking. We will present evidence that major contributions to blink rate are made by cognitive and affective variables. We will also demonstrate that aspects of blinking other than rate, such as blink timing and blink closure duration, provide additional information about aspects of cognition and affect.

The idea that movements of the eyelid convey information to the beholder dates back to antiquity. Gifford (1958), in an interesting monograph *The Evil Eye: Studies in the Folklore of Vision,* provides us with the quotation from the Book of Proverbs that suggests that more than the eyes of the beholder are involved in the

This research was supported by the United States' Air Force School of Aviation Medicine (USAF-SAM) Contract #F33615–87–R0603; William F. Storm, Ph.D., was the project officer.

art of seduction. He also reports on a Sumerian clay tablet dating from the third millennium B.C. that describes Iauana, goddess of love, dressing herself:

> *On her eyelids she placed an ointment with a strangely modern name. It was called, "Let him come, let him come." (p. 185)*
>
> *A somewhat later user of cosmetics, Jezebel painted her eyes when she heard that the rebel who had slain her husband was approaching. It was a brave gesture which did her no good. She was thrown from her window, and a troop of horse rode over the body. When they came to bury her, nothing remained but the skull, and the feet, and the palms of her hands. (p. 185)*
>
> *Other women have been more successful with eye paint than was Jezebel. Egyptian women used it lavishly, to judge from ancient Egyptian painting and sculpture." (p. 185)*

Gifford suggests that the act of painting the eyes to enhance beauty evolved from the application of ointments to avert eye disease and to repel insects. For the Egyptians it gradually became more important for decorative purposes. Women painted their upper eyelids black (lead sulphide) and their lower eyelids green (copper carbonate). Ancient Greek women used mulberry juice to paint their eyelids and Roman women in the days of Pliny the Elder painted their eyelids and eyelashes with powdered antimony or ashes. The use of belladonna to dilate the pupil also has been traced to Roman days. The eyes, eyelids, eyelashes, and eyebrows have been accentuated since antiquity to enhance beauty in the eye of the beholder.

The folklore of vision apparently has little to say about blinking. The notion that feelings of anxiety are associated with a high frequency of blinking is a fairly recent item of folklore, one whose roots we have not investigated.

BLINK TYPOLOGY

One can identify three types of blinks: reflex blinks, instructed blinks, and spontaneous blinks. Reflex blinks occur in response to unexpected, novel, and intense stimuli and are a component of the startle response. According to Landis and Hunt (1939), they are one of the more sensitive indicators of startle. For example, people who frequently shoot firearms continue to show the blink component of startle long after other muscle groups have ceased responding. Also listed under the rubric of reflex blinks are blinks produced by "threat" to the eyes. A blast of air to an eye invariably produces a blink. This finding has been used extensively by investigators concerned with the phenomenon of eyelid conditioning (Cason, 1922). The *voluntary eye blink* occurs in response to instruction, this instruction can come from another person in the form of a direct command to blink or it can be self-instructed. We blink when we experience a foreign object in our eye.

The *spontaneous* or *periodic* eye blink category includes all blinks that are not accounted for by reflex or voluntary blinks. How it came to be known as the "periodic" blink is somewhat of a mystery. Cranach (1969) demonstrated that there is no periodicity to these blinks; we thus prefer to label them spontaneous. This is not meant to imply that these blinks are not triggered by external or internal events, rather that experimenters have no direct control over them.

BLINKING AND COGNITION

An ingenious series of observations on the act of blinking, Ponder and Kennedy (1928) came to the conclusion that "mental tension" is the major determiner of blink rate. Most of their results have been confirmed by later, methodologically more sophisticated studies. These authors first demonstrated that one must tally blinks for at least 5 minutes per observation to obtain a reliable index of blink rate, and that even minor alterations in the experimental condition leads to alteration in the blink rate.

Ponder and Kennedy investigated blinking under a variety of experimental conditions and concluded that:

1. The presence of cigarette smoke leads to a marked increase in blink rate.

2. Variations in humidity (produced by taking subjects into the hothouses of the botanical department of the University of Edinburgh where conditions were either arid or humid) had no effect on blink rate.

3. Anesthetizing the cornea (2% cocaine solution) had no effect on blink rate; however, in the presence of tobacco smoke subjects did not show the customary increase in blink rate.

4. Manipulating light intensity (within reasonable limits) has no effect on blink rate. We blink as frequently in the dark as we do in a lighted room.

5. Blindness does not affect blinking, that is, blinking movements of normal frequency are observed in both congenitally blind individuals as well as those afflicted with optic nerve atrophy.

6. Blinks are controlled by the central nervous system rather than being reflex in nature, and are caused by impulses discharged through the seventh cranial nerve.

7. Lesions of the basal ganglia, especially the globus pallidus of the caudate nucleus and the lentiform nucleus, markedly inhibit blinking.

8. Making a subject "excited" or "angry" produces marked increases in blink rate.

9. Making a subject "mentally tense" (anxious) produces marked increases in blink rate.

10. Gender differences in blink rate were obtained, with men showing higher blink rates under some conditions and women showing higher blink rates under other conditions. They found blink rates of 10.4 per minute in women and 22.7 per minute in men riding in trolley cars. The lower rate in women was accounted for by the suggestion that they actively avoided looking at the men and engaged in introspective activity. The men focused their attention on the world around them. These differences in attentional focus were used to rationalize the observed differences in blink rate. In the library reading room the average blink rate of women was 8.96 per minute while that for men was 5.36 per minute. Their "explanation" needs to be read to get their full (sexist) flavor.

> . . . *in reading-rooms the attention of the women, or at least the women who came under our examination, is obviously much more externalised than that of the men, probably because the latter tend to study more closely than the former. The continual wandering of attention in women, accompanied by movements of the head and eye, constituted the whole difficulty of the experiment."* (pp. 106–107)

Ponder and Kennedy (1928) "explain" increases in blink rate in terms of increases in "mental tension" and this rationale sounds quite modern. They are attributed to "motor overflow" from other CNS foci. They suggest that in some subjects this may be the "preferred" path for such motor overflow whereas in other subjects such tension may be relieved by increased activity of the masseter and/or facial muscles as well as finger and foot movements. One might inquire into the number of subjects one has to test in order to demonstrate reliably the effects of mental tension on blinking. The experiments reported in this chapter dealing with sex differences used 50 male and 50 female subjects. Unfortunately, the chapter provides no statistical comparisons and thus it is not possible to evaluate this issue. However, research in the past 60 years has substantiated most of the *results* obtained by these investigators although the interpretation of the results has shifted somewhat. For example, the obvious sexist interpretation in the quoted passage dealing with differences in blink rate between men and women while studying goes further than current investigators would venture. A more exhaustive review dealing with the spontaneous eye blink is the article by Stern, Walrath, & Goldstein (1984), which documents much of the research dealing with spontaneous eye blinks through the early 1980s.

RECENT RESEARCH
AT WASHINGTON UNIVERSITY
ON COGNITIVE ASPECTS OF THE EYE BLINK

In all of the studies reviewed in Stern et al. (1984), the major or sole emphasis was on blink frequency. For over 10 years we have used oculomotor measures to make inferences about cognitive variables. Most of our research has dealt with the eye blink, although our interest also includes eye and head movements. Our major concern is with the strategies used by humans to acquire, process, and store information, and how physiological measures can be used to make inferences about these processes.

Our research suggested that variables other than blink frequency might be usefully related to aspects of perception and thought. For a number of reasons we singled out blink closure duration and timing as potentially relevant variables. We have demonstrated that blink closure duration is sensitive to task demands. It came as no great surprise to us that closure durations were significantly shorter when subjects were engaged in a visual vigilance task as compared to an auditory vigilance task of comparable difficulty. Somewhat more interesting was the finding of time-on-task effects. For example, there is a significant increase in average closure duration over a 40-minute vigilance task. Most interesting were studies on aircraft pilots. In aircraft with a pilot and co-pilot we found that blink closure durations of the pilot in control of the aircraft were significantly shorter than was true of the co-pilot. The nature of task requirements also affects closure duration. In a study conducted in a U.S. Air Force Flight Simulator, pilots were required to fly a lengthy mission involving segments of normal flight, terrain avoidance, threat avoidance, and attacking a target. Average blink closure durations were significantly shorter during the latter two types of flight segments than during either normal flight or terrain avoidance. It should be pointed out that the differences in closure duration across conditions involving visual activity seldom exceed 10% (i.e., 10–15 m/sec); nevertheless, they are statistically reliable (Stern & Skelly, 1984). Significant differences in blink frequency were also obtained in this study: the pilot flying the aircraft blinked significantly less frequently than the co-pilot.

Also, blink rate during threat avoidance was significantly less frequent than during other segments of the flight.

A second variable of interest concerns the timing of blinks and/or the inhibition of blinking. Do blinks occur randomly or are they influenced by psychologically relevant events? Informal observation suggests that blinks are influenced by perceptual/cognitive processes. Observe a person engaged in the act of reading. It has been known for a long time that people blink significantly less frequently when engaged in the act of reading than when not reading (Ponder & Kennedy, 1928). Many of the blinks occur as the reader shifts from one page of text to the next. Preliminary studies (Orchard & Stern, 1991) suggest that blinks that occur during the reading of text also do not occur at random points in time. They are most likely to occur as the reader shifts from one line of text to the next, in association with regressive saccades, or as the reader shifts from one page of text to the next. It thus appears that readers blink when they can inhibit momentarily the acquisition of new information (line change saccade and page change) or where recently acquired information makes no sense and the reader is forced to return to an earlier segment of the text for clarification (regressive saccade). Here, too, the reader momentarily suspends the taking in and processing of information. Thus blinks occur at points where one can take time out from attending to and processing information. Based on other data we have collected, this phenomenon is not unique to reading but occurs in situations involving the processing of auditorily as well as visually presented information.

We have conducted a series of laboratory studies in which there is tighter control over aspects of information processing than is true of the reading process. We examined blinking as subjects are required to perform the Sternberg memory task (Bauer, Goldstein, & Stern, 1987). This task involved committing to memory a set of letters or other stimuli. After a delay period, a single stimulus is presented. The subject has to decide whether this stimulus is, or is not, a member of the set committed to memory. In our paradigm, the first stimulus is a CUE, a stimulus that identifies the number of items to be presented in the memory set. After a fixed period, the MEMORY set is presented, followed after a fixed period by the TEST stimulus. The TEST stimulus is followed after a fixed period by the next CUE stimulus. In one such study involving 18 male university students (Goldstein, Bauer, & Stern, 1990), the stimuli to be memorized were letters; the set consisted of either two or six letters. The interval between STIMULUS periods was 6 or 10 seconds. Stimuli were presented for 700 msec at the beginning of each stimulus period. What effect does the task of committing a small and large set of letters to memory have on blink latency? What effects do the presentation of CUE and TEST stimuli (in each case a single letter) have on blink latency following stimulus onset?

Table 1 depicts blink latencies (in m/sec) for the first blink following stimulus onset for each of the three periods for the two set sizes used. An analysis of variance demonstrated a significant set size effect ($p < .02$) and a significant period effect ($p < .05$). The set size effect was significant for the MEMORY period, that is, subjects inhibited blinking significantly longer for the large as compared to the small memory set size.

The significant period effect is a function of longer blink inhibition associated with the MEMORY set as compared to the CUE and TEST periods. Although it appears that blink latencies for the TEST stimuli were longer than those for the

Table 1 Blink latencies (in m/sec) from onset of CUE,
MEMORY, and TEST stimulus presentation

	CUE	MEMORY	TEST
Two items	772	865	874
Six items	800	1039	865

Note. Memory set size consisted of two and six items.

CUE stimuli, these differences were not statistically reliable. These results, and those of similar studies, indicate that blinking is inhibited longer when we are required to commit information to memory than when required to read a single item (CUE) or required to read and compare the test item with information stored in memory.

If the timing of the first blink following MEMORY SET presentation is affected by the nature of task demands and set size, one would suspect that the timing of blinks throughout the three periods also might be nonrandom. Figure 1 depicts blink frequencies during successive seconds of the three periods. It is readily apparent that blinks are not distributed randomly during any of the three periods. What can we conclude from this figure (and the appropriate statistical analyses)? First, the anticipation of any stimulus input leads to a significant reduction in blinking. The closer we get to the point where information is expected, the lower the likelihood of blink occurrence. What is expected, be it the MEMORY, CUE, or TEST stimulus or whether the set size is large or small has no differential effect on blink rate immediately preceding presentation of a stimulus. Subjects also appear to "judge" the duration of the 6- and 10-second intervals reliably because blink rate at the 6-second point in time is significantly higher for the 10-second as compared to the 6-second stimulus presentation periods.

Other evidence for a set size effect occurs during the memory period where blink rate is consistently higher for the large as compared to small memory set size, except, of course, for the first 2 seconds of the period. This suggests that the retention of information for short periods affects blink rate. My interpretation of the increase in blink rate during information retention currently is based on my subjective impression. Its validity is thus suspect and badly in need of objective testing. How do we retain a set of meaningless letters in memory when the requirement is to forget the set as soon as a decision about a test letter has been made? To retain the information, after seeing the letter set, people may use "inner" speech to maintain it in memory. They rehearse it repeatedly throughout the 6- or 10-second delay period. It is my impression that the frequency with which persons have to repeat the letter set is a function both of set size and time. The larger set size has to be repeated more frequently than the small one, whereas the set has to be repeated less frequently as time elapses. I believe that one is most likely to blink immediately following a rehearsal of the letter set. Thus the greater decrease in blink rate for the smaller set size is attributed to a faster reduction in the frequency with which the letter set is rehearsed to maintain it in memory.

Is the third measure, blink duration, affected by our experimental manipulations? As is apparent from Figure 2, it is. Blink closure duration, like rate, decreases as one approaches stimulus presentation, with closure durations being shortest immediately before presentation of the memory set (regardless of size)

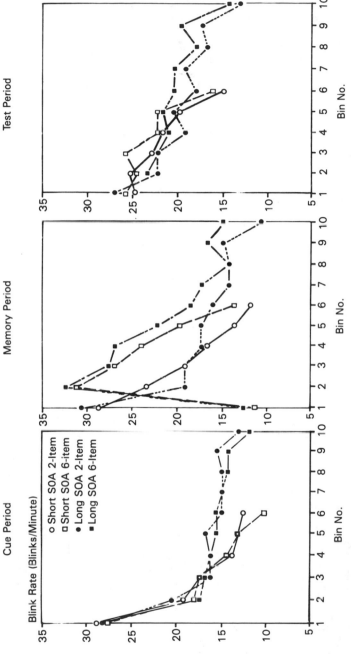

Figure 1 Blink rate following CUE, MEMORY, and TEST stimulus presentation for two levels of difficulty (○, 2 items; □, 6 items) and two levels of information retention (○□, 6 sec; ●■, 10 sec).

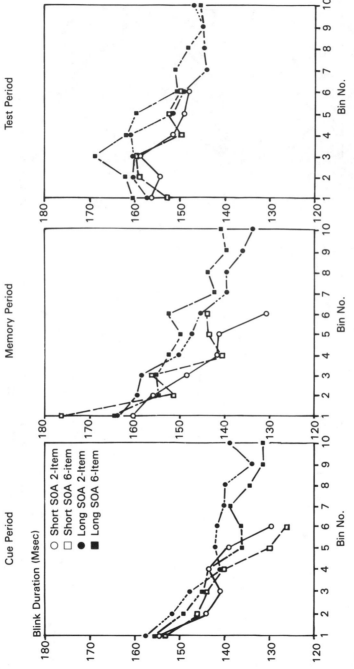

Figure 2 Blink closure duration (50% window) following CUE, MEMORY, and TEST stimulus presentation for two levels of difficulty (○●, 2 items; □■, 6 items) and two levels of information retention (○□, 6 sec; ●■, 10 sec).

and longest in anticipation of the next CUE stimulus. One might infer from this that if a subject has difficulty inhibiting a blink in anticipation of a stimulus, he does the next best thing that will ensure detection and perception of the stimulus, namely blink as rapidly as possible.

Although not as robust as the blink frequency effect, one sees that closure duration during the MEMORY period also demonstrates a reliable set size effect. Closure durations are reliably longer during the retention of a large as compared to small set size. Thus the nature (i.e., waveform) of the blink is also affected by stimulus processing demands.

Our speculation about the meaning of the longer closure duration is even further removed from objective reality than our interpretation of the blink frequency effect. Fortunately, it is also amenable to experimental verification. We believe the reason for the long closure duration blinks associated with the more difficult task is a "relief" phenomenon associated with the successful retention of information. After repeating the letter set successfully, one can momentarily relax. If longer duration blinks are associated with larger set size one can make the inference that such "relaxation" is greater for the larger set size.

To summarize, our research to date has demonstrated that cognitive variables affect not only blink rate, but the timing as well as closure duration of blinks. As task demands increase, blink frequency and closure duration decrease; as memory demands increase, blink latency increases. We blink when we momentarily are not required to or abort the taking in or processing of information, and we blink at times when expectancies are not met.

BLINKING AND AFFECT

What effect will feelings of anxiety have on the timing of blinks and blink closure duration? Does anxiety lead to poorer inhibition of blinking, as may be suggested by the finding that anxiety leads to an increase in blink rate? Does anxiety lead to shorter or longer closure duration blinks or does it have no effect on this variable? As is readily apparent, we have little information on the effect of anxiety on these variables. Research by others, it is hoped, will shed light on these questions and will allow us to say more about the relationship between aspects of blinking and feelings of anxiety in the not-too-distant future.

The idea that symptoms of anxiety can be categorized into two or more "syndromes" has a long history. Alexander (1950) conceived of patterns of symptoms associated with the sympathetic nervous system and those associated with the parasympathetic nervous system symptom predominance. Eysenck (1961) distinguished between autonomic hyperactivity or conditioned anxiety responses on the one hand and somatic or visceral anxiety on the other. Hamilton (1959) discriminated between somatic and psychic anxiety, and Buss (1962) as well as Fenz & Epstein (1965) described similar clusters of symptoms. Buss (1962) associated somatic anxiety with physiological arousal, subjective feelings of discomfort, somatic complaints, and distractibility. Psychic anxiety was manifested by feelings of restlessness and worry as well as muscle tension. Fenz and Epstein (1965) accorded muscle tension a separate category of anxiety in addition to categories of autonomic arousal and psychic anxiety (feelings of fearfulness and insecurity).

More recently, Cloninger (1986) arrived at a somewhat different constellation of symptoms associated with what he refers to as *somatic anxiety* and *cognitive anxiety.* He differs with other anxiologists in suggesting that patients in both groups report both psychological and physical complaints. He suggests that patients with somatic anxiety manifest "prominent and diverse bodily pains" (p. 169), whereas the physical complaints of those with cognitive anxiety "involve fatigue, muscle tension and slow recuperation from minor illness." The psychological distress symptoms of those with cognitive anxiety are characterized by "avoidance of novelty and anticipation of harm contingent on specific warning signals" (p. 169). Those with somatic anxiety have symptoms involving "vague feelings of alarm and global uneasiness without specific premonitory cues" (p. 169). In spite of these vague and global feelings of alarm they are described as novelty seekers who are characterized by impulsive behavior.

Thus one can say that people manifest different constellations of symptoms, which are all labeled *anxiety,* or that there is more than one kind of anxiety. In any case, researchers interested in physiological or behavioral patterns associated with anxiety need to be careful to define the type or types of anxiety they are investigating. From my cursory review of the literature dealing with the spontaneous eye blink and anxiety, this has not been done.

The Eye Blink and Anxiety

Relatively few studies have looked at blink rate as it relates to aspects of anxiety. Although most of those reviewed demonstrate significant relationships between blinking and anxiety there are some with nonsignificant results. We will review the latter first.

Jackson and Bloomberg (1958) evaluated blink rate in a group of psychiatric patients composed principally of schizophrenics (60%), and anxiety neurotics (32%). The Taylor Manifest Anxiety Scale (TMAS) was administered as well as the digit span test of the Wechsler–Bellevue Scales of Intelligence. Electrodermal activity was also measured. These variables were intercorrelated and not one significant correlation was found. Unfortunately, only the table of correlations is presented in the report. The best that can be concluded with respect to our concern for eye blink–anxiety relationships is that when the TMAS is administered to a mixed group of psychiatric patients, its scores do not correlate with blink rate, nor do they correlate with digit span.

Martin (1958) conducted a study to evaluate blink rate and anxiety. She points out that "it is a common clinical impression that a high blink rate is present in states of anxiety" (p. 123). Martin sampled subjects at the extremes of the neuroticism and introversion–extroversion continua, and studied blink rate under resting conditions and while subjects were responding to questions dealing with the presence of neurotic symptoms. No difference in blink rate between groups was obtained. She did find that blink rate was markedly elevated (doubled) during the answering of questions as compared to the two rest periods. Her conclusion is that the widely held impression of differences in blink rate between neurotics and normals is in error. One can infer from her data that either situational anxiety, change in experimental condition, or both, have significant effects on blink rate. A graph is presented showing alterations in blink rate over successive 10-second periods during rest and while subjects were responding to questions. There is a rapid reduction in blink rate over the first 30 seconds in all three periods (rest 1, question, rest 2). In all cases, the drop is approximately 10 blinks per minute.

Interestingly, this reduction in blinking is not mirrored in another measure presumed to be associated with anxiety, namely activity recorded from the frontalis muscle group. Frontalis muscle activity was similar across the three time periods and "manifests no observable trends" (p. 129). Thus if the reduction in blink activity over the 30-second period is associated with the reduction of situational anxiety, one would come to the conclusion that blink frequency is a better measure of such anxiety than frontalis EMG activity.

Kanfer (1960) evaluated blink rate in 38 married female psychiatric patients during a structured interview dealing with various topics, some of which were designed to arouse feelings of anxiety. Marginal support for a higher blink rate associated with discussing an anxiety-arousing topic was obtained ($p = .10 > .05$). Psychiatrists familiar with the patient were asked to rate degree of conflict experienced by each patient for the five topics that were discussed. For half of the 32 patients studied, the highest blink rate coincided with the topics of greatest discomfort; for 15 patients the lowest blink rate was associated with topics predicted to be the least disturbing. Kanfer's study thus provides suggestive data that blink rate is affected by manipulations that increase feelings of anxiety in women regardless of diagnosis.

Weiner and Concepcion (1975) manipulated anxiety by having subjects view or listen to a graphic description of an automobile–truck crash or a tranquil landscape scene. Subjects were exposed to one of those four conditions and blink rate was measured before, during, and following exposure to the material. Anxiety levels were measured preexposure and postexposure by use of the Multiple Affect Adjective Check List (MAACL). Results from the MAACL demonstrated a significant change in anxiety level as a function of stimulus material (accident vs. landscape).

Blink rate showed a significant stimulus presentation effect (auditory stimulus presentation led to greater blink frequency than visual stimulus presentation), a significant effect for periods with higher blink rate during information presentation as compared to rest periods, and a significant modality by periods and content by period interaction. The difference between auditory accident and auditory landscape was significant, the accident producing higher blink rates than the landscape. The differences for the visual mode of information presentation, although in the right direction, were not significant.

Thus in the auditory mode of information presentation heightened anxiety was reflected in an increase in blink rate. The nonsignificant effect for visual stimulus presentation is rationalized in terms of a competition between blink suppression associated with attending to important stimuli and to an increase in blinking associated with tension release.

Thus this study suggests that momentary or short-lived alterations in feelings of anxiety are reflected in an increase in blinking, a phenomenon similar to that seen in chronically anxious subjects.

Muscle Tension and the Eye Blink

Three studies will be reviewed in which either muscle tension or situational anxiety was experimentally manipulated and blink rate evaluated. The basis for manipulating muscle tension was an influential paper by Meyer (1953). Meyer had suggested that because motor centers controlling the vocal apparatus and other musculature are located close to those that control the eyes, activation of motor cortical centers may lead to an "overflow" or "spreading activation" (in the current vernacular) into the oculomotor area, leading to an increase in blink rate. King and Michels (1957) demonstrated that muscle tension, induced by squeezing a hand dynamometer, led to an increase in blinking. Lovaas (1960) administered the TMAS to a large group of subjects and selected 32 with the lowest and 32 with the highest scores on this test. He had subjects engage in a paired–associate learning task under four conditions of muscle tension. Subjects high in scores on the TMAS had blink rates twice as great as those that had low scores on the TMAS under the condition of no induced muscle tension. Subjects were required to increase muscle tension (by squeezing a hand dynamometer); the subjects with high TMAS scores demonstrated a decrement in blink rate as muscle tension increased while subjects with low TMAS scores demonstrated an increase. Using a nonlinear correlation procedure (η), he found a significant correlation between TMAS scores and blink rate ($r = .37$). The reliability of blink rate measurement was $r = .76$.

Harris, Thackray, and Shoenberger (1966) administered the TMAS and the Maudsley Personality Inventory (MPI) to 25 male college students. They recorded blink rate, heart rate, respiration, and electrodermal activity under conditions of "rest" and while subjects squeezed a hand dynamometer at one fourth their maximal effort for 4 minutes. Blink rate was the only measure that correlated significantly with performance on both the TMAS and the neuroticism scale of the MPI. Under conditions of rest, blink rate correlated .50 and .49, respectively, with the TMAS and the MPI. Under the muscle tension condition, the correlation for neuroticism as measured by the MPI remained significant ($r = .43$), whereas that for the TMAS fell below an acceptable level of significance. In both the rest and the muscle tension conditions, the relationships were highest for the first and second minute. The significant relationship did not persist for minutes three and four. The lack of correlation for the last 2 minutes for both the "rest" and the muscle tension conditions may be attributed to feelings of physical discomfort. Both conditions are reported to produce an increase in blink rate over the 4-minute period. In the relaxed condition, subjects were instructed to fixate a small dim indicator light located about 4 feet away. Maintaining fixation on a small object for 4 minutes produces feelings of ocular discomfort that may well produce an increase in blink rate. Although it is unclear from the paper, it is possible that subjects were also instructed to fixate the light during the muscle tension task. Thus the lack of significant effects for the last 2 minutes of task performance may be attributed to feelings of discomfort, which produced increases in blink rate for both groups of subjects. This study suggests that one does not have to sample extremes of the anxiety continuum in order to obtain differences in blink rate between those "high" and those "low" in anxiety.

Situational Variables and the Eye Blink

Appel, McCarron, and Manning (1968) manipulated anxiety experimentally by having subjects exposed to high- and low-threat conditions. The subjects were 30 high school counselors attending a counseling and guidance institute. In the high-threat condition they had to role play contending with an irate parent. They were instructed that the interview was to be televised so that members of the class could view each other's performance. The task was described as part of their final counseling evaluation. The low-threat condition involved a discussion between the subject and a member of the institute's staff concerning their counseling experiences prior to attending the institute.

Eye blinks were evaluated from videotapes with blinks counted for the first 3 minutes of the "threat" interview. Blink rates for the 30 subjects were rank-ordered and the nine highest and lowest blinkers were selected to constitute the high eye blink (HEB) and the low eye blink (LEB) groups. The average blink rate for the HEB and LEB groups was 42 and 11.7 blinks per minute, respectively. High blinkers in the high-threat condition demonstrated a significant decrease in blinking when shifted to the low-threat condition (x blink rate of 47.6–36.4) while the LEB group demonstrated no change in blink rate (x blink rates of 11.2 and 12.2, respectively). This study also evaluated anxiety as measured by the TMAS and the correlation between TMAS and blink rate ($r = -.21$) was not significant.

Other procedures have been studied for inducing anxiety or for making use of "natural" conditions in which anxiety as well as cognitive variables are varied. The earliest, and perhaps most ingenious, is a report by Ponder and Kennedy (1928) of blink rate of witnesses in a court of law being interrogated by the opposition lawyer or "friendly" lawyer. Blink rate was significantly higher during questioning by the "unfriendly" lawyer. In a symposium presentation at the Annual Meeting of the Society of Psychophysiological Research (1989), Tecce reported on the blink rate of President Bush, then an aspirant to the presidency, and of Michael Dukakis, during one of their presidential "debates." Tecce used videotaped recordings of these debates to evaluate blinking. The average blink rate of both Bush and Dukakis was high throughout the debate (67/min and 75/min respectively). Speaking about topics that were congenial to both candidates led to significantly lower blink rates than speaking about topics on which there was considerable debate. When speaking of his vice presidential running mate, Bush had an average blink rate of 44/min. When talking about his stance on a woman's right to have or not have an abortion, an emotionally charged topic, Bush's blink rate went to 89/min. Similarly, when Dukakis was asked to list some of his sterling qualities, such self-praise was associated with blink rates of 53/min. On the topic of taxes, a loaded topic on which he and his adversary differed vehemently, his blink rate was 92/min. The average blink rate of both men appeared to be considerably elevated during the debate. Although not formally studied, the blink rate of both men under less "stressful" television appearances was below 30/min.

Fatigue

Fatigue, a feeling state frequently associated with both anxiety and depression, has been studied with respect to its influence on aspects of blinking. The earliest report of blinking as a measure of eye fatigue found by us dates back to a paper by Katz (1895). This author, using himself as sole subject, asked whether the subjective feeling of "tired eyes" can be studied objectively. He mechanically coupled the orbicularis muscle to a Mareymyograph and studied blinking under three lighting conditions while reading. Reading was conducted for 10 minutes under each of the three conditions. In the lowest light intensity condition (reading was difficult) blink rate was 5 and 8.6 per minute, respectively, for successive 5-minute periods. Under the medium lighting condition (reading under a gas light) mean rate for the first and second 5-minute period was 1.8 and 3.8. Using an Edison glow light (best illumination), the rate was 1 and 2.6 blinks per minute, respectively. Katz came to the conclusion that visual fatigue could be indexed by blink rate. In a brief paper based on a dissertation presented to the Medical Faculty of the George-August University of Gottingen, Buttger (1923) suggested that blink frequency is useful not only as a measure of ocular fatigue but as a measure of imposed "workload" as well. He reported that changes in light intensity while subjects were reading produced differences in blink rate during the first 10 minutes of reading, with no appreciable further change during a 1-hour reading period. Slowest blink rates occurred when the text was illuminated with between 40 to 70 lux. Reducing light intensity below 40 lux initially produced a slow increase in blinking, and then a rapid increase. When intensity exceeded 70 lux, blink rate increased rapidly. Subjects also reported subjective discomfort when light intensity exceeded this limit. When subjects were required to read for a 4-hour period, blink rate increased approximately two to three times over the initial rate.

Carpenter (1948) evaluated blink rate in subjects performing the Mackworth Clock Test over a 2-hour period. The major increase in blinking occurred after the first half hour of task performance. The increase was approximately 30%. After 2 hours the average blink rate was 50% higher than at the start. Of 20 participants only 1 showed a decrease in blink rate. He reported that the curve depicting performance on the Mackworth Clock Test (missed signals) was "very similar to that of the blink rate found here" (p. 589). Two studies will be reviewed, in which fatigue was induced by sleep deprivation. Research from our laboratory has suggested that time-on-task effects in areas other than reading are reflected in a significant increase in blink rate. Slater, Neville, Whitmore, French, and Schiflett (1990) evaluated blink rate in subjects performing a variety of tasks under sleep deprivation conditions. The study involved 36 hours of continuous activity in which light intensity was manipulated. One group was subjected to dim and the second to bright light during the 36-hour vigil. They demonstrated that subjects run under the more intense light condition showed less impairment in task performance and, what is more interesting in the present context, significantly less of an increase in blink rate than subjects run under the dimmer lighting conditions.

A study by Morris (1984) deprived pilots of sleep for the major portion of their normal night of sleep and required them to fly a simulated cross-country flight in a General Aviation Trainer flight simulator. Errors in performance as reflected by deviation from prescribed altitude, heading, air speed, and so forth were combined into a single score and this measure was correlated with aspects of blinking, including blink amplitude, frequency, closure duration, and the occurrence of long-closure duration blinks. A stepwise regression analysis of the above variables as predictors of impaired performance identified blink amplitude as the best single predictor ($R^2 = .36$). The best two variables fit paired blink amplitude with frequency of long-closure duration blinks ($R^2 = .61$). Adding other variables did not appreciably add to the predictive equation.

These data suggest then that both blink rate and measures of blink closure duration may index aspects of fatigue and workload. We suspect that a combination of these two measures would allow one to discriminate between workload-induced and fatigue-induced alterations in blinking. Blink frequency appears to increase (under some conditions) as a function of visual workload as well as with feeling of fatigue or simply time-on-task effects. Blink closure duration, on the other hand, decreases as a function of workload and increases as a function of fatigue. Thus, we would recommend that both measures be used in attempts at evaluating and discriminating between workload and fatigue effects.

Blink Rate as a Diagnostic Aid

It would be convenient if an elevation in blink rate was diagnostic of anxiety. Unfortunately, this is not the case. There are marked individual differences in blink rate. Differences in psychopathology and neuropathology, in addition to "state" variables, significantly affect blink rate.

Stevens (1978a) and Karson, Freed, Kleinman, Bigelow, and Wyatt (1981) have demonstrated that patients diagnosed as schizophrenic have a significant elevation in blink rate when compared to normal subjects. These results also have been reported by others (Andresen, Seifert, Lammers, & Thom, 1988; Cegalis & Sweeney, 1979; Helms & Godwin, 1985). Karson (1983) and, earlier, Ponder and Kennedy (1928) presented evidence linking activity of the central nervous system nigrostriatal area to blink activity. Karson also reported that removing the (rat's) cerebellum produces a significant increase in blinking. By manipulating drugs that affect central dopaminergic pathways, Karson and collaborators were able to determine that the acute administration of agents affecting central dopamine production significantly affected blinking. Reducing CNS dopamine reduced blink rate whereas increasing it produced increases in blink rate.

Involvement of the nigrostriatal system is inferred from the finding that patients suffering from Parkinsonism demonstrate a significant reduction in blink rate, and that the reduction in blink rate is related to severity of symptom, with those more severely affected having lowest blink rates. Levodopa, a drug used in the treatment of Parkinsonism, has been found to produce significant increases in blink rate in these patients. It is believed that these symptoms are due to increased central dopaminergic activity.

Schizophrenia

The blink rate of schizophrenics is reported to be higher than that of normals. Whether this finding is secondary to other variables or is causally implicated in schizophrenia (e.g., as a reflector of increased central dopaminergic activity) is unclear. Ostow and Ostow (1945) studying medication-free schizophrenics report a higher blink rate in schizophrenics ($x = 27$) than in other psychiatric groups ($x = 18$–22). Stevens (1978b) reported higher levels of blinking in medication-free schizophrenics as compared to controls. Similar results were obtained by Karson (1983). Both these latter authors equivocate on whether the higher level of blinking in their schizophrenic patients was pathognomonic of schizophrenia or whether it could be linked to a neuroleptic–drug-induced symptom of tardive dyskinesia. Karson further reports that when patients are returned to a neuroleptic medication they showed a significant reduction in blink rate (premedication $x = 31$; postmedication $x = 24$), and their average blink rate while on medication was similar to that of normal control subjects ($x = 23$). Mackintosh, Kumar, and Kitamura (1983) report that schizophrenics have a lower-than-normal blink rate and suggest that this is "probably a result of neuroleptic administration" (p. 55). It is obvious that there is some confusion concerning differential blink rates in schizophrenia as well as concern for the basis of the increase or decrease in blink rate.

Mackert, Woyth, Klaus-Malte, & Volz (1990) studied a group of drug-naive acutely ill schizophrenic patients (n = 15), a group (n = 8) treated with a neuro-leptic drug, and a group of age- and gender-matched control subjects while per-forming a visuomotor task. There were no differences in visuomotor reaction times or accuracy between groups. Significant differences in blink rate were ob-tained between the unmedicated schizophrenic and the control and medicated group. Mean blink rate was 16, 9, and 8 blinks per minute, respectively. These authors correlated blink rate with performance on the Brief Psychiatric Rating Scale (BPRS) administered both before and after treatment. Before treatment, blink rate correlated significantly with anxiety (rho = .49) and hostility–suspicion (.42). Posttreatment these two variables correlated .75 and .78, respectively, with blink rate and a third variable, "unusual thought content," correlated .59 with blink rate.

Bartko, Herczeg, and Zador (1990) related blink rate to variables evaluated with the BPRS. Blink rate was evaluated while subjects gazed at a neutral picture for 3 minutes. The BPRS was administered approximately 14 days after blink frequency evaluation. Subjects in the study were 18 newly admitted research-diagnosis-criteria (RDC) diagnosed schizophrenic patients with a history of schizophrenia. Blink rate was evaluated 4 hours after intramuscular (IM) injection of 5 mg of haloperidol. Patients were then treated daily for the next 14 days with haloperidol. Significant correlations were obtained between blink frequency and thought disturbance (r = .69), suspiciousness (r = .59), G.A.S. global assessment (r = 61), total score on the rating scale (r = .63), and activation (r = .48). This study and the one by Mackert et al. suggest that blink rate is sensitive to aspects of personality as mea-sured by the BPRS.

The evidence generally suggests a higher-than-normal blink rate in schizophren-ics but equivocates on whether this elevation is secondary to prior or concurrent treatment with neuroleptics. Most studies evaluated blink rate during psychiatric interviews. Whether the elevations in blink rate are secondary to higher levels of "arousal" or discomfort on the part of the patients subjected to such interviews is unclear, although the study by Mackert et al. obtained relatively elevated blink rates in unmedicated schizophrenics performing a visuomotor task. Andresen (1991) points out that cigarette smoking is a habit of 80 to 90% of all schizophrenics in western industrialized countries. Andresen suggests that the elevated blink rate seen in schizophrenia (as well as elevated platelet MAO levels) may be secondary to smoking rather than a primary "symptom" of disturbed physiological processes.

Depression

Mackintosh et al. (1983) report on blink rate in clinically depressed (n = 23) patients studied on three occasions, 14 days apart. Blink rate was evaluated over a 15-minute period on each occasion while the subject was interviewed with the Present State Examination (PSE). Comparisons were made with a control group of nonpatients matched for age, sex, race, and socioeconomic status evaluated with the same PSE. Depressed patients blinked significantly more frequently on the first interview than controls (x = 26 vs. x = 15). On the second interview blink rates were no longer significantly different although average blink rate for the depressed group remained above that for the normal sample (x = 21 vs. x = 15). At the third interview average blink rates for the two groups were nearly the same (x = 17 vs. x = 15). Reduction in blink rate in the depressed group was related to clinical improvement. Dividing the group into 17 "improved" and 6 "unimproved" (grouping was done by an independent evaluator), the blink rate of the unimproved group did not show a significant reduction over the three interviews. Patients received a variety of medications including major and minor tranquilizers (not specified) and tricyclic antidepressants. Grouping patients according to medications received produced no differences in blink rate between groups.

These authors refer to a report in Trethowan and Anderson's book (1973) about a major reduction in blink rate in depressed patients. The present authors suggest that the patients reported by Trethowan and Anderson were suffering from severe psychomotor retardation. Mackintosh et al. (1983) divided their group of depressed patients into endogenous depression without psychomotor retardation ($n = 7$), endogenous depression with psychomotor retardation ($n = 9$), a neurotic depression group ($n = 7$), and a group of schizophrenics with depressive symptoms ($n = 5$). Average blink rates of these groups was 29, 20, 17, and 43, respectively. They suggest that "blink rate may therefore increase with depression, but reduce again as symptoms of psychomotor retardation appear" (p. 56).

Although these authors do not comment on it, we found it interesting that a group of schizophrenic patients ($n = 20$) only interviewed at intake had a blink rate of 8 blinks per minute while their subgroup of schizophrenics with depressive symptoms had a rate of 43 blinks per minute. Whether this is attributable to differences in nature or differences in duration of taking psychoactive medication cannot be inferred from their paper.

Posttraumatic Stress Disorder (PTSD)

Resick, Churchill, Schnicke, and Olevitch (1991) studied a group of women suffering from PTSD and a control group. Blink frequency was evaluated during four phases of the study: a baseline rest period while responding to neutral questions, a second baseline period, and a third period while responding to questions about the trauma that had precipitated PTSD in that group. The PTSD group blinked more frequently before answering questions about trauma than before answering neutral questions. The PTSD group had comparable blink rates across the four conditions whereas the control group blinked more frequently when answering questions than during baseline period. Although not reliably so, the PTSD group blinked more frequently than the control group. Thus if PTSD can be thought of as an "anxiety" disorder we have further evidence suggesting that elevated blink rates may be implicated not only in phasic or situational anxiety but in chronic anxiety as well.

CONCLUDING COMMENTS

We hope that this review of the literature relating aspects of blinking to issues of cognition and affect has provided convincing evidence for such relationships. We are, of course, left with more unanswered than answered questions. For example, restricting ourselves to the issue of anxiety we need to ask whether the increase in blinking associated with both traits and situational anxiety is as time-locked to specifiable events as is true of normal subjects engaged in the act of reading. During reading by competent readers, the vast majority of blinks occurs in association with page turns, line changes, and regressive saccades. Will the anxious readers show the same pattern of major inhibition of blinking characteristic of normal readers? Or does anxiety lead to a reduction or lessening of such inhibitory control? Such lessening of inhibitory control may be manifested in two ways. The most drastic would be a more random distribution of blinks for the anxious as compared to the normal reader. A second possibility would be a higher likelihood of blinking concurrent with these events. It might be possible that one could gauge the degree of impairment in inhibitory control from the properties of randomly occurring blinks as compared to blinks that are time-locked to psychologically meaningful events. Because both anxiety and schizophrenia lead to an increase in blink rate, the latter measure might well discriminate between these two conditions (presuming that the elevation in blinking on the part of schizophrenics is not mediated by anxiety). We would expect schizophrenics to have poorer inhibitory control than would be characteristic of anxiety states. If anxious subjects are more "aroused" or alert to environmental events, we would expect average blink closure durations to be significantly shorter than would be true of normal subjects dealing with the same environmental events. With respect to blink timing, if such timing is, as we suspect, time-locked to the point in time at which information has been abstracted, and if anxiety neurotics have no difficulty in the acquisition of information but have trouble with the processing of such information, we would suspect that blink latencies would not discriminate between normals and anxiety neurotics. If anxiety neurotics have difficulty in the processing of information, we would expect more blinks and probably longer closure duration blinks during this portion of task performance than is true of normal subjects.

These are a few examples of how this relatively simple measure might be used in the study of aspects of anxiety. Generating such hypotheses is relatively easy. Converting them into sound research protocols is somewhat more difficult. Let me encourage anxiologists to explore the utility of this and other measures of oculomotor function.

REFERENCES

Alexander, F. (1950). *Psychosomatic medicine.* New York: Norton.

Andresen, B. (1991). Clinical psychophysiology and uncontrolled status variables in schizophrenia research. *Journal of Psychophysiology, 5,* 98(a).

Andresen, B., Seifert, R., Lammers, C. H., & Thom, E. (1988). Lidschlagfrequenz, Schizophrenie und Schizotype Personlichkeitsstorung. *Jahrestagung der Deutschen Gesellschaft fur Psychopysiologie und irhe Anwendungen, 2,* 129–130(a).

Appel, V. H., McCarron, L. T., & Manning, B. A. (1968). Eyeblink rate: Behavioral index of threat? *Journal of Abnormal & Social Psychology, 15*(2), 152–157.

Bartko, G., Herczeg, I., & Zador, G. (1990). Blink rate response to haloperidol as possible predictor of therapeutic outcome. *Biological Psychiatry, 27,* 113–115.

Bauer, L. O., Goldstein, R., & Stern, J. A. (1987). Effects of information-processing demands on physiological response patterns. *Human Factors, 29*(2), 213–234.

Brandt, K., & Fenz, W. D. (1969). Specificity in verbal and physiological indicants of anxiety. *Perceptual & Motor Skills, 29,* 663–675.

Buss, A. H. (1962). Stimulus generalization with aggressive verbal stimuli: A new paradigm. *Journal of Psychology, 53*(2), 417–424.

Buttger, W. (1923). *Uber die Lidschlagfrequenz als Mass Fur die Ermudung des Auge und uber den Einfluss von Beleuchtungsstarke und lichtfarbe auf die Ermudung.* Unpublished dissertation, Medical Faculty, George-August University, Gottingen, Germany.

Carpenter, A. (1948). The rate of blinking during prolonged visual search. *Journal of Experimental Psychology, 38,* 587–591.

Cason, H. (1922). The conditioned eyelid reaction. *Journal of Experimental Psychology, 5,* 153–195.

Cegalis, J. A., & Sweeney, J. A. (1979). Eye movements in schizophrenia: A quantitative analysis. *Biological Psychiatry, 14*(1), 13–26.

Cloninger, C. R. (1986). A unified biosocial theory of personality and its role in the development of anxiety states. *Psychiatric Developments, 3,* 167–226.

Cranach, M., Schmid, R., & Vogel, M. W. (1969). The relationship between gaze movements and eye blink under various conditions. *Psychologische Forschung, 33,* 68–78.

Eysenck, H. J. (1961). *The handbook of abnormal psychology.* New York: Basic Books.

Fenz, W. D., & Epstein, S. (1965). Manifest anxiety: Unifactorial or multifactorial composition. *Perceptual & Motor Skills, 20,* 773–780.

Gifford, E. S. (1958). *The evil eye; studies in the folklore of vision.* New York: MacMillan.

Goldstein, R., Bauer, L. O., & Stern, J. A. Effect of task difficulty and stimulus onset asynchrony on blinking and cardiac activity. Unpublished manuscript, Washington University, St. Louis.

Hamilton, M. (1959). The assessment of anxiety states by rating. *British Journal of Medical Psychology, 32,* 50–59.

Harris, C. S., Thackray, R. I., & Shoenberger, R. W. (1966). Blink rate as a functon of induced muscular tension and manifest anxiety. *Perceptual & Motor Skills, 22*(1), 155–160.

Helms, P. M., & Godwin, C. D. (1985). Abnormalities of blink rate in psychosis: A preliminary report. *Biological Psychiatry, 20*(1), 103–106.

Jackson, D. N., & Bloomberg, R. (1958). Anxiety: Unitas or multiplex. *Journal of Consulting Psychology, 22,* 225–227.

Kanfer, F. H. (1960). Verbal rate, eyeblink, and content in structured psychiatric interviews. *Journal of Abnormal Social Psychology, 61,* 241–247.

Karson, C. N. (1983). Spontaneous eye-blink rates and dopaminergic systems. *Brain, 106,* 643–653.

Karson, C., Freed, W. J., Kleinman, J. E., Bigelow, L. B., & Wyatt, R. J. (1981). Neuroleptics decrease blinking in schizophrenic subjects. *Biological Psychiatry, 16*(7), 679–682.

Katz, R. (1895). Ueber das Blinzeln als Maasstab fur die Ermudung des Auges (The eyeblink as a measure of visual fatigue). *Klinische Monatsblatter fur Augenheilkunde,* 154–157.

King, D. C., & Michels, K. M. (1957). Muscular tension and the human blink rate. *Journal of Experimental Psychology, 53,* 113–116.

Landis, C., & Hunt, W. A. (1939). *The startle pattern.* New York: Farrar & Rinehart.

Lovaas, O. I. (1960). The relationship of induced muscular tension, tension level and manifest anxiety in learning. *Journal of Experimental Psychology, 59,* 145–152.

Mackert, A., Woyth, C., Klaus-Malte, F., & Volz, H. (1990). Increased blink rate in drug-naive schizophrenic patients. *Biological Psychiatry, 27,* 1197–1202.

Mackintosh, J. H., Kumar, R., & Kitamura, T. (1983). Blink rate in psychiatric illness. *British Journal of Psychiatry, 143,* 55–57.

Martin, I. (1958). Blink rate and muscle tension. *Journal of Mental Science, 104,* 123–132.

Meyer, D. R. (1953). On the interaction of simultaneous responses. *Psychological Bulletin, 50,* 204–220.

Morris, T. L. (1984). An evaluation of three electrooculographic measures as indices of decrements in flying performance. Report GS-00K-830262903, Task Order EP-10 to Air Force School of Aerospace Medicine, Brooks Air Force Base, Texas.

Orchard, L. N., & Stern, J. A. (1991). Blinks as an index of cognitive activity during reading. *Integrative Physiology and Behavioral Sciences, 26,* 108–116.

Ostow, M., & Ostow, M. (1945). The frequency of blinking in mental illness: Measurable somatic aspect of attitude. *Journal of Nervous Mental Disease, 102,* 294–301.

Ponder, E., & Kennedy, W. P. (1928). On the act of blinking. *Quarterly Journal of Experimental Physiology, 18,* 89–110.

Resick, P., Churchill, M., Schnicke, M. K., & Olevitch, B. (1991, October). *Behavioral correlates of PTSD: A pilot study.* Paper presented at the annual meeting of the ISTSS, Washington, DC.

Slater, T., Neville, K., Whitmore, J., French, J., & Schiflett, S. (1990). Electrophysiological correlates of performance improvement by light intensity. Poster presented at the annual meeting of the Human Factors Society, CITY.

Stern, J. A., & Skelly, J. J. (1984). The eye blink and workload considerations. In *Proceedings of the 28th Annual Meeting of the Human Factors Society* (pp. 942–944). Santa Monica, CA: Human Factors Society.

Stern, J. A., Walrath, L. C., & Goldstein, R. (1984). The endogenous eyeblink. *Psychophysiology, 21,* 22–33.

Stevens, J. R. (1978a). Disturbances of ocular movements and blinking in schizophrenia. *Journal of Neurology, Neurosurgery, & Psychiatry, 4*(11), 1024–1030.

Stevens, J. R. (1978b). Eye blink and schizophrenia: Psychosis or tardive dyskinesia. *American Journal of Psychology, 135,* 223–226.

Tecce, J. J. (1989). Contingent negative variation and eyeblinks. *Clinical EEG, 20,* 71–72.

Trethowan, W. H., & Anderson, E. W. (1973). *Psychiatry* (3rd ed.). London: Balliere, Tindall.

Weiner, E., & Concepcion, P. (1975). Effects of affective stimuli mode on eye blink rate and anxiety. *Journal of Clinical Psychology, 31,* 256–259.

9

Skin Conductance, Heart Rate, and Active-Passive Coping

Tytus Sosnowski
University of Warsaw, Poland

The active-passive coping continuum is undoubtedly one of the fundamental dimensions of human behavior set. Depending on how one evaluates a situation (i.e., gratification value of an object, task demands, and behavior reinforcement ratio), people may either act or withdraw from activity. Therefore, the active-passive coping dimension plays an important role in many conceptions of emotion and motivation, including conceptions of anxiety (cf. Chapters 2, 13, & 16 in this volume).

According to Lacey (1967), and in opposition to the classical theory of activation (cf. Duffy, 1962, 1972), psychophysiological activity results not only from the energetic dimension of behavior but also from the content-related "nature of the subject's set and expectation of his intended response to stimulus" (Lacey, 1967, p. 25; cf. also Fahrenberg, 1986; Venables, 1984). Based on these assumptions, we may predict that the set to cope actively or passively in a given situation will involve differently organized physiological processes. This safeguards the best possible implementation of the intended behavior at the lowest possible physiological cost.

Obrist (1976, 1981; Obrist & Light, 1984) was one of the first researchers to draw attention to the role of active-passive coping in the regulation of psychophysiological activity, specifically cardiovascular activity. A broader approach to this problem may be found in conceptions proposed by Gray and Fowles.

GRAY'S THEORY

Gray (1975, 1982a, 1982b) postulates the existence of three basic systems that control behavior: the behavioral inhibition system (BIS), the behavioral approach system (BAS), and the fight/flight system. The last system will not be discussed here because it does not fall within the scope of the present study.

According to Gray (1982a, 1982b, 1991), specific structures in the central nervous system can be identified as being the neurophysiological counterparts of the three regulatory systems. We shall focus only on the behavioral aspect of Gray's theory.

According to Gray, the BIS is responsible for responses to negative conditioned

This work was supported by Grant RPBP.III.25/VI from the Polish Ministry of National Education and Grant BST 91/91 from the Polish Committee for Scientific Research.

stimuli, that is, signals of punishment and signals of frustrative nonreward, as well as responses to novel stimuli. The arousal of this system results in the inhibition of ongoing behavior (passive avoidance or extinction), increased attention focused on the surroundings (orienting response), and in increment in nonspecific arousal.

The BAS is responsible for responses evoked by positive conditioned stimuli (i.e., signals of reward (incentives) and signals of relieving nonpunishment). The BAS arousal effect is behavioral activation aimed at positive reinforcement (approach or active avoidance) and, like the BIS effect, an increase of nonspecific arousal. Moreover, Gray's conception presupposes a mutually inhibitory effect of BIS and BAS.

The aim of Gray's concept is to explain not only a subject's reactions to different situational cues but also individual differences in such responses. According to Gray, sensitivity of the BIS may be regarded as the factor responsible for individual differences in anxiety, whereas sensitivity of the BAS may be regarded as the factor responsible for individual differences in impulsivity (Gray, 1982a, 1991; Wilson, Barrett, & Gray, 1989). However, to date, empirical data supporting the applicability of Gray's concept in the explanation of individual differences—particularly in human beings—are scant.

APPLICATION OF GRAY'S MODEL
TO PSYCHOPHYSIOLOGY: FOWLES' APPROACH

The original version of Gray's theory makes no reference to psychophysiology. It was Fowles who gave it its psychophysiological elaboration. According to Fowles (1980, 1983, 1988), electrodermal activity (particularly the number of nonspecific fluctuations and the amplitude of evoked exosomatic responses) may be regarded, under certain circumstances at least, as an index of activity of the behavioral inhibition system, whereas tonic heart rate changes serve as an index of activity of the behavioral approach system (also called *the behavioral activation system*). However, Fowles does not mention any psychophysiological variable associated with nonspecific activation.

Reviews of research to date (Fowles, 1980, 1982, 1983, 1988) provide much support for Fowles' interpretation. Special attention should be paid to the studies of Obrist and his collaborators (Obrist, 1976, 1981; Obrist et al., 1983; Obrist, Lawler, Howard, Smithson, Martin, & Manning, 1974; Obrist & Light, 1984; Obrist, Light, Langer, Grignolo, & Koepke, 1982). These authors have shown that when punishment avoidance is response contingent, for example, when the subject must make a motor response as fast as possible in order to avoid an electric shock, a very considerable increment of tonic cardiovascular activity (heart rate and systolic blood pressure), mediated by activation of the sympathetic (beta-adrenergic) system, is observed. Individual differences in cardiovascular reactivity are also most pronounced in such conditions (cf. Obrist & Light, 1984; Manuck & Garland, 1980). When punishment is not response contingent (e.g., during aversive classical conditioning), the parasympathetic system predominates and increments in cardiovascular activity are relatively small. According to Obrist (1976), this switch in the psychophysiological response pattern is determined primarily by the subject's set to cope actively or passively.

Similar changes in heart rate are also found in conditions requiring active responding if reward is to be gained (cf. Belanger & Feldman, 1962; Ehrlich &

Malmo, 1967; Elliott, 1969, 1974; Fowles, 1980, 1982, 1983, 1988; Fowles, Fisher, & Tranel, 1982; Hahn, Stern, & Fehr, 1964; Tranel, Fisher, & Fowles, 1982). Moreover, as Fowles (1980) claims, a review of the relevant data from the literature implies that the organism's response to incentive is often much more clearly visible in heart rate changes than in motor activity. This is particularly interesting because Hull and Spence's incentive motivation theory was constructed precisely to explain the energizing effect of rewards on motor behavior (Hull, 1952; cf. also Bolles, 1979; Madsen, 1974).

The mechanism underlying tonic cardiovascular changes in situations demanding active coping is very interesting psychologically. First, these changes cannot be explained satisfactorily in terms of activation of the somato-motor system. It has been determined that pharmacological blocking of the beta-adrenergic system, which inhibits the increment of tonic heart rate, does not cause any marked changes in skeletal muscle tension (Obrist et al., 1974; cf. also Obrist, 1976).

Second, these changes cannot be explained as the effect of tuning of the cardiovascular system to current metabolic demands of the organism. It has been shown in many studies (Blix, Stromme, & Ursin, 1974; Brener, Philips, & Connally, 1977; Moses, Clemens, & Brener, 1986; Obrist & Light, 1984; Obrist et al., 1983; Turner, 1989; Turner, Carroll, Hanson, & Sims, 1988) that although there is a very strong correlation between activity of the heart and oxygen consumption during simple physical effort, the correlation disappears in conditions of psychological stress, particularly when the situation requires active coping in a stressful task. In the latter case, heart rate increases far beyond the level predictable from oxygen consumption (so-called "additional heart rate").

The changes in heart rate and systolic blood pressure discussed above cannot be treated as responses of the cardiovascular system to disruption of homeostasis. They are clearly contingent upon the psychological evaluation of the meaning of the situation to the subject and the subject's set.

Fowles' interpretation of electrodermal changes is more problematic. On the one hand, there are many data indicating that the electrodermal system is very sensitive to stimuli critical for BIS, that is, punishment, frustrative nonreward, and orienting stimuli (cf. Dawson & Schell, 1985; Ohman, 1979, 1983; Prokasy & Kumpfer, 1973; Raskin, 1973; Roberts & Young, 1971). On the other hand, this system responds to other stimulus categories: unconditional aversive stimuli (cf. Fowles, 1980), nonaversive meaningful stimuli, for example, imperative stimuli (Maltzman, 1977, 1979), and positive reinforcements in instrumental conditioning (Kimmel, 1973), although some authors doubt the reliability of the last category. The nonspecific nature of electrodermal responses need not in itself undermine Fowles' interpretation. As Fowles (1983) himself says, BIS may not be treated as the only mechanism responsible for changes in electrodermal activity (cf. also Edelberg, 1972, 1973; Fowles, 1986).

INTERRELATIONSHIP BETWEEN ACTIVITY OF THE ELECTRODERMAL AND CARDIOVASCULAR SYSTEMS

According to Gray, BAS and BIS are two potentially reciprocally inhibitive systems. If so, and if Fowles' psychophysiological interpretation of Gray's theory is correct, we are entitled to expect, at least in certain conditions, a negative relationship between phasic changes in skin conductance and tonic changes in heart rate. In other words, a greater increment in heart rate should go hand in hand with smaller electrodermal changes and vice versa.

To date, the data indicating that such a relationship is possible are scant (Hare, 1978; Szpiler & Epstein, 1976). However, the problem itself is seldom investigated. Also, certain additional conditions must be fulfilled in order for the relationship between cardiovascular and electrodermal activity to appear. Three such conditions seem to be of particular importance.

First, according to Fowles (1980, 1983), BAS is only one of many mechanisms responsible for changes in heart rate; similarly, BIS is only one of many mechanisms responsible for electrodermal changes (cf. also Edelberg, 1972, 1973; Fowles, 1986). Hence, we may only expect reciprocal relationships between activity of these two physiological systems when they are, in fact, activated by BAS and BIS.

Second, it seems to be that a reciprocal relationship between activity of the cardiovascular and electrodermal systems is only observable when both regulatory systems (BAS and BIS) are activated simultaneously. Only then can we observe the effect of decrement of the (previously elevated) activity of one system as a result of inhibition by the other system.

Finally, we must remember that the data in the literature showing lack of correlation between heart and electrodermal activity (cf. Lacey, 1967; Mitchell, Venables, Mednick, Schulsinger, & Cheaneebash, 1983) are based on linear correlation. However, as we shall attempt to show later, there is reason to think that the relationship between the activity of these two response systems may be curvilinear.

Both the literature and our own findings suggest that there are at least two types of situations conducive to a relationship between cardiovascular and electrodermal activity.

1. There are situations in which one system (BAS or BIS) dominates because of specific situational (stimulus, task) factors. In this case we may expect most people to manifest a similar, situation-specific psychophysiological response pattern.

2. There are ambiguous or conflict situations where both factors critical for BAS and for BIS are present but neither is dominant enough to evoke the same direction of response in most subjects. In such cases, the actual response should be contingent first and foremost upon individual properties of the subject, that is, the subject's relative sensitivity of BAS or BIS to critical stimuli and his previously acquired response habits. We may expect that people whose BAS predominates over BIS will show a large increment in tonic heart rate and simultaneous low skin conductance responses, whereas those whose BIS predominates over BAS will show relatively strong electrodermal responses and, at the same time, a small increment in heart rate. In people for whom neither regulatory system is sufficiently activated and no reciprocal inhibition is present, changes in heart rate and electrodermal activity should be small and they should not correlate with each other. (For a discussion of individual differences in BAS or BIS dominance, cf. Gray, 1991.)

The hypotheses mentioned in points 1 and 2 were tested in three experiments, which will be presented below.

RELATIONSHIPS BETWEEN CHANGES
IN SKIN CONDUCTANCE AND HEART RATE:
TASK DEMAND EFFECTS

The first study (Sosnowski, Nurzynska, & Polec, 1991) examined the effect of active versus passive coping with the task situation, as defined by the experimental instruction, on tonic changes in heart rate and phasic changes in skin conductance.

Sixty women, students of a medical high school in Warsaw, participated in the experiment. Subjects were tested in pairs, that is, two subjects took part in a session at the same time. The active member of the pair independently solved problems from the Raven Progressive Matrices, which were presented by means of a projector. The passive subject in the pair was merely an observer of the task situation.

Heart rate of the two groups of subjects across eight blocks of trials is given in Figure 1. Analysis of these data revealed that the level of heart rate was significantly higher in active than passive subjects, but only at the beginning of the experimental session (block 1): $F(1,27) = 4.86, p = < .05$. In addition, a significant Active/passive task role × Blocks of trials linear trend interaction was found: $F(1,27) = 6.50, p = < .05$. The interaction indicates that the descending linear trend of heart rate changes is steeper in the group of active subjects than in the group of passive subjects.

The findings for skin conductance, especially differences between phases of the task activity, were quite interesting. The magnitudes of three responses evoked by task presentation (phase 1), solving a task by the active participant (phase 2), and

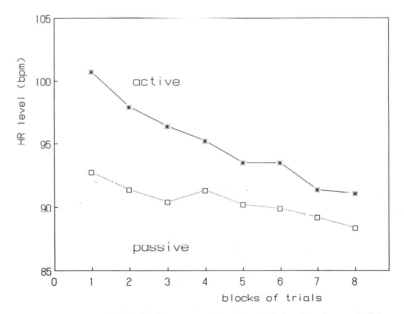

Figure 1 Heart rate level of active and passive subjects during the subsequent eight blocks of tasks (each block equals four tasks). Reproduced from Sosnowski, T., Nurzynska, M., & Polec, M. (1991). *Psychophysiology.*

feedback on correctness of response (phase 3), were compared. Statistical analysis revealed (cf. Figure 2) a significant Task role × Phase linear trend interaction: $F(1,27) = 24.72, p = < .001$. In the active group, the magnitudes of consecutive responses revealed a descending linear trend, $t(27) = 3.62, p = < .001$, whereas in the passive group the trend is ascending, $t(27) = 2.70, p = < .05$. The results of this study seem very consistent with predictions from both Gray's and Fowles' theories.

Taking both these theories as our starting point, we may assume that the task role induced by the experimenter should lead to relatively stable differences in subjects' sets. This should result in a more pronounced activation of BAS in the active group than in the passive group. This seems to be true in terms of the changes in heart rate. On the other hand, analysis of the task demands implies that the degree of activation of one or the other regulatory system should differ in particular phases of task activity. We may assume that the first two phases (task presentation and task solving) should activate the BAS more strongly than the BIS, whereas the third response, that is, the response to feedback, should primarily activate the BIS. If inhibition of the BIS by the BAS did in fact predominate in the active group, this should result first and foremost in responses that were most strongly mediated by the BIS, that is, responses to feedback.

INTERRELATIONSHIPS BETWEEN CHANGES IN SKIN CONDUCTANCE AND HEART RATE: THE ROLE OF INDIVIDUAL DIFFERENCES

The two studies presented later in this paper were based on almost identical experimental designs. In each case subjects waited for 1 minute for a prospective aversive stimulus (a 100-dB sound), announced each time by a special perceptual message. The message consisted of two slides, each presenting a black circle on a white background. The subjects had been instructed that the aversive stimulus would be presented each time the second circle was larger than the first (standard). The sound would not be presented if the second circle were smaller than the first. Subjects had also been instructed that the circles would definitely not be identical. In fact, however, in the test trials the two circles were identical (ambiguous message).

The first study was conducted on a sample of 18 male students at the University of York (UK) (see Sosnowski, 1988, 1991, for a detailed description of the experimental procedure). The results, based on only the first experimental trial, are presented in Figure 3. The results of further trials were less clear because of a fast habituation of psychophysiological changes.

The y axis shows the increments in skin conductance evoked by the message. The x axis shows the mean tonic changes in heart rate during the period when the subject is waiting for the prospective aversive stimulus. In order to deal with two different units of measurement, the two variables are presented in standardized score form (z).

As can be seen in Figure 3, subjects who showed a large increment in heart rate also showed small changes in skin conductance. On the other hand, subjects who had large changes in skin conductance had small changes in heart rate. Some subjects showed small changes in both psychophysiological parameters. The data distribution indicates high consistency with the hypothesis presented earlier.

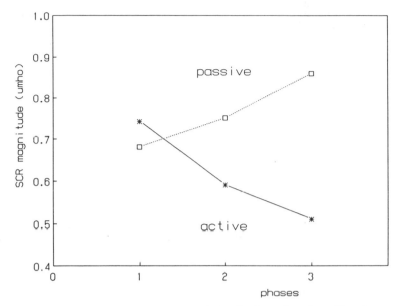

Figure 2 Skin conductance response magnitude of active and passive subjects in response to: projection of the task (phase 1), answer given by the active subject (phase 2), and feedback given by the experimenter (phase 3). Reproduced from Sosnowski, T., Nurzynska, M., & Polec, M. (1991). *Psychophysiology.*

The data plot presented some problems for statistical analysis. A glance at the results suggest that the points in Figure 3 represent a parabola, rotated by about 45 degrees to the right. However, the relationship represented by this curve does not fulfill the condition that only one value of Y exists for each X value. To eliminate this problem, a transformation of the scores was done equivalent to the rotation of the axes by an angle of -45 degrees. The transformed data are presented in Figure 4.

Analysis of regression of the nontransformed scores revealed a lack of a linear trend, $R^2 = .03$, $F(1,16) = .53$, or of a quadratic trend, $R^2 = .03$, $F(1,15) = .05$. No linear trend was found for the transformed data either, $R^2 = 0$, $F(1,16) = 0$. However, the quadratic trend was very significant, $R^2 = .51$, $F(1,15) = 15.62$, $p = <.001$.

Because the results of this study were provocative, we replicated it (Sosnowski, 1991; Zarnecka, 1988) on a second, independent, and larger sample ($N = 45$). This time the subjects were females, students of a medical college in Warsaw. Because the main aim of the study was to replicate the previous results, the experiment consisted of one trial only. The results are presented in Figures 5 and 6; the study followed the same procedures as for the first study.

Analysis of regression of the untransformed data again revealed a lack of either a linear trend, $R^2 = .03$, $F(1,43) = 1.52$ or a quadratic trend, $R^2 = .04$, $F(1,42) = .20$. Again, no linear trend was found for the transformed data, $R^2 =$

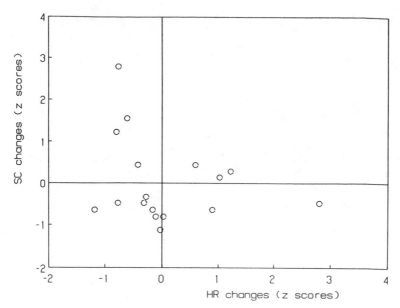

Figure 3 Interrelationship between skin conductance changes (evoked by presentation of an ambiguous message) and tonic heart rate changes (averaged for the entire trial) (N = 18).

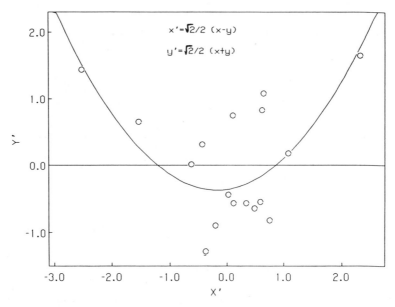

Figure 4 Interrelationship between skin conductance and heart rate changes, following axes rotation by −45 degrees (N = 18).

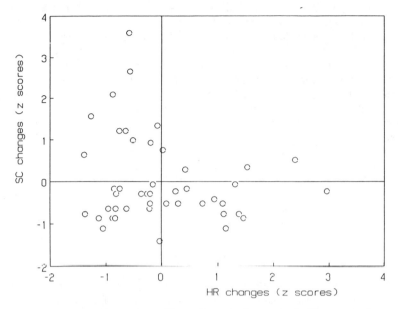

Figure 5 Interrelation between skin conductance changes (evoked by presentation of an ambiguous announcement) and tonic heart rate changes (averaged for the entire trial) (*N* = 45).

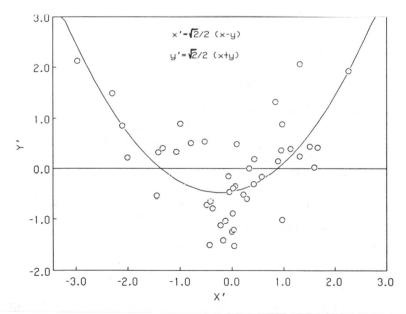

Figure 6 Interrelationship between skin conductance and heart rate changes, following axes rotation by −45 degrees (*N* = 45).

0, $F(1,43) = .06$. However, a significant quadratic trend was found as before, $R^2 = .50$, $F(1,42) = 42.54$, $p = < .0001$.

Despite different populations and different sample sizes, the results of these two latter experiments were very consistent. Thus the relationship studied seems robust and supports the hypothesis that in certain specifically defined conditions there is an interrelationship between changes in heart rate and electrodermal activity. However, this relationship is not linear but curvilinear. The fact that it occurred only in the first trial is understandable because it is at the beginning of an experiment that subjects are most uncertain of the situation and of their decisions on possible courses of action.

We must treat these findings with certain reservations, however. We know that regression analysis is very sensitive to extreme values. Even a few extreme values, especially in a small sample, may substantially change the regression line and lead to an inappropriate assessment of the strength of the relationship between variables. Thus the studies should be replicated on a larger sample and perhaps even more sophisticated methods of statistical analysis should be used.

DISCUSSION

The aim of these three studies was to test a hypothesis about the relationship between cardiac and electrodermal activity under strictly defined conditions. This hypothesis was based on two main assumptions: (a) Gray's hypothesis that the two regulatory systems he postulates—the Behavioral Approach System (BAS) and the Behavioral Inhibition System (BIS)—are reciprocally inhibitory; and (b) Fowles' hypothesis that tonic changes in heart rate and phasic changes of skin conductance may be interpreted as indicators of BAS or BIS activation, respectively.

Our results were largely consistent with theoretical expectations. In the first study, we found that subjects actively coping with the task showed higher heart rate level in the initial phase of the experimental situation than subjects who were only passive observers. On the other hand, magnitude of the skin conductance response to experimenter's feedback was lower in active than passive subjects.

Results of the two other studies showed the existence of individual differences in combined changes of both psychophysiological variables in a new, ambiguous situation. Subjects responding with higher skin conductance to a message announcing an aversive stimulus showed smaller heart rate increase while awaiting the stressor, whereas subjects responding with higher increase in heart rate show smaller skin conductance magnitude.

First of all, our results may be regarded as empirical support for Fowles' psychophysiological interpretation of Gray's model. Besides, they show that BAS/BIS imbalance, caused by critical situational factors or (under strictly defined conditions) by individual differences, may result in combined changes in the activity of both autonomic response systems.

What is interesting, however, is that the interrelationship between skin conductance and heart rate changes is visible only in an initial phase of the stressful situation. This phenomenon may be explained partly by a relatively fast habituation of psychophysiological activity. However, such a nonspecific explanation does not seem fully satisfactory. Another interpretation is that this relationship between skin conductance and heart rate changes appears at the moment of making a decision about behavior direction (or coping set) in the CNS. If so, the described response pattern would be an index of the conflict between two simultaneously activated (mutually inhibitory) systems, that is, the BAS and BIS, or—on the psychological level—between two opposite (i.e., active or passive) coping sets. In the next phase, after the decision is made and one regulatory system is activated much more than the other, the relationship between skin conductance and heart rate changes would not be visible.

This interpretation is consistent with the common point of view that a subject's reaction to a stressful situation is of a dynamic nature and varies as a function of time. Such an opinion now has more and more proponents, and also is reflected in other domains of stress research, including psychometric studies (cf. Hagtvet, Chapter 6). Simultaneously, it forces us to take a hard look at studies that examine psychophysiological response patterns or psychophysiological indices of psychological constructs (e.g., the indices of anxiety) that would be considered to be independent of the temporal dimension of the subject–situation interaction.

REFERENCES

Belanger, D., & Feldman, S. M. (1962). Effects of water deprivation upon heart rate and instrumental activity in the rat. *Journal of Comparative and Physiological Psychology, 55,* 220–225.

Blix, A. S., Stromme, S. B., & Ursin, H. (1974). Additional heart rate—an indicator of psychological activation. *Aerospace Medicine, 45,* 1219–1222.

Bolles, R. C. (1979). *Learning theory.* New York: Holt, Rinehart, & Winston.

Brener, J., Philips, K., & Connally, S. R. (1977). Oxygen consumption and ambulation during operant conditioning of heart rate increases and decreases in rats. *Psychophysiology, 14,* 483–491.

Dawson, M. E., & Schell, A. M. (1985). Information processing and human classical conditioning. In P. K. Ackles, J. R. Jennings, & M. G. H. Coles (Eds.), *Advances in psychophysiology* (Vol. 1, pp. 89–166). Greenwich, CT: JAI Press.

Duffy, E. (1962). *Activation and behavior.* New York: Wiley.

Duffy, E. (1972). Activation. In N. S. Greenfield & R. A. Sternbach (Eds.), *Handbook of psychophysiology* (pp. 577–622). New York: Holt, Rinehart, & Winston.

Edelberg, R. (1972). The electrodermal system. In N. S. Greenfield & R. A. Sternbach (Eds.), *Handbook of psychophysiology* (pp. 367–418). New York: Holt, Rinehart, & Winston.

Edelberg, R. (1973). Mechanisms of electrodermal adaptation for locomotion, manipulation, or defense. *Progress in Psychophysiological Psychology, 5,* 155–209.

Ehrlich, D. J., & Malmo, R. B. (1967). Electrophysiological concomitants of simple operant conditioning in the rat. *Neuropsychologia, 5,* 219–235.

Elliott, R. (1969). Tonic heart rate: Experiments on the effects of collative variables lead to a hypothesis about its motivational significance. *Journal of Personality and Social Psychology, 12,* 211–228.

Elliott, R. (1974). The motivational significance of heart rate. In P. A. Obrist, A. H. Black, J. Brener, & L. V. DiCara (Eds.). *Cardiovascular psychophysiology: Current issues in response mechanism, biofeedback, and methodology* (pp. 505–537). Chicago: Aldine.

Fahrenberg, J. (1986). Psychophysiological individuality: A pattern approach to personality research and psychosomatic medicine. *Advances in Behaviour Research and Therapy, 8,* 43–100.

Fowles, D. C. (1980). The three arousal model: Implications of Gray's two-factor learning theory for heart rate, electrodermal activity, and psychopathy. *Psychophysiology, 17,* 87–104.

Fowles, D. C. (1982). Heart rate as an index of anxiety: Failure of a hypothesis. In J. Cacioppo & R. Petty (Eds.), *Perspectives in cardiovascular psychophysiology* (pp. 93–126). New York: Guilford Press.

Fowles, D. C. (1983). Motivational effects on heart rate and electrodermal activity: Implications for research on personality and psychopathy. *Journal of Research in Personality, 17,* 48–71.

Fowles, D. C. (1986). The eccrine system and electrodermal activity. In M. G. H. Coles, E. Donchin, & S. W. Porges (Eds.), *Psychophysiology: Systems, processes, and applications* (pp. 51–96). Amsterdam: Elsevier.

Fowles, D. C. (1988). Psychophysiology and psychopathy: A motivational approach. *Psychophysiology, 25,* 373–391.

Fowles, D. C., Fisher, A. E., & Tranel, D. T. (1982). The heart beats to reward: The effect of monetary incentive on heart rate. *Psychophysiology, 19*, 506–513.

Gray, J. A. (1975). *Elements of a two-process theory of learning.* London: Academic Press.

Gray, J. A. (1982a). *The neuropsychology of anxiety: An enquiry into the functions of septo-hippocampal system.* New York: Oxford University Press.

Gray, J. A. (1982b). Precis of the neuropsychology of anxiety: An enquiry into the functions of the septo-hippocampal system. *The Behavioral and Brain Sciences, 5*, 469–534.

Gray, J. A. (1991). The neuropsychology of temperament. In J. Strelau & A. Angleitner (Eds.), *Explorations in temperament: International perspectives in theory and measurement* (pp. 105–128). New York: Plenum Press.

Hahn, W. W., Stern, J. A., & Fehr, F. S. (1964). Generalizability of heart rate as a measure of drive state. *Journal of Comparative and Physiological Psychology, 58*, 305–309.

Hare, R. D. (1978). Electrodermal and cardiovascular correlates of psychopathy. In R. D. Hare & D. Schalling (Eds.), *Psychopathic behaviour: Approaches to research* (pp. 107–143). New York: Wiley.

Hull, C. L. (1952). *A behavioral system.* New Haven, CT: Yale University Press.

Kimmel, H. D. (1973). Instrumental conditioning. In W. F. Prokasy & D. C. Raskin (Eds.), *Electrodermal activity in psychological research* (pp. 255–282). New York: Academic Press.

Lacey, J. I. (1967). Somatic response patterning and stress: Some revisions of activation theory. In M. H. Appley & R. Trumbull (Eds.), *Psychological stress: Issues in research* (pp. 14–44). New York: Appleton-Century-Crofts.

Madsen, K. B. (1974). *Modern theories in motivation.* Copenhagen: Munksgaard.

Maltzman, I. (1977). Orienting in classical conditioning and generalization of the galvanic skin response to words: An overview. *Journal of Experimental Psychology: General, 106*, 111–119.

Maltzman, I. (1979). Orienting reflexes and classical conditioning in humans. In H. D. Kimmel, E. H. van Olst, & J. F. Orlebeke (Eds.), *The orienting reflex in humans* (pp. 323–351). Hillsdale, NJ: Erlbaum.

Manuck, S. B., & Garland, F. N. (1980). Stability of individual differences in cardiovascular reactivity: A 13-month follow-up. *Physiology and Behavior, 24*, 621–624.

Mitchell, D. A., Venables, P. H., Mednick, S. A., Schulsinger, F., & Cheaneebash, K. (1983). *Aspects of the development of electrodermal and cardiac activity between 5 and 25 years: IV, inter- and intrarelationships.* Unpublished manuscript, University of York, Department of Psychology, York.

Moses, J., Clemens, W. J., & Brener, J. (1986). Bidirectional voluntary heart rate control during static muscular exercise: Metabolic and respiratory correlates. *Psychophysiology, 23*, 510–520.

Obrist, P. A. (1976). The cardiovascular-behavioral interaction—as it appears today. *Psychophysiology, 13*, 95–107.

Obrist, P. A. (1981). *Cardiovascular psychophysiology—A perspective.* New York: Plenum Press.

Obrist, P. A., Grignolo, A., Hastrup, J. L., Koepke, J. P., Langer, A. W., Light, K. C., McCubbin, J. A., & Pollack, M. H. (1983). Behavioral-cardiac interactions in hypertension. In D. S. Krantz, A. Baum, & J. E. Singer (Eds.), *Handbook of psychophysiology and health, vol. III: Cardiovascular disorders and behavior* (pp. 199–229). Hillsdale, NJ: Erlbaum.

Obrist, P. A., Lawler, J. E., Howard, J. L., Smithson, K. W., Martin, P. L., & Manning, J. (1974). Sympathetic influences on the heart in humans: Effects on contractility and heart rate of acute stress. *Psychophysiology, 11*, 405–427.

Obrist, P. A., & Light, K. C. (1984). Active-passive coping and cardiovascular reactivity: Interaction with individual differences and types of baseline. In A. Baum, W. Gordon, & J. A. Herd (Eds.), *Proceedings of the Academy of Behavioral Medicine Research,* 1981–1982. New York: Academic Press.

Obrist, P. A., Light, K. C., Langer, A. W., Grignolo, A., & Koepke, J. P. (1982). Behavioral-cardiovascular interaction. In O. A. Smith, R. A. Galosy, & S. M. Weiss (Eds.), *Circulation, neurobiology and behavior* (pp. 57–76). New York: Elsevier.

Ohman, A. (1979). The orienting response, attention, and learning: An information processing perspective. In H. D. Kimmel, E. H. van Olst, & J. F. Orlebeke (Eds.), *The orienting reflex in humans* (pp. 443–471). Hillsdale, NJ: Erlbaum.

Ohman, A. (1983). The orienting response during pavlovian conditioning. In D. A. T. Siddle (Ed.), *Orienting and habituation: Perspectives in human research* (pp. 315–369). Chichester, UK: Wiley.

Prokasy, W. F., & Kumpfer, K. L. (1973). Classical conditioning. In W. F. Prokasy & D. C. Raskin (Eds.), *Electrodermal activity in psychological research* (pp. 157–202). New York: Academic Press.

Raskin, D. C. (1973). Attention and arousal, In W. F. Prokasy & D. C. Raskin (Eds.), *Electrodermal activity in psychological research* (pp. 125–155). New York: Academic Press.

Roberts, L. E., & Young, R. (1971). Electrodermal responses are independent of movement during aversive conditioning in rats, but heart rate is not. *Journal of Comparative and Physiological Psychology, 77,* 495–512.

Sosnowski. T. (1988). Patterns of skin conductance and heart rate changes under anticipatory stress conditions. *Journal of Psychophysiology, 2,* 231–238.

Sosnowski, T., Nurzynska, M., & Polec, M. (1991). Active-passive coping and skin conductance and heart rate changes. *Psychophysiology, 28,* 675–682.

Sosnowski, T. (1991). *Wzorce aktywnosci psychofizjologicznej w warunkach kròtkotrwalego stresu antycypacyjnego* [Patterns of psychophysiological activity under conditions of anticipatory, short-circulating stress]. Wroclaw: Ossolineum.

Szpiler, J. A., & Epstein, S., (1976). Availability of an avoidance response as related to autonomic arousal. *Journal of Abnormal Psychology, 85,* 73–82.

Tranel, D. T., Fisher, A. E., & Fowles, D. C. (1982). Magnitude of incentive effects on heart rate. *Psychophysiology, 19,* 514–519.

Turner, J. R. (1989). Individual differences in heart rate response during behavioral challenge. *Psychophysiology, 26,* 497–505.

Turner, J. R., Carroll, D., Hanson, J., & Sims, J. (1988). A comparison of additional heart rates during active psychological challenge calculated from upper body and lower body dynamic exercise. *Psychophysiology, 25,* 209–216.

Venables, P. H. (1984). Arousal: An examination of its status as a concept. In M. G. H. Coles, J. R. Jennings, & J. A. Stern (Eds.), *Psychophysiological perspectives: Festschrift for Beatrice and John Lacey* (pp. 134–142). New York: Van Nostrand.

Wilson, G. D., Barrett, P. T., & Gray, J. A. (1989). Human reactions to reward and punishment: A questionnaire examination of Gray's personality theory. *British Journal of Psychology, 80,* 509–515.

Zarnecka, A. (1988). *Wzorce reakcji konduktancji skòry i szybkosci rytmu serca na wieloznaczny komunikat, sygnalizujacy bodziec awersyjny* [Patterns of skin conductance and heart rate response to ambiguous message announcing aversive stimulus]. Unpublished master's thesis, University of Warsaw, Department of Psychology, Warsaw.

10

Anxiety and Inhibition: A Psychophysiological Approach

Janick Naveteur and Esteve Freixa i Baqué
Université de Lille, France

INTRODUCTION

The recording of physiological indices developed early in anxiety research. As in the case of many other psychopathologies, the initial goal was laudable: to find an appraisal more objective than a self-report. Unfortunately, this expectation has not been fulfilled and studies in this area mainly provide information about the functioning of the nervous system in relation to disease. Such an issue remains of great interest in the case of anxiety because of the importance of somatic symptoms reported by anxious people.

One of the oldest of recorded indices is electrodermal activity (EDA), which reflects the activation of the eccrine sweat glands when sympathetically innervated. Following Odegard's pioneering work in 1932, relevant publications were numerous, but for several years now interest in this research area has waned and it may be argued that this topic is somewhat out of date. The reasons for the decline in such research must be questioned. Perhaps it was believed that final conclusions had already been made to which nothing could be added, or that no clear conclusion could be drawn in this area. Both types of reasoning may be appropriate. Indeed, indisputable significant effects showing an increase of EDA as a function of anxiety have been described. However, experiments leading to nonsignificant differences have also been reported (Naveteur & Freixa i Baqué, 1987).

From their review of the literature in this area, Stern and Janes (1973) concluded that significant relationships existed for pathologically anxious subjects. Most of the subjects of these studies were under medical care for anxiety and they were compared to normal controls selected from the hospital staff. Similar studies performed on subjects selected from a normal population who scored extremely high or low on anxiety tests, and generally students, were very often nonsignificant. Stern and Janes' conclusion, therefore, was based on a dichotomy between subjects evidencing pathological and normal anxiety.

Initially at least this dichotomy proves to be relevant for all electrodermal parameters: tonic EDA, phasic spontaneous, or evoked activity. However, a closer inspection of the experimental designs of these studies (Naveteur & Freixa i Baqué, 1987) allowed us to mitigate this conclusion. In fact, for tonic EDA and spontaneous responses, the differences observed between pathologically anxious subjects and normal controls disappeared when a period of relaxation preceded the experimentation, as in the studies of Goldstein (1964) and Kelly, Brown, and Shaffer (1970). A second point in question concerns phasic EDA and, especially, amplitude of response. Response amplitudes have been typically recorded following the presentation of tones, and higher overall amplitudes in pathologically anxious subjects have sometimes been observed. Furthermore, the hypothesis of slower habituation rates in pathologically anxious subjects than in normal subjects should not be dismissed totally, although that effect appears to be limited to cases of exposure to auditory stimuli of high intensity (90–100 dB). It must also be noted that many studies on nonpathological subjects used stimuli of low or average intensity (20–80 dB), whereas the intensity of stimulation used with pathological subjects was generally higher.

Our own review led us to reconsider Stern and Janes' (1973) conclusion. It is possible that the differences previously observed are mainly caused by state anxiety, which would have been experimentally higher in research dealing with pathologically anxious subjects.

When one considers this mainly quantitative dimension of anxiety, the classical framework of the theory of activation appears to be relevant. However, the influence of trait anxiety on EDA is more controversial. It is possible that trait anxiety acts as a kind of "catalyst," increasing both the number of situations that induces state anxiety and the anxious reaction itself. However, the findings of Wilson and Dykman (1960) indicate an opposite influence of trait and state anxiety on spontaneous EDA during an emotional question task. Subjects whose spontaneous EDA was weak showed at the same time a higher trait anxiety and a lower state anxiety than the subjects whose spontaneous EDA was strong. This surprising effect suggests that the influence of trait anxiety on EDA could be more complex than previously supposed.

Thus we consider that previous studies addressing the issue of influence of anxiety on EDA have yielded a great amount of data but they have failed to distinguish between the separate influences of trait and state anxiety on this index. We conclude that these studies have mainly provided evidence for the increasing effect of state anxiety, but results leading to a better understanding of the influence of trait anxiety are still lacking. The following series of studies focuses on trait anxiety and attempts to dissociate its influence from that of state anxiety.

EXPERIMENTAL STUDIES

For all our experiments subjects were selected on the basis of their trait anxiety score, using a French adaptation of Cattell's Self Analysis Sheet (1957). A pool of 768 applicants screened by this method yielded a study sample of 102 subjects who were then used in the experiments. Approximately half were low scorers (categories 0, 1, or 2) and the other half were high scorers (categories 9 and 10). All subjects were right handed, and were students of psychology and speech therapy. Only female subjects were selected because the screened population consisted largely of females. The subjects' state anxiety during the experiment always was assessed at the end of the session. The subjects were asked to rate 20 anxiety-laden adjectives, taken from de Bonis and Freixa i Baqué's Q-sort (1978), on a seven-point scale.

The EDA was recorded from the right hand in conductance units. The accuracy of the apparatus was a tenth of a micromho. The measures taken were as follows:

1. Prestimulus skin-conductance level recorded just before each stimulus.

2. Interstimuli spontaneous skin-conductance responses referring to each response equal to or greater than 0.02 micromhos occurring between two consecutive stimuli, with the exception that the first one was considered to be a response elicited by the stimulus itself. This measure was recorded only in study 1.

3. Skin-conductance response amplitude, which is the first response equal or superior to 0.02 micromhos that occurred in an interval of 1–5 seconds after the start of the stimulus.

4. Skin-conductance response latency is defined as the time period recorded between 1 and 5 seconds separating the beginning of the stimulus from the onset of the response.

Study 1: Induction of Negative Emotions by the Presentation of Aversive Slides

Our first experiment (Naveteur & Freixa i Baqué, 1987) was an attempt to repeat Wilson and Dykman's (1960) singular observation of the opposite influences of trait and state anxiety on EDA. However, instead of asking emotional questions, emotional slides were presented to the subjects, allowing better measurement of electrodermal response amplitude. As indicated above, subjects were selected on the basis of their trait anxiety. A total of 46 subjects actually were included in the data analysis: 24 anxious and 22 nonanxious.

Four slides representing the woof of a mottled fabric were first presented in order to habituate the subject. Then 16 slides constituting the experimental material were projected in a randomized order for each subject. Eight slides were neutral and represented landscapes; the remaining eight were emotional and showed unpleasant pictures (disfigured babies, bloody faces, insects, and so forth). The neutral or emotional quality of the slides had been determined in previous research.

For all the EDA measures trait anxiety proved to be a significant variable, as shown in Figure 1. Compared to the nonanxious subjects, the anxious subjects showed significantly lower skin conductance levels (SCL) [$F(1/44) = 9.22$, MSe $= 118.69$, $p < .01$], a smaller number of interstimulus spontaneous skin conductance responses (SSCR) [$F(1/44) = 4.51$, MSe $= 26.04$, $p < .05$], and smaller skin conductance responses (SCR) [$F(1/44) = 12.87$, MSe $= 1.46$, $p < .01$]. The significantly longer latencies of the anxious subjects [$F(1/44) = 7.25$, MSe $= 3190465$, $p < .01$] were of course also compatible with lowered responsiveness in these subjects. Another significant effect was found. There is a significant interaction [$F(1/44) = 44.9$, MSe $= 0.27$, $p < .01$] between anxiety and the type of slide for the skin conductance response amplitude. Figure 2 shows that the difference between the anxious and nonanxious subjects was stronger following an emotional slide than following a neutral one, and it appears that the reaction to the emotional slide has been reduced differentially in the high trait anxiety subjects. Results based on state anxiety will be dealt with later.

Effects obtained as a function of trait anxiety coincided with our expectations and were interpreted as resulting from electrodermal inhibition in high trait anxiety subjects as compared to low trait anxiety subjects. These effects appeared to be enhanced by induced emotions. Although several interpretations of such effects could be proposed, they are consistent with an extension to EDA of the behavioral

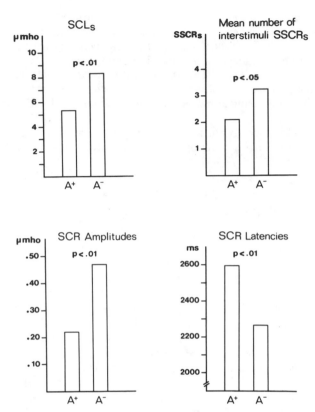

Figure 1 Skin conductance parameters as a function of the
subjects' trait anxiety. A⁺: high trait anxiety subjects;
A⁻: low trait anxiety subjects; SCL: skin conductance
levels; SSCR: spontaneous skin conductance responses;
SCR: skin conductance response.

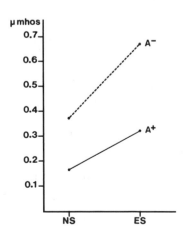

Figure 2 Mean SCR amplitude as a function of the
subjects' trait anxiety and the type of slide. A⁺:
high trait anxiety subjects; A⁻: low trait anxiety
subjects; NS: neutral slide; ES: emotional slide.

inhibition system (BIS) described by Gray (1982). The BIS action could not only concern the motor field but could, directly or indirectly, induce an inhibition of EDA.

Based on this interpretation, a second experiment was carried out. Because Gray (1982) considers that the BIS is activated in situations of punition or frustrative nonreward, we attempted to put low and high trait anxiety subjects in a frustrative nonreward situation.

Study 2: Induction of Frustration During a Frustrative Video Game

Sixteen low trait anxiety and 17 high trait anxiety subjects, measured as described above, took part in this experiment. They were invited to play a mathematical video game presented as quite easy and were provided a monetary gain. At the beginning of the game, the subject received a sum of around $50. The game was composed of 10 rounds. The purpose of each round was to discover the logical rule according to which a series of numbers was supposed to be constructed. Figure 3 summarizes the game. The subjects had to indicate whether the missing number in a series was 0 or 1. At most, three series of numbers were presented successively in each round, each presentation constituting a trial; a rule was assumed to have been understood if three right answers were given.

In fact, the game had been faked completely; there was nothing logical in it and the subjects never reached the criterion of success [i.e., they never gave three consecutive right answers (RA)]. Each response considered a wrong answer (WA) meant that the subject lost 10% of the sum previously given, or about $5, and a new round began in the next trial.

In the first round, all the subjects lost in the second trial, and this round of habituation was not included in the data processing. In the following nine rounds, the subjects lost randomly: three times in a third trial (i.e., the sequence "RA RA WA" was presented three times); three times in a second trial (i.e., the sequence "RA WA" was presented three times); and three times in a first trial (i.e., the sequence "WA" was presented three times). So there were 18 experimental trials: 9 were right answers and 9 were wrong answers; {[3 × (RA, RA, WA)] + [3 × (RA, WA)] + [3 (WA)] = 9RA + 9WA}. Supposed right or wrong answers were indicated by a tone of 2,000 and 1,000 Hz, respectively. EDA was recorded in response to these tones.

The principal significant result obtained in this experiment concerns SCR am-

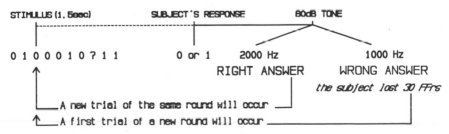

Figure 3 Summary of the game's experimental protocol.

plitude and it is presented in Figure 4. The trait anxiety score interacts with the trials of the game [$F(5/155) = 3.85$, MSe $= 0.026$, $p < .01$]. In the nonanxious subjects this parameter was constant from the beginning to the end of the game, but in the anxious subjects SCR amplitude decreased linearly as the game proceeded, as assessed by a trend test [$F(1/16) = 13.01$, MSe $= 0.108$, $p < .01$]. This effect is once more compatible with an interpretation in terms of EDA inhibition in the high trait anxiety subjects. An extensive presentation of this experiment can be found in Naveteur and Roy (1990a).

Study 3: Induction of Positive Emotions by the Presentation of Erotic Slides

In both the first and second experiment, results were compatible with an interpretation suggesting that trait anxiety was able to induce a decrease in EDA. This observation was made when negative emotions were induced experimentally. We wondered about the effect of trait anxiety on EDA in a positive emotional context. Having taken into account that the BIS is not activated in such circumstances, a lack of significant difference between subjects with low and high trait anxiety was to be expected.

In order to test this hypothesis, slides of positive emotional valence were projected onto a screen in an experimental context that was as close as possible to that of the first experiment. Eleven subjects were nonanxious and 12 were anxious. Erotic slides were selected as positive emotional stimuli. They were chosen carefully in a pretest as being very positive to see and nonshocking. No significant difference was found between subjects with high and low trait anxiety with regard to the EDA. With the caution usually applied to the interpretation of nonsignificant statistical results, the present experiment suggests that the effect of inhibition previously discussed is limited, as predicted, to a negative emotional context. In addition to the above analyses, product–moment correlations were calculated, on the one hand, between each electrodermal parameter and, on the other hand, the scores attributed to the adjectives of the state anxiety test. Whereas these coefficients were always low and nonsignificant in both the first and second experiments, an acceptable significance level was reached for skin conductance levels in

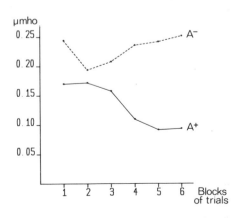

Figure 4 Mean SCR amplitude pooled in blocks of three trials for each group of subjects (low- and high-trait anxiety subjects).

this third study ($r = .42$, $df = 21$, $p < .05$) and for skin conductance latencies ($r = -.43$, $df = 21$, $p < .05$). These results suggested higher tonic EDA and faster responses for high state anxiety subjects.

DISCUSSION

The results of these experiments on trait anxiety can be integrated within the framework of Gray's anxiety theory (1982) by a parallel in the situations where an inhibition of behavior and vegetative activity appeared. Moreover, additional results obtained with heart rate (HR) recorded in similar experimental situations also showed reduced HR in high trait anxiety subjects compared to low trait anxiety subjects (Naveteur & Roy, 1990b). It is possible, then, that the BIS action might not be limited to the behavioral system (motor) but also could be applied to the vegetative system as well.

Such an extrapolation of the BIS to the vegetative field has already been suggested by Fowles (1980). Nevertheless, contrary to the hypothesis proposed above, Fowles (1980) stipulates that BIS activation should lead to an increase and not to an inhibition of EDA. With respect to this discrepancy in interpretation, some physiological results may support our hypothesis. In the field of the somato-vegetative coupling, Roy, Sequeira-Martinho, and Brochard (1984) have shown that, in cats, electrodermal responses can be elicited by a motor cortex stimulation through the pyramidal tract only, with all other ways being cut off. If such a coupling exists for activation, it could also exist for inhibition. It also has been reported that systematic inhibitions of EDA have been obtained by an electrical stimulation of the bulbar area (Roy, Delerm, & Granger, 1974; Wang & Brown, 1956) and stimulation of the anterior cortex (Wilcott & Bradley, 1970). Given that connections between these subcortical structures are numerous and that their role is manifest in emotional behaviors, of which anxiety is one particular aspect, it is possible that BIS activation, anchored in the septo-hippocampic structures, could lead directly or indirectly to an inhibition of EDA.

However, the parallel between a situation inducing a motor inhibition and one that induces a vegetative one does not prove that an explanation by the BIS is the correct or only explanation. One can argue that high trait anxiety subjects used active coping strategies to calm themselves. Such mechanisms were suspected previously in such subjects by Lazarus (1966). One of these could be that of diverting attention from the task. According to Beck, Laude, and Bohnert (1974), trait anxiety subjects could overestimate the potential danger of some situations, which could stimulate coping strategies, whereas this could not occur in nonanxious people. It is also possible that an attempt to reduce the vegetative reactions is a direct strategy used by the anxious in order to calm themselves (cf. the James-Lange theory; James, 1892).

In situations particularly relevant for the subject, the state anxiety effect seems preponderant. This point refers to the relationships between trait and state anxiety and the high sensitivity of subjects with high trait anxiety to threats to their self-esteem as described by Spielberger (1972). As regards the strong vegetative reactions presented in such cases by the anxious, the vegetative inhibition that was observed also could appear as a mechanism of adaptation or compensation.

To return to state anxiety influences: in these three nonstressful situations, relationships between state anxiety and EDA parameters were evaluated on the basis of correlation analyses. Although such designs are not the best for testing this influence, stronger positive correlations were observed in the third experiment when no effect of inhibition caused by trait anxiety was noted. On the contrary, in the second experiment, when because of the threat to self-esteem the high trait anxiety subjects were mainly among the high state anxiety subjects, the correlations were weak and nonsignificant following the inhibition exerted by trait anxiety on EDA. This supports once more the idea that trait and state anxiety always interact and that all research done in this field must take these two dimensions into account.

In summary, this chapter presents the results of three studies in which EDA was recorded in high and low trait anxiety subjects. It has been shown that when the experimental design induced negative emotions, as in the case of viewing aversive slides (study 1) or in the case of a frustrating video game (study 2), significant differences always reflect lower EDA in the high trait anxiety subjects compared with low trait anxiety ones. The induction of positive emotions by the projection of erotic slides (study 3) produced no significant difference between both groups of subjects. In these studies, state anxiety was correlated poorly with EDA measures. However, significant correlations, indicating an increase of EDA activity with higher state anxiety, occurred in the positive emotional context where trait anxiety did not induce a significant effect on EDA (study 3).

Taken as a whole, these experiments cast a new light on the relationships between EDA and anxiety, especially as a personality trait. Results have been interpreted in terms of EDA inhibition in the high trait anxiety subjects and suggest that the activity of the sympathetic nervous system is reduced in these subjects in response to negative emotions. However, considering that the EDA/trait anxiety relationship interacts with the induced emotions, it is necessary to examine our studies in terms of a wider range of emotional situations. One can argue that the emotional contexts that we created were not neutral (as in the case of the classical delivery of tones), nor were they stressful because the potential threat was low. Also, students often are solicited for experiments, so their participation in our studies probably did not constitute a new experience for most of our subjects. Moreover, this participation had no consequences on their own lives. Consequently, it can be stated that EDA inhibition is linked to a fairly moderate level of negative emotions. It is interesting that the level is not critical because it does not lead to important difficulties for the anxious subjects who, consequently, do not require help in these circumstances. Our psychophysiological investigations have successfully provided evidence for a significant effect of trait anxiety, which had not been suggested in the past. The process is opposite to that which had been described previously. People experiencing state anxiety reported high physiological reactivity, and psychophysiologists tried to verify and quantify these symptoms in a variety of psychological investigations. The present psychophysiological results are only a beginning and they require explanation at both physiological and psychological levels. The explanations we have suggested are highly speculative. We have demonstrated that high trait anxiety subjects showed a high frequency of high-anxious states linked, indeed, to high autonomic activity. They differed from low trait anxiety subjects in stressful contexts or contexts perceived as such. In response to low-negative emotions, they begin to react differently and, at least for EDA, in an opposite way to what has been described when emotions are more intense. The explanation of this phenomenon is still unclear and this is an area that needs to be researched more extensively.

REFERENCES

Beck, A. T., Laude, R., & Bohnert, M. (1974). Ideational components of anxiety neurosis. *Archives of General Psychiatry, 31,* 319–325.

Bonis, M. de, & Freixa i Baqué, E. (1978). Activité électrodermale spontanée et variations de l'état affectif. [Spontaneous electrodermal activity and mood variations]. *Neuropsychobiology, 4,* 15–25.

Cattell, R. B. (1957). Manuel de l'échelle d'anxiété (Feuille d'auto-analyse). [Handbook for the IPAT anxiety scale]. French adaptation (1962). Paris, CPA.

Fowles, D. C. (1980). The three arousal model: Implications of Gray's two-factor learning theory for heart rate, electrodermal activity and psychopathy. *Psychophysiology, 17,* 87–104.

Goldstein, I. B. (1964). Physiological responses in anxious women patients: A study of autonomic activity and muscle tensions. *Archives of General Psychiatry, 10,* 382–388.

Gray, J. A. (1982). *The neuropsychology of anxiety: An enquiry into the functions of the septo-hippocampal system.* Oxford: Clarendon Press.

James, W. (1892). What is an emotion? *Mind, 19,* 188–205.

Kelly, D. H., Brown, C. C., & Shaffer, J. W. (1970). A comparison of physiological and psychological measurements on anxious patients and normal controls. *Psychophysiology, 6,* 429–441.

Lazarus, R. S. (1966). *Psychological stress and the coping process.* New York: McGraw-Hill.

Naveteur, J., & Freixa i Baqué, E. (1987). Individual differences in electrodermal activity as a function of subjects' anxiety. *Personality and Individual Differences, 8,* 615–626.

Naveteur, J., & Roy, J. C. (1990a). Electrodermal activity of low and high trait anxiety subjects during a frustrative video game. *Journal of Psychophysiology, 4,* 443–449.

Naveteur, J., & Roy, J. C. (1990b, July). Trait-anxiety and heart rate in a frustrative video game. Abstracts of the Fifth International Congress of Psychophysiology, Budapest.

Odegard, O. (1932). The psychogalvanic reactivity in affective disorders. *British Journal of Medical Psychology, 12,* 132–150.

Roy, J. C., Delerm, B., & Granger, L. (1974). L'inhibition bulbaire de l'activité électrodermale chez le chat. [Bulbar inhibition of electrodermal activity in the cat]. *Electroencephalography and Clinical Neurophysiology, 37,* 621–632.

Roy, J. C., Sequeira-Martinho, A. H., & Brochard, J. (1984). Pyramidal control of skin potential responses in the cat. *Experimental Brain Research, 54,* 283–288.

Spielberger, C. D. (1972). Anxiety as an emotional state. In C. D. Spielberger (Ed.), *Anxiety: Current trends in theory and research* (pp. 23–49). New York: Academic Press.

Stern, J. A., & Janes, C. L. (1973). Personality and psychopathology. In W. F. Prokasy & D. C. Raskin, (Eds.), *Electrodermal activity in psychological research* (pp. 284–337). New York: Academic Press.

Wang, G. H., & Brown, V. W. (1956). Suprasegmental inhibition of an autonomic reflex. *Journal of Neurophysiology, 19,* 564–572.

Wilcott, R. C., & Bradley, H. H. (1970). Low-frequency electrical stimulation on the cat's anterior cortex and inhibition of skin potential responses. *Journal of Comparative and Physiological Psychology, 72,* 351–355.

Wilson, J. W. D., & Dykman, R. A. (1960). Background autonomic activity in medical students. *Journal of Comparative and Physiological Psychology, 53,* 405–411.

11

Detector Mechanisms of Perceptions and Emotions

E. N. Sokolov
Moscow State University

INTRODUCTION

Feature detectors are neurons that selectively extract different aspects of the external and internal environment. In vertebrates, detectors are organized as detector maps constituting a mechanism to represent stimuli in the brain. The detector map is based on principles of a channel-dependent code. A local excitation maximum arising on the detector map evoked by sensory stimulation corresponds to a specific sensation. The modification of the stimulus results in a shift of the excitation maximum on the detector map.

The subjective threshold equals a change in a stimulus that results in a shift of the excitation maximum from a given feature detector to the neighboring one. The subjective difference between two stimuli measured by the sum of just noticeable differences is characterized by a number of feature detectors separating the loci of excitation maxima evoked by respective stimuli on the detector map.

The selective tuning of detectors is performed by predetector neurons that link receptors with feature detectors. The stimulus at the predetector level generates a set of excitations that constitutes an excitation vector, which acts in parallel on all feature detectors of the detector map. Each feature detector is characterized by a set of synapses linking it with predetectors. The set of synapses constitutes a link vector of the detector. The link vectors of different detectors having a constant length differ with respect to their orientations, which depend on the location of the detector on the detector map.

The excitation of the feature detector evoked by a single synapse equals the excitation of a predetector multiplied by the strength (weight) of a respective synapse. The total response of the feature detector equals the sum of products obtained by pairwise multiplication of predetector excitations and synaptic weights. In terms of linear algebra, the sum of the obtained pairwise products of predetector excitations and synaptic weights is a scalar product of excitation vector and link vector. The excitation maximum evoked by a stimulus on the detector map will be reached with a feature detector having a link vector collinear to an excitation vector evoked in predetectors. A constant length of link vectors of detectors constituting a detector map suggests that the detector map is a hypersphere in n-dimensional euclidian space. The input signals are projected on the hypersphere as perceptual space. The dimensionality of such a perceptual space is defined by the number of independent predetectors. A spherical model of perceptual space is based on detector mechanisms of stimulus coding. The detector mechanism of perception can be examined in two different ways. It can be tested either through multidimensional scaling, assuming that the subjective differences between signals equal the euclidian distances between respective detectors, or by electrophysiological identification of neurons at predetector and detector levels.

The detector theory of perception presented above can be extended to emotions by suggesting that different emotional experiences depend on specific detector neurons. The main difference between feature detectors and emotion detectors consists in the organization of their predetectors. Sensory feature detectors are supplied by excitations coming from predetectors linked with extero- and interoceptors. Emotion detectors seem to be supplied by excitations coming from predetector neurons, which operate as direct sensors of biologically active substances within the brain.

The composition of these biologically active substances constitutes an input signal for emotion predetectors, resulting in the excitation of a set of emotion predetectors. These excitations constitute an excitation vector acting in parallel on a map of emotion detectors. A specific emotion is evoked when an excitation maximum is reached on an appropriate emotion detector. The mechanism for generating an excitation maximum on the emotion-detector map is assumed to be similar to detector mechanisms of perception. This means that link vectors composed of synaptic weights of emotion detectors are also of constant lengths, which suggests that different emotions represented by emotion detectors are localized on the surface of a hypersphere in emotional euclidian space analogous to perceptual euclidian space. The dimensionality of the emotional space is determined by the number of predetectors constituting the basis of an emotional space. The subjective differences between emotions are measured by euclidian distances between the emotion detectors responsible for evocation of respective emotional experiences.

This conclusion, based on detector theory concerning localization of emotions on a hypersphere in an n-dimensional euclidian space, is a unique opportunity to test psychophysically the detector theory of emotion using multidimensional scaling procedures. This approach to the study of emotions is close to the multidimensional scaling of perceptual phenomena. The matrix of subjective differences between stimuli contains information concerning cartesian coordinates of points representing perceived stimuli in euclidian space. The coordinates of each stimulus point define excitations of respective predetectors evoked by a given stimulus. The number of coordinates needed for reproduction of initial perceptual differences characterizes the number of predetectors involved in perceptual coding. At the same time, the number of coordinates specifies the number of synapses characterizing each feature detector. Testing a spherical model of emotional space involves many difficulties related to the evocation of emotions under experimental conditions. One way to overcome these difficulties is to analyze the semantic space of emotions.

The semantic space of perceptual phenomena is constructed by using the verbal symbols of these phenomena. The matrix of subjective differences between names of respective stimuli makes it possible to represent the names of stimuli in euclidian space in such a way that subjective differences between the semantic content of names correspond with euclidian distances between the points representing these names in the semantic space. The semantic space is isomorphic to the respective perceptual space. Thus from the semantic space one can extract data concerning the respective perceptual space. Such a strategy can be applied to the study of emotions as well. By substituting an emotional space with a semantic space of emotional terms one can get information concerning emotional space. This strategy is based on the assumption that the semantic space of emotional terms is isomorphic to emotional space. Thus the coordinates of emotional terms found in an analysis of emotional semantic space can be regarded as coordinates of respective emotions corresponding to excitations of emotional predetector neurons.

A second approach to the study of emotional space is based on the extraction of emotional coordinates by comparison with perceptual data. The matrix of subjective differences between emotional terms and perceptual data can be used to reveal characteristics of emotional predetectors operating in emotional detector mechanisms. A direct demonstration of detector mechanisms of emotions is based, however, on finding emotion-selective neurons. Let us start this search by a direct evaluation of detector mechanisms of sensory coding and emotional representation in the simple nervous system of a snail.

LOCALITY DETECTORS

The skin and intestinal organs of a snail are projected on a map of neurons characterized by local pointlike receptive fields. Penetrating the cell body with a microelectrode and touching different points of the snail's body with a hair, one can find a specific area from which spikes can be triggered. Stimulation of neighboring points of the skin results in slight hyperpolarizing effects that contrast with the local excitation. Such a neuron can be called a *locality detector*. The locality detector can be identified by injection of cobalt ions into its cell body through the microelectrode. Such identifiable locality detectors with pointlike receptive fields have been found in the snail. The diverging axons of the locality detector reach giant command neurons, resulting in the execution of different behavioral acts. Microelectrode recording from an identified command neuron of defensive behavior shows that direct electric stimulation of the locality detector brings about excitatory postsynaptic potentials (EPSP). The synapse between the locality detector and the defensive command neuron can be identified by injecting different dyes into a locality detector and a defensive command neuron.

Each locality detector selectively responds to stimulation of a particular locus of the skin. All the locality detectors that independently converge on the defensive command neuron operate in parallel. The receptive field of the defensive command neuron is composed of inputs from parallel locality detectors. By using EPSPs to local skin stimulations, this makes it possible to evaluate the organization of the detector map representing external and internal organs. In the defensive command neuron, slight local tactile stimulation of the foot skin results in two independent EPSPs, indicating that each point of the skin is represented by at least two parallel channels. Repeated stimulation of this point results in a habituation of these EPSPs, demonstrating plastic properties of the respective synapses. A minimal shift of the stimulus with respect to its position on the skin shows a recovery of the EPSPs. Such a selective habituation is evidence that the information from every point of the skin is handled in parallel. The increase of stimulus intensity produces a new late EPSP in the defensive command neuron. The late nociceptive component is not habituated by repeated stimulation, which may be indicative of unplastic synapses. The data show two different detector maps: a plastic one for nonpainful stimuli and an unplastic one for nociceptive stimuli (Sokolov, 1981).

The sets of locality detectors form detector maps on which local stimuli of different intensities are represented. The feature-detector maps constitute inputs for different command neurons. The other population of cells is represented by modulating neurons, which are tuned selectively either to positive or negative values of stimuli. The modulating neurons of feeding behavior are excited by sweet food or by injected glucose, which demonstrates the neuronal basis of simple positive emotional states. The aversive substances, nociceptive stimuli, and norepinephrine result in an inhibition of spiking in these positive neurons, activating in turn modulating neurons of the defensive reflex corresponding to a negative emotional state (Sokolov, at press). Thus in the simple nervous system of a snail, sensory and emotional coding are accomplished by two different sets of neurons: sensory-selective feature detectors and emotionally selective cells.

The data obtained in the simple neuronal system of a snail can be applied to more complex organisms. The difference between feature detectors and emotion-dependent neurons has been demonstrated by Yamamoto, Matsuo, Kiyomitsu, and Kitamura (1989). They have found that taste-selective neurons and emotion-dependent neurons separately represent the sensory and emotional aspects of taste stimulation. Two types of cortical taste-responsive neurons have been identified in rats: Type 1 neurons responded in excitatory or inhibitory fashion to one or more of the basic taste stimuli and the response of Type 2 neurons depended upon the palatability (preference or aversion, acceptance or rejection) of liquids. Type 1 neurons were arranged within the cortical gustatory area in a chemotopic manner. Type 2 neurons are located in the periphery of the gustatory area. Taste quality is coded by Type 1 neurons. The hedonic tone of taste stimuli is represented by Type 2 neurons. A similar dichotomy of taste-responsive neurons exists in the lateral hypothalamus. Some Type 1 neurons showed enhanced responses to conditioned tastes. Type 2 neurons changed the character of the response from excitation to inhibition, and vice versa, after positive or negative conditioning. The difference between taste-selective and emotion-selective neurons consists in the state-dependence of emotional units. Emotion-selective neurons change their responses in accordance with the state of satiation for specific substances, evaluating their positive or negative values with respect to internal states. Thus the basic principles of the organization of feature detectors and emotion detectors seem to be similar.

SENSORY INFORMATION PROCESSING

To develop a sensory information processing plan, let us first consider a formal model of sensory representation based on the integration of subjective and neurophysiological data. The basic unit of the sensory information model is a formal feature detector (see Figure 1). The relationship between the detector map and perception can be found by means of multidimensional scaling. Estimating the subjective difference between two stimuli, the subject can express this value in numbers. The matrix of subjective differences between pairwise presented stimuli obey the axioms of metric space. The perceived stimuli are represented as points in an n-dimensional metric space. Experiments performed with different stimuli have shown that the points representing the stimuli are located in euclidian perceptual space. The euclidian distances between the points of respective stimuli calcu-

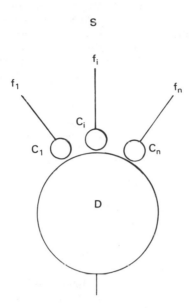

$$D = f_1C_1 + f_iC_i + \ldots f_jC_j = (\vec{F}, \vec{C}) = |\vec{F}| |\vec{C}| \cos \varphi$$

Figure 1 Detector. Detector neuron D is a formal neuron with $i = 1 \ldots n$ synaptic contacts characterized by $c1 \ldots ci \ldots cn$ synaptic weights. The $f1 \ldots fi \ldots fn$ are inputs from predetector neurons. The stimulus S generates, at the predetector level, a combination of excitations constituting an excitation vector $\vec{F}$. The excitation vector acts through a set of synaptic contacts that make up a link vector $\vec{C}$ in a parallel manner on the detector D. The response of the detector equals the sum of products of respective excitations and synaptic weights. In terms of linear algebra, the response of the detector equals the scalar product of excitation vector $\vec{F}$ and link vector $\vec{C}$. Such formalization suggests a selective characteristic of the detector with a response maximum at the point where the excitation vector $\vec{F}$ becomes collinear to the specific detector for the link vector $\vec{C}$.

lated from their cartesian coordinates closely matched their respective subjective differences (Izmailov & Sokolov, 1991; Sokolov & Izmailov, 1984). The points representing signals did not occupy the space randomly but rather lay in a thin spherical layer. One might say that the signal points are located on the surface of a hypersphere in an n-dimensional euclidian space.

The position of the sphere with respect to orthogonal axes cannot be obtained directly from a matrix of subjective differences. Its orientation is based on additional information extracted from an analysis of the neuronal mechanisms that determined the spherical representation of stimuli. The basic principle of information processing in neuronal nets is a channel-dependent code: Each particular stimulus parameter excites a selectively tuned detector neuron (Fomin, Sokolov, & Vaitkyavichus, 1979). A population of differently tuned detectors constitutes a detector map. The modification of input signals results in a shift of excitation maximum on the detector map; in this way, a set of signals is projected on the detector map.

The response of the detector neuron results from the summation of excitations evoked at each synaptic contact. Unitary synaptic excitation is a product of synaptic input and synaptic weight. The synaptic inputs converging on the detector neuron constitute the excitation vector. The set of synaptic weights of a detector corresponds to its link vector. The response of the detector equals the scalar product of the excitation vector and the link vector. The link vectors of detectors of a particular detector map are of constant length. A particular stimulation generating an excitation vector affects all detectors of a detector map in a parallel manner.

The response of a detector is defined as a scalar product of the excitation vector and the detector link vector. The detector having link vector collinearity with the evoked excitation vector will generate an excitation maximum on the detector map (see Figure 2). The position of the excitation maximum on the detector map determines a channel-dependent code of the input signal. Each detector characterized by a particular link vector of constant length can be represented by a point on the hypersphere in the n-dimensional euclidian space. The sphere in an n-dimensional euclidian space where the detectors are located corresponds to the detector map.

The study of the neuronal organization of a detector map suggests that the excitation that affects in parallel all detectors of the detector map is generated by predetector neurons. The components of the excitation vector reaching the detector map are composed of the responses of such predetectors. The length of an excitation vector is of constant value.

At the predetector level, the input signal is coded by the orientation of an n-dimensional excitation vector of a constant length. At the detector level, the input signal generates an excitation maximum on the detector map. The angle between two neighboring detectors is a measure of the subjective threshold between stimuli that excite respective detectors.

An equivalence of the subjective difference between two signals at the detector level is measured by a euclidian distance between respective excitation maxima on the detector map. Such a distance between excited detectors parallels the euclidian distance between their link vectors or the euclidian distance between corresponding excitation vectors (see Figure 3). The matrix of subjective differences between the presented signals corresponds to a matrix of euclidian distances between excitation vectors evoked by respective stimuli. This means that the matrix of subjective differences between signals contains, implicitly, information on the characteristics of the predetector neurons and the synaptic weights of the respective detectors.

COLOR CODING

Such a model can be tested by using color stimuli. The multidimensional scaling procedure applied to the matrix of subjective differences between monochromatic colors of different intensities has shown that each color can be represented

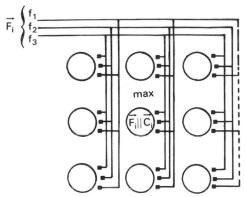

Figure 2 Detector map. The detector map consists of formal neurons having *C1, C2,* and *C3* weights that constitute their link vectors. For different detectors, the link vectors having different orientation are of equal length. The stimulus *Si* generates, at the predetector level, an excitation vector $\vec{F_i}$ with excitations *f1, f2, f3* as its components. The excitation vector, $\vec{F}$, reaching in parallel manner all detectors of the detector map, generates an excitation maximum on the detector characterized by the link vector $\vec{C_j}$. The response maximum is reached in the detector having link vector $\vec{C_j}$ collinear to excitation vector $\vec{F_i}$. The change of the stimulus results in a modification of the excitation vector and a shift of the excitation maximum on the detector map. Thus a local stimulus on a set of predetectors is transformed into a specific position of the excitation maximum on the detector's map. The link vectors of the detectors are of constant length. It suggests that the detector map is represented by a sphere in multidimensional space. The number of dimensions is determined by the number of predetectors and the number of respective synaptic contacts on the detector. The maximally excited detector is characterized by a link vector collinear with the excitation vector acting on the detector map.

by a four-dimensional vector of a constant length. The euclidian distances between the points representing different colors closely correspond to subjective differences between respective colors. The orientation of the axes was based on the neuronal channels participating in color coding. Two orthogonal cartesian coordinates paralleling responses of opponent cells represent colors according to wavelength. The

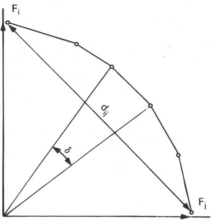

Figure 3 Subjective threshold and subjective difference. The detectors on the detector map represent input signals. The just noticeable difference between two signals is measured by the angle, δ, between two neighboring detectors characterized by link vectors $\vec{C}i$ and $\vec{C}i + 1$. The sum of just noticeable difference between two signals equals the angle, α, between detectors excited on the sphere by respective signals. The subjective difference between two signals is evaluated as a euclidian distance between the detectors selectively excited on the sphere by these stimuli. The spherical model of the detector map suggests that the matrix of subjective differences, regarded as a matrix of euclidian distances between detectors, contains information concerning the link vectors of detectors and excitation vectors generated by predetectors.

horizontal angle corresponds to the hue of respective colors. Two other orthogonal axes representing brightness (B neuron) and darkness (D neuron) characterize colors with respect to their intensity. The angle on the plane built up by these axes corresponds to the subjective estimation of color luminosity. The spherical model of color vision suggests that the subjective estimation of the luminosity of achromatic light stimuli is measured by euclidian distances between the ends of two-dimensional vectors of constant length representing stimuli of different intensity along a semicircle. The set of equally luminous colors is located on the sphere in three-dimensional space.

The third angle of the four-dimensional sphere parallels the saturation of colors.

Thus four orthogonal cartesian axes of the color space closely match four types of color-coding cells, and three spherical coordinates correspond to three subjective aspects of perceived colors: hue, value, and saturation (Izmailov & Sokolov, 1991; Izmailov, Sokolov, & Chernorizov, 1989; Sokolov & Izmailov, 1984) Differential color thresholds are measured by a constant spherical angle. The sum of thresholds between two colors equals the arc separating respective color points; however, the subjective difference between colors equals the euclidian distance between color points (see Figures 4, 5, and 6).

The color predetectors are composed of two stages. At the receptor level, the responses of three types of cones build up a nonorthogonal coordinate system that is orthogonalized by means of horizontal cells that constitute the first stage of predetectors. At this stage, the three-dimensional vector has intensity-dependent length. At the second stage of predetectors, the three-dimensional vector is transformed into a four-dimensional vector of a constant length represented by bipolar cells.

The four-dimensional color space is composed of selectively tuned color detectors. Each color detector is characterized by a specific four-dimensional link vector of a constant length. The four-dimensional excitation vector evoked by light stimulation generates an excitation maximum on a particular detector having a link vector collinear with the excitation vector. The subjective differences between colors are equal to the euclidian distances between the link vectors of respective

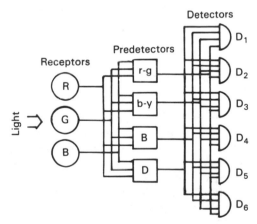

Figure 4 The four-dimensional color space. The matrix of subjective differences between pairwise presented colors treated by multidimensional scaling procedures shows that the color stimuli are located on the hypersphere in four-dimensional euclidian space. Four coordinates of the color space correspond to red-green (*RG*), blue-yellow (*BY*), brightness (*B*), and darkness (*D*) neurons, respectively. A particular color is characterized by a four-dimensional excitation vector, which can be projected on the three planes.

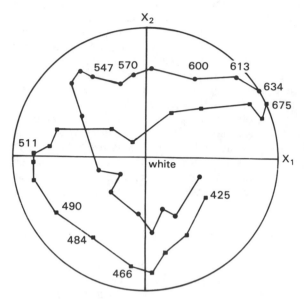

Figure 5 The projection of monochromatic colors on the
RG-BY plane. *X1* corresponds to the red-green
system and *X2* to the blue-yellow system. The
achromatic colors are located in the center of the
plane. The monochromatic lights from 675 nm up to
425 nm of two different intensities are presented on
the *X1X2* plane. An intensity-depending shift of the
trace characterizes the influence of the stimulus
brightness on its hue.

detectors or the euclidian distances between the excitation vectors. This means that
the matrix of subjective differences between colors implicitly contains information
on characteristics of predetectors on the one hand, and on link vectors of color
detectors on the other.

Behavioral experiments on the discrimination of colors of different brightness
in monkeys were accomplished to construct a matrix of probabilities of instrumental reactions to different colors. Analysis revealed four factors. The colors are
located on a sphere in four-dimensional space. On the plane composed of the first
and second factors, color points are situated in accordance with a Newtonian color
circle. These two factors are the blue-yellow and red-green cells. The third and
fourth factors were interpreted as excitations of brightness (B) and darkness (D)
neurons (Latanov, Polyansky, & Sokolov, 1991). Color detectors located in the
visual cortex of primates are selectively tuned to particular combinations of excitations evoked by light stimulation in cones that are sensitive to short, middle, and
long waves (Zeki, 1990). The three hyperpolarization responses evoked in three
types of cones are transformed into excitations of achromatic, blue-yellow and red-
green horizontal cells. At this level the luminosity is coded by the length of the
three-dimensional vector. At the bipolar cell level the three-dimensional vector
with intensity-dependent length is transformed into a four-dimensional vector of a

constant length. This transformation is achieved by the addition of a bipolar cell, which generates spikes during darkness (D neuron). At the same time, each color opponent cell is divided into a pair of reciprocally operating bipolar cells: R + G−, R − G+, B − Y+, and B + Y−. These four parallel channels are used for spike generation in such a way that only one pair is active at a time. Thus the light is coded by a four-dimensional excitation vector composed of excitations of B, D, RG, and BY cells that affect all color detectors at the cortical level in a parallel manner. Each color detector is characterized by a four-dimensional link vector composed of synaptic weights. The link vectors of color detectors are of constant length.

Selective color perception is determined by the position of an excitation maximum on the four-dimensional sphere built up by color detectors. The excitation maximum on the particular detector is reached when the excitation vector and link vector of the detector are collinear.

EMOTIONAL SPACE

Now that the detector mechanisms of perception have been explicated, let us return to the problem of emotions. The evocation of emotions under experimental conditions involves many obstacles. Assuming that the names of emotions consti-

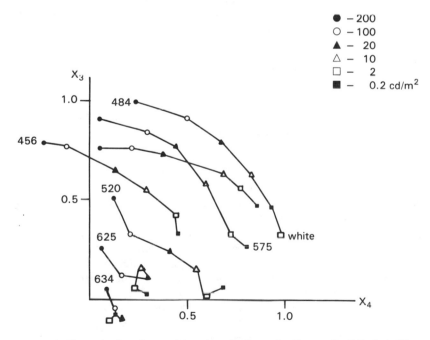

Figure 6 The projection of monochromatic and achromatic colors on the *B-D* plane. The *X4* corresponds to the *D* neuron and *X3* to the *B* neuron. The angle on the plane composed of *X4* and *X3* axes characterizes the subjective aspect of light intensity, its lightness, or its value. The achromatic colors are located on the external arc with respect to stimulus intensity.

tute a semantic emotional space isomorphic to emotional space, one may construct a semantic emotional space and deduce from these data the structure of emotional space. Another approach is to construct emotional space based on the emotional aspects of colors. In this case, additional information is obtained from perceptual color space. To do this, a 19 × 25 matrix of subjective similarity estimations between 19 equiluminant monochromatic colors and 25 emotional terms was constructed.

Every emotional term was represented by a set of estimations regarded as a vector of differences with respect to presented color stimuli. Differences between emotional terms were measured by euclidian distances between the ends of these vectors. The results were integrated into a 25 × 25 matrix of differences between emotional terms, which was analyzed by a metric multidimensional scaling procedure. We found that all 25 emotional terms are located on the sphere in three-dimensional space. In a similar way, the 19 colors represented by emotional estimations were used to compose a 19 × 19 matrix of color differences. Multidimensional scaling of the matrix demonstrated that the equiluminant monochromatic colors are positioned on the sphere in a three-dimensional emotional space. The coordinate systems for colors and emotions were parallel in the following way: enthusiasm with blue (475 nm), calm with green (500 nm), disgust with yellow (570 nm), and anger with red (675 nm) (Izmailov, in press). Thus emotions can be represented on a color sphere. Conversely, colors can be located on a sphere of emotional terms. The correspondence of color space and semantic emotional space suggests the analogy of neuronal mechanisms operating in the perception of colors and in the generation of emotions. The results suggest that any particular emotion is coded by a specific emotion detector in the same way as a color is coded. The predetectors linked with emotion detectors constitute a spherical emotional space that can be revealed by using the semantics of emotional terms.

So far only equiluminant colors have been related to emotional terms. A problem to be considered in the future is the relationship between the brightness of colors and their emotional characteristics.

SUMMARY

Processing of sensory information occurs in a parallel manner in multilayered networks. At the predetector level the signal is coded by orientation of an excitation vector of constant length. At the detector level the signal is coded by the position of an excitation maximum on the detector map. The detector map is composed of detectors having link vectors of constant lengths. The output responses of feature detectors equal scalar products of the excitation and link vectors. The set of detectors having constant lengths of the link vectors constitutes a sphere in an n-dimensional space with the dimensionality equal to the number of synaptic contacts on the detector. The difference between signals on the sphere are characterized by euclidian distances between excited detectors. The principles of sensory information processing were demonstrated in color vision. The cartesian coordinates of colors correspond to excitations of predetector-opponent color cells. Color perception is determined by the selective excitation of color detectors constituting the sphere. The subjective differences of colors are measured by euclidian distances between points representing the colors. The matrix of subjective differences between colors contains the information concerning neuronal channels for color coding. The map of color detectors constitutes a basis for color perception. Studying the similarity between colors and emotional terms demonstrates the correspondence between color space and semantic emotional space. The isomorphic spherical structure of both spaces indicates the common principles of their organization. Isoluminant colors and emotions are coded by selective detectors receiving inputs from predetectors whose excitations constitute three-dimensional excitation vectors.

The total set of emotional terms can be represented on the surface of a sphere in a three-dimensional color space of equiluminant colors. The cartesian coordinates of emotional terms corresponds to the excitations of three color predetector neurons. In the same way, color stimuli can be given by points in three-dimensional semantic emotional space. The cartesian coordinates of the semantic emotional space correspond to excitations of assumed emotional predetectors. The similarity of color space and semantic emotional space suggests a detector mechanism of emotions. According to this detector theory of emotions, a set of emotions is represented by a set of selective detectors of emotions. The selective excitation of a particular detector of emotion is determined by a combination of excitation of the three emotion predetectors assumed on the basis of experimental data. Color stimuli affect the emotional predetectors, and thus constitute a basis for the emotional tone of colors.

REFERENCES

Fomin, S. V., Sokolov, E. N., & Vaitkyavichus, G. G. (1979). *Iskusstvennye organy chuvstv.* [Artificial sensory organs]. Moscow: Nauka.

Izmailov, C. A. (1992). *Color-emotion relationship.* Manuscript submitted for publication.

Izmailov, C. A., & Sokolov, E. N. (1991). Spherical model of color and brightness discrimination. *Psychological Science, 2,* 249–259.

Ismailov, C. A., Sokolov, E. N., & Chernorizov, A. M. (1989). *Psikhofisiologiya tsvetovogo zreniya* (Psychophysiology of color vision). Moscow: Moscow University Press.

Latanov, A. S., Polyansky, V. B., & Sokolov, E. N. (1991). Chetyryekhmyernoye sferichaskoye tsvetovoye prostranstvo obezyany. [Four-dimensional spherical color space of the monkey]. *Journal of Higher Nervous Activity, 41,* 636–646.

Sokolov, E. N. (1981). *Neyronnye mechanizmy pamyati i obucheniya* (Neuronal mechanisms of memory and learning). Moscow: Nauka.

Sokolov, E. N. (at press). Vector coding in neuronal nets.

Sokolov, E. N., & Izmailov, C. A. (1984). *Tsvetovoe zrenie.* [Color vision]. Moscow: Izdatelstvo MGU.

Yamamoto, T., Matsuo, R., Kiyomitsu, Y., & Kitamura, R. (1989). Taste responses of cortical neurons in freely ingesting rats. *Journal of Neurophysiology, 1,* 1244–1258.

Zeki, S. (1990). Colour vision and functional specialisation in the visual cortex. *Discussions in Neuroscience.* Vol. VI. Amsterdam: Elsevier (pp. 1–64).

12

Genetic and Environmental Effects on the Need for Sensory Stimulation and Emotional Reactivity in Rats

Jan Matysiak, Pawel M. Ostaszewski, Wojciech Pisula,
and Sniezyna Watras
University of Warsaw, Poland

INTRODUCTION

Many human characteristics have been studied with the goal of determining the relative contributions of heredity and environment. The methods employed are, of course, necessarily less direct than the techniques of animal studies. In our study, we used inbred strains of rats reared in different environmental conditions.

A number of theories of personality and temperament proposes a relationship between the need for sensory stimulation and emotional functioning (Eysenck, 1970; Strelau, 1983). Generally, both features are regarded as strongly genetically determined. However, environmental factors also are claimed to contribute to their development.

There are both theoretical and empirical reasons for considering light-contingency bar-pressing behavior as an expression of the need for light stimulation (Matysiak, 1979, 1985; Wong, 1976). There are also grounds for treating locomotor activity in the running wheel as a specific measure of the need for tactile–kinesthetic stimulation (Matysiak, 1985). In addition, the open-field test and active-avoidance task are used widely as measures of emotionality in animals (Brush, Baron, Froehlich, Ison, Pellegrino, Phillips, Sakellaris, & Williams, 1985; Walsh & Cummins, 1976).

A number of experiments has revealed the influence of genetic and environmental factors on stimulus-seeking behavior. Studies by Hennessy, Hershberger, Bell, and Zachman (1976) and Tees, Midgley, and Bruinsma (1980) have shown that rats reared in enriched environments tend to choose more stimulating surroundings. Lockard (1962) found that rats with different genotypes reared in the same environmental conditions differ also in light-contingent bar-pressing activity. Ebimara and Tsuji (1976) and Festing (1977) obtained similar results when testing locomotor activity in the running wheel in different strains of mice.

Wax (1977) found strains of mice to differ in activity level in the running wheel in different light-stimulation conditions. Oakeshott and Glow (1980) claim that

This work was financed by the Research Program of the Polish Ministry of Education No. III.25/VII.

71% of individual difference variability in need for light stimulation is determined by genetic factors. Matysiak and Toeplitz (1990) have shown that the modality of stimulation preference also is determined genetically. Experiments on the need for tactile–kinesthetic stimulation have revealed that rat strains that are very active in the running wheel have a lower need for light stimulation than low-active ones, and vice versa.

Experiments involving the open-field test have suggested a strong effect of social isolation on emotionality and exploratory behavior in rats (Koch & Arnold, 1972; Parker & Morinan, 1986). Renner and Rosenzweig (1986) have reported that rats reared in enriched environments show stronger and more diverse exploratory behavior than animals reared under standard environmental conditions. Manosevitz and Montemayor (1972), in a three-factorial experiment that seems to be of great importance, found that environmental conditions that differ in their stimulation level affect exploratory behavior, open-field activity, and running wheel activity in various ways depending on the mouse strain.

The influence of genetic and environmental factors on emotionality in animals also was revealed in experiments using escape and avoidance conditioning measures. Findings suggesting genetic determination of avoidance learning behavior are presented by Satinder (1976) and Brush et al. (1985). Satinder and Hill (1974) have shown the influence of genotype and stimulation during early development of such behavior.

Matysiak and Toeplitz (1990) have hypothesized that simple forms of behavior that do not require special training such as exploration and stimulus seeking are under the separate control of genetic and environmental factors. On the other hand, the interaction of both factors should influence more complex behavior that requires learning. Empirical verification of this hypothesis was one of the purposes of this experiment.

METHOD

Subjects

Subjects were 54 male rats, of whom 18 were homozygotic BN/Han, 18 were homozygotic LEW/Han, and 18 were heterozygotic Wistar rats.

Apparatus

Four behavioral measures were made. The self-exposure chamber was used to measure the level of need for light stimulation. Modified, coupled running wheels were used both to measure the level of need for kinesthetic and tactile stimulation and to reveal any preference for motor activity that yields a lower level of stimulation (kinesthetic and tactile only) or a higher level (kinesthetic, tactile, and light). The open-field test was used to measure behavioral characteristics related to exploratory behavior and emotional reactivity. Emotional reactivity also was examined during avoidance reaction training.

The self-exposure chamber (Matysiak, 1985) was constructed from a breeding cage 40 × 30 × 20 cm in size. Two identical levers were mounted symmetrically on two opposite walls, 10 cm above the base. Applying pressure to one of them (experimental) caused the switching on of one light that was 1.6 lux in intensity. The exposure time was equal to the duration of lever press. Pressing the other lever (control) produced no effect. The number of presses of the experimental lever (NPe) and of the control lever (NPc) was recorded. The overall time of pressing the experimental lever (Te) and the control lever (Tc) during the whole test period also was recorded.

A chamber equipped with two running wheels also was built from a breeding cage. Two wheels of similar construction, 32 cm in diameter, and a 15-cm track were mounted on opposite walls of the chamber. The only difference between wheels was the effect of their revolution. The revolution of one wheel turned on the light in the cage; the revolution of the "control" wheel did not.

A low–fear-producing open-field apparatus was used. It was painted white and its floor (a 160-cm diameter circle) was divided into several squares, 20 × 20 cm each. The entire apparatus was surrounded by a white wall 35 cm high. In the central part, 120 cm above the floor, a glow bulb (200 W) was placed. The number of squares crossed, urination, defecation, and rearing up were registered. Latency of leaving the central start position of the open field also was measured.

Avoidance reaction training was done in a typical shuttle box, 48 × 22 × 23 cm. The floor was made of metal bars. One of the walls was transparent to enable the experimenter to view the animals during the experimental trials. In the cover, behind frosted glass, several small glow bulbs were placed. This cover was a source of the conditioned stimuli (intensity light of 5 lux). The unconditioned stimulus, an electric shock, was delivered by the floor bars. The intensity of shock was stabilized for each individual rat and ranged from 1.5 to 2.5 mA. Each shock was preceded by a 3.6 second light period. Both light and current were turned off when the rat had crossed a 3-cm high band in the middle of the cage. Escape reaction time, avoidance reaction time, and the number of trials needed by the subject to reach the avoidance reaction criterion were measured. The criterion was seven consecutive avoidance reactions.

Procedure

A few days after weaning, all subjects were divided into nine subgroups as illustrated in Table 1.

Six Wistar rats, six LEW/Han, and six BN/Han rats were placed in standard breeding cages, 40 × 30 × 20 cm, in groups of six (subgroups SW, SL, and SB). Another six Wistar, six LEW/Han, and six BN/Han rats were placed individually in small cages, 50 × 13 × 14 cm (subgroups IW, IL, and IB). Finally, rats from all strains were placed in big (80 × 30 × 20 cm) cages equipped with balance, seesaw, and ladder, in groups of six (subgroups EW, EL, and EB). These subjects were exposed to handling during the whole pretesting period. All animals were

Table 1 Experimental subgroups

Environment	Strain		
	(W)istar	(L) EW/Han	(B) N/Han
(I)mpoverished	IW	IL	IB
(S)tandard	SW	SL	SB
(E)nriched	EW	EL	EB

kept in the same breeding room with light–darkness cycle (24 hours) beginning at 8 A.M. Food and water were available ad libitum.

When subjects were approximately 90 days old, the behavioral tests were run.

Stage 1 in the self-exposure chamber and running wheels lasted 23.5 hours. The measurement sequence was randomized and began at 1 P.M. Intervals between experimental trials ranged from 3 to 5 days. The experimental room was dark. The experimental procedure and data recording were conducted automatically by an MSM Impol computer.

One week after the previously described tests were completed, the open-field test was done as the second step of the study. Subjects were placed at the central point of the open field. During a 3-minute session the spontaneous behavior of animals was recorded. Between the successive subjects, the open field was cleaned. This test was run at 6 P.M.

The third and last step of this investigation was the avoidance reaction training. The high pain threshold of BN/Han rats rendered it impossible to use these subjects in this part of the experiment, and only Wistar and LEW/Han rats were tested. After being placed in the experimental cage, the subject had 3 minutes to adapt to the new situation. Light stimuli were then turned on. Following the light (after 3.6 seconds) the electric shock was turned on. A 1-minute interval between trials was used ($+/-10$ seconds). If the rat avoided the shock by appropriate behavior the break lasted only 30 seconds. Daily sessions consisted of 10 trials. The experimental session was prolonged if the rat started to perform the avoidance reaction at the close of a session. If the subject did not achieve the criterion (seven avoidance reactions in succession), the training was continued the following day. The experimental room was dark. Stimulus exposure and data recording were conducted by apparatus constructed at our laboratory.

RESULTS

The data were analyzed by the ANOVA method followed by the least significant difference (LSD) range test. It has been shown previously (Matysiak, 1979, 1985) that the self-exposure chamber yields two kinds of information: the total number of presses of both levers, and a ratio measure that reflects the need for light stimulation. The latter is determined by using a special coefficient described by Matysiak (1979, 1985) and computed according to the formula: $NS = NPe/NPt \times Te/Tt$, where NS is the need for light stimulation coefficient, Ne is the number of presses of the experimental (light) lever, NPt is the total number of presses of both levers, Te is the time of all presses on the experimental lever, and Tt is the total time of the presses on both levers. Data based on these two indicators are presented in Figure 1.

As illustrated in Figure 1a, subjects bred in the impoverished conditions showed higher activity in general in the self-exposure chamber than subjects raised in a normal environment, $F(2,53) = 4.37$, p $< .05$. Statistical analysis also revealed an interaction of heredity and environment on general activity, $F(4,53) = 2.99$, $p < .05$. Wistar rats bred in normal conditions showed higher motor activity than the BN/Han and LEW/Han subjects bred in the same conditions; BN/Han subjects bred in restricted conditions showed higher activity than the rats of the same strain bred in normal and enriched conditions.

The measure of the need for sensory stimulation (NS) was influenced only by

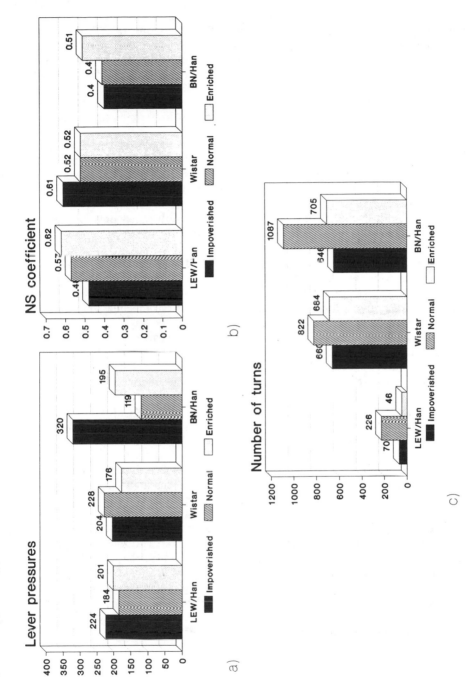

Figure 1 Mean values of need for sensory stimulation and general activity indicators in different strains bred in impoverished, normal, and enriched environments: (*a*) number of presses of both levers in self-exposure chamber, (*b*) NS coefficient value, and (*c*) number of turns of both wheels.

the genetic factor, $F(2,53)$ = 3.235, $p < .05$ (see Figure 1b). BN/Han rats presented a lower level of need for stimulation than their counterparts.

Figure 1c presents the results of the measurement of activity in the running wheels. This kind of activity was also affected by the genetic factor only. LEW/Han subjects showed a lower level of activity than their counterparts, both in the experimental (light) wheel, $F(2,53)$ = 11.724, $p < .001$, and in the control wheel, $F(2.53)$ = 12.481, $p < .001$. There was no preference for activity on either wheel.

Figure 2 presents the results of avoidance reaction training. Each of the analyzed indicators appeared to be under a different influence. Escape reaction time was affected only by rearing conditions, $F(2,34)$ = 4.449, $p < .05$ (Figure 2a). Rats reared in enriched conditions showed slower performance of this reaction than their counterparts.

On the other hand, avoidance reaction time was influenced only by genetic characteristics, $F(1,34)$ = 13.176, $p < .001$ (Figure 2b). LEW/Han rats avoided shocks more slowly than Wistar rats.

The indicator of the speed of learning (number of trials needed by subjects to achieve the criterion) was affected only by the interaction of heredity and environment, $F(2,32)$ = 5.918, $p < .001$ (Figure 2c). LEW/Han subjects bred in normal conditions learned more slowly than their counterparts of the same strain bred in impoverished and enriched environments.

Figure 3 presents the results of the open-field tests measurements. Wistar rats showed lower ambulation than BN/Han and LEW/Han subjects, $F(2,53)$ = 6.853, $p < .01$ (Figure 3a). Ambulation of rats was also affected by environmental influences. Animals bred in the restricted conditions presented a lower level of ambulation than their counterparts, $F(2,53)$ = 5.823, $p < .01$. There was also a significant effect of interaction between the two experimental factors on ambulation, $F(4,53)$ = 3.607, $p < .05$. LEW/Han subjects bred in the enriched conditions showed a higher level of ambulation than both BN/Han and Wistar rats bred in the same conditions and LEW/Han rats bred in the remaining kinds of environment. BN/Han rats bred in normal conditions also showed a higher level of ambulation than their counterparts bred in the same conditions and than the BN/Han subjects bred in impoverished and enriched conditions.

Latency in the central area of the open field was affected independently by the experimental factors (Figure 3b). LEW/Han rats escaped the central area more quickly than other subjects, $F(2,53)$ = 9.72, $p < .001$. Animals bred in the restricted conditions escaped significantly more slowly than the subjects bred in the normal and enriched environments, $F(2,53)$ = 4.481, $p < .05$.

Although there was no significant effect on defecation, it was found that subjects bred in impoverished conditions showed a higher level of urination than their counterparts, $F(2,53)$ = 10.179, $p < .001$ (Figure 3c). It was also found that rats bred in restricted conditions reared up less than other subjects, $F(2,45)$ = 4.604, $p < .05$ (Figure 3d).

DISCUSSION

In the present study, the hypothesis of an additive effect of genetic and environmental factors on simple forms of behavior (stimulation inflow regulation) was

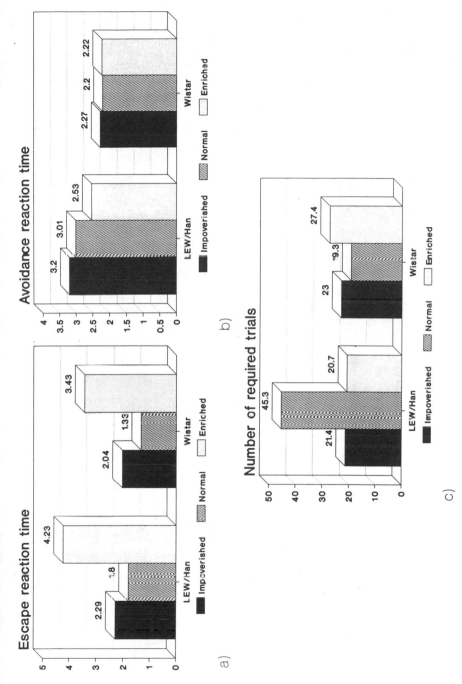

Figure 2 Mean values of defensive reactions indicators in different strains bred in impoverished, normal, and enriched environments: (*a*) escape reaction time, (*b*) avoidance reaction time, and (*c*) number of trials required to achieve sufficient avoidance reaction performance.

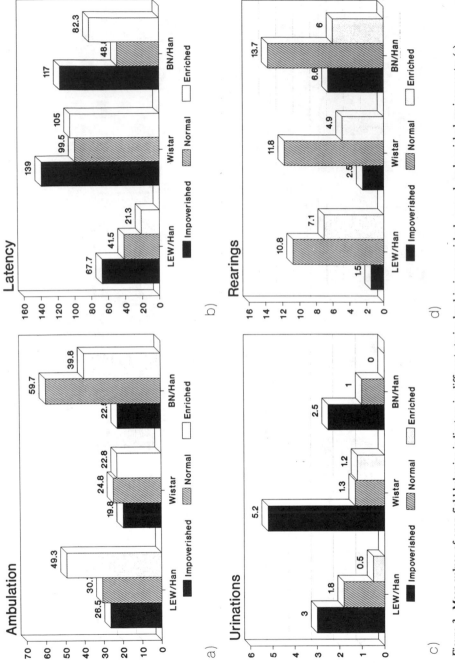

Figure 3 Mean values of open-field behavior indicators in different strains bred in impoverished, normal, and enriched environments: (*a*) ambulation, (*b*) latency to escape the center of open field, (*c*) urinations, and (*d*) rearings.

confirmed. It also was found that the interaction of both factors influences more difficult behavior, especially stress-related behavior.

Our results have confirmed only partly the hypothesis of separate effects of genotype and environment on the need for light stimulation, because only a genetic influence was statistically significant here. This result is in agreement with data obtained by Lockard (1962) and Oakeshott and Glow (1980), who suggested a strong genetic determination of the need for light stimulation in rats. Lack of an environmental effect may be explained by the fact that the subjects were exposed to different environmental conditions later in life than in our prior research. The pertinent literature suggests that the influence of environments differing in stimulation can be realized only when animals are reared in special conditions from the very beginning of their lives (DeNelski & Denenberg, 1967; Tees, Midgley, & Bruinsma, 1980).

Present results concerning running wheel activity are similar to those from our previous study (Matysiak & Toeplitz, 1990). That type of behavior (which shows the level of the need for tactile–kinesthetic stimulation) seems to be strongly genetically determined. The same finding was made by Festing (1977) and Ebimara and Tsuji (1976). On the other hand, it contradicts data from Manosevitz and Montemayor (1972), who showed that both genetic and environmental factors and their interaction affect mouse activity in the running wheel. This lack of agreement could be caused by interspecies differences or by the fact that the animals in the study by Manosevitz and Montemayor (1972) were exposed to different environmental conditions just after birth. In our experiment, rats were placed in different rearing conditions 4 weeks after birth. It is possible that there is a crucial period in the life of the organism when exposure to different environmental conditions causes development of individual differences in the need for sensory stimulation. Further study is needed to clarify these possibilities.

The influence of the interaction of genetic and environmental factors on the general activity in the self-exposure chamber is noteworthy. The results of greater activity of BN/Han rats reared in impoverished environmental conditions in comparison to subjects from the same strain reared in other environments is in agreement with data presented by Manosevitz and Montemayor (1972). In their experiment, mice reared in impoverished conditions showed stronger exploratory behavior than animals reared in an enriched environment. Matysiak and Toeplitz (1990) also found a similar effect. Rats from a relatively poorer environment (standard conditions) were more active in the self-exposure chamber than animals reared in an enriched environment. However, our results are contrary to data reported by Renner and Rosenzweig (1986), who found that rats from enriched environmental conditions displayed more diverse exploratory behavior than animals from a low-stimulation environment. This may be accounted for by differences in the methods of measurement of exploratory behavior used by Renner and Rosenzweig (1986) and ourselves.

Data from the open-field test also did not confirm the increase of general activity shown by rats from the impoverished environment in the self-exposure chamber. In the open-field test, general activity measures are ambulation and rearing up. In our study, ambulation was influenced by a complex interaction of heredity and environment. On the other hand, the frequency of rearing up was influenced only by the environmental factor. The effect was opposite to that obtained in the self-exposure chamber: Animals reared in the impoverished environment were less active than those from standard and enriched environmental conditions. This difference probably is caused by the fact that in the open-field test emotional factors such as exposure to illumination and wide open areas play a significant role in controlling behavior. It seems that rats from an impoverished environment have a higher level of anxiety than animals from other environments that have been investigated. This is probably the reason that they are less active in the open field. It has been shown that animals with high levels of anxiety show freezing behavior in stress situations (Brush et al., 1985; Satinder, 1976; Satinder & Hill, 1974). In the present study, animals reared in the impoverished environmental condition had longer latency in the open-field test than rats from other environments. Higher frequency of urination shown by isolated rats strongly supports the hypothesis of their high level of anxiety. It is noteworthy that the relationship of isolation to high level of anxiety has been noted by other authors (Parker & Morinan, 1986).

The influence of the genetic factor on open-field latency, which is one of the indicators of emotional reactivity, is worth emphasizing. The obtained relationships correspond to the data from the self-exposure chamber. BN/Han rats, which had the lowest level of need for light stimulation, showed the longest latency in the open field. This suggests that they were the most emotionally reactive, which may be interpreted as revealing some relationship between both these features. A genetically determined low level of need for stimulation corresponds to a high level of emotional reactivity, which also is inherited.

As was stated earlier, the basic hypothesis of this experiment concerned the influence of the interaction of genetic and environmental factors on avoidance learning behavior. The results of our experiment confirmed the hypothesis. At the same time, separate effects of genetic and environmental factors on time variables of escape and avoidance performance were revealed. Here, the escape from pain stimulus latency was influenced by the environmental factor. However, this does not exclude the role of a genetic factor in controlling this behavior. The results of research by Satinder and Hill (1974) demonstrated the existence of inter-strain differences in time of escape from a pain stimulus. The lack of a genetic effect in our study may be due to an accidental selection of rat strains that do not differ in escape latency. This may be the reason why only an environmental effect was obtained. This effect, which shows that animals reared in enriched environmental conditions can withstand pain longer, may be attributable to their lower emotional reactivity, the latter being confirmed by their lower frequency of urination and shorter open-field latency.

In the present study, latency of avoidance behavior was affected only by the genetic factor. This result runs contrary to data presented by Brush et al. (1985), who found no differences between two rat strains in avoidance latency. However, our data are in agreement with the results of Satinder and Hill (1974). These authors revealed the effect of a genetic factor, together with the interaction of genetic and environmental factors, on avoidance latency. In our research, such an interaction was obtained for rate of avoidance learning. Thus the influence of the genetic factor and the interaction of genetic and environmental factors for variables strongly connected with learning appears to be qualitatively different from escape behavior, which is much closer to being an unconditioned reaction. The effect of an interaction between genetic and environmental factors leads us to the hypothesis that different genotypes are influenced by environmental factors in different ways. Moreover, our results suggest that the more complex the behavior is, the stronger the influence of an interaction between genetic and environmental factors. However, both these issues require further investigation.

Psychologists study the behavior of so-called lower animals with the hope of finding principles that can be generalized to the behavior of humans. The general assumption is that principles derived from animal research can be used as hypotheses for human behavior. We believe that this is true for our results.

REFERENCES

Brush, F. R., Baron, S., Froehlich, J. C., Ison, J. R., Pellegrino, L. J., Phillips, D. S., Sakellaris, P. C., & Williams, V. N. (1985). Genetic differences in avoidance learning by *Rattus norvegicus*: Escape/avoidance responding, sensitivity to electric shock, discrimination learning, and open-field behavior. *Journal of Comparative Psychology, 99,* 60–73.

DeNelsky, G. Y., & Denenberg, V. H. (1967). Infantile stimulation and adult exploratory behaviour in the rat: effects of handling upon visual variation seeking. *Animal Behaviour, 15,* 568–573.

Fhimara, S., & Tsuji, K. (1976). Strain differences in the mouse's wheel running behavior. *Japanese Psychological Research, 18,* 20–29.

Eysenck, H. J. (1970). *The structure of human personality.* London: Methuen.

Festing, M. F. W. (1977). Wheel activity in 26 strains of mouse. *Laboratory Animals, 11,* 257–258.

Hennessy, M. B., Hershberger, W. A., Bell, R. W., & Zachman, T. A. (1976). The influence of early auditory experience on later auditory and tactual variation seeking in the rat. *Developmental Psychobiology, 9,* 255–260.

Koch, M. D., & Arnold, W. J. (1972). Effects of early social deprivation on emotionality in rats. *Journal of Comparative and Physiological Psychology, 78,* 391–399.

Lockard, R. B. (1962). Some effects of maintenance, luminance and strain differences upon self-exposure to light by rats. *Journal of Comparative and Physiological Psychology, 55,* 1118–1123.

Manosevitz, M., & Montemayor, R. J. (1972). Interaction of environmental enrichment and genotype. *Journal of Comparative and Physiological Psychology, 79,* 67–76.

Matysiak, J. (1979). Self-exposition of sensory stimuli of different modalities in rats. *Polish Psychological Bulletin, 10,* 159–165.

Matysiak, J. (1985). Need for sensory stimulation: Effects on activity. In J. Strelau (Ed.), *Temperamental bases of behavior: Warsaw studies on individual differences* (pp. 141–180). Lisse: Swets & Zeitlinger.

Matysiak, J., & Toeplitz, Z. (1990). Influence of genetic and environmental factors on self-exposure to sensory stimuli in rats. *Ricerche di Psicologia, 2,* 19–28.

Oakeshott, J. G., & Glow, P. H. (1980). Genetic and environment determinants of sensory contingent bar pressing in laboratory rats. *Australian Journal of Psychology, 32,* 31–43.

Parker, V., & Morinan, A. (1986). The socially isolated rat as a model for anxiety. *Neuropharmacology, 25,* 663–664.

Renner, M. J., & Rosenzweig, M. R. (1986). Object interactions in juvenile rats (*Rattus norvegicus*): Effects of different experimental histories. *Journal of Comparative Psychology, 100,* 229–236.

Satinder, K. P. (1976). Sensory responsiveness and avoidance learning in rats. *Journal of Comparative and Physiological Psychology, 90,* 946–957.

Satinder, K. P., & Hill, K. D. (1974). Effects of genotype and postnatal experience on activity, avoidance, shock threshold, and open-field behavior of rats. *Journal of Comparative and Physiological Psychology, 86,* 363–374.

Strelau, J. (1983). *Temperament, personality, activity.* London: Academic Press.

Tees, R. C., Midgley, G., & Bruinsma, Y. (1980). Effect of controlled rearing on development of stimulus-seeking behavior in rats. *Journal of Comparative and Physiological Psychology, 94,* 1003–1018.

Walsh, R. N., & Cummins, R. A. (1976). The open-field test: A critical review. *Psychological Bulletin, 83,* 482–504.

Wax, T. M. (1977). Effects of age, strain, and illumination intensity on activity and self-selection of light-dark schedules in mice. *Journal of Comparative and Physiological Psychology, 91,* 51–62.

Wong, R. (1976). *Motivation: A biobehavioral analysis of consumatory activities.* New York: Macmillan.

III

HEALTH DEVELOPMENTS

13

Motivational Approach to Anxiety Disorders

Don C. Fowles
University of Iowa

In an earlier publication (Fowles, 1988), I proposed that motivational constructs provide a general theoretical framework for understanding psychopathology. These motivational constructs were borrowed from the animal learning and motivation literature, more specifically from the writings of Jeffrey Gray. This argument was supported by the ability to cite already published work applying motivational concepts to the affective disorders, psychopathy (antisocial personality disorder), conduct disorder, drug abuse (especially of opioids and stimulants), and, to some extent, schizophrenia. Applying motivational concepts to anxiety disorders was less satisfactory, however, because only limited reference to the clinical literature was possible. As a result, the discussion of anxiety disorders did not do justice to the complexity of this topic. The purpose of the present paper is to address that shortcoming, that is, to reexamine the use of motivational constructs in the light of extensive research on anxiety disorders. This effort has been facilitated greatly by Barlow's (1988) definitive review and integration of research on anxiety disorders, and the present analysis is based on this work. Before presenting Barlow's conclusions, it will be helpful to briefly summarize Gray's motivational constructs and to describe the major phenomena seen in anxiety disorders.

GRAY'S THEORY

The cornerstone of Gray's theory is a fundamental distinction between appetitive and aversive motivational systems. The focus of Gray's work has been on the aversive motivational system or, as he calls it, the *behavioral inhibition system* (BIS). The aversive motivational system inhibits behavior in response to conditioned stimuli (CS) for punishment and frustrative nonreward, and to novel stimuli and innate fear stimuli (Gray, 1982). In addition to inhibiting behavior, BIS activity increases arousal, allocates attention to "the maximum possible analysis of current environmental stimuli, especially novel ones" (Gray, 1982, p. 13), and prepares for vigorous action (Gray, 1987). Gray sometimes calls the BIS the "stop, look, and listen" system (1987, pp. 263-264) to emphasize the redirection of attention to the environment. The arousal increases the vigor of those responses that occur in spite of the threats of punishment or nonreward. In terms of inhibitory effects on behavior, the prototypical paradigms are passive avoidance and extinction. Passive avoidance is attributed to inhibition of behavior by the BIS in response to cues for punishment, whereas extinction is attributed to inhibition of behavior by the BIS in response to cues for frustrative nonreward. Note that there is an anticipatory quality to BIS activity: It is activated by conditioned stimuli (CSs) for threats and even by uncertain threats in the form of novelty, and it promotes a vigilant scanning of the environment for potential threats. Similarly, it is involved centrally in appraising the threat value of the environment. These features are prominent in generalized anxiety disorder, which will be discussed in this chapter.

A great deal of literature has demonstrated that anxiolytic drugs (alcohol, barbiturates, and the minor tranquilizers) specifically disinhibit behavior in paradigms believed to elicit activity in the BIS (e.g., passive avoidance, extinction). Consequently, Gray (1977, 1982, Chapter 2) argues that the anxiolytic drugs have in common the property of diminishing the efficacy of the BIS. In view of this specificity and the nature of the stimuli to which the BIS responds (threats of punishment and frustration), Gray argues that activity in the BIS is associated with anxiety; that is, the BIS constitutes the neurophysiological substrate for anxiety.

The appetitive motivational system activates behavior in response to conditioned stimuli for reward and relieving nonpunishment. The prototypical paradigms are approach and active avoidance. Gray calls the appetitive system the *approach system*. In my 1980 article on the three-arousal model, I called it the *behavioral activation system* (BAS) to emphasize its parallelism with the BIS. There is a positive hedonic tone to activation of the BAS: The emotional labels applied to this positive affect are "hope" in the case of approach for rewards and "relief" in the case of active avoidance.

Gray (1982) describes a third system, called the *fight/flight system*. This system responds to unconditioned punishment and nonreward with greatly increased activity, for example, running, jumping, hissing, or attacking a suitable target (Gray, 1987). These behaviors are characterized as centering around defensive attack (fight) or attempts at escape (flight) (Gray, 1982). Gray's use of fight/flight terminology refers to Cannon's well-known work on the emergency reaction. Cannon found that animals exposed to immediately stressful stimuli (e.g., a cat exposed to a barking dog) showed a massive reaction of the sympathetic branch of the autonomic nervous system in preparation for vigorous activity. To anticipate material presented in this chapter, one would expect strong cardiovascular activity in connection with activity in this third system (Gray, 1987).

Gray makes a sharp distinction between the BIS and the fight/flight system. He emphasizes that the behavioral effects of unconditioned and conditioned aversive stimuli are often diametrically opposed to each other: vigorous behavior (fight/flight) versus "tense, silent immobility" (1987, p. 254). The two systems are seen as having different neurophysiological substrates: the septo-hippocampal system and the dorsal ascending noradrenergic bundle for the BIS and the amygdala, ventromedial hypothalamus, and central gray of the midbrain for the fight/flight system. Gray (1987) argues that fear and anxiety are related to the BIS and not to the fight/flight system. This argument relies heavily on the finding that the antianxiety drugs attenuate responses mediated by the BIS while having little effect on escape and defensive aggression. To this argument might be added the consideration that pathological anxiety is, by definition, not associated with unconditioned punishment and frustration. Rather, pathological anxiety is irrational, being experienced in the absence of real threats or frustrations. For these reasons, Gray and others using his theory, including the present author, have not incorporated the fight/flight system into a theory of anxiety. In strong contrast, Barlow (1988) has made the fight/flight system an important component of his theory of panic, as will be detailed later in this chapter.

DIAGNOSTIC CRITERIA FOR THE ANXIETY DISORDERS

DSM-III-R, the American diagnostic system, specifies diagnostic criteria for three major aspects of the anxiety disorders seen clinically (American Psychiatric Association, 1987): *panic disorder, agoraphobia,* and *generalized anxiety disorder.* Panic disorder is defined as the rapid onset of intense anxiety accompanied by a number of somatic and cognitive symptoms of acute anxiety. A requirement that the attacks occur in the absence of an identifiable stimulus differentiates panic from simple phobias. Agoraphobia refers to a fear of being trapped in places from which escape might be difficult or embarrassing, or in which help might not be available (Barlow, 1988). Quite often, agoraphobia is seen in connection with panic, in which case the core fear is of having a panic attack in such a place (Barlow, 1988). Although DSM-III-R makes a distinction as to whether panic and agoraphobia occur alone or in combination, Barlow (1988) concludes that panic with and without agoraphobia is essentially the same disorder. Whereas agoraphobia is a prominent aspect of the clinical picture, it probably does not constitute a separate disorder.

The third major aspect of the anxiety disorders is generalized anxiety disorder. This disorder involves unrealistic or excessive chronic anxiety or worry (apprehensive expectation) about life circumstances (e.g., misfortune to one's child, worry about finances) (American Psychiatric Association, 1987). There must be associated symptoms of motor tension, autonomic hyperactivity, and/or vigilance and scanning (6 out of a list of 18 symptoms). Chronic worry in this population focuses on possible future negative or traumatic events and methods of coping with them (Barlow, 1988). In other words, this type of anxiety is anticipatory (Barlow, 1988). Thus we have a contrast between the rapid onset, phasic, acute anxiety of panic disorder versus the chronic, worrying, future-oriented anxiety of generalized anxiety disorder.

BARLOW'S THEORY OF PANIC DISORDER AND GENERALIZED ANXIETY DISORDER

As indicated above, Barlow (1988) has presented an ambitious theory of the nature and etiology of panic disorder and generalized anxiety disorder. The starting point in this theory is Barlow's distinction between two types of anxiety, which he calls *anxiety* and *fear.* Anxiety prepares the organism to cope with the challenges and stresses of everyday life. Invoking the Yerkes-Dodson law, Barlow (1988) suggests that moderate levels of anxiety facilitate performance, whereas higher levels cause deterioration of performance. At least in major respects, this preparatory anxiety resembles Gray's BIS. Both involve anticipation of aversive outcomes (punishment, failure) and produce arousal that invigorates behavior. Although Gray's emphasis on behavioral inhibition is not prominent in Barlow's account of preparatory anxiety, the role of the BIS in conflict situations (approach–avoidance conflict) and in situations of uncertain reward (potential frustration in the form of partial reinforcement schedules) is consistent with Barlow's emphasis on preparation for stresses and challenges, as is Gray's comment that the BIS prepares for vigorous (future) action.

Fear is a massive alarm reaction to potentially life-threatening situations. The most frequent alarm reaction involves strong behavioral and cardiovascular activation, which Barlow (1988) equates with Cannon's (1929) fight-or-flight response. Less frequently, the alarm reaction consists of "freezing" or "tonic immobility" with decreased cardiovascular activity. Fainting is an extreme version of freezing, sometimes seen in simple phobics with fears of blood, injury, and injection, and attributable to a drop in heart rate and blood pressure. For the most part, Barlow (1988) focuses on the behaviorally active version of the alarm reaction, which he calls the ancient alarm reaction of *fear*. Because he equates this alarm reaction with Cannon's fight-or-flight response, there necessarily is considerable overlap with Gray's fight/flight system (see also Barlow, 1988).

Having defined two types of anxiety—called *anxiety* and *fear*—Barlow (1988) relates them to the processes involved in the anxiety disorders. To begin with, panic attacks are viewed as alarm reactions. An alarm reaction that occurs in response to a life-threatening event is a "true alarm." When this same reaction occurs without such an event, it is a "false alarm." Thus an uncued panic attack is a false alarm. These false alarms are almost identical to true alarms phenomenologically, except that the person cannot identify an antecedent triggering event; that is, false alarms also include a sudden burst of anxiety accompanied by somatic symptoms and by a fear of dying and/or losing control. Barlow (1988) argues that false alarms constitute an intense unconditioned stimulus (UCS), one intense enough to bring about one-trial conditioning.

Panic attacks, cued or uncued, are common both among patients with anxiety disorders and in the general population—that is, they are not limited to patients with panic disorder. Among 108 consecutive patients with a diagnosis of anxiety or affective disorder, at least 83% in each diagnostic category reported having had a panic attack (defined as "a sudden rush of intense fear or anxiety or feelings of impending doom"), and at least 75% also met the four-symptom criterion from DSM-III. (The diagnostic categories in this study included panic with agoraphobia, panic disorder, social phobia, simple phobia, generalized anxiety disorder, obsessive-compulsive disorder, and major depression.) In the general population, surveys have found that about 35% of the population report at least one cued or uncued panic attack within the last year. The cued panic attacks were associated with such situations as public speaking, interpersonal conflict, high stress, and tests and examinations. Perhaps of greatest interest, Rapee, Ancis, and Barlow (1987) found that about 14% of the population has experienced uncued panic or false alarms (Barlow, 1988).

These dual assumptions—that uncued panic is common in the population and that it constitutes a powerful UCS for further conditioning—permit the development of a theory of panic disorder. The traditional behavioral approach to understanding the learning of phobias, and also of uncued panic attacks, is to invoke a past traumatic event. This traumatic event is hypothesized to act as the UCS, with any associated stimuli becoming CSs for future attacks of anxiety. A major problem with this hypothesis has been the difficulty of obtaining evidence of such traumatic conditioning. The two major variations on this theme have been the preparedness hypothesis and the suggestion that fear conditioning can occur through observational learning (Mineka, 1985). The preparedness hypothesis, dating from Seligman (1971), argues that through a process of evolutionary selection we are prepared to condition fear more readily to some objects (e.g., snakes, spiders) than to others. This hypothesis has inspired a large number of laboratory studies of classical conditioning to presumably prepared stimuli versus neutral stimuli (e.g., Cook, Hodes, & Lang, 1986; Ohman, Erixon, & Lofburg, 1975; Pitman & Orr, 1986). The extension of the conditioning hypothesis to observational learning, documented in an elegant series of experiments with primates by Mineka (Cook & Mineka, 1989; Cook, Mineka, Wolkenstein, & Laitsch, 1985; Mineka & Cook, 1986; Mineka, Davidson, Cook, & Keir, 1984), greatly expands the opportunities to acquire fears from adult models. Even with these changes, the conditioning model has not been able to account for all fears seen in the clinic, and this has been especially true in the case of panic attacks.

Barlow (1988) suggests that false alarms—the initial uncued panic attacks—*may* serve as the "missing link" in this approach (p. 228)—a replacement for the elusive hypothesized traumatic event. That is, no external traumatic event is necessary to account for learned fear. The initial traumatic event may be an unlearned, uncued panic attack. This panic attack constitutes the UCS for conditioning, leading to conditioned panic attacks or "learned alarms" as Barlow calls them. (See Gray, 1987, pp. 365–366, for a similar proposal that panic attacks may serve as a UCS and that the fight/flight system is implicated in panic attacks.)

In the case of simple phobias, either a true alarm or a false alarm may serve as the initial event. If the alarm is true, the traditional conditioning model adequately explains the conditioned anxiety. If the alarm is false, the individual may nevertheless condition the response to whatever external stimuli are present and salient. This conditioning is more likely to happen with prepared stimuli, such as small animals. In vicarious or observational conditioning, the intensity of the model's fear elicits similarly strong alarm in the observer. It is the strength of the observer's alarm reaction that predicts future phobic behavior (Barlow, 1988).

An important additional factor in many initial episodes of panic is a feeling of being trapped. The nature of the ancient alarm reaction of fear is to produce flight or escape. Blocking escape will intensify and prolong the alarm, with a subsequent facilitation of learning. Examples of this are fears of flying or driving, in which the initial false alarm occurred while flying or driving, causing the person to feel unable to escape. There is no particular purpose to the impulse to escape, because there is no objective threat, but escape is a very strong component of the alarm reaction and is therefore a compelling concern during the alarm. Having this survival-based impulse blocked greatly increases the severity of the trauma.

In the case of panic disorder, there is no obvious external cue for the panic attacks. Citing the literature on interoceptive conditioning (Martin, 1983; Razran, 1961), in which internal physiological cues become conditioned stimuli for anxiety, Barlow (1988) suggests that uncued panic attacks derive from learning an association between an initial false alarm and internal cues. A similar proposal was offered by Mineka (1985). Thus uncued panic attacks actually are just as cued as phobic panic attacks, but the cues are less obvious. In support of this hypothesis, a large literature documents the sensitivity of panic patients to internal physiological cues (Barlow, 1988). This conditioning to internal cues is most likely to take place in the absence of salient external stimuli, such as prepared stimuli or stimuli that prevent escape. Consequently, interoceptive conditioning is more likely to occur when the initial false alarm is experienced at home, where the absence of external cues allows attention to be directed to the internal cues associated with the panic attack (Barlow, 1988). An intermediate case occurs where the initial false alarm occurs outside the home but in the absence of obvious phobic stimuli, which is associated with the development of panic with agoraphobia (Barlow, 1988).

In panic disorder, it is obvious that patients fear the reoccurrence of the uncued panic attack. Even with simple animal phobias, however, interviews with patients revealed that it was not attack from the animal they feared that concerned them. Rather, they feared another panic attack and its consequences, should they be unable to avoid the phobic stimulus. Thus in both panic disorder and simple phobias, patients are primarily anxious about future panic or false alarms. In simple phobias, this fear leads to passive avoidance of the external conditioned stimulus. In panic with agoraphobia, this fear leads them to avoid situations in which they would feel trapped in the event of a panic attack or in which it would be embarrassing to have a panic attack, and to seek places in which and people with whom it is safe to experience a panic attack.

The conditioning model presented above accounts for the occurrence of learned alarms in the population, but Barlow (1988) suggests that something more is needed to account for the development of a panic disorder. Many individuals experience learned and/or unlearned alarm reactions, yet they are not disabled by them and do not seek treatment. The difference between these nonclinical panickers and those who seek treatment, he proposes, is that the latter become anxiously apprehensive about possible future panic attacks. That is, panic disorder develops in individuals who experience learned and/or unlearned alarms and who also have temperaments involving a high degree of preparatory anxiety (anxious apprehension). This point brings us to a more extensive discussion of preparatory anxiety.

Barlow (1988) refers to the anxiety associated with the preparatory or organizing function of anxiety as *anxious apprehension* and views it as the process underlying generalized anxiety disorder. Anxious apprehension is a complex phenomenon involving several features. First, Barlow (1988) assumes a continuity between pathological anxiety and the trait of mild generalized anxiety. This trait is variously called *nervousness* or *emotionality* and is reflected in the factor of anxiety or neuroticism on self-report measures of personality. Second, anxious apprehension consists of a diffuse cognitive–affective structure including negative affect, high arousal, perceptions of helplessness or uncontrollability of future events, and the allocation of attention to negatively valenced self-evaluative concerns and/or the autonomic correlates of the arousal itself. Following Borkovec (1985) and Sarason (1985), this focusing of attention on negative affective material is called worry. The internal focus of attention is believed to be a particularly important contributor to performance decrements. Finally, this anxious apprehension often will have become associated with so many different situational contexts that effective avoidance is precluded, that is, there will be no clear stimulus and the anxiety will appear to be free-floating.

The connection between panic disorder and anxious apprehension is suggested particularly by three observations. First, marked generalized anxiety is characteristic of almost all panic disorder patients (Barlow, Blanchard, Vermilyea, Vermilyea, & Di Nardo, 1986), that is, most of these patients are severely anxious even when not experiencing panic attacks. Second, across a wide range of techniques for inducing panic attacks in panic disorder patients in the laboratory, the best predictor of which patients develop a panic attack is a high level of baseline anxiety, indicated by self-reports of anxiety and high heart rates. Barlow (1988) argues that this combination of subjective apprehension and high autonomic arousal serves as a necessary "platform" for panic attacks (p. 155), and that panic may "spike off" such a baseline of high anxiety (p. 177, 220). Third, as mentioned previously, panic disorder patients are apprehensively anxious about future alarm reactions. Taken together, these observations suggest that among those individuals who experience alarm reactions (cued or uncued), only those with high levels of the trait of anxious apprehension will develop a panic disorder.

Finally, Barlow (1988) offers a vulnerability–stress model for the etiology of anxious apprehension (or generalized anxiety disorder). The vulnerability risk factors include a high level of biologically based stress reactivity of genetic origin, perceptions that the alarms and/or negative events are neither predictable nor controllable, an absence of good coping skills, and inadequate social support.

THE PERCEPTION OF CONTROL

From a psychological perspective the perception of uncontrollability is a particularly interesting risk factor, especially with regard to its developmental antecedents. That is, the experiential determinants of a generalized perception of lack of control constitute a major psychological contribution to the etiology of anxious apprehension. The development of a sense of mastery and control has widely been thought to depend on success during early development in controlling the environment, especially the social environment (Mineka, 1985; Mineka & Kelly, 1989). Even though highly suggestive, the evidence for this proposal has been entirely correlational in nature. For that reason, Mineka, Gunnar, and Champoux's (1986) experimental manipulation of control in a study with rhesus monkeys is critically important.

The monkeys were raised with peers in groups of four. Between the ages of 6 and 11 months, the master groups could operate manipulanda at specific times to deliver a variety of reinforcers. The yoked control groups received the reinforcers at the same time, but had no control over them. Between the ages of 6.5 and 11 months, the groups were tested in several ways to determine the effects of a history of control or lack thereof. The master group monkeys showed:

1. Less fear of a toy monster placed in front of the home cage.
2. More exploratory behavior in a novel environment.
3. Better adaptation to an intruder test. As intruders, they explored the environment more and ate and drank more. As hosts, they showed fewer fearful and submissive behaviors to the intruder.

These results support the hypothesis that a history of control exerts a general effect of diminishing the impact of threatening situations. Mineka et al. (1986) and Mineka and Kelly (1989) also emphasize that this result was obtained even when the mastery was over appetitive events and inanimate aspects of the environment, which the researchers see as a more stringent test of the hypothesis. As Mineka and Kelley (1989) assert, this experiment strongly suggests that an early history of control may reduce vulnerability to developing anxiety disorders in adulthood. That is, a history of control reduces vulnerability to current stressors, which, in turn, reduces the risk of developing anxiety disorders.

Additionally, Mineka and Kelley (1989) review studies indicating that there is greater anxiety in response to controllable than to uncontrollable current stressors. One approach to this question has been the induction of "experimental neurosis" in animals. The common element in these studies is that "environmental events of vital importance to the organism became unpredictable, uncontrollable, or both" (Mineka & Kelly, p. 171; see also Mineka & Kihlstrom, 1978). A second approach to examining the beneficial effects of control employs master and yoked animals, in which both receive the same shock but only the masters can terminate it. The yoked animals show much greater fear conditioning, as indicated by freezing in response to the conditioned stimulus. Both effects have been replicated widely. Thus extensive research employing two rather different paradigms converge to confirm the beneficial effects of perception of control over current stressors.

In view of the conclusions reached above, one can assert that negative expectancies concerning the efficacy of reward-seeking and punishment-avoiding behavior increase vulnerability to threats of punishment and frustrative nonreward. At least to some extent then, this conclusion points to weak activation of appetitive motivation via reduced expectancies as a contributor to the development of anxiety disorders.

HEART RATE AND ANXIETY

The relationship between heart rate and anxiety should also be addressed. In view of the limitations of verbal self-report, anxiety researchers often have employed measures of autonomic nervous system activity as a means of assessing the physiological component of anxiety. Of the physiological measures, heart rate is the most commonly used. Thus the relationship between anxiety and heart rate is a central issue when considering anxiety disorders. As it happens, basic research on psychological influences on heart rate has challenged the use of heart rate as a simple index of anxiety.

In 1976, Obrist concluded that cardiac acceleration did not reflect anxiety, but rather was to be seen when the organism is actively coping with a threatened punishment. A key finding was that heart rate does not accelerate during classical aversive conditioning as long as the animal does not struggle, even though one must assume such conditions produce anxiety. In contrast, cardiac acceleration is seen if the organism believes that instrumental responding can result in avoidance of the shock. Taking off from these findings and borrowing Gray's motivational constructs, I (1980, 1982) proposed that heart rate is tied more strongly to the appetitive motivational system than to the aversive motivational system (see also Fowles, 1988). It was suggested that anxiety-induced drive contributes to the cardiac acceleration seen in Obrist's active coping tasks, but that heart rate is also influenced by the subject's tendency to avoid actively the anxiety-provoking situation (Fowles, 1982). Heart rate is not, it was argued, a simple index of anxiety.

Barlow's (1988) review contributes a new element to this analysis. If he is correct in viewing panic as a primitive fight/flight alarm reaction, strong cardiac acceleration is to be expected in connection with the strongly motivated somatic activity. Data confirm this expectation: during both naturally occurring and induced panic attacks, there is a strong tendency toward cardiac acceleration (Barlow, 1988). In a major study by Taylor et al. (1986), heart rate was monitored during daily activities and patients reported both panic attacks and anticipatory anxiety (Barlow, 1988). When the two types of anxiety were matched on rated intensity, it was found that heart rate during anticipatory anxiety showed little increase and was significantly lower than that seen in connection with panic attacks. From this evidence it appears that there is greater cardiac acceleration during activation of the fight/flight system than during activation of the aversive motivational system, even when rated intensity is matched.

On the other hand, baseline differences in heart rate between anxiety patients and controls were reported by Liebowitz et al. (1985): 84 BPM for patients who panicked during the experiment, 75.3 BPM for patients who did not panic, and 62.8 BPM for controls (Barlow, 1988). To what can these elevated heart rates be attributed in the absence of panic, that is, when the patient is at rest? As suggested above, it may be that it is the combination of anxiety and action tendencies (active avoidance) that results in cardiac acceleration in these patients. Support for this proposal comes from comparison of anxiety and depression. Citing evidence from Riskind, Beck, Brown, and Steer (1987), Barlow (1988) concludes that anxiety involves "engagement and activation" and "implies effort to cope with difficult situations, and the physiology is there to support active attempts at coping" (p. 69; see also p. 277 for a similar statement). Depression, in contrast, involves "disengagement and inactivity" and "is characterized by behavioral retardation and an associated lack of physiology" (p. 69). These conclusions, in combination with Obrist's research, suggest that action tendencies contribute to the elevation of cardiovascular activity in anxiety patients. Thus it still seems reasonable to suggest that coping tendencies contribute to the cardiac acceleration in anxiety disorders. What is needed is a method of separately assessing the severity of negative affect and the strength of action tendencies in order to determine their relative contributions to heart rate. Perhaps patients would be able to report these two components with reasonable accuracy. For example, they might be asked how anxious they were when they came to the experiment, and to what extent they felt an impulse to leave. Alternatively, it might be possible to compare the heart rates of anxious and (retarded) depressed patients who were matched on the level of negative affect. Differences in heart rate would presumably reflect differential action tendencies.

MOTIVATIONAL HYPOTHESES
AND THE ANXIETY DISORDERS

To return to the original question, it appears that motivational concepts are quite valuable in understanding anxiety disorders. Two motivational systems are critically important for understanding these disorders: (a) Barlow's fear or alarm reaction and Gray's fight/flight system, and (b) Barlow's (preparatory) anxiety and Gray's behavioral inhibition system. Although Gray and Barlow use somewhat different names for these two systems and sometimes describe them in somewhat different ways, it is clear that the concepts are essentially very similar.

Although both systems can be said to be involved in anxiety, they have very different properties. Perhaps the sharpest contrast is the temporal dimension: the fight/flight system is concerned with an imminent threat and with mobilization of bodily resources for vigorous behavior in the present, whereas the BIS is concerned with the anticipation of and preparation for future threats. The second major contrast is in the effects on behavior, the BIS producing behavioral inhibition in contrast to the vigorous behavior associated with fight/flight. Finally, the vigilance and worry associated with BIS activity are not seen in fight/flight system reactions. Thus when studying anxiety disorders it is important to consider which type of anxiety is involved.

A major advantage of adopting the motivational approach to understanding psychopathology is the link it provides to neurophysiological substrates, making possible an integration of psychological approaches with genetic and especially pharmacological approaches. This advantage is particularly true of Gray's (1987) theorizing, because such integration is a major focus of his writing. The link between anxiolytic drugs and diminished BIS activity has already been mentioned. Another example is Gray's (1987) suggestion that anxiolytic drugs do not affect panic attacks, because these are mediated by the fight/flight system; antidepressant drugs do control them by facilitating serotonergic transmission which, in turn, causes inhibition of the central gray of the midbrain (involved in the fight/flight response).

Thus the motivational perspective facilitates an integrated and therefore more comprehensive model of anxiety disorders. Generalized anxiety disorder is seen as a manifestation of anxious apprehension, an anxious temperament reflecting stronger reactions of the preparatory anxiety system (or BIS), combined with stress, perceptions of lack of control, poor coping skills, and lack of social support. A prior developmental history of control over reinforcements lends a generalized sense of perceived control, providing protection against severe anxiety reactions. Conversely, a history of lack of control constitutes a vulnerability factor when facing current stress.

Panic disorder derives from a combination of uncued alarm reactions (fight/flight system) and anxious apprehension such that individuals with anxious apprehension become morbidly concerned about future panic attacks. As a result of this conditioned anxiety, internal physiological cues come to serve as conditioned stimuli for future panic attacks. Similarly, when external stimuli are conditioned, the fear of panic attacks leads to passive avoidance, as in the case of agoraphobia and simple phobias. This approach to panic disorder accounts for the co-morbidity of panic attacks and generalized anxiety so often seen in patients. A simple medical model approach that treats generalized anxiety disorder and panic disorder as two discrete diseases has difficulty explaining this co-morbidity.

Finding parallels between Barlow's (1988) theory of anxiety disorders and Gray's (1987) motivational approach to anxiety enriches both perspectives. Barlow's (1988) review is more thorough and sophisticated on the clinical side, whereas Gray's (1987) is more thorough and sophisticated with respect to the behavioral and physiological aspects. Integrating the two perspectives offers the hope of a fully integrated psychobiological theory in the future, one in which the neurophysiological substrates for a variety of important clinical phenomena are delineated and both environmental and pharmacological influences are understood.

REFERENCES

American Psychiatric Association (1987). *Diagnostic and statistical manual of mental disorders* (3rd ed.). Washington, DC: Author.

Barlow, D. H. (1988). *Anxiety and its disorders: The nature and treatment of anxiety and panic.* New York: Guilford Press.

Barlow, D. H., Blanchard, E. B., Vermilyea, J. A., Vermilyea, B. B., & Di Nardo, P. A. (1986). Generalized anxiety and generalized anxiety disorder: Description and reconceptualization. *American Journal of Psychiatry, 143*, 40–44.

Borkovec, T. D. (1985). The role of cognitive and somatic cues in anxiety and anxiety disorders: Worry and relaxation-induced anxiety. In A. H. Tuma & J. D. Maser (Eds.), *Anxiety and anxiety disorders*. Hillsdale, NJ: Lawrence Erlbaum.

Cannon, W. B. (1929). *Bodily changes in pain, hunger, fear, and rage* (2nd ed.). New York: Appleton-Century-Crofts.

Cook, E. W., III, Hodes, R. L., & Lang, P. J. (1986). Preparedness and phobia: Effects of stimulus content on human visceral conditioning. *Journal of Abnormal Psychology, 95*, 195–207.

Cook, M., & Mineka, S. (1989). Observational conditioning of fear to fear-relevant versus fear-irrelevant stimuli in rhesus monkeys. *Journal of Abnormal Psychology, 98*, 448–459.

Cook, M., Mineka, S., Wolkenstein, B., & Laitsch, K. (1985). Observational conditioning of snake fear in unrelated rhesus monkeys. *Journal of Abnormal Psychology, 94*, 591–610.

Fowles, D. C. (1980). The three arousal model: Implications of Gray's two-factor learning theory for heart rate, electrodermal activity, and psychopathy. *Psychophysiology, 17*, 87–104.

Fowles, D. C. (1982). Heart rate as an index of anxiety: Failure of a hypothesis. In J. T. Cacioppo & R. E. Petty (Eds.), *Perspectives in cardiovascular psychophysiology* (pp. 93–126). New York: Guilford Press.

Fowles, D. C. (1988). Psychophysiology and psychopathology: A motivational approach. *Psychophysiology, 25*, 373–391.

Gray, J. A. (1977). Drug effects on fear and frustration: Possible limbic site of action of minor tranquilizers. In L. L. Iversen, S. D. Iversen, & S. H. Snyder (Eds.), *Handbook of psychopharmacology: Vol. 8. Drugs, neurotransmitters, and behavior* (pp. 433–529). New York: Plenum.

Gray, J. A. (1982). *The neuropsychology of anxiety: An enquiry into the functions of the septo-hippocampal system*. Oxford: Oxford University Press.

Gray, J. A. (1987). *The psychology of fear and stress* (2nd ed.). Cambridge: Cambridge University Press.

Liebowitz, M. R., Gorman, J. M., Fyer, A. J., Levitt, M., Dillon, D., Levy, P., Appleby, I. L., Anderson, S., Palij, M., Davies, S. O., & Klein, D. F. (1985). Lactate provocation of panic attacks: II. Biochemical and physiological findings. *Archives of General Psychiatry, 42*, 709–719.

Mineka, S. (1985). Animal models of anxiety-based disorders: Their usefulness and limitations. In A. H. Tuma & J. D. Maser (Eds.), *Anxiety and anxiety disorders* (pp. 199–244). Hillsdale, NJ: Lawrence Erlbaum.

Mineka, S., & Cook, M. (1986). Immunization against the observational conditioning of snake fear in Rhesus Monkeys. *Journal of Abnormal Psychology, 95*, 307–318.

Mineka, S., Davidson, M., Cook, M., & Keir, R. (1984). Observational conditioning of snake fear in rhesus monkeys. *Journal of Abnormal Psychology, 93*, 355–372.

Mineka, S., Gunnar, M., & Champoux, M. (1986). Control and early socioemotional development: Infant rhesus monkeys reared in controllable versus uncontrollable environments. *Child Development, 57*, 1241–1256.

Mineka, S., & Kelly, K. A. (1989). The relationship between anxiety, lack of control, and loss of control. In A. Steptoe & A. Appels (Eds.), *Stress, personal control, and worker health*. New York: Wiley.

Mineka, S., & Kihlstrom, J. (1978). Unpredictable and uncontrollable aversive events. *Journal of Abnormal Psychology, 87*, 256–271.

Obrist, P. A. (1976). The cardiovascular-behavioral interaction—as it appears today. *Psychophysiology, 13*, 95–107.

Ohman, A., Erixon, G., & Lofburg, I. (1975). Phobias and preparedness: Phobic versus neutral pictures as conditional stimuli for human autonomic responses. *Journal of Abnormal Psychology, 84*, 41–45.

Pitman, R. K., & Orr, S. P. (1986). Test of the conditioning model of neurosis: Differential aversive conditioning of angry and neutral facial expressions in anxiety disorder patients. *Journal of Abnormal Psychology, 95*, 208–213.

Rapee, R. M., Ancis, J., & Barlow, D. H. (1988). Emotional reactions to physiological sensations: Comparison of panic disorder and nonclinical subjects. *Behaviour Research and Therapy, 26*, 265–270.

Riskind, J. H., Beck, A. T., Brown, G. B., & Steer, R. A. (1987). Taking the measure of anxiety and depression: Validity of reconstructed Hamilton Scales. *Journal of Nervous and Mental Disease,* *175,* 474–479.

Sarason, I. G. (1985). Cognitive processes, anxiety, and the treatment of anxiety disorders. In A. H. Tuma & J. D. Maser (Eds.), *Anxiety and anxiety disorders* (pp. 87–107). Hillsdale, NJ: Lawrence Erlbaum.

Seligman, M. E. P. (1971). Phobias and preparedness. *Behavior Therapy, 2,* 307–320.

Taylor, C. B., Sheikh, J., Agras, W. S., Roth, W. T., Margraf, J., Ehlers, A., Maddock, R. J., & Gossard, D. (1986). Self-report of panic attacks: Agreement with heart rate changes. *American Journal of Psychiatry, 143,* 478–482.

14

Emotional Quality of Life
After Myocardial Infarction

Tadeusz M. Ostrowski
Jagiellonian University, Poland

The quality of life of people who have suffered severe illness is an important problem, one that should be the subject of multidisciplinary research, including the fields of medicine, sociology, philosophy, and psychology (Mayou, Bryant, & Turner, 1990; Moody, McCormick, & Williams, 1990). Many dimensions should be taken into consideration, including physical status (physical capabilities, improvement in treatment and rehabilitation), psychological characterization, social behavior (realization of social roles, extension of social support), and economic aspects of life (Bech, 1987).

Psychological issues related to quality of life are many; they include, for example, cognitive systems (self-concept, world concept), emotions (anxiety, depression, aggression, fatigue, irritability), emotional–cognitive structures such as self-attitude and attitude toward illness (Ostrowski & Sniezek-Maciejewska, 1983), intellectual and psychophysiological variables (memory, alertness, visual latency), and changes in personality as a result of illness.

The quality of life should be examined from a positive viewpoint that emphasizes, among other things, psychological well-being, and takes into account a healthy emotional and intellectual state, an optimistic attitude toward the future, and ensures that the patient has enough energy to realize life plans. Bech (1987) has stated that in the majority of relevant research, quality of life usually is pictured as a negative variable. However, applied research is based on the real problems of people who come to psychologists or physicians; such people typically are unhappy.

These same considerations are relevant to the present study. Our approach to quality of life is positive; nevertheless, operationalization of our research plan to actual measures resulted in an emphasis on anxiety and hostility. Even a presumably neutral variable such as attitude toward illness has assumed a negative meaning in patients in terms of anxiety or denial of illness.

The main goal of our study was to focus on the emotional aspects of the quality of life in people suffering myocardial infarction without complication (MI) in comparison with people after infarction complicated with ventricular fibrillation,

The author is grateful to the late Professor Wladyslaw Krol, M.D., Maria Sniezek-Maciejewska, M.D., and the staff of the First Cardlological Hospital of the School of Medicine in Cracow for their support in conducting this research program.

which has resulted in the state of clinical death for at least a brief period (CMI).

Our main expectation was that an event such as clinical death would have some implications for the psychological components of the quality of life, which would remain long after restoration of life. We felt that such effects could be measured as significant differences in pertinent dependent variables between MI and CMI patients for at least a few years following myocardial infarction. Thus the independent variable in the study was the kind of infarction experienced, complicated or noncomplicated, that is, with or without clinical death.

This study was stimulated by our observations of the Cardiological Institute in Cracow, Poland. After reanimation, patients seemed to be different: more anxious, less ready to perform rehabilitation exercises involving effort, but more willing to cooperate with staff in medical and psychological matters, including research.

METHOD

Subjects

This investigation was carried out on a group of 51 people who had experienced myocardial infarction. Of them, 23 had had infarctions complicated with ventricular fibrillation (Group CMI), and 28 had noncomplicated infarctions (Group MI). The groups are comparable in gender, age, education, and time since infarction (see Table 1). Their myocardial infarctions had occurred from 1 to 8 years before this study was conducted.

All CMI subjects had experienced clinical death and had undergone reanimation, and each had been informed about it. The reanimation had been performed on the street for 7 people, in the hospital immediately after reception for 11 patients, and during their stay in the hospital for 5 patients.

The period of unconsciousness after effective reanimation varied. It lasted less than 1 minute for 10 patients, less than 10 minutes for 3 patients, less than 1 hour for 3 patients, from 2 to 3 hours for 3 patients, about 20 hours for 1 patient, from 2 to 3 days for 2 patients, and for about 3 weeks for 1 patient.

Materials

Each subject was given a standardized interview, which included questions about the history of illness, current somatic and neurotic disorders, and family, occupational, and social circumstances. As part of the interview procedure, the following test data were collected.

The State Trait Anxiety Inventory (STAI) (Sosnowski & Wrzesniewski, 1983; Spielberger, Gorsuch, & Lushene, 1970) was used to measure anxiety level. The Eysenck Personality Questionnaire (EPQ) (Eysenck & Eysenck, 1975) was used to measure extraversion, neuroticism, psychoticism, and lie. The Hostility–Guilt Inventory developed by Buss (1961) was used as a measure of aggression and guilt awareness.

We also used the Attitude Towards Illness Questionnaire (ATI), which was prepared by Wrzesniewski (1975), and consists of 70 items. It has been used to assess the emotional and cognitive components of that attitude. There are two separate scales: The emotional component is estimated as a whole score and as

Table 1 Demographic information for the two patient groups

Variable	CMI	MI	t
n	23	28	
Gender:			
Male	19	24	
Female	4	4	
Age:			
M	58.30	57.25	.41
SD	9.32	9.19	
Education:			
Primary	9	10	
Secondary	10	13	
University	4	5	
Time since infarction:			
M	2.99	3.86	1.43
SD	1.62	2.50	
n^a	20	20	
Gender:			
Male	16	16	
Female	4	4	
Age:			
M	57.88	54.69	1.04
SD	8.85	8.80	
Education:			
Primary	8	6	
Secondary	9	11	
University	3	3	
Time since infarction:			
M	2.94	4.00	1.29
SD	1.89	2.79	

[a]The groups after the 11 subjects with high lie score have been removed.

scores on subscales, including accepting the diagnosis and treatment, sense of wrong after falling ill, anxiety towards the future, current mood, demanding care from other people, and level of anxiety. The cognitive component is estimated by tapping general knowledge about illness.

Procedure

The investigation was carried out within the Medical School of Cracow at the First Hospital of Cardiology. The patients were invited to undergo a follow-up examination at the hospital from 1 to 8 years after their infarction.

RESULTS

ANOVA analyses were accomplished for each scale score, with components being type of infarction (CMI/MI), gender, and their interaction. Results indicate that there are significant differences between the MI and CMI groups on state and trait anxiety (see Table 2). That analysis was done on all 51 subjects, divided into the two groups. The gender effect was not significant. For the extraversion scale, only the interaction of CMI/MI and gender was significant. The only other significant finding was that for time since infarction. Such limited results were inconsistent with our observations of these patient groups.

According to Eysenck and Eysenck's (1975) prescriptions for the interpretation of the EPQ, subjects with extremely high scores on the lie scale are likely to have invalidated all their EPQ scales, and perhaps other data from these persons should be regarded with great caution. On this basis, we excluded all subjects with lie scores equal to or above 8 sten (11 subjects), and were left with two comparable 20-person groups (see Table 1). We repeated the ANOVA analyses on these smaller groups and these results are presented in Table 3. As seen there, several significant differences between the CMI and MI groups were found in the ANOVA analysis. Significant effects were not found for gender or the interaction of CMI/MI and gender for any variables and hence these results are not reported.

The CMI and MI groups differ significantly on the measures of state anxiety ($p < .004$) and trait anxiety ($p < .0009$). These scores are higher in the CMI group. The neuroticism score is also significantly higher in this group ($p < .013$).

The attitude toward illness is significantly worse in the CMI group ($p < .002$). A component of that attitude—current mood—is also significant in the same direction ($p < .04$). The CMI group also has more anxiety about another infarction and less knowledge about illness ($p < .007$). The scale of knowledge is a separate one, but its questions are related strongly to the emotional component of that attitude.

Time Since Infarction and Quality of Life

The objective of the second part of our analyses was to evaluate the relationship of time since infarction to the 12 dependent variables of the study to see if there might be a different pattern of relationship between the CMI and the MI groups. Initially we used a linear regression model, but only the relationship between time and extraversion turned out to be significant ($r = -0.46; F = 8.15, p < .008$). We then tested other regression shapes, including quadratic, cubic, logarithmic, compound, and exponential. Most relationships were best described by the quadratic function. Multiple R, estimated from the polynomial regression model, was the measure of the adequacy of the regression line, and significance of R was tested by ANOVA. Results of these analyses are given in Table 4.

The regression lines between time since infarction and measures of the emotional quality of life are different for the two patient groups. Although the relatively small size of each of the two samples ($n = 20$) makes any far-reaching interpretation of the shapes of these regression lines questionable, the results are quite interesting.

In the CMI group there was a systematic increasing trend over time in trait anxiety, whereas the trends for extraversion and knowledge about illness decreased for this group. In the MI group, significant quadratic trends were found for anxiety about the future and for mood. In both cases there is a decrease in score until about the fifth year after infarction, and then an increase.

Table 2 Results of the ANOVA analysis

Variable	CMI		MI		ANOVA[a]
	M	SD	M	SD	F
State anxiety	43.43	10.77	36.93	11.21	4.26*
Trait anxiety	45.91	6.28	40.36	8.90	6.14**
Lie scale	15.65	4.38	16.79	5.74	.59
Neuroticism	24.52	11.92	20.32	9.67	1.90
Extraversion	25.74	8.71	27.25	5.99	.51
Psychoticism	13.43	4.80	11.46	3.91	2.76
Aggression	50.65	18.95	53.96	22.64	.29
Attitude toward illness	96.35	26.62	108.57	37.84	1.64
Knowledge about illness	17.82	7.49	20.86	7.06	2.15
Anxiety about the future[b]	6.78	3.68	7.39	4.21	.05
Anxiety about another infarction[b]	2.61	1.88	4.18	2.57	5.72**
Mood	39.90	8.70	41.53	9.20	.07

Note. Results are based on all 51 MI subjects broken down into complicated MI (CMI) and uncomplicated (MI) subgroups.

[a]A column for gender results is not included because no significant gender effects were found for any variable. In addition, only one significant interaction effect was found, that for MI/CMI × gender for the extraversion scale ($F = 4.03$). *$p < .05$; **$p < .02$.

[b]Lower numbers indicate higher anxiety.

DISCUSSION

Our hypothesis about a possible difference in the emotional quality of life in these two groups of patients is confirmed by these results, including the measures of state and trait anxiety, neuroticism, introversion, and attitude toward illness (both emotional and cognitive aspects). The emotional aspects of quality of life a

Table 3 Results of the ANOVA analysis

Variable	CMI		MI		ANOVA[a]
	M	SD	M	SD	F
State anxiety	44.47	12.12	33.06	8.00	9.36***
Trait anxiety	46.94	6.15	37.56	6.22	17.57***
Lie scale	14.59	4.05	13.94	5.10	.06
Neuroticism	27.76	9.55	20.44	9.10	3.08**
Extraversion	25.53	10.06	27.75	6.78	.34
Psychoticism	14.18	5.03	12.06	4.78	1.96
Aggression	56.35	13.12	56.25	23.70	.01
Attitude toward illness	98.12	16.05	123.37	24.08	11.57***
Knowledge about illness	17.82	6.86	23.00	5.45	5.33*
Anxiety about the future[b]	8.06	2.11	9.44	2.34	3.53
Anxiety about another infarction[b]	2.70	2.02	5.00	2.39	8.01**
Mood	40.06	8.78	46.62	8.26	4.50*

Note. Results of analysis are after the 11 subjects with high lie scores had been removed. $N = 20$ in each group.

[a]A column for gender results is not included because no significant gender effects were found.

[b]Lower numbers indicate higher anxiety.

*$p < .05$; **$p < .02$; ***$p < .005$.

Table 4 Estimation of quadratic regression (multiple R and F tests) between time after infarction and each of the emotional and personality variables

	CMI		MI	
Variable	R	F	R	F
State anxiety	.31	.76	.36	.95
Trait anxiety	.73	8.13***	.21	.31
Lie scale	.19	.27	.49	2.05
Neuroticism	.12	.10	.20	.29
Extraversion	.64	4.97**	.44	1.55
Psychoticism	.44	1.69	.27	.51
Aggression	.41	1.42	.44	1.53
Attitude toward illness	.32	.83	.51	2.31
Knowledge about illness	.58	3.57*	.28	.56
Anxiety about the future	.23	.41	.60	3.61*
Anxiety about another infarction	.12	.11	.16	.16
Mood	.36	1.07	.65	4.66*

$*p < .05; **p < .02; ***p < .005.$

few years after infarction is worse for CMI patients than for MI patients. But the question we were interested in was the influence of clinical death as a traumatic event in promoting these differences. That question cannot be answered directly on the basis of our data, but indirect suggestions are present.

A higher level of trait anxiety and neuroticism might be expected for CMI persons before the beginning of their disease. That would be in keeping with psychosomatic hypotheses concerning the etiology of ventricular fibrillation, which have been verified experimentally on both animal and human subjects (Corbalan, Verrier, & Lown, 1974; Lown, DeSilva, & Lenson, 1978; Lown, Verrier, & Rabinowitz, 1977; Skinner, Lie, & Entman, 1975). The general conclusion of these studies is that emotional stress can induce a significant decrease in the threshold of ventricular fibrillation. Our results support this position.

In addition to the differences we found on personality measures (state anxiety, neuroticism), there are additional data from the interviews we conducted. For example, job satisfaction of CMIs before illness appears to be significantly lower than for MIs ($\chi^2 = 6.32$, $n = 40$, $p < .05$) (Krol, Sniezek, & Ostrowski, 1981).

Our results also indicate that the experience of clinical death has a clear influence on the attitude toward illness. It was considerably worse in the CMI group in both emotional and cognitive dimensions. The traumatic influence of complicated infarction is greater than that of noncomplicated infarction. All the CMI patients had been informed about reanimation. They knew that the recurrence of ventricular fibrillation was possible at any moment—during the next infarction or without infarction—so they were more anxiety-ridden about their disease than the MI patients. That anxiety had been projected generally to the future. It is possible, of course, that the emotional consequences of a traumatic event such as complicated infarction had overlaid the more anxious personality of people prone to ventricular fibrillation.

Gender did not seem to contribute to the effects that we observed. This may be due to the number of females studied relative to the number of males, but this proportion (1:5) is quite typical for the population of MI cases.

The regression lines that we obtained on the time variable permitted us to examine the direction of change on our dependent variables across time since infarction, from 1 to 8 years. Five variables were correlated significantly with time: trait anxiety, extraversion, knowledge about illness, anxiety about the future, and mood. With time increase since infarction, the CMI patient has a higher level of trait anxiety, is more introverted, and his or her knowledge about illness decreases. Changes after noncomplicated infarction seem to be parabolic. With more time after infarction, anxiety about the future in the MI patient group decreases, but only for a few years, and then significantly increases. The same is true for the mood measure for this group.

It is difficult to explain why only these five variables were correlated significantly with time, and further research is required to corroborate and explicate these results.

The increase in trait anxiety across time in the CMI group was surprising. Wrzesniewski (1986) has reported that the level of state anxiety is highest in the hospital immediately after infarction, that it goes down during hospitalization, and that it increases again before discharge. He further reports that state anxiety decreases again during rehabilitation in a sanitarium. However, in his study trait anxiety did not change significantly in the period of hospital and posthospital treatment. The present study dealt only with the early period after infarction. Research performed by Myrtek (1987) studied the period after infarction and was more similar to our research than Wrzesniewski's research was. Myrtek (1987) found that life satisfaction was the most significant variable influencing the resumption of work of 83 cardiac patients. Life satisfaction was studied in terms of health, occupation, financial circumstances, leisure time, spouse/partnership, children, satisfaction with oneself, and sexuality. Except for health and leisure time all these variables decreased meaningfully and significantly ($p < .05$) 1 year after discharge.

The present research adds evidence to the well-known finding that high scores on the Eysenck Lie Scale should be taken into account when one uses self-report data in a research paradigm. Our results have also indicated that people after MI cannot be treated as a single group. Using cluster analysis, Havik and Maeland (1990) have done a 3- to 5-year follow-up study of 283 MI patients and found six groups with different patterns of emotional reaction to disease, including such dimensions as anxiety, depression, and irritability. The majority of these groups showed decreasing measures during follow-up, but one of them, consisting of 45 people (16%), was characterized by increasing measures during follow-up. This means that for them the level of assessed emotions was higher 3 to 5 years after infarction than during hospitalization. Our CMIs displayed a similar pattern of decreasing quality of emotional life. It was necessary to provide psychotherapeutic intervention for some of these patients, beginning in the hospital and continuing in the posthospital period.

REFERENCES

Bech, P. (1987). Quality of life in psychosomatic research: A psychometric model. *Psychopathology, 20,* 169–179.

Buss, A. H. (1961). *The psychology of aggression.* New York: Wiley.

Corbalan, R., Verrier, R., & Lown, B. (1974). Psychologic stress and ventricular arhythmias during myocardial infarction in the conscious dog. *American Journal of Cardiology, 34,* 692–696.

Eysenck, H. J., & Eysenck, S. B. G. (1975). *Manual of the Eysenck personality questionnaire*. London: Hodder & Stoughton.

Havik, O. E., & Maeland, J. G. (1990). Patterns of emotional reactions after a myocardial infarction. *Journal of Psychosomatic Research, 34,* 271–285.

Krol, W., Sniezek, M., & Ostrowski, T. M. (1981). Psychologiczne aspekty smierci klinicznej w przebiegu zawalu miesnia sercowego powiklanego migotaniem komor. *[Psychological aspects of clinical death during myocardial infarction complicated with ventricular fibrillation].* Kardiologia Polska, 24, 333–341.

Lown, B., DeSilva, R. A., & Lenson, R. (1978). Roles of psychological stress and autonomic nervous system changes in provocation of ventricular premature complexes. *American Journal of Cardiology, 41,* 979–985.

Lown, B., Verrier, R. L., & Rabinowitz, S. H. (1977). Neural and psychologic mechanisms and the problem of sudden cardiac death. *American Journal of Cardiology, 39,* 890–902.

Mayou, R., Bryant, B., & Turner, R. (1990). Quality of life in non–insulin-dependent diabetes and a comparison with insulin-dependent diabetes. *Journal of Psychosomatic Research, 34,* 1–11.

Moody, L., McCormick, K., & Williams, A. (1990). Disease and symptom severity, functional status, and quality of life in chronic bronchitis and emphysema (CBE). *Journal of Behavioral Medicine, 13,* 297–306.

Myrtek, M. (1987). Life satisfaction, illness behavior, and rehabilitation outcome: Results of a one year follow-up study with cardiac patients. *International Journal of Rehabilitation Research, 10,* 373–382.

Ostrowski, T. M., & Sniezek-Maciejewska, M. (1983). Postawa wobec choroby u osob po przebytym zawale miesnia serca powiklanego migotaniem komor. [Attitude toward illness in persons after myocardial infarction complicated with ventricular fibrillation]. *Przeglad Psychologiczny, 26,* 925–938.

Skinner, J. E., Lie, J. T., & Entman, M. L. (1975). Modification of ventricular fibrillation latency following coronary artery occlusion in the conscious pig: The effects of psychological stress and beta-adrenergic blockade. *Circulation, 51,* 656–667.

Sosnowski, T., & Wrzesniewski, K. (1983). Polska adaptacja inwentarza STAI do badania stanu i leku cechy. [Polish adaptation of The State-Trait Anxiety Inventory]. *Przeglad Psychologiczny, 26,* 393–412.

Spielberger, C. D., Gorsuch, R. L., & Lushene, R. E. (1970). *Manual for the State Trait Anxiety Inventory.* Palo Alto: Consulting Psychologists Press.

Wrzesniewski, K. (1975). Skala do badania postaw wobec choroby pacjentow po zawale serca. [A scale to study attitudes toward illness of patients after myocardial infarction]. *Studia Psychologiczne, 14,* 99–122.

Wrzesniewski, K. (1986). *Psychologiczne problemy chorych z zawalem serca.* [Psychological problems of myocardial infarction patients. A selection from theory and practice] (2nd ed.). Warsaw: PZWL.

15

Emotional Responses
to Illness Involving High or Low Risk of Life
in Type A Patients

Kazimierz Wrzesniewski
Warsaw Medical Academy, Poland

Any stress situation is directly followed by changes in emotional processes, which affect three aspects of emotion: cognitive, physiological, and behavioral. The present report deals with stress situations that are associated with the occurrence of a somatic illness. From the psychological point of view, any disease and its consequences may be regarded as a stress situation because any disease involves: (a) a more or less marked physical threat, for example, the risk of life or a permanent disability; (b) psychological threat, for example, frustration of many needs or a decreased sense of self-value; and (c) social threat, for example, the possibility of being rejected by one's family or workmates and of having to change one's routine social roles. At the same time, any illness disturbs the usual way of life and imposes upon the individual a certain treatment or rehabilitation regime.

Understandably, the stressful factors suggested above would depend on the type of illness, its course, and prognosis. The study to be presented here deals with emotional responses of patients whose illnesses involve various degrees of risk to life.

According to one theory of stress (Lazarus & Folkman, 1984), people's responses depend not only on the type of stress situation, but also on individual differences. Among the individual factors that can influence reactions to stress, there is the Type A Behavior Pattern (TABP); this term is used here to denote a certain way of regulating the individual's relationship with his or her environment, with the following underlying characteristics: a strong need for achievement, aggressiveness, and a tendency to dominate and control one's environment. Formal characteristics of this type of regulation of the individual's relationship with the environment include a high energy output, speed, hurry, and impatience (Wrzesniewski, 1991).

Reviews of research into how Type A subjects respond to stress situations (Contrada, Krantz, & Hill, 1988; Contrada, Wright, & Glass, 1985; Houston, 1988; Matthews, 1982; Matthews & Haynes, 1986; Pittner, Houston, Spiridigliozzi, 1983) reveal a variety of responses. In the vast majority of studies conducted so far, stress situations were investigated under laboratory conditions.

This work was supported by Grants RPBP.III.25/VI and IIB/36.

Results of these studies are more consistent than findings yielded by research into stress under natural conditions. In studies included in the reviews cited above, physiological and somatic indices were used most often; cognitive indices of emotion were employed less frequently.

Significant differences between emotional responses of TA and TB subjects were found to depend on the type of situation. In neutral or relaxed conditions, there were usually no significant differences. However, such differences emerged in stressful situations involving the TABP syndrome characteristics, for example, situations in which varying degrees of control were possible, situations involving provoked competitiveness or aggression, situations involving time pressure, and so forth. No differences between the responses of TA and TB subjects were noted if a physical stressor was used, for example, the cold pressor test. The choice of physiological–somatic indices of emotions also played a role. Responses of the two groups were found to differ most often on some measures of circulatory and endocrine functioning. TABP assessment by means of the structured interview yielded significant differences more often than that using the Jenkins Activity Survey. In terms of subjects, significant differences in emotional responses were found more frequently in male than in female subjects, and in older rather than in younger age groups.

In the majority of studies in which significant differences were found between the response of TA and TB subjects, emotional responses expressed in terms of physiological and behavioral indices were more pronounced in TA people. Data concerning cognitive aspects of emotions are less clearcut.

No research into the emotional response of TA people to stress caused by the onset and treatment of a somatic illness has been described in any of the reviews cited above.

The aim of the present study was to examine whether TA and TB patients differ in their emotional responses to illnesses involving various degrees of risk to life. The study focused on cognitive aspects of emotions, that is, the subject's awareness of the signs, contents, and intensity of experienced emotions.

Because of the exploratory nature of the study, no detailed hypotheses have been proposed. The results of this research are expected to contribute to a better understanding of the functioning of TA people in stress situations. In addition, the empirical data obtained here may suggest hypotheses for further research, and such data may also be useful in clinical practice.

METHOD

Subjects

Subjects were three groups of patients matched for gender, age, education level, and type of occupation prior to illness. The patients were males aged 35 to 60, with either a secondary or university education; all were white-collar workers.

Group I consisted of 113 patients undergoing sanitarium rehabilitation, following their hospitalization after their first myocardial infarction (MI). The MI was uncomplicated and had occurred within 4 to 12 weeks (mean of 5.6 weeks) prior to their sanitarium admission. The sanitarium rehabilitation lasts 4 weeks and the program is complex, including medication, physical rehabilitation, and psychotherapeutic interventions. Because of their recent MI, this group of patients runs a high risk of sudden death.

Group II was composed of 37 patients who had experienced amputation (AP) of either one (76% of sample) or both legs (24% of sample). The extremities were lost in accidents that had occurred within 12 to 98 weeks (mean of 54.7 weeks) prior to admission to the rehabilitation center. Duration of stay for these patients at the center varied, but amounted to several weeks on an average. The patients undergo physical rehabilitation and psychotherapy. They are not at risk of imminent death.

Group III included 32 patients suffering from various rheumatic diseases (RP), who had been provided a 4-week sanitarium rehabilitation. The onset of their illness was between 52 and 1,030 weeks (mean of 215.6 weeks) prior to their admission. Their rehabilitation involved calisthenics, massages, and balneotherapy. Rheumatic diseases are chronic, but do not involve any direct risk of life.

None of the patients under study suffered from any concomitant disease other than their main illness.

Measures

For the assessment of TABP, an original Polish questionnaire, AATAB Scale, Form B (Wrzesniewski, 1990) was used. According to the theory underlying the questionnaire development, TABP is regarded as the individual's specific mode of regulation of his or her relationship with the environment (Wrzesniewski, 1991). The following variables are considered to be crucial aspects of TABP: a strong need for achievement, aggressiveness, and a tendency to dominate and control one's environment. Formal characteristics of TABP include considerable dynamics of behavior, haste, and impatience. Initially a questionnaire for TABP assessment in children, adolescents, and young adults was designed (Wrzesniewski, Forgays, & Bonaiuto, 1990). With some modification of the scale and the addition of a few items, a new version was developed for adults; the latter consists of 22 items. Each item includes mutually contradictory descriptions denoting two extremes. Between them there is a five-point rating scale on which the subject is to check to what extent his behavior conforms to the descriptions given on the left or on the right of the answer sheet. For each item a single number is circled. The total score is a sum of weights obtained using the response key. The higher the score, the more the subject's behavior tends to conform to the TABP. The questionnaire was standardized on a random sample of 1,438 women and 1,211 men between the ages of 35 and 64. Reliability and validity of the AATAB Scale, Form B, were found to be satisfactory (Wrzesniewski, 1990).

The patients' emotional states were assessed using the Profile of Mood States (POMS) developed by McNair, Lorr, and Droppleman (1981), as well as Spielberger's State–Trait Personality Inventory, Part I (Spielberger et al., 1979).

The Profile of Mood States consists of 65 adjectives describing various emotional states or moods. The subject's task is to rate, on a five-point rating scale (0–4), the intensity of a given emotional state as described by adjectives. Six scales were determined by factor analysis performed by the questionnaire authors: (a) tension–anxiety (9 items), (b) depression–dejection (15 items), (c) anger–hostility (12 items), (d) vigor–activity (8 items), (e) fatigue–inertia (7 items), and (f) confusion–bewilderment (7 items). Seven items of the questionnaire were not diagnostic, but were retained as buffer items. The mood dimensions were not defined by the authors, who refer to only the content of the adjectives relevant to the six subscales. The Polish adaptation of the POMS was published in 1987 (Dudek & Koniarek, 1987).

The State–Trait Personality Inventory (STPI) consists of six subscales: anxiety, curiosity, and anger as states, and anxiety, curiosity, and anger as traits. Each subscale consists of 10 items. The first part of the questionnaire (SPI) deals with emotional states, the second part (TPI) with personality traits. The rationale and development of the STPI are the same as those of the well-known State–Trait Anxiety Inventory. Psychometric studies on the Polish version of the STPI were carried out from 1982–1983 (Wrzesniewski, 1984).

Procedure

Patients' case records were analyzed in terms of the selection criteria adopted in the study. The eligible patients were contacted individually by a psychologist working in a given center who requested their participation in the research. The request was refused in only a few instances. Data were collected from each patient by a psychologist employed in the respective centers.

Results

The first step in the data analysis involved a comparison of scale scores of the three groups of patients, without differentiation into the TABP and TBBP subgroups. This allowed us to examine to what extent situational factors inherent in these diseases, which involved varying risk to life, evoke different affective responses in the three patient groups, irrespective of individual differences, that is, the TA/TB dimension. These data also provide information about similarities and differences in the emotional responses of two different groups of patients at low risk of sudden death. The next step in the analysis consisted of a comparison of the emotional responses of TA and TB subjects for each of the three groups separately. These data allow us to evaluate to what extent the emotional response pattern in each patient group is modified by the TABP. The last analysis involves a comparison of TA patients' scores in groups at high and low risk to life. Statistical analyses were based on the ANOVA model. Where necessary, multiple comparisons made use of the Scheffe test.

Means and standard deviations of the various scale scores for the three groups of patients are given in Table 1. Also shown are the ANOVA results and the results of subgroup comparisons. These data indicate that myocardial infarction (MI) patients, as compared with the other two groups of subjects, have the highest TABP score. The result is in agreement with the TABP concept and requires no comment. However, it should be noted that MI patients' scores differ significantly only from those of AP patients, and not from those of RP patients. This finding seems to corroborate the thesis that TABP may be a risk factor not only for coronary heart disease, but also for other illnesses (Wrzesniewski, 1991; Wrzesniewski, Wonicki, & Turlejski, 1988). Moreover, among the statistically significant differences between myocardial infarction patients and amputees indicated in Table 1 are the following: the MIs manifested less of a tendency to depression-dejection and anger–hostility as well as a stronger tendency to vigor–activity, as

Table 1 Means and standard deviations of the various scale scores of the three patient groups

	MI (N = 113)		AP (N = 37)		RP (N = 32)			
Variables	Mean	SD	Mean	SD	Mean	SD	F	p
TABP	73.91	11.54	66.05	13.73	68.69	14.34	6.383	.0002
	x----------------x							
POMS								
Tension–anxiety	8.63	8.26	9.62	5.96	6.66	6.26	1.387	NS
Depression–dejection	12.91	10.67	18.70	10.63	15.41	9.34	4.423	.013
	x----------------x							
Anger–hostility	10.59	6.63	15.43	6.88	11.00	7.37	7.205	.001
	x----------------x----------------x							
Vigor–activity	19.50	5.55	16.35	5.53	17.59	5.32	5.095	.007
	x----------------x							
Fatigue–inertia	7.19	5.40	8.78	4.81	8.97	6.26	2.054	NS
Confusion–bewilderment	5.33	5.25	5.03	4.07	4.72	4.29	.211	NS
SPI								
State anxiety	19.34	5.38	21.41	6.23	19.44	6.07	1.909	NS
State curiosity	29.25	4.77	26.84	4.18	28.53	5.39	3.567	.030
	x----------------x							
State anger	14.89	4.89	16.62	5.86	15.69	7.03	1.427	NS

Note. ANOVA results and subgroup comparisons are also shown.
x-------x: $p < .05$.

assessed by the POMS. Their curiosity state level on the SPI scale was also higher. It should be noted that both groups of low-risk patients differ from each other in only one emotional dimension of the nine studied. As compared with the AP patients, the RPs tended to be less prone to anger–hostility, as measured by the POMS.

To distinguish TA and TB people within particular groups, a decision had to be made about the criteria to be used. In the AATAB Scale, Form B, there are no norms for such patient groups. A criterion involving a mean score or quartile deviation of the total score of all these subjects would be questionable because the MI group is almost 1.5 times as numerous as the other two groups combined. Moreover, the MI group has the highest TABP scores of the three groups. Consequently, another criterion was used, based on the norms previously obtained for the random sample of 1,211 male subjects aged 35 to 64. The distribution of the AATAB Scale, Form B, in this group of subjects was normal, with a mean score of 68.31 (SD = 14.22). The mean score was assumed as the cut-off point, that is, subjects scoring above 68 points were included in the TA group; those scoring 68 points or less were included in the TB group.

Scale scores on the POMS and SPI for MI patients, differentiated for TA and TB, are given in Table 2. As seen there, the ANOVA results indicate significant differences in only two POMS scales—the vigor–activity and the confusion-bewilderment scales. As compared with the TB MI patients, the TAs scored higher on vigor and lower on confusion.

A similar analysis was performed on the AP group and the results are shown in

Table 2   Scale scores and ANOVA results of MI patients differentiated as TA and TB subjects

Variables	TA (N = 74)		TB (N = 39)		F	p
	Mean	SD	Mean	SD		
POMS						
Tension–anxiety	8.32	8.04	9.20	8.74	.288	NS
Depression–dejection	12.71	10.21	13.28	11.62	.071	NS
Anger–hostility	10.73	6.34	10.33	7.23	.090	NS
Vigor–activity	20.32	4.78	17.92	6.56	4.949	.028
Fatigue–inertia	6.72	4.96	8.05	6.14	1.534	NS
Confusion–bewilderment	4.61	4.85	6.69	5.75	4.140	.044
SPI						
State anxiety	19.74	5.11	18.59	5.85	1.16	NS
State curiosity	29.63	5.04	28.51	4.17	1.42	NS
State anger	15.38	4.96	13.97	4.65	2.13	NS

Table 3. As seen there, no significant differences in the intensity of emotions as assessed by the POMS and SPI were found between TA and TB amputees.

A third similar analysis was done on the RP group and these results are shown in Table 4. As seen there, in these patients, TA as compared to TB subjects manifested statistically significant more intense anxiety and confusion, as assessed by the POMS, as well as more intense anger and less marked curiosity, as assessed by the SPI.

It follows from these analyses that the emotional responses of TA and TB people as measured here do not differ a great deal within patient groups characterized as either high or low risk to life. However, our data permit an additional comparison of the emotional responses of TA patients at high and low risk to life. We can combine the two groups of low-risk patients and compare them with the MIs. The rationale for such a step is provided by the data shown in Table 1, which indicate that the two groups in question (the APs and the RPs) do not differ significantly from each other in terms of either the TABP intensity or their emotional responses. The only significant difference was found for the anger–hostility

Table 3   Scale scores and ANOVA results of patients after amputation, differentiated as TA and TB subjects

Variables	TA (N = 13)		TB (N = 24)		F	p
	Mean	SD	Mean	SD		
POMS						
Tension–anxiety	9.00	3.92	9.96	6.88	.213	NS
Depression–dejection	15.31	5.91	20.54	12.19	2.106	NS
Anger–hostility	13.54	5.80	16.46	7.31	1.542	NS
Vigor–activity	16.31	4.57	16.37	6.08	.001	NS
Fatigue–inertia	7.15	3.55	9.67	5.23	2.386	NS
Confusion–bewilderment	3.54	2.54	5.83	4.55	2.813	NS
SPI						
State anxiety	19.77	5.49	22.29	6.54	1.140	NS
State curiosity	26.85	4.04	26.83	4.34	.001	NS
State anger	16.31	5.84	16.79	5.99	.056	NS

Table 4 Scale scores and ANOVA results of rheumatic patients, differentiated as TA and TB subjects

Variables	TA (N = 14)		TB (N = 18)		F	p
	Mean	SD	Mean	SD		
POMS						
Tension–anxiety	9.29	6.94	4.61	4.94	4.958	.034
Depression–dejection	18.79	10.39	12.78	7.74	3.521	NS
Anger–hostility	13.36	8.92	9.17	5.47	2.687	NS
Vigor–activity	15.86	5.97	18.94	4.46	2.805	NS
Fatigue–inertia	10.43	7.87	7.83	4.57	1.372	NS
Confusion–bewilderment	6.86	5.08	3.06	2.67	7.477	.010
SPI						
State anxiety	21.43	6.64	17.89	5.26	2.837	NS
State curiosity	26.43	6.15	30.17	4.19	4.179	.050
State anger	18.64	9.29	13.39	3.36	4.957	.034

dimension. In the newly combined group, TA and TB patients were determined by using the same cut-off point as in the previous analysis. Twenty-seven patients were classified as TA and 42 were classified as TB. A comparison of the emotional response scores of TA and TB patients at low risk to life reveals no significant differences between these groupings on any of the nine variables under study. This finding is consistent with the data presented in Tables 3 and 4.

We then compared the scores of TA patients whose illness involved a high risk to life with those whose illness involved a low risk to life. These data are presented in Table 5. As seen there, statistically significant differences were found between the two groups for three variables, and close to significant differences were found on two other variables. High-risk TAs as compared with low-risk TAs scored lower on scales of depression–dejection, anger–hostility, and fatigue–inertia, but these patients had higher scores on the vigor–activity and state curiosity scales. The results are rather surprising because high-risk patients could be expected to be

Table 5 Scale scores and ANOVA results of TA patients with high and low threat of imminent death

	Threat					
	High (N = 74)		Low (N = 27)		F	p
	Mean	SD	Mean	SD		
POMS						
Tension–anxiety	8.32	8.04	9.15	5.59	.246	NS
Depression–dejection	12.71	10.21	17.11	8.55	4.179	.044
Anger–hostility	10.73	6.34	13.44	7.44	3.037	.083
Vigor–activity	20.32	4.78	16.07	5.25	15.104	.001
Fatigue–inertia	6.72	4.96	8.85	6.29	3.333	.071
Confusion–bewilderment	4.61	4.85	5.26	4.33	.453	NS
SPI						
State anxiety	19.74	5.11	20.63	6.06	.778	NS
State curiosity	29.63	5.04	26.63	5.14	6.631	.011
State anger	15.38	4.96	17.52	7.77	2.805	NS

more prone to depressive states, fatigue, and anger, as well as to show a less marked tendency to activity and curiosity. Our results may be due to an interaction between TABP and some specific situational factors associated with myocardial infarction, rheumatic diseases, and whatever state occurs after amputation of the lower limbs. This possibility seems to be corroborated by TB patients' scores. A comparison of TB patients' scores in subgroups involving either a high or low risk to life yielded no statistically significant intergroup differences for any of the nine variables under study.

DISCUSSION

Comparisons of TA and TB people within each of the three patient groups suggest that in TA patients disease that involves a high risk to life (MI) is associated with a more intense feeling of well-being and energy, as assessed by the vigor–activity scale, and also a lower sense of perplexity and of being muddled, as expressed by the confusion–bewilderment scale. In other words, in the MI group, TA patients manifest more positive emotions than do TB patients. The pattern is reversed in one of the low-risk patient groups (RP), where TA patients as compared with TB people manifest stronger negative emotions, such as tension, anxiety, anger, and bewilderment. Such relationships are confirmed by a comparison of TA patients' scores in subgroups at high and low risk to life (Table 5). High-risk TA patients, as compared with low-risk TA patients, manifest more pronounced positive emotions, such as a sense of well-being, vigor, and curiosity, and less intense negative affects, such as fatigue or anger. The findings are seemingly paradoxical. However, they become more understandable on the basis of a more detailed psychological analysis, when both the circumstances of particular patient groups and some TABP characteristics are taken into account.

First of all, the illness of the MI patient has few external manifestations, in contrast to the other two patient groups. Those who do not know an MI patient's health history are unable to detect any symptoms of ill health. The patient does not attract attention in public, and is not assessed adversely by other people in the environment. At the same time, limitations imposed on the MI patient's physical activity are gradually diminishing both because of the lapse of time since the heart attack and because of the process of physical rehabilitation. In the rehabilitation center, these patients are aware of their returning health daily. They also lack coronary pain; absence of the latter is a condition of the sanitarium rehabilitation referral. The absence of signs of illness allows these patients to develop an optimistic view of their condition. On the other hand, the situation of patients suffering from rheumatic diseases and that of amputees is entirely different. Their health problems are perfectly visible to the public and so they are exposed to a more or less open negative assessment of their physical fitness and of their difficulties in accomplishing the ordinary tasks of living. Neither during their sanitarium rehabilitation nor after they leave the program do these patients have a chance of improving significantly. The general prognosis of rheumatic patients in particular is unfavorable and they can expect a deterioration of their health and a further decrement in their physical abilities.

In order to better understand the results obtained in our study, the circumstances of MI, AP, and RP patients just described should be seen from the viewpoint of TA patients, and with consideration of their premorbid functioning level. Glass (1977) and other authors (e.g., Smith & Rhodewalt, 1986; Vingerhoets & Flohr, 1984) point out that TA patients have a strong tendency to dominate and control, which is accompanied by their pronounced need for achievement. From this perspective, the situation for MI patients seems to be different from that of the two other patient groups. TA patients after myocardial infarction believe that many changes for the better are occurring in the rehabilitation center as compared with the hospital. In the hospital, immediately following the heart attack, they were immobilized, had little control over their situation, and in many respects were totally dependent on other people. Simultaneously, they lost control over their occupational and domestic affairs. However, their plight slowly improved as treatment progressed. On discharge from the hospital and before their admission to the sanitarium, they usually had some contact with their workplace, partially regaining their old status in the world of work. Similarly, they were gradually regaining control over what went on at home. These experiences were then enhanced by the first positive effects of the sanitarium rehabilitation. These patients gradually begin to realize that the outcome of treatment and rehabilitation depends to a large extent upon their own behavior, such as not smoking, changing their eating habits, or taking up systematic physical exercise, all of which contribute to their health improvement. Thus these patients have a growing sense of control and they are provided with many opportunities for gratifying their strong need for achievement. This is not the case with amputees and rheumatic patients. Their ability to control and influence their own circumstances is very limited in both the hospital and sanitarium environments. The prognosis for rheumatic patients is generally unpromising and their ability to control their lives can be expected to decrease with deterioration of their condition. In both AP and RP patients, the ability to control professional and domestic affairs is reduced considerably. Amputees usually have not been to their workplace since the accident; many of them never can resume their previous employment. In both these groups, the patients' gratification of their strong needs for achievement is dramatically limited because of their physical condition; this is true for the future as well as the present.

Based on laboratory research, Glass (1977) concluded that TA patients respond with strong negative emotions to stress situations over which they lose control. Our findings corroborate this conclusion.

As a final interpretation of our results, it is worthwhile to refer to the view shared by Pittner and Houston (1980) and Smith and Rhodewalt (1986). According to these authors, TA patients use denial as their defense mechanism of choice. This mechanism seems to be of importance in our TA patients after MI. A rapid relief from coronary pain, even during hospitalization, as well as an evident increase in physical activity during sanitarium rehabilitation may facilitate the repression of the awareness that the risk of sudden death is still present. For TA amputees and TA rheumatic patients denial is not very feasible because their illness-induced limitations are too evident and treatment can bring about no essential improvement. Under the circumstances, denial cannot be used efficiently.

In summary, the high risk to life associated with MI and the low risk to life associated with rheumatic disease and lower-limb amputation had no significant effect on emotional states manifested by TA patients. On the other hand, interaction between situational characteristics specific to particular patient groups and TABP features had a significant effect. Type A MI patients, when compared with other patients who were Type A, manifested more positive emotions. This finding could also have been influenced by the defense mechanism of denial, which in the Type-A patient groups under study would be expected to play different roles.

Our results and the conclusions we have drawn from them are based only on the investigation of cognitive aspects of emotion. Therefore, future research should also take into account physiological aspects of emotion. Attention to both aspects of emotion will permit more general conclusions.

REFERENCES

Contrada, R. J., Krantz, D. S., & Hill, D. R. (1988). Type A behavior, emotion, and psychophysiologic reactivity: Psychological and biological interactions. In B. K. Houston and R. C. Snyder (Eds.), *Type A behavior pattern: Research, theory, and intervention* (pp. 254–274). New York: Wiley.

Contrada, R. J., Wright, R. A., & Glass, D. C. (1985). Psychophysiological correlates of Type A behavior. Comments on Houston (1983) and Holmes (1983). *Journal of Research in Personality, 19,* 12–30.

Dudek, B., & Koniarek, J. (1987). Adaptacja testu D. M. McNair'a, M. Lorr'a, L. F. Droppleman'a—Profile of Mood States. [Adaptation of D. M. McNair, M. Lorr, and L. F. Droppleman Test Profile of Mood States]. *Przeglad Psychologiczny, 30,* 753–763.

Glass, D. C. (1977). *Behavior patterns, stress and coronary disease.* Hillsdale, NJ: Erlbaum.

Houston, B. K. (1988). Cardiovascular and neuroendocrine reactivity, global Type A, and components of Type A behavior. In B. K. Houston & R. C. Snyder (Eds.), *Type A behavior pattern: Research, theory, and intervention* (pp. 212–253). New York: Wiley.

Lazarus, R. S., & Folkman, S. (1984). *Stress, appraisal, and coping.* New York: Springer.

Matthews, K. A. (1982). Psychological perspectives on the Type A behavior pattern. *Psychological Bulletin, 91,* 293–323.

Matthews, K. A., & Haynes, S. G. (1986). Type A behavior pattern and coronary disease risk. *American Journal of Epidemiology, 123,* 923–960.

McNair, D. M., Lorr, M., & Droppleman, L. F. (1981). *Profile of mood states. Manual.* San Diego: Educational and Industrial Testing Service.

Pittner, M. S., & Houston, B. K. (1980). Response to stress, cognitive coping strategies, and the Type A behavior pattern. *Journal of Personality and Social Psychology, 39,* 147–157.

Pittner, M. S., Houston, B. K., & Spiridigliozzi, G. (1983). Control over stress, Type A behavior pattern, and response to stress. *Journal of Personality and Social Psychology, 44,* 627–637.

Smith, T. W., & Rhodewalt, F. (1986). On states, traits and processes: A transactional alternative to the individual difference assumptions of Type A behavior and physiological reactivity. *Journal of Research in Personality, 20,* 229–251.

Spielberger, C. D., Barker, L., Russel, R., & Marks, E. (1979). *Preliminary manual for the State--Trait Personality Inventory.* Tampa: University of South Florida.

Vickers, R. R., Herving, L. K., Rahe, R. H., & Rosenman, R. H. (1981). Type A behavior pattern and coping and defense. *Psychosomatic Medicine, 45,* 381–396.

Vingerhoets, A. J. M., & Flohr, P. J. (1984). Type A behavior and self reports of coping preferences. *British Journal of Medical Psychology, 57,* 15–21.

Wrzesniewski, K. (1984). Development of the Polish Form of the State–Trait Personality Inventory. In H. M. van der Ploeg, R. Schwarzer, & C. D. Spielberger (Eds.), *Advances in test anxiety research* (Vol. 3, pp. 265–275) Hillsdale, NJ: Erlbaum.

Wrzesniewski, K. (1990). Badanie Wzoru zachowania A przy uzyciu polskiego kwestionariusza. [Polish questionnaire for the assessment of the Type A behavior pattern]. *Przeglad Lekarski, 447,* 538–541.

Wrzesniewski, K. (1991). *Wzor zachowania A jako czynnik predysponujacy do chorob somatycznyh.* [Type A behavior pattern as a risk for somatic diseases]. Warsaw: Warszawska Akademia Medyczna.

Wrzesniewski, K., Forgays, D. G., & Bonaiuto, P. (1990). Measurement of the Type A behavior pattern in adolescents and young adults: Cross-cultural development of AATAB. *Journal of Behavioral Medicine, 13,* 111–135.

Wrzesniewski, K., Wonicki, J., & Turlejski, J. (1988). Type A behavior pattern and illness other than coronary heart disease. *Social Science and Medicine, 27,* 623–626.

16

Test Anxiety Can Harm Your Health: Some Conclusions Based on a Student Typology

Eric Depreeuw and Hubert De Neve
University of Leuven, Belgium

INTRODUCTION

About 25,000 students enroll each year at the University of Leuven, Belgium; they represent more than 25 different study departments. Since the early 1950s, a broad offering of psychological, medical, and social services has been assembled to help these students maximize their study results by optimizing their personal and material well-being. In 1986, the staff of these services set up a comprehensive research project to analyze students' problems and needs. The study also focused on the adequacy of the services in meeting students' needs.

This practical field study followed some important guidelines. Although the primary aim was the eventual readjustment of the psycho–medico–social department's policy, the project also needed a valid theoretical and methodological foundation. Another aim of the study was to stress student well-being and not, as is frequently the case, academic grades and a successful study career. Consequently, the sample was limited to more senior students, and excluded first-year students. As the university entrance criteria in Belgium are rather liberal, the first-year population is quite heterogeneous. On the other hand, the first year program is highly selective. In the research at hand, it was opportune to study the eventual influence of range of intellectual capacities on the students' well-being. A final option was to focus on a broad spectrum of the students' lives: the staff of the services had their own interests and hypotheses, which were transformed into questions and alternatives.

In the first phase of the project, an extensive questionnaire was developed. It contained 233 Likert-type items and 12 open questions. The structure of the questionnaire was as follows. After several student identification items (e.g., gender, age, department and year, socioeconomic variables), behavioral variables concerning different areas of student life were assessed. Important examples are the estimated time spent in study, leisure, and rest; the frequency of contacts with parents; consumption of several items (coffee, alcohol, cigarettes, etc.); and intake of medical drugs. For most of these variables, distinction was made between the frequency of use during the academic year versus the examination period. The third part of the questionnaire focused on subjective experiences and estimations of somatic, psychological, and study-related (dys)functioning and well-being or ill-

ness. In contrast to the former more neutral parts, this segment was more evaluative, asking the students explicitly to indicate eventual problems. The respondents
had to rate items on a five-point agreement scale, ranging from 1 (statement is not
true or not applicable to me) to 5 (fully true or applicable). Examples of items
include "I get nervous when I hear other students talk about their study," "It is not
clear to me what I am expected to do for my study," "I have the impression that
other students have less difficulties with their study than I have," and "Studying in
higher education is of great importance to my parents."

Academic success was not the central focus of this research project; its central
focus was the subjective experience of different aspects of the student role, including the impression of success or failure. The questions in this area were inspired
by an explorative or descriptive achievement process model that will be described
later. In this model the cognitive and emotional components of motivation and
achievement behavior are central, especially in relation to test anxiety.

The last part of the questionnaire was oriented to the solutions students look for
in order to solve their eventual problems. The contribution of the immediate social
network (parents, friends, peers, etc.) was explored, as well as the appeal of the
professional services offered to them.

THE ACHIEVEMENT PROCESS MODEL

Sixty-one items were based on a descriptive achievement process model described elsewhere (Depreeuw, 1988, 1989). In this model, the interaction of motivational components and test anxiety is of crucial importance. There is overwhelming theoretical and clinical evidence that cognitive and emotional
components of both motivation and test anxiety seem to be of considerable influence for student functioning and well-being in general (Depreeuw, 1984), and for
study achievement in particular (Hembree, 1988; Tryon, 1980).

We based our phenomenological achievement process model on the Heckhausen
cognitive model of achievement motivation (Heckhausen, 1977) and the Salamé
heuristic process model of test anxiety (Salamé, 1984). Our model consists of eight
components. The first two components are primarily cognitive appraisal or inter-
pretative decoding processes. The tendency to achievement starts, rises, or de-
clines after the actual activation of motivational states by perceived or interpreted
incentive situations. This means that the student first has to appraise or decode
some task aspect. Second, the task itself and/or its consequences must be related to
one or more motives. Examples of the latter are the achievement motive, obedi-
ence or loyalty to parents, financial needs, altruism, and so forth. In earlier experiences, for the most part, motives have been associated with positive and/or aversive emotional states. The decoding of the objective situation results in a
motivational state with an intensity but also with an affective color, that is, a
positive or negative emotional load.

The next appraisal relates to the balance between the perceived task demands
and the perceived self resources, including the social network. Level of abstrac-
tion, time pressure, familiarity, material context, and oral or written evaluation are
common examples of task demands. On the other hand, the perceived personal,
intellectual, somatic, and social potential and skills, including the energy supply
and an effort-related attitude, are only a few examples of the counterweight in the
balance.

According to expectancy–value theories, achievement behavior will or will not develop in a situation and it may take the concrete form of a task-related approach versus non–study-related acts, which may be accompanied by self-related worry. For intellectual tasks, attention, in interaction with achievement motivation and test anxiety, is an important variable in performance (Sarason, 1988; Wine, 1980). Anxiety will emerge when the task situation is decoded as related to one or more vital motives and when the probability of success is less than perfect. If anxiety occurs, attempts to reduce this aversive feeling can influence performance considerably. Anxiety plays the role of an interactional variable or even a central motive. Anxiety-related behavior can interfere with task-related behavior in several ways (Depreeuw, 1991).

Both these appraisal processes are related clearly to the two appraisal processes described by Lazarus and Launier (1978), which result in implicit or explicit goals. The difference between anxious and nonanxious people lies in the extremeness and rigidity of the goal setting. Only with perfect mastery or total resignation can the anxiety level be reduced to zero. The task-oriented student will formulate flexible goals that fall between these two extremes, for the most part.

Goal setting is followed by and influences task preparation and performance itself. During both phases the appraisals are renewed almost continuously, resulting in rising or declining motivational or anxiety levels. The switch from one extreme to another can happen suddenly.

The last model components are subjective self-evaluation and causal attribution, differentiating again between test-anxious and non–test-anxious persons. High test-anxious persons tend to evaluate themselves more negatively, partly as a consequence of their goal setting. In addition, they have an unfavorable attribution style for success and for failure (Abramson, Seligman, & Teasdale, 1978; Weiner, 1985).

Finally, the total cognitive, emotional, and behavioral experience is registered in long-term memory, closing the loop to the motivational and personal expectancy dispositions.

DESIGN AND SUBJECTS

The research data presented in this chapter form part of a more comprehensive study (Depreeuw, De Neve, & Bracke, 1988). Here we will only describe briefly the general methodological strategy and discuss some of the main results from the perspective of the relationship between test anxiety and the included health variables.

The extensive questionnaire was presented to second- and third-year students of different departments of Leuven University during oral examination time. This approach, of course, has some limitations (e.g., no information about the absent students), but other strategies (e.g., individual sampling and interview) are more time consuming and expensive, with comparable or greater disadvantages. Anonymous and valid questionnaires were collected from 1,144 respondents, 63% filled out by second-year students and 37% by third-year students. Many of these respondents were members of the departments of Law, Medicine, Civil Engineering, and German Philology. Fifty-seven percent of the total second-year population and 49% of the total third-year population of these departments were participants, and

52% of the sample were males. The mean age was between 20 and 21 years. Based on these characteristics, the sample seems satisfyingly representative.

The statistical analysis was done in three stages. In the first, the amount of information had to be reduced. Three separate factor analyses were applied: (a) on 90 items that referred to the subjective study experiences based on the descriptive process model (61 items), together with the social interactional items (29); (b) on a pool of 16 items referring to the frequency of some emotional or mood-related self experiences; and (c) on a pool of 16 items concerning rather aversive (psycho)somatic sensations and symptoms, such as trembling hands, stomachache, headache, sweaty hands, and so forth.

In stage two, it was decided for theoretical and practical (service) reasons to use cluster analysis on those factors of the first analysis related to the achievement process model. We felt that an interesting theoretical issue related to whether some relevant and recognizable student types would emerge. There was also a practical concern as to whether delineation of such types could be of some value in the development of future policy of the welfare department (e.g., providing specific or differentiated help). Student types could then be compared on different criteria, and this was done in the third phase. We planned to maximize the theoretical and practical relevance of student types in the event that clear and significant differentiations could be demonstrated. The latter analysis was also developed more extensively in relation to student test anxiety characteristics.

ANALYSES AND RESULTS

Factor Analyses

Factor Analysis I: Study Process and Social Network

For the first group of items, a principal factor analysis with iteration was applied, followed by varimax rotation. The orthogonal rotation revealed seven factors with an eigenvalue greater than 1.00 and accounting for at least 5% of common variance. The seven factors were quite interpretable. Table 1 illustrates each factor with some high loading items.

The first factor (14 items, explaining 21% of common variance) refers to different experiences of *test anxiety:* physiological reactions such as nervousness, tension, and feeling sick, as well as cognitive and emotive components (panic when thinking about examinations) and some behavioral items (not taking examinations) are apparent. It clearly demonstrates the complexity of this dimension.

Students rating themselves high on factor 2 (15 items: 26% of common variance) have a tendency to postpone their study activity. They clearly lack the self-discipline that is necessary to study hard and regularly. Only when external pressure is high enough can they bring themselves to study intensively. As a consequence, a lot of other activities are used as an excuse for not studying. This factor was labeled *study avoidance*.

High ratings on factor 3 (seven items: 10% of common variance) reflect student opinion that failing in a task in general, or in an examination or test in particular, is "catastrophic," both for students themselves and for their parents or other people close to them. This threat of being unsuccessful is always present. A student's experience is imbued with the conviction that he or she *must* pass the exams.

Factor 4 (20% of common variance) groups 13 items expressing a student's

Table 1 Seven-factor solution of the questionnaire items on Study and Social Experiences: Examples of high loading items on each factor

Dimension	Five high loading items
Test anxiety	I feel sick when I am too busy with my study. While studying, feelings of panic assail me. I feel severely tense when studying. I'd rather not take an exam than risk giving stupid answers. I get stressed only by thinking of exams.
Study avoidance	I have a tendency to postpone study activities. I find it difficult to start studying. I lack discipline in my study habits. I work in bouts. I keep myself from studying by doing odd jobs.
Must	Failing in my study would be a terrible experience. I think my parents would be shocked if I do not succeed in my studies. I can't stand the feeling of failing in a job. People that are close to me consider studying as extremely important. I try to learn course content in all its details.
Negative self-evaluation	I need more time than other students to master a course. I have the impression of not being able to cope with study requirements. I don't have the right skills for studying effectively. I wonder greatly if I use a good study method. I find it difficult to memorize what I have learned.
Demotivation	This study does not come up to my expectations. If I could have my own way, I would stop this study and do something else. I really consider dropping out of this study. I am not highly interested in this study program.
Social isolation	I have a lot of friends in this university town(−). I feel isolated in this university town. I have a lot of contacts with fellow students(−). This study prevents me from having the social contacts I want.
Conflicts with family	I come into conflicts with my parents. My parents stimulate me to continue my studies.(−) My parents do accept my personal choices and values(−). I grew up in a family with problems. My parents are apprehensive for me(−).

perception of being (un)able to cope with study requirements. It relates manifestly to the student's self-confidence. As most of the items are formulated in a problem-oriented manner, the dimension was labeled *negative self-evaluation*.

The fifth dimension (eight items: 11% of common variance) is also bipolar. It refers to the way a study situation and the attending study behavior is experienced as significant, enriching, and hence personally satisfying, versus the experience producing disillusion because it did not meet personal needs and expectations. The factor was labeled as *demotivation*.

Factors 6 and 7 were quite specific. Only four and seven items, respectively, were highly loaded, and each factor accounted for 6% of common variance.

Whereas factor 6 refers to feelings of *social isolation* versus integration in the study environment, factor 7 groups items expressing experiences of *conflicts with family* versus a positive and warm familial relationship.

Before calculating scores on each group of items, internal consistency was verified for each item group. A Gulliksen item analysis and selection (Verhelst & Vander Steene, 1972) was performed to control the homogeneity of each scale and eventually to increase the consistency to an acceptable level. None of the items was eliminated. The internal consistency allowed the computation of scale results (Cronbach's α was high for five out of seven scales, varying between .88 and .92, and was moderate for the *must* scale and the *social isolation* scale, being .72 and .64, respectively).

We will not discuss the external validity of the scales at this time but will return to this issue more extensively in an indirect but more meaningful way in the last part of this chapter, which deals with differentiation among student types. Many psychologically meaningful and statistically significant relationships were found between the scores on the seven scales on the one hand, and the behavioral variables and subjective experiences on the other.

Although we did not accomplish a confirmatory factor analysis, the construct validity of the five model-related factors can be supported. Two factors relate to the first model component, namely, the *demotivation* and the *must*. The first has to do with intrinsic study motivation or interest, the other with eventual negative, even catastrophic consequences in the event of a failure. These consequences are related to different motives (e.g., personal career, self-worth, social environment, parents). The second model component is clearly manifested in the (negative) *self evaluation* factor. Probably this factor is crucial in the appearance of state test anxiety and regulates the influence of the *must* factor, for example, as an expectancy value interaction. Only when the subject predicts or anticipates a failure do the catastrophic consequences become relevant, and anxiety rises. Manifestly this self-evaluation factor reveals an important aspect of the test anxiety *worry* dimension (Sarason, 1988). The influence of the self evaluation factor seems comparable to the self efficacy notion (Bandura, 1986) and the optimism–pessimism differentiation (Carver & Scheier, 1988). We hypothesize that the final evaluation component of the model is integrated in the self-evaluation factor, which is not surprising, given the continuous and repetitive character of evaluation. Further, we have observed an important behavioral factor that is labeled *study avoidance/effort*. The differentiation made in the model between *preparation* and *performance* is not revealed, however. Finally, there is a strong anxiety factor, illustrating the autonomous and emotional component of the descriptive model.

Factor Analyses II and III: Self Experience and Psychosomatic Complaints

Because the second and third groups of items (recent mental self-experiences and psychosomatic complaints) were limited in number (only 16 items in each case), principal component factor analyses were calculated as attempts to explain total variance.

The extraction of principal components revealed two components in the items about mental self experiences and only one in the items about physical sensations or psychosomatic complaints. For that reason, only for the first group was the original factor matrix varimax rotated for interpretive reasons. Six items had a high loading on component 1: "being blocked, lonely, confused, helpless, feeling down and having a difficult time." The factor was labeled *Depression*. The second component referred to *general anxiety* with five high loading items: "being restless and anxious, nervous, lack of self confidence and lack of relaxation."

As these two scales and the one resulting from the physical sensation/psychosomatic complaint analysis are only of minor importance in the study at hand, no further details on the technical characteristics of these scales will be provided here.

In Search of a Typology of Students: Cluster Analysis

The scale results for different subgroups of students already indicated the large amount of interindividual differences on the dimensions of study experiences. However, the issue of intra-individual differences, of the "patterns of dimensional scores," remained. Cluster analysis is a technique that can provide useful information on this issue because it allows one to explore the existence of different subgroups of students, if, for example, they show a distinct and relatively homogeneous pattern of scores on the dimensions. Scores on the five scales, which refer to the theoretical model described, were subjected to this level of analysis. For interpretive reasons, all scores were standardized ($M = 50$; $SD = 10$). Because the group of participants was large, the SAS FASTCLUS procedure was used for disjoint clustering of the data set. Based on the "Cubic Clustering Criterion" and by exploring solutions with different number of clusters, the seven-cluster solution was preferred. In Table 2, mean scores on the five scales are reported for each of the seven clusters; the profiles of the seven groups are shown in graphical form in Figures 1, 2, and 3. It should be noticed, however, that two kinds of mean scores are used: the standardized scores (Ss) used for clustering, and the percentage scores (Ps). The latter are obtained by dividing raw scores by the number of items and by linearly transforming them on a scale ranging from 0 (not at all applicable) to 100 (fully applicable).

The Model, the Mean, and the Choice Disillusioned Student

We start our description of clusters with the student types that are represented most frequently. The first one, the *model* student, accounts for 331 or 29% of all

participants. Their scores are in all ways propitious. Such students are motivated to study and call themselves hard workers. The high score on *must* seems to indicate that failing in their studies would be a serious event. This pressure apparently prevents them from minimizing the importance of study. Because such students are quite confident about their personal abilities to cope with study requirements (balance), they do not live under the subjective threat of failure, and their test anxiety is low.

The *mean* student's scores (sample size of 361 or 32% of total) show a tendency toward the average of the entire group, except for the *study avoidance* scale. Students of this largest or "modal" group experience their study behavior as rather uncomplicated, although they admit that they could and perhaps should work somewhat harder because of the demands of their study program.

A third group is called the *choice disillusioned* students. In several aspects they are similar to the *mean* student. For them, studying in higher education is consid-

Table 2 Mean standardized and mean percentage score of seven student types on the five scales on study experiences

Cluster	N	%	Test anxiety		Study avoidance		Must		Negative self-evaluation		Demotivation		Cluster interpretation
			Ss	Ps	Ss	Ps	Ss	Ps	Ss	Ps	Ss	Ps	
1	331	29.1	43	18	41	23	54	82	41	25	43	8	Model student
2	361	31.7	49	28	57	54	47	73	52	43	49	20	Mean student
3	119	10.5	54	35	50	41	51	79	53	45	62	41	Choice disillusion
4	136	12.0	61	46	46	33	59	89	57	52	47	16	Active test anxious
5	75	6.6	68	56	62	64	55	83	66	67	67	50	Passive test anxious
6	26	2.3	54	35	63	66	32	52	60	57	72	60	Apathetic student
7	90	7.9	44	19	48	37	32	52	44	29	47	15	Happy-go-lucky

Note. Ss = Standardized score; M = 50/SD = 10; Ps = Percentage score on a scale ranging from 0 (not applicable) to 100 (fully applicable).

ered to be an important opportunity, hence, failing "must" be avoided. On the other hand, they experience test anxiety; however, it does not prevent them from feeling self-confident. They believe that being a student calls for an active approach, and that excuses for avoiding study should be avoided. Surprisingly, this student type is rather unmotivated or demotivated. Their motivational expectations clearly are not fulfilled but because they have already progressed quite far, they can see no clear reason to quit the program.

The Active and the Passive Test Anxiety Student

Two out of the seven clusters are characterized by a high score on test anxiety. However, these two groups differ remarkably on most of the other dimensions. Scale scores for these groups are shown in Figure 2.

The *active test* student (N = 126; 12% of total) gets the highest score on the *must* scale. For such students and their parents, failure would indeed be catastrophic. Taking into account that these students lack self-confidence, it is understandable that their "doom" is combined with a high score on test anxiety. They describe themselves as hard workers with high study interest (lower scores for *avoidance* and *demotivation*).

Passive test anxiety students (N = 75; 7% of total), on the other hand, characterize themselves as demotivated for study. Bad academic grades are perceived as very negative events, but for one reason or another these students fail to get actively involved in study. They avoid study effort; there is "always something else to do." Their extremely high scores on *test anxiety* are combined with low self-esteem. These students clearly lack confidence in their own capabilities, although to some extent they have already demonstrated some competence in previous study results. In our opinion, such students are paralyzed by anxiety that is so high that it borders on panic. Something should be done about the situation, but whatever one will do, it will still result in failure.

The Happy-Go-Lucky and the Apathetic Student

The last two groups are clearly opposite to each other. Their scale scores are graphed in Figure 3. For *happy-go-lucky* students (N = 90; 8% of total), the sky

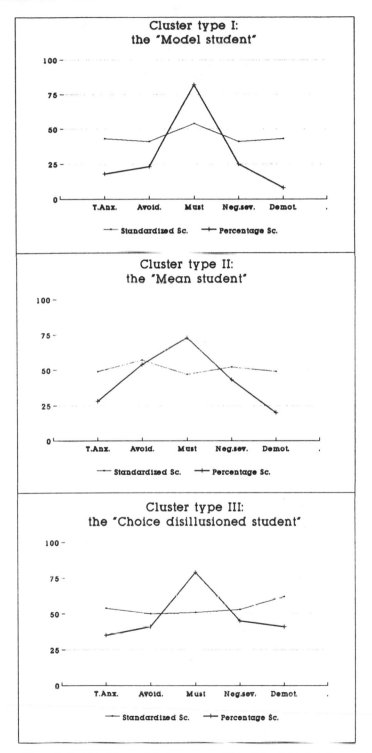

Figure 1 Profile of the *model*, the *mean*, and the *choice disillusioned* student.

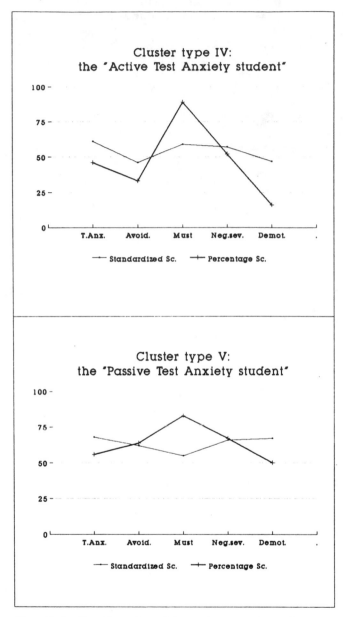

Figure 2 Profile of the *active* and the *passive test anxiety* student.

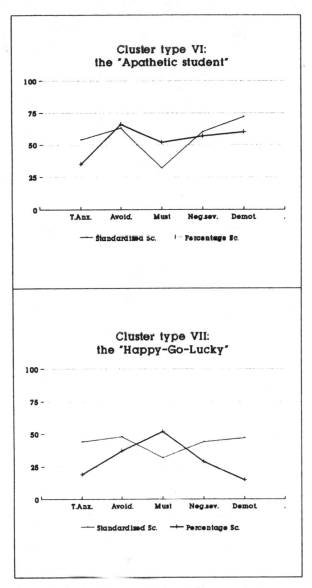

Figure 3 Profile of the *apathetic* and the *happy-go-lucky* student.

is always blue. Being successful students might be personally important, but failure is not perceived as being the end of the world. If these students should fail, it would be a negative experience but certainly not a catastrophe. It is not surprising that such students are quite confident in their studies and are free of test anxiety. The odds for a failure are estimated to be low, based on the fact that they are active in their studies. In this respect, these students resemble the *model* students.

Score profiles of the *apathetic* students, on the other hand, are quite problematic. Their scores for *must* are as low as for *happy-go-lucky* students, but combined with the other scores, they reveal a conviction that nothing is important enough to strive for. Apathetic students are extremely demotivated. If it were up to them, they probably would stop their study careers and drop out. This is why their scores for *study avoidance* are so high while their *test anxiety* scores are moderate. Why should one be anxious about something that is personally unimportant and not worthy of one's effort?

Further Analysis of the Test-Anxious Student Types: Some Health Criteria

In this section, active and passive test-anxious students will be explored further. Both types are characterized by an extremely high level of negative study emotions, especially anxiety, and by a strong awareness of catastrophic outcome consequences (failure). Both types lack self-confidence. However, the active type shows a moderate-to-positive study satisfaction and works very hard. The passive types, on the other hand, are extremely unsatisfied and show a very low discipline for study effort, that is, they procrastinate considerably.

It was hypothesized that the statistical differentiation between these two anxiety types and its psychological relevance would be more valid, and hence more supported, if they scored differently on additional criteria that were explored simultaneously in the questionnaire. We emphasized the health criteria in particular. Five data groups will be examined: identity variables (sex, study program, and study career of respondents), mental health scale results, use of medical drugs, use of "luxury stimulants," and study behavior.

Identity Characteristics

Table 3 reports the distribution of the seven student types in different subgroups of respondents; we will comment only on the two anxiety types.

As regards gender differences, Table 3 shows that the active test anxiety student (TAA) is found more frequently in the female group than in the male group (15.7% and 8.4%, respectively: $z = -3.770$; $p = < .001$), and this difference could have been expected. Females score higher on anxiety-related variables. The difference between the proportions for males and females on the passive test anxiety type (TAP) is not significant.

TAAs are relatively most frequently enrolled in the Medical program, and least frequently in Engineering ($z = 2.140$; $p = < .05$). It should be noticed, however, that this difference probably coincides with the sex difference, as there are almost no female students in Engineering. TAPs, however, are found more frequently in the Law (9%) than in the Medical program (4.6%) and Engineering studies (3.6%). Both these differences are significant ($p = < .05$).

Finally, TAA is slightly but positively related to the previous study career of students, whereas TAP is most frequently found among the group of students with 2 or more years of study retardation (12.8% vs. 5.5% of the students without retardation) and less in the group without retardation. Retardation is defined as the difference between the number of years a student has already spent on his particular program, and the nominal number of years that is prescribed for this part of the study program.

Mental Health: Scale Results

In Table 4, mental health scale results are reported for the seven student types. The scales have been described already: social isolation, conflicts with family, psychosomatic complaints, depression, and general anxiety. To facilitate the interpretation of the first three scales, results have been transformed to a percentage scale, ranging from 0 (not at all applicable) to 100 (fully applicable). In addition to these scales, measures of time spent on study are also reported.

Results in Table 4 show that nearly all measures differ significantly across the seven student types. However, we will again limit discussion to the anxiety types. High scores on psychosomatic complaints and general anxiety characterize both the TAA and the TAP student. It should also be noted that the TAP students obtain the highest scores on depressive feelings, which to a less extent are also characteristic of the TAA students. TAP students feel most isolated from other students; in that respect, they even exceed the apathetic students. Similar to the latter type, TAP students also report frequent conflicts with their families, especially with their parents.

Table 3 Relative frequency of seven student types in different subgroups

| | | | | | Student type | | | |
| | | | | | | Active test anxiety student | Passive test anxious student | | |
Group	N	Model student	Mean student	Choice disillusioned student				Apathetic student	Happy-go-lucky
Total group	1138	29.1	31.6	10.3		11.9	6.6	2.3	8.0
Sex									
Male	580	30.5	31.0	10.2		8.4	6.0	3.1	10.7
Female	542	27.7	32.3	10.5		15.7	7.2	1.5	5.2
Study program									
Law	467	22.3	35.1	13.1		10.9	9.0	2.1	7.5
Humanities	219	28.3	27.9	12.3		11.4	6.4	5.9	7.8
Medicine	259	37.8	27.8	4.6		16.2	4.6	0.8	8.1
Engineering	193	34.7	33.2	9.8		9.3	3.6	0.5	8.8
Study career[a]									
None	805	32.5	29.6	10.1		12.8	5.5	1.9	7.7
One	242	22.3	38.0	10.3		9.1	8.3	3.3	8.7
Two or more	86	16.3	34.9	14.0		11.6	12.8	3.5	7.0

Note.[a] Years of retardation = number of years of study exceeding the nominal number, as prescribed in the program.

Table 4 Mean scores of seven student types on a number of scales on mental health, on study time, and on behavioral items

| | | | | Student type | | | | | ANOVA | |
Scale	Model student	Mean student	Choice disillusioned student	Active test anxiety student	Passive test anxious student	Apathetic student	Happy-go-lucky	Total group	F	p
Social isolation[a]	11.25	12.53	10.35	14.98	18.10	16.25	11.40	13.20	22.02	0.000
Conflicts with family[a]	5.87	9.21	9.71	7.44	11.30	12.69	8.96	8.29	27.98	0.000
Psychosomatic complaints[a]	4.92	7.71	10.01	12.69	15.88	10.70	5.78	8.19	77.92	0.000
Depressive feelings[b]	−0.43	0.03	0.17	0.31	1.13	0.43	−0.35	0.00	36.70	0.000
General anxiety[b]	−0.41	−0.07	0.19	0.69	0.94	−0.06	−0.28	0.00	39.26	0.000
Study effort[c]										
Class attendance	24.20	21.71	24.95	24.09	21.70	21.90	22.03	23.09	2.636	0.016
Personal study (acad. year)	27.18	20.79	23.06	28.84	21.18	18.13	21.91	23.94	11.62	0.000
Exertion in exam period	71.12	67.52	72.10	70.04	70.03	68.77	71.75	69.88	0.928	0.474

Note. [a]Mean item score, transformed on a scale ranging from 0 (= never) to 100 (= always); [b]factor scores; [c]self reported time (hours per week).

Medical Drug Use

Compared with the total group, both TAAs and TAPs use medical drugs more frequently (all differences are significant) (Table 5). This holds true for sleeping drugs (hypnotics), tranquilizers, and stimulants, as well as for sedatives and vitamins, both during the academic year and in the examination period. Both groups are clearly the most frequent users of medical drugs. However, some differences exist between both test anxiety types. For example, during the academic year passive anxiety students use more tranquilizers ($p = <.10$) and stimulants ($p = <.05$) than the active anxiety students. In the examination period, the passive group is still using more stimulants (39.2%) than the active group (28.9%, $p = <.10$).

Use of Cigarettes, Alcohol, Coffee, and Cola

Active test anxiety students are certainly not conspicuous in their use of cigarettes, alcohol, coffee, or cola (Table 6). Compared with the total group, they use even less light alcohol (pilsner beer) and cola ($p = <.05$ and .01, respectively) during the academic year. During the examination period they do not differ from the total group. About one out of every five TAPs is a smoker, which is significantly more than in the TAA group or in the total group. Only in the apathetic student group is the proportion of smokers higher. Members of the TAP group are also "heavy cola drinkers" during the examination period, a finding that is consistent with the equally higher use of medical stimulants in this group.

Study Time Management

Students were asked to estimate how much time in hours they spent weekly on attending classes, on personal study during the academic year, and on personal study in the examination period. Data concerning study effort are shown in Table 4. Of all groups, TAPs spend the least time attending class. TAAs, on the other hand, regularly attend class and report the highest number of hours spent in per-

Table 5 Medical drug use of seven student types during academic year and exam period (in percentages)

Medical drug use[a]	Model student	Mean student	Choice disillusioned student	Active test anxiety student	Passive test anxious student	Apathetic student	Happy-go-lucky	Total group
During academic year								
Soporific	1.8	1.1	3.4	5.9	10.7	4.0	2.2	2.9
Tranquilizer	1.8	3.3	4.2	11.0	17.3	4.0	0.0	4.6
Stimulant	0.9	2.5	4.2	9.6	18.7	0.0	2.2	4.1
Sedative (pain)	19.8	26.7	28.6	30.9	33.3	12.0	15.7	24.6
Tonic/vitamin	28.7	37.8	45.4	53.7	62.7	36.0	27.0	38.6
During exam period								
Soporific	3.6	4.4	8.4	10.4	14.9	0.0	5.6	6.0
Tranquilizer	4.9	6.4	10.9	26.7	25.7	7.7	5.6	10.1
Stimulant	6.1	15.2	22.7	28.9	39.2	19.2	7.8	16.0
Sedative (pain)	5.8	6.1	9.2	18.4	18.9	3.8	10.0	8.9
Tonic/vitamine	46.0	56.5	65.3	70.6	75.7	61.5	46.7	56.7

Note. [a]Percentages of student types that report the use of one or more medical drugs.

Table 6 Use of cigarettes, light alcohol, coffee, and cola by seven types of students (in percentages)

Use of items[a]	Model student	Mean student	Choice disillusioned student	Active test anxiety student	Passive test anxious student	Apathetic student	Happy-go-lucky	Total group
During academic year								
Cigarettes	9.9	13.4	11.0	11.2	19.2	28.0	9.1	12.3
Light alcohol	2.8	9.5	2.5	2.2	5.5	11.5	11.2	5.8
Coffee	14.2	18.5	24.5	19.9	19.2	7.7	14.4	17.7
Cola	11.1	7.6	3.6	3.3	10.0	23.1	12.5	9.1
During exam period								
Cigarettes	10.5	14.0	12.9	10.4	19.7	28.0	9.1	12.7
Light alcohol	0.3	0.0	1.7	0.0	1.4	0.0	0.0	0.4
Coffee	24.2	29.6	34.8	31.2	30.6	23.0	23.3	28.2
Cola	12.1	18.5	8.3	15.6	27.3	26.0	18.9	16.0

Note. [a] Percentages of student types that use: more than five cigarettes per day; more than two glasses of beer per day; more than four coffees per day; more than two glasses of cola per day.

sonal study during the year. As could be expected, during the examination period there are no differences.

DISCUSSION AND CONCLUSION

Earlier in this chapter we described and differentiated a university student population by means of scores on five scales, combined into student types. This typology does not pretend to be exhaustive or definitive. The items included are related to the descriptive process model, which is motivational in nature and emphasizes test anxiety, neglecting other dimensions, such as study skills. Therefore, replication of these analyses is necessary. Nevertheless, the resulting typology has some merit: it is based on theoretical concepts, the analyses are done on a large student sample, and the different types are psychologically meaningful and valid. It is expected that this typology can aid the mental health program at the university, especially in the provision of study guidance and counseling. Finally, the results of this project uncover new areas for research, for example, on a sharper and more detailed elaboration of the types or on the effectiveness of differentiated or specific training programs. General outcome data of differentiated help programs, related to student typology, have been described elsewhere (Depreeuw, 1991).

The relationship between test anxiety and some health criteria is overwhelming. Both test anxiety student types, active and passive, describe themselves as suffering a good deal from (psycho)somatic complaints, such as headaches and disorders of digestion or respiration. They score higher than all other student types and the passive test-anxious students clearly score higher than the active ones. TAA and TAP students also seem to have generally poorer mental health; their mean scores on general anxiety and on depression tend to be higher than those of most other student types. Again, these relations are more pronounced for the TAP students than for their TAA counterparts. In addition, the social network of the TAP students is problematic. These students have more conflict with the primary social environment, that is, parents, and are more isolated in the university community. Finding that test-anxious students are vulnerable in a general way is in agreement with earlier research data based on the MMPI (Depreeuw, 1984).

Considering these factors, it is not at all surprising that test-anxious students are heavy consumers of medical drugs. Not only do they use anxiety-related drugs such as tranquilizers and hypnotics, they also use other drugs such as sedatives, tonics, and stimulants. Although most of the heavier use occurs during the examination period, heavy use also occurs during the academic year as well. Although we are not in possession of data on the frequency and intensity of the drug-taking behavior, this relationship with test anxiety is alarming.

The unfavorable health profile described above can be supplemented with several other pieces of research data. The TAP students in particular behave less optimally in relation to the consumption of cigaretts and other items that threaten mental and physical health. During the academic year and the examination period, TAP students smoke more than the population mean and drink far more coffee and cola. The TAP students consume an average amount of alcohol during the year, and slightly more during the examination period. The TAA students, on the contrary, behave in a more healthy way in this regard, with the exception of coffee drinking.

A final interesting note is that the TAP types tend to procrastinate. TAP students probably are worse prepared for examinations, they attend classes less, and they study less during the academic year than the student population mean (which is not the same as the mean student type). Other research (Depreeuw, 1991) suggests that the procrastination of the TAP students does not only manifest itself in a quantitative way (study time), but in a qualitative way as well (effective study skills and concentration). In addition, Table 3 shows that the study careers of the TAP students are worse than the population mean. They are overrepresented in the category of the 2 or more years' study average. In contrast, TAA students tend to attend classes and to study more and have slightly better study careers than the population mean.

The interaction and causal relationship between anxiety level, active and passive study avoidance, health characteristics, medical and other harmful item consumption, study career, and differences in social network can furnish interesting hypotheses for future research. For example, one can hypothesize that TAP students postpone study effort because of lower achievement motivation and higher anxiety level; consequently they experience high-stress situations regularly (e.g., intermediate tests) but do not really succeed in compensating for their procrastination in spite of an intensified use of external aids (drugs, coffee, cola, etc.) Bad study results stir up conflicts with parents and negatively influence their lives, at times in interaction with a lowered need for achievement and self-confidence or raised test anxiety. Further research is clearly indicated in this area.

We suggested above that the research at hand could be of value to the psycho-medical-social staff. In an extensive outcome study on high test-anxious students (Depreeuw, 1989), it was shown that a specific group behavior therapy treatment not only resulted in a sharp decline in test anxiety, but in an amelioration of several health criteria as well. A follow-up inquiry on 56 ex-participants 8 to 24 months after the end of the therapy revealed that, whereas 61% used all kinds of medical drugs before the treatment, 26% said that they took less or much less drugs after the treatment; 27% were unchanged, and 9% consumed more or much more. A similar questionnaire filled out by significant others of the students shows even more favorable results. These people report that of the former therapy participants, 70% of them were medical drug consumers in the pretreatment period, 46% took less to much less after therapy, 21% did not change their habits, and only 4%

took more or much more. Further, significant others respond that out of 79% of participants with pretreatment sleeping disorders, 44% ameliorated afterwards, 26% stagnated, and 10% slept worse. In 64% of the participants digestion problems were observed by the significant others, with a more or less considerable amelioration after treatment in 36% of the cases, stagnation in 25%, and worsening in 25%.

Our data suggest that test anxiety must be considered far more complex and dysfunctional for health than it has seemed to be. The relationship between test anxiety and health definitely seems to be causally interactive, a conclusion that is additionally supported by the amelioration of several psychosomatic disorders in large percentages of participants of a behavior therapy treatment program for test anxiety.

REFERENCES

Abramson, L. Y., Seligman, M. E., & Teasdale, J. D. (1978). Learned helplessness in humans: Critique and reformulation. *Journal of Abnormal Psychology, 87*, 49–74.

Bandura, A. (1986). *Social foundations of thought and action: A social cognitive theory.* Englewood Cliffs, NJ: Prentice Hall.

Carver, C. S., & Scheier, M. F. (1988). A control–process perspective on anxiety. *Anxiety Research, 1*, 17–22.

Depreeuw, E. A. (1984). A profile of the test-anxious student. *International Review of Applied Psychology, 33*, 221–232.

Depreeuw, E. A. (1988). Sociale angst en faalangst: een gemeenschappelijk procesmodel met implicaties voor behandeling. [Social phobia and fear of failure: A common process model with implications for treatment]. *Gedragstherapie, 21*, 125–140.

Depreeuw, E. A. (1989). *Faalangst: Theorievorming, testconstructie en resultaatonderzoek van de gedragstherapeutische behandeling.* [Test anxiety: Concept building, test construction, and outcome study of the behavior therapeutic treatment]. Unpublished doctoral dissertation, Catholic University, Leuven, Belgium.

Depreeuw, E. A. (1991). On the fear of failure construct: Active and passive test anxious students behave differently. In K. Hagtvet (Ed.), *Advances in test anxiety research* (Vol. 7, pp. 31–43). Amsterdam: Swets & Zeitlinger.

Depreeuw, E. A., De Neve, H., & Bracke, E. (1988). *Psycho-medisch-sociaal welzijn aan de universiteit. Een onderzoek van welzijn bij ouderejaarstudenten aan de K. U. Leuven.* [Psycho-medical-social health at the university. An examination of well-being of undergraduate students at the University of Leuven, Belgium.] Leuven, K.U. Studentenvoorzieningen.

Heckhausen, H. (1977). Achievement motivation and its constructs: A cognitive model. *Motivation and Emotion, 1*, 283–329.

Hembree, R. (1988). Correlates, causes, effects, and treatment of test anxiety. *Review of Educational Research, 58*, 47–77.

Lazarus, R. S., & Launier, R. (1978). Stress and related transactions between person and environment. In L. Pervin & M. Lewis (Eds.), *Perspectives in interactional psychology* (pp. 287–327). New York: Plenum.

Salamé, R. F. (1984). Test anxiety: Its determinants, manifestations, and consequences. In H. Van der Ploeg, R. Schwarzer, & C. Spielberger (Eds.), *Advances in test anxiety research* (Vol. 3, pp. 83–120). Lisse: Swets & Zeitlinger.

Sarason, I. G. (1988). Anxiety, self-preoccupation and attention. *Anxiety Research, 1*, 3–7.

Tryon, G. S. (1980). The measurement and treatment of test anxiety. *Review of Educational Research, 50*, 343–372.

Verhelst, N., & Vander Steene, G. (1972). A Gulliksen item analysis program. *Behavior Science, 17*, 491–493.

Weiner, B. (1985). An attributional theory of achievement motivation and emotion. *Psychological Review, 92*, 548–573.

Wine, J. D. (1980). Cognitive-attentional theory of test anxiety. In I. Sarason (Ed.), *Test anxiety: Theory, research and applications* (pp. 349–385). Hillsdale, NJ: Erlbaum.

17

Isolation, Anxiety Reduction, and Health

Donald G. Forgays and Deborah K. Forgays
University of Vermont

In the third section of this book, we are concerned with the relationship of anxiety to health. This theme would appear to be somewhat more applied in its orientation than the themes of the first two parts of the book. This is not really so, however, because the application of basic theory and the resulting feedback to theory is a reciprocal process. Strictly applied studies of significant issues are important in their own right in addition to contributing to the generation of theory.

The influence of isolation on human behavior has been of concern for hundreds of years, at least from an anecdotal point of view. Interpretations of the curious behavior observed in shipwrecked sailors, prisoners of war, and even of Admiral Byrd in the Antarctic usually have emphasized the role of isolation in the changes of behavior observed. These changes have included an increase in anxiety, irritability, anger, cognitive dysfunctioning, and even hallucinatory type activity.

Systematic isolation studies began in the 1950s with the work of Donald Hebb and John Lilly. Hebb used the soundproofed room as his isolation environment and Lilly used the deep immersion tank. This early research has been summarized by Zubek (1969, 1973). These were not well-controlled studies, and they led to the development of a stereotype that this form of isolation, called *sensory deprivation* at the time, frequently produced negative cognitive, affective, and consciousness-altering effects. This negative view of isolation has persisted, as Suedfeld and Coren (1989) have emphasized recently, even though a number of studies, including some quite early ones, did not report adverse effects for most of their subjects.

Suedfeld (1980) has reviewed relevant research on the influence of a variety of isolation environments on behavior and has concluded that the negative stereotype associated with isolation is entirely unwarranted. Although some people do not find such environments to be positive, most do. A good deal of positive change can be aided through the use of these environments.

It is not clear why important individual differences exist with respect to the influence of isolation environments. Forgays (1989) has reported that people who stayed in underwater isolation tended to be extroverts and maintained a better orientation to the environment, whereas quitters tended to be introverted and anxious. Physiological differences between these two groups of subjects are consistent with the notion that short-term subjects were more aroused and felt more anxiety than did the long-term subjects. Thus isolation may be stress inducing for some people and stress reducing for others. This may result from an interaction of the specific characteristics of the environment itself, important personality characteristics of the subjects, the amount of time spent in isolation (either on a single run or on multiple runs), and the attitudes and expectations that subjects have about the isolation experience. In the early studies there was reason to believe that subjects anticipated that the environment would cause disturbance. It was no surprise that disturbance was reported by most of these subjects. Recent, better-controlled research indicates that this old stereotype should be laid to rest because most subjects report certain isolation environments to be very relaxing (Forgays & Belinson, 1986).

Explanations of isolation effects have included psychodynamic process change, disturbance of social interaction patterns, and individual difference reactions, among others. One of the more reasonable explanations had associated isolation effects with the arousal system and, more specifically, with the disruption of ongoing neurophysiological substrata involved in the mediation of normal functioning. Studies to test these kinds of possibilities were difficult to design and carry out, and research interest in the isolation area began to wane in the early 1970s.

However, interest was rekindled with Lilly's introduction of a new form of isolation, the flotation tank, in 1977. The focus of interest at that time appeared to be quite applied. Lilly had developed the flotation tank as an acceptable substitute for the more cumbersome and complicated deep immersion procedure. In his 1977 book, he proposed that most people can relax thoroughly in flotation, but, unfortunately, he provided no research data in support of that claim. Later on, others, including Suedfeld (1980) and Thackray (1981), also suggested that reduced stimulation environments are not damaging in terms of stress, arousal increase, and consciousness alteration, and that they may actually be potentially therapeutic.

Although systematic research had not demonstrated that the flotation environment was a relaxing, anxiety-reducing one, the technique was employed as an intervention for a variety of stress-related behaviors during the early 1980s. For example, Fine and Turner (1982) and Stanley and Francis (1984) used flotation isolation as an intervention for essential hypertension; Jacobs, Heilbronner, and Stanley (1984) used it to reduce arousal level; and Turner and Fine (1984a) used it to control pain, and used it again (1984b) to modify heart rate. More recently, the flotation technique has been used by Taylor (1985) to improve learning; by Suedfeld, Metcalfe, and Bluck (1987) to augment scientific creativity; and by Suedfeld and Bruno (1990), coupled with imagery training, to improve athletic performance.

Most of these studies report relaxation and subjective anxiety/stress reduction as a result of flotation. However, many of them were pilot studies with small samples of subjects. In addition, observations were frequently made in less-than-rigorous conditions, and rarely was a control group used. Thus it appeared to be important to accomplish a systematic and well-controlled examination of the supposed benefits of the flotation environment, employing appropriate behavioral and physiological measures.

In this report, this first study (Forgays & Belinson, 1986) will be reviewed briefly. This will establish that flotation isolation is a relaxation environment for most persons. After this, data from several other recent studies will be presented in which flotation was used as an intervention for heavy cigarette smoking and for muscle contraction headache. Then a brief review will be provided of studies examining the habituation process of subjects who floated at least once a week for 6 months, an examination of the comparative benefits of the salt water tank with a dry tank in which the subject rests on a waterbed mattress, and a comparison of the responses of Type A and Type B subjects in flotation. Finally, a brief review of two very recent studies will be made; in them flotation has been used as a creativity-enhancing as well as an anxiety-reducing environment.

FLOTATION AS A RELAXING ENVIRONMENT

The first study in this series was designed to respond to the question: Is flotation isolation a relaxing environment? The subjects were 20 males and 20 females between the ages of 18 and 48, with a mean age of 30 years for the males and 29 for the females. Most were students, faculty, and staff members at the University of Vermont; none were from the Department of Psychology.

The apparatus is a closed tank 1.22 by 2.44 meters in size, holding approximately 400 liters of water mixed with 400 kilograms of magnesium sulfate. The water is heated to 34.5 °C and the tank is in a quiet space. Brain waves are recorded on a Grass polygraph by surface electrodes, with the signals passing through photo-isolator connections for subject safety.

A week or so before floating, each subject completed the Eysenck Personality Inventory,[1] the Jenkins Activity Survey, the Zuckerman Sensation Seeking Scale, the Edwards Personal Preference Schedule, the SCL-90-R, the Spielberger Trait Anxiety Inventory, and the Taylor Manifest Anxiety Scale.

Each subject has three floats, each a week apart. The maximum trial length is specified as 150 minutes but the subject could terminate a trial at any time. After each float the subject estimates time spent in the tank, fills out the Spielberger State Anxiety Inventory, the Zuckerman Multiple Affect Adjective Check List, and the Myers Isolation Symptom Questionnaire, and lastly, responds to a short interview about the float experience.

Results of this study will only be summarized here; the actual data and full results are available in the 1986 report (Forgays & Belinson). Was flotation found to be relaxing? Yes, for most subjects. Subjects spent, on average, about 1 3/4 hours in the tank on each float, out of a possible 2 1/2 hours. This fact alone would suggest that they found the environment acceptable. Subjects tend to underestimate time in tank by about 15 minutes per float. Such underestimation was more typical of older female subjects and occurred least in younger males who are more accurate estimators. Female subjects spent more time in isolation introspecting and in self-appraisal than did the males. Heart rates dropped within and across floats but increased slightly at the end of each float, which seems to be a preparation for exiting, and also for the third float relative to the first two, which may be a result of a boredom factor gradually increasing.

In the post-float interviews, 90% of the trials were rated as having gone well and 83% as being quite pleasant. The only irritation on occasion was the salt solution, especially if some of it got into the subjects' eyes. About half the subjects slept briefly, thinking was relaxation-oriented rather than task-oriented, time passed quickly, and many subjects reported the sensations of "seeing" or "hearing" something. Over 90% stated that they looked forward to the next float.

The personality data reinforce the idea that general emotional stability and low anxiety is characteristic of those who spend more time in the tank, who show a

---

[1]Full references for all specific test measures listed in this chapter can be obtained from general test sources or by writing to the authors.

reduction of heart rate asociated with floating, and indicate a sense of well-being after floating.

The data, then, seem to be quite clear. Most subjects are very positive about the float experience, and the physiological data and length of stay in the tank confirm this appraisal. However, important individual differences exist in this general picture; the sex and age of the subject and also some specific personality characteristics affect just how relaxing and pleasant the float experience is.

FLOTATION AS AN INTERVENTION FOR CIGARETTE SMOKING

After this first study in which the relaxation merits of flotation were established, we used the technique as an intervention for heavy cigarette smoking (Forgays, 1987). If cigarette smoking is stress related, at least for some smokers a stress-reducing environment may be useful as an intervention for this health-injurious behavior.

The subjects were 22 females, between the ages of 20 and 64 years, with a mean age of 40 years. They reported that they had smoked an average of 30 cigarettes per day for an average of 20 years but wished to stop. Each had tried an average of 2.5 systematic attempts to stop before enrolling in our study; usually these attempts were formal interventions.

The characteristics of the flotation environment are as already described. There were two groups of subjects, massed and distributed floats, and each subject had five floats. The first float of all subjects was up to 150 minutes in duration. Thereafter, half (12 subjects) received four more floats of up to 60 minutes duration, one each on consecutive days (massed floats). The other half (10 subjects) received four more floats of up to 150 minutes each, each one separated by a week (distributed floats). Half of each of these subject groups (five subjects in each of two groups) received four brief taped messages in their last four floats and the other half did not. The messages are an attempt to stimulate imagery associated with quitting smoking. After each float, the subject estimated time in tank, filled out questionnaires, and was interviewed briefly. The principal dependent measure in this study related to changes in smoking behavior. Changes in other measures can be found in the article reporting this research (Forgays, 1987). Table 1 shows the mean level of initial smoking, mean smoking level after five floats, the mean smoking level and percentage reduction of initial level at 12 months after the floats, and the mean level of smoking and percentage reduction of initial level at 24 months after intervention. All these measures are based on self-report.

As seen in Table 1, all groups reduce smoking appreciably after any of the interventions. Twelve months later, however, the two massed groups show less of a smoking reduction than the two distributed float groups, and this difference is statistically significant. This pattern continues for the 24 month follow-up data. Differences between the two massed groups and between the two distributed groups are not significant, indicating that the messages we used had no measurable effect. Variability is reasonably high in the data because some subjects do not change their smoking pattern at all, whereas others stop smoking completely.

Although this study is limited in the number and gender of subjects used, it does demonstrate the relative efficacy of flotation as a smoking intervention. The finding of more than a 40% reduction in smoking after 2 years compares very favor-

Table 1 Smoking pattern changes for the six groups of subjects

	Mean level of initial smoking[a]	Mean level of smoking after five interventions[a]	Mean level of smoking 12 months later[a]	Reduction (%) at 12 months of initial level	Mean level of smoking 24 months later[a]	Reduction (%) at 24 months of initial level
Group 1 (*N* = 5) Massed 60-minute floats with messages	36.00	16.40	30.00	16.67	32.00	11.11
Group 2 (*N* = 7) Massed 60-minute floats without messages	32.14	12.60	25.00	22.22	28.00	12.88
Group 3 (*N* = 5) Distributed 150-minute floats with messages	34.00	12.60	22.00	35.29	20.00	41.18
Group 4 (*N* = 5) Distributed 150-minute floats without messages	32.00	14.20	19.00	40.63	18.00	43.75

[a]Number of cigarettes per day.

ably with virtually all other attempts to intervene in cigarette-smoking behavior. This study needs to be replicated on a larger number of subjects of both sexes and with an improved approach to promote cognitive restructuring (the messages).

FLOTATION AS AN INTERVENTION FOR MUSCLE CONTRACTION HEADACHE

While we were studying flotation and cigarette smoking we also examined flotation as an intervention for muscle contraction headache. This is the most common type of headache throughout the world and accounts for about 80% of all headaches. These chronic disturbances usually are treated with muscle relaxant, analgesic, and antidepressant drugs, often with undesirable side effects. The cost for nonprescription pain killers used by these sufferers is estimated to be over $500,000,000 in the United States alone. Therefore it seems to be very important to find a behavioral intervention for this ailment. Various relaxation techniques have shown the greatest promise in past research.

One of the University of Vermont graduate students in my laboratory, Randy Rzewnicki, did pilot work on this problem in Vermont and then had the good fortune to be able to continue the work at the University of British Columbia, under the direction of Professor Peter Suedfeld. In their study, they recruited 6 male and 25 female subjects, each of whom had been diagnosed by a physician as having chronic muscle contraction/tension headaches and each of whom had at least three headaches per week (Rzewnicki, 1991). These subjects were assigned randomly to one of four experimental conditions lasting 4 weeks each. In the first condition, the subjects underwent 1-hour sessions twice a week in a dark sound-proofed room, reclining on a cot. In the second condition, the subject spent 1 hour in a soundproofed room and 1 hour each week in the flotation tank. In the third condition, the subject spent 1 hour in the soundproofed room and underwent 1 hour of Progressive Muscle Relaxation (PMR) training each week. In the fourth condition, the subject spent 1 hour in the flotation tank and 1 hour undergoing PMR training each week.

The dependent variable in this study was a Headache Index, which reflected a combination of submeasures of the frequency, intensity, and duration of headache activity. This was obtained from a daily record kept by each subject.

The much-simplified results of this study are shown in Table 2. There were no significant differences between groups on the Headache Index at baseline. Follow-up at 2 and 6 months shows some interesting changes. At 2 months after intervention, the headache activity of the two groups receiving the flotation tank intervention is reduced much more than that of the other two groups. At 6 months' follow-up, all groups show improvement in the index over that of the earlier follow-up. The 79% reduction for the combination of PMR and flotation tank is considerably higher than the comparable figures for the other three groups. In addition, the percent reductions for the second and third conditions are much higher than that for the soundproof room alone.

These data compare very favorably with recently reported data based on a meta-analysis of various relaxation treatments for headache. The meta-analysis found that headache reduction averaged 59%. This figure is considerably lower than the "best" intervention reduction of 79% reported above. We thus conclude that relaxation is a meaningful nonchemical intervention for chronic muscle contraction headache and that flotation isolation is a meaningful contributor to a relaxation intervention.

HABITUATION IN FLOTATION

Several years ago, we began to speculate about the possible habituation process across exposures in the tank. Because floating was shown to be relaxing for most

Table 2 Percent reduction in headache activity from preintervention baseline to postintervention follow-up at 2 and 6 months for the four subject groups

Group	Follow-up time	
	2 months	6 months
Soundproofed room ($N = 5$)	$-9\%^a$	19%
Soundproofed room and flotation tank ($N = 6$)	26%	39%
Soundproofed room and progressive muscle relaxation training ($N = 10$)	$-8\%^a$	48%
Flotation tank and progressive muscle relaxation training ($N = 10$)	21%	79%

[a]Negative sign indicates an increase in headache activity over the baseline measure.

people, would the relaxation benefits and the anxiety and stress reduction be accumulative across repeated floats or would the benefits disappear after the subject had been exposed to the technique for a number of trials? This is an important question because, for certain purposes such as blood pressure or headache interventions, it may be necessary to provide float trials over relatively long periods of time.

To study habituation phenomena in the tank, we floated six male and six female subjects at least once a week for up to 150 minutes per float for a period of 6 months (Forgays, Rzewnicki, & Pudvah, 1991). The subjects were 19 to 43 years old, with an average of 29 years. They were recruited through poster advertising. The total number of floats per subject varied between 29 and 35 over the 6-month period. Conditions of flotation are as described above except that after the first few floats subjects were given access to the laboratory and were trained to float themselves. Before and after each float, the subject filled out the Spielberger State Anxiety Inventory and the abbreviated form of the Zuckerman Multiple Affect Adjective Check List (MAACL), which has submeasures of state anxiety, state depression, and state hostility.

If there is an accumulation effect of this relaxation technique, the preflotation measures should decrease over the 6-month period. If the tank continues to have a relaxing effect on subjects the pre- and postflotation differences in the measures should continue until a ceiling effect is reached if the preflotation measures continue to drop.

The Spielberger State Anxiety and the MAACL measures of state anxiety correlated highly; for all the preflotation measures, the Pearson r was 0.656, and for the postflotation measures it was 0.555—both significant at the $p < .001$ level. Pre- and postflotation comparisons were made by t test, collapsing the data by month and then by week. All these differences were significant at the $p < .001$ level. This indicates that the tank continues to have relaxation benefits over the 6-month period with repeated floats. ANOVA analysis of all the preflotation measures, all the postflotation measures, the difference between pre- and postflotation measures, and of the actual time spent in the tank across all floats revealed no significant differences. Thus there were no systematic changes in the preflotation measures across exposure and no accumulation effect of repeated exposure. This was also true for the postflotation measure and the differences between pre- and postflotation measures.

These results seem to be quite clear. Although there is no accumulated benefit of the float experience over many trials, there does continue to be benefit for each trial even after repeated exposures. Thus, although the typical subject does not improve in emotional status across time, at least as measured here, on each occasion of floating there is a significant drop in the measures used. This finding, coupled with the lack of significant change in the postflotation measures, the difference measures, and the time spent in the tank suggests that these measures do not display the usual habituation phenomena expected with repeated exposure. This is a most unusual finding.

COMPARISON OF "WET" AND "DRY" FLOTATION ENVIRONMENTS

In the last few years, commercial firms have introduced a "dry" version of the wet tank. In it, the subject does not come in contact with the salt solution; rather, the subject rests on a water bed liner that may be filled with salt solution or ordinary water. The chamber is similar to the wet tank although somewhat larger and more handsomely finished. Firms have advertised that the dry tank affords the same benefits as the wet one but without the nuisances associated with the salt solution. Like in the case of our first study, such positive claims were not based on research, only on speculation. We believed once again that we had to evaluate these claims under controlled conditions. If a dry tank is as beneficial as the wet one, it would be easier and less expensive to use. This study is an attempt to compare the relative influence of these two "flotation" environments in a controlled protocol (Forgays, Forgays, Pudvah, & Wright, 1991).

The subjects were 14 male and 10 female undergraduate students between 18 and 22 years of age, recruited though class announcements. The float for the "wet" exposure is as described above. To provide the most adequate control that we could, in the "dry" exposure we drained about 300 L of the salt solution from the tank and pumped it into a waterbed mattress that was "floated" on top of the remaining 4 cm of solution. Temperature and other variables of the tank environment remain the same for the two conditions except that the subject did not come into contact with the salt solution in the dry float.

Each subject made two floats, one in the wet condition and one in the dry condition in a balanced design. Time for each float was up to 60 minutes and the runs were usually about 1 week apart. Preflotation and postflotation measures included the Spielberger State Personality Inventory; the Profile of Mood States (POMS), which has six scales: *tension, vigor, anger, confusion, depression,* and *fatigue;* and heart rate, which was obtained for 2-minute periods just before entering and after leaving the tank.

Means and standard deviations for each of these measures for male and female subjects in the two environments are given in Table 3. As seen there, pre- and postflotation decreases generally occur for both sexes in both environments. ANOVA analyses reveal that the pre- and postflotation POMS scales differences are not significant. For the SPI scales, there was an overall significant decrease in anxiety from pre- to postflotation and a greater pre- to postflotation decrease in anxiety in female subjects over male subjects for both environments. For the *curiosity* scale, a significant wet/dry interaction with sex was found, reflecting a greater pre- and postflotation decrease in curiosity among female subjects in the wet environment and a greater decrease in curiosity among male subjects in the dry environment. No significant effects were found for the *anger* scale. For heart rate, the wet/dry effect was highly significant. This reflected a greater decrease in the wet tank pre- and postflotation than in the dry tank for both sexes. The interaction of sex with wet/dry environment was also significant, reflecting the fact that female subjects decreased heart rate pre- and postflotation more in the wet tank than in the dry tank in contrast to male subjects, whose decrease was more similar in the two environments.

The remaining measures were obtained by interviews with the subjects after the two floats. The interviews confirm the test and heart rate data. Whereas floats of either type are rated highly, wet floats are rated more highly than dry and are reported to produce more consistently higher degrees of relaxation. Both environments had their irritations but these did not appear to mitigate the positive effects of "floating" in either environment. Virtually all subjects said that these isolation experiences were pleasant.

Table 3 Means and standard deviations (in parentheses) for the various POMS and SPI scales and the heart rate measure for the two environments by gender and for combined gender

| | Wet environment | | | | | | Dry environment | | | | | |
| | Male subj. (N = 14) | | Female subj. (N = 10) | | All subj. (N = 24) | | Male subj. (N = 14) | | Female subj. (N = 10) | | All subj. (N = 24) | |
	Pre	Post	Pre	Post	Pre	Post	Pre	Post	Pre	Post	Pre	Post
POMS												
Tension	14.14 (8.07)	7.14 (2.96)	15.00 (5.87)	8.20 (3.12)	14.50 (7.10)	7.58 (3.01)	13.00 (6.85)	7.21 (3.07)	16.00 (6.63)	7.90 (2.42)	14.25 (6.78)	7.50 (2.78)
Vigor	6.07 (2.84)	10.00 (4.87)	6.00 (2.75)	8.80 (4.92)	6.04 (2.74)	9.50 (4.82)	5.07 (3.08)	9.57 (3.61)	5.30 (3.33)	8.40 (4.70)	5.17 (3.12)	9.08 (4.04)
Anger	4.36 (5.73)	1.50 (2.95)	1.70 (1.77)	1.10 (1.10)	3.25 (4.65)	1.33 (2.33)	2.50 (2.95)	2.71 (4.43)	1.50 (1.08)	1.10 (1.60)	2.08 (2.38)	2.04 (3.57)
Confusion	2.36 (2.13)	6.29 (4.27)	1.90 (1.20)	5.90 (2.85)	2.17 (1.79)	5.13 (3.67)	2.07 (1.86)	6.50 (4.22)	3.00 (2.79)	6.60 (3.84)	2.46 (2.28)	6.54 (3.98)
Depression	10.71 (5.64)	7.07 (3.47)	10.00 (4.76)	7.60 (2.72)	10.42 (5.19)	7.29 (3.13)	8.57 (4.03)	8.00 (6.25)	7.80 (1.81)	6.10 (1.10)	8.25 (3.26)	7.21 (4.85)
Fatigue	4.64 (3.34)	6.50 (6.49)	4.90 (3.07)	4.20 (3.36)	4.75 (3.17)	5.54 (5.44)	5.50 (4.40)	5.86 (4.93)	4.70 (4.00)	5.00 (5.19)	5.17 (4.17)	5.50 (4.94)
SPI												
Anxiety	21.00 (2.75)	20.86 (1.51)	22.00 (2.71)	20.40 (2.01)	21.42 (2.72)	20.67 (1.71)	20.50 (2.85)	20.86 (2.54)	21.70 (1.42)	20.20 (1.87)	21.00 (2.40)	20.58 (2.26)
Curiosity	22.79 (6.29)	22.71 (5.77)	23.50 (4.12)	20.90 (4.93)	23.08 (5.40)	21.96 (5.40)	24.71 (4.87)	21.79 (4.54)	22.30 (2.71)	21.50 (3.89)	23.71 (4.22)	21.67 (4.20)
Anger	12.57 (4.16)	10.42 (0.76)	10.70 (1.06)	10.80 (1.62)	11.79 (3.36)	10.58 (1.18)	11.71 (2.95)	10.43 (1.09)	11.20 (1.81)	10.20 (0.42)	11.50 (2.50)	10.33 (0.87)
Heart rate	79.14 (3.92)	73.43 (4.03)	90.80 (3.01)	83.00 (3.62)	84.00 (6.83)	77.42 (6.13)	80.71 (4.55)	76.71 (4.14)	89.20 (2.49)	84.80 (4.18)	84.25 (5.70)	80.08 (5.76)

Thus both environments appear to be acceptable with respect to their potential utility as therapeutic intervention environments. Because it is far easier to produce and maintain a dry environment, it would seem to be indicated for many purposes. However, generally, the wet environment was superior in terms of relaxation and pleasantness ratings and in terms of heart rate decrease, and this was especially so for female subjects. Thus, for certain purposes such as producing a relaxed state, especially for male subjects, perhaps the dry tank would be acceptable, whereas for the modification of physiological process, especially for female subjects, the wet tank is more likely to be recommended. Further research needs to be done to evaluate these possibilities.

This study and an earlier one have examined the effects over time on behavior of four different isolation environments. In the earlier study (Forgays & McClure, 1974), we compared the quiet room with a water-immersion isolation technique in the same subjects and found the underwater experience to be associated with greater arousal and stress.

TYPE A/TYPE B SUBJECTS IN FLOTATION

In the first of these two studies, we focused on subjects who were high Type A and subjects who were low Type A (Type B). Because important Type A characteristics include hurriedness, impatience, competitiveness, and hostility, and because anxiety is frequently associated with this classification, we wished to see if Type A and Type B subjects would react to flotation in different ways, especially on anxiety and related measures. Our expectation was that, because of a floor effect, Type Bs would not show reduced anxiety and related measures to any degree but that Type As would show greater pre- and postflotation changes in anxiety.

About a year ago we accomplished two pilot studies in which we selected subjects on the basis of either Type A/Type B or *creativity* measures and floated them in the wet tank to examine pre- and postflotation changes on relevant measures. The results were quite promising and since that time we have done full studies following the same subject selection process (Forgays & Forgays, 1991a).

We selected 23 female and 16 male subjects on the basis of their Type A/Type B scores on the AATABS measure (Wrzesniewski, Forgays, & Bonaiuto, 1990). Twenty of them (9 males, 11 females) scored at least 1 standard deviation above and 19 (7 males, 12 females) scored at least 1 standard deviation below the normative mean. Half of these subjects were given one float of up to 60 minutes in the wet tank and half were controls who spent a similar period of time in a lighted waiting room. Before and after each condition, each subject responded to the Spielberger State Personality Inventory, the Profile of Mood States, and the Guilford Creativity scales. They also were tested with a 2-minute trial on a Pursuit Rotor, 1 minute of which provided a soft click when on target and 1 minute of which provided a loud buzz when on target.

Means and standard deviations of these various groups of subjects on pre- and postflotation conditions on the various measures are given in Table 4. As seen there, all subject groupings show decreases in emotional state measures after either environmental condition and positive increases in creativity and in pursuit motor performance.

Table 4 Means and standard deviations (in parentheses) for preflotation and postflotation measures

Tests		Floater (N = 19) Pre	Post	No float (N = 20) Pre	Post	Type A (N = 20) Pre	Post	Type B (N = 19) Pre	Post	Females (N = 23) Pre	Post	Males (N = 16) Pre	Post
Spielberger SPI	Anxiety	18.95 (4.21)	14.05 (4.60)	20.20 (8.31)	18.45 (6.24)	19.75 (6.66)	15.80 (3.58)	19.42 (6.67)	16.84 (7.66)	18.70 (6.16)	16.83 (6.82)	20.88 (7.14)	15.56 (4.26)
	Curiosity	28.74 (6.09)	25.37 (5.79)	24.00 (4.58)	21.85 (4.43)	27.05 (5.74)	23.70 (6.05)	25.53 (5.95)	23.42 (4.72)	26.35 (5.77)	23.48 (4.99)	26.25 (6.06)	23.69 (6.05)
	Anger	10.16 (0.69)	10.00 (0.00)	11.65 (2.41)	11.10 (1.45)	11.05 (2.46)	10.50 (1.28)	10.79 (1.18)	10.63 (1.07)	10.57 (0.99)	10.52 (0.99)	11.44 (2.73)	10.63 (1.41)
Guilford	Creativity	54.53 (12.65)	62.84 (12.11)	53.50 (12.06)	58.90 (12.54)	54.95 (12.41)	62.10 (12.72)	53.00 (12.22)	59.47 (12.11)	54.70 (10.43)	61.17 (13.21)	53.00 (14.67)	60.31 (11.35)
Pursuit rotor	No buzz	11.61 (10.10)	27.11 (10.96)	11.45 (8.02)	28.50 (10.10)	12.79 (7.60)	28.68 (12.46)	10.26 (10.16)	27.00 (8.08)	10.86 (9.98)	25.68 (9.57)	12.44 (7.50)	30.81 (11.05)
	Buzz	14.17 (10.00)	26.56 (9.39)	12.85 (9.68)	25.95 (10.04)	16.47 (9.59)	27.37 (11.43)	10.47 (9.12)	25.11 (7.51)	11.73 (9.01)	23.55 (8.28)	15.88 (10.44)	29.94 (10.33)
POMS	Tension	9.11 (5.33)	3.74 (6.19)	10.55 (8.19)	7.05 (6.55)	10.15 (7.11)	3.60 (3.47)	9.52 (6.83)	7.37 (8.31)	9.13 (6.94)	6.30 (7.95)	10.88 (6.91)	4.19 (3.45)
	Depression	4.21 (6.02)	1.89 (4.31)	9.15 (10.95)	7.25 (10.58)	5.20 (7.90)	3.95 (6.71)	8.37 (10.23)	5.37 (10.18)	6.22 (8.97)	4.13 (9.40)	7.50 (9.60)	5.38 (7.22)
	Confusion	5.68 (3.82)	4.11 (3.09)	8.25 (4.99)	7.95 (4.67)	6.80 (5.20)	5.90 (4.27)	7.21 (3.98)	6.26 (4.62)	6.30 (3.82)	6.22 (4.02)	8.00 (5.49)	5.88 (4.99)
	Vigor	15.47 (6.79)	15.26 (5.75)	14.45 (6.85)	11.25 (6.13)	14.35 (6.52)	13.10 (6.23)	15.58 (7.11)	13.32 (6.36)	15.70 (7.08)	13.35 (6.06)	13.88 (6.31)	13.00 (6.61)
	Hostility	2.53 (6.21)	0.89 (1.91)	5.00 (6.51)	3.00 (3.95)	5.20 (8.45)	2.35 (3.48)	2.32 (2.63)	1.58 (3.06)	1.70 (2.27)	1.35 (2.84)	6.81 (8.94)	2.88 (3.70)
	Fatigue	7.47 (7.93)	5.05 (5.87)	10.15 (6.65)	9.30 (6.55)	9.50 (7.67)	8.10 (7.11)	8.16 (7.10)	6.32 (5.87)	8.17 (7.21)	6.57 (5.56)	9.81 (7.64)	8.19 (7.77)

ANCOVA analyses were performed with the preflotation measure as the covariate and the postflotation measure as the dependent variable. The principal findings are that those who floated decrease significantly more than those who did not on two of the three SPI measures, the *anxiety* and the *curiosity* scales, but there is no difference on the *anger* scale. Floaters also decrease significantly more than non-floaters on five of the POMS scales: *tension, depression, confusion, hostility,* and *fatigue.* On the *vigor* subscale, interestingly enough, the control subjects decrease significantly more than the floaters who stay quite the same from pre- to postflotation. The floaters also show a significant pre- to postflotation increase over the controls on the Guilford Creativity scales but not on Pursuit Rotor performance. As for the Type A/B subjects, the only significant difference on the SPI scales is for the *curiosity* scale, where the Type A subjects decrease pre- to postflotation more than the Type B subjects. On the POMS, the Type A subjects decrease significantly more than the Type B subjects on the *tension* subscale. No Type A/B differences were found on the creativity scales, and on the Pursuit Rotor the Type B subjects increased their pre- to postflotation performance significantly more than the Type A subjects but only under the no-buzz condition.

The interaction terms are complicated and too detailed for presentation here. For the most part they reflect significant interactions of gender with other terms such as Type A/B or float/no float and suggest interesting hypotheses to be followed up in additional research.

Once again, we provide evidence for the tension-reducing qualities of the float tank over an appropriate control condition, and some additional benefits as well, such as the increase in creativity measures. We also have found some evidence that Type A and Type B subjects respond differently to the float condition on two of the emotional scales and on the Pursuit Rotor measure. These are meaningful differences. Type As decrease more than Type Bs on the SPI curiosity subscale, suggesting that Type As become less aroused in the tank while Type Bs remain at about the same level. Similarly, Type As decrease their POMS tension score more than Type Bs. Both these changes are consistent with the conclusion that flotation is a stress-reducing environment. The Pursuit Rotor finding is interesting. One might expect that Type As would try to improve their performances; they do so here, but only on the less stressful no-buzz condition, again suggesting that they are in a relatively calm state after the float. Type Bs change more than Type As on the Pursuit Rotor on both buzz and no-buzz conditions, but appreciably more under the buzz condition.

FLOTATION AND CREATIVITY

Suedfeld (1980) has speculated that isolation environments might be associated with an increase in creativity expression. We have had floaters reporting subjective increases in creative processes during and after the isolation experience. Several have described vivid and varied sweeps of imagination, similar to watching a film without knowing what scene would occur next.

Suedfeld, Metcalfe, and Bluck (1987) have studied creativity enhancement associated with flotation. The self ratings of their subjects suggested that novel ideas generated after floating were more creative than those developed in a control condition. This study had only five subjects, all of whom were psychology faculty, and the procedures and measures used were somewhat imprecise. Thus a more sharply controlled investigation of the relationship of the influence of flotation on creativity expression was in order.

The design of our study is similar to the Type A/B study outlined above. Here, however, we selected subjects on the basis of preflotation scores on the Guilford Creativity scales. We wished to examine whether flotation would have a differential effect on creativity scores as compared with the quiet control condition (Forgays & Forgays, 1991b). Thirty subjects were selected from among student volunteers, 17 female and 13 male. Half were given one float in the tank of up to 60 minutes while the other half enjoyed quiet time resting on a couch in a darkened room. This was quite different from the waiting-room control used in the Type A/B study, where the control subject was allowed to read.

Each subject responded to the Spielberger Personality Inventory and the Profile of Mood States before and after the intervention condition, float or control. The two groups of subjects were matched roughly on the basis of preflotation scores on the Guilford Creativity Scales, and they were given an alternate form of this measure in the postflotation period.

Means and standard deviations of these various measures for pre- and postflotation intervention are given in Table 5 for the float and no-float subjects. As seen there, both groups decrease their SPI and POMS scale scores from pre- to postflotation conditions, with only two exceptions. The float group increases its *vigor* score while that for the controls decreases. In addition, the float group increases its *creativity* score while the control subjects do not change.

These data were analyzed by ANCOVA with each preflotation measure as the covariate, and the postflotation measure as the dependent variable. We found that creativity increased significantly from pre- to postflotation measure ($p <$ .001); this was because the float group increased significantly more than the control group ($p <$ .03); the control group had not changed. In addition, all the SPI scales and all the POMS scales, except for *vigor* and *fatigue*, decreased significantly from pre- to postflotation measures. With respect to subgroup effects, the control group decreased its *curiosity* score postflotation over preflotation significantly more than the float group ($p <$ .03), while the float group decreased

Table 5 Means and standard deviations (in parentheses) of the float and no-float subjects on pre- and post-creativity, SPI, and POMS scales

	Float		No float	
	Pre	Post	Pre	Post
Guilford creativity	58.80 (6.99)	62.20 (6.93)	59.00 (6.38)	58.75 (7.59)
Spielberger SPI				
Anxiety	15.13 (4.66)	13.20 (5.52)	21.33 (5.91)	14.87 (4.37)
Curiosity	32.80 (5.63)	32.20 (6.11)	29.20 (4.33)	26.93 (5.62)
Anger	10.80 (2.34)	10.80 (2.14)	12.20 (6.04)	11.33 (4.89)
Profile of mood states				
Tension	7.87 (4.49)	5.20 (4.04)	13.00 (7.76)	5.60 (3.09)
Depression	4.13 (6.11)	0.93 (1.62)	7.20 (10.35)	4.00 (6.94)
Anger	2.87 (3.98)	0.60 (1.45)	4.87 (8.97)	3.07 (8.59)
Vigor	18.47 (5.40)	22.20 (5.07)	16.13 (5.89)	13.53 (6.52)
Fatigue	5.33 (4.50)	1.87 (2.80)	9.40 (7.96)	6.33 (5.85)
Confusion	5.93 (3.81)	5.20 (2.51)	7.80 (5.07)	4.47 (3.04)

significantly more than the control group on the *depression* ($p < .02$), *hostility* ($p < .05$), and *fatigue* ($p < .0001$) scales of the POMS. However, the float group increased significantly more than the control group on the *vigor* scale ($p < .01$).

DISCUSSION

This review of recent flotation studies demonstrates the efficacy of this technique in effecting change in a variety of behaviors. Flotation clearly is associated with relaxation and stress reduction in most persons. Subjects have been males and females from 18 to over 60 years of age, and most show positive change after floating. It must be emphasized, however, that there are important individual differences in these effects with some subject groupings, for example, younger males. The influence of individual differences on flotation effect must be examined more systematically in the future.

In addition, flotation appears to be a possible effective intervention for several health conditions. We evaluated flotation as an intervention for cigarette smoking and others have used the technique as an intervention for patients with chronic tension headaches. In both instances, flotation was as effective an intervention for these conditions as any other techniques that have been examined systematically to date. For headaches, it must be remembered, flotation should be accompanied with relaxation training to be most efficacious. Others have found flotation to be effective in the management of essential hypertension and in pain control. Clearly, this method should be studied systematically as a possible intervention for other health conditions.

It is likely that emotional/personality factors contribute to the effectiveness of flotation in the modification of important behaviors. We reported, for example, that Type A and Type B people respond differently to this environment. Research should be undertaken to study how people with other emotional/personality characteristics respond to this type of isolation. Characteristics that are likely targets for early study include sensation seeking, introversion/extroversion, neuroticism, and self-esteem.

It is an intriguing notion that flotation isolation may be used to enhance creative effort. In the studies reported above, we found a significant increase in measured creativity associated with flotation. Our studies, however, were pilot studies. Thus they should be replicated and extended with larger samples and additional measures of creativity. If our results are corroborated, attempts to examine the possible underlying factors that may contribute to this positive effect should be undertaken. It is important to determine if the effect is caused by relaxation alone, with an attendant reduction in anxiety/stress, by some kind of subtle practice effects, by a distraction or incubation effect such as that described by Poincaré many years ago, or by physiological changes that continue after the float is over and influence behavior for a time. These are complex issues and a good deal of well-designed research needs to be done to evaluate them.

Finally, we must try to explain why flotation isolation should have any effect at all on any process or behavior. We frankly do not know at this time, but several possibilities exist; some are cognitive and some are physiological.

One cognitive possibility has been provided by Lilly (1977). He proposed that flotation leads to relaxation through psychodynamic changes that occur during the float. Presumably the self becomes better integrated in some way; such a speculation is difficult to assess.

A different kind of cognitive process is one that we observed in many of the subjects of our smoking intervention study. These subjects were females and several of them were married and had children. In the interview that we conducted after the float, many of these subjects commented that floating was a very positive experience because they could be quietly alone, without the noise and interruptions of children, telephone, or even a husband. They were able to think, plan, and indulge in self-examination. This latter aspect has been mentioned by subjects in most of our float studies, males and females of all ages. For most of us, everyday life involves continuous sensory bombardments and it is frequently sought out by many as a response to potential boredom. However, this state of affairs does not permit effective self-evaluation. Indeed, high sensation seeking may well occur as an avoidance of self-examination processes. Such processes, however, may be necessary before appropriate behavioral changes can take place. Flotation may have its effect, at least in part, by providing a comfortable environment in which such cognitive restructuring can occur. In future studies we will look at our data with self-evaluation processes in mind, for example, by breaking subject groups down on the basis of whether self-evaluation processes had occurred or not.

Physiological changes may also be taking place in the float experience. We reported heart rate reductions associated with flotation in two of the studies mentioned. In other studies we have found blood pressure reductions and brain wave pattern changes consistent with relaxation in the subject. It is possible that flotation may operate in the manner of biofeedback to provide greater self-control of physiological process (cf. Turner & Fine, 1984b). Floating also may produce a change in metabolic rate and in heart rate because of autonomic processes. However, one must keep in mind that heart rate changes occur only in some subjects. It is clear that careful measurement of physiological changes should be part of future flotation studies.

A distinct possibility exists that neurotransmitter changes are associated with the flotation experience. These in turn may bring about cognitive or behavioral changes. Turner and Fine (1984a), for example, have found systematic corticosteroid changes in pain patients after floating. These chemical changes may well have been the basis for the positive pain changes observed.

Another neurotransmitter change that may occur in flotation is an increase in the production of endorphins. The comfortable, relaxed state of many subjects in flotation may reflect such a chemical increase, which in turn may be associated with a variety of cognitive and behavioral changes, including the sense of well-being, a reduction in the perception of pain, or a reduction in emotional state, with specifically an increase in anxiety or anger thresholds.

It is, of course, quite likely that both cognitive and physiological changes result from the float experience and that they operate in an interactive manner. In our search for conditions that promote a reduction in anxiety, stress, and anger and an increase in perceived positive quality of life, it is important that we research aspects of the float experience that are essential to the occurrence of positive change. The specific features of the float environment, including the state of confinement and the salt used, may be incidental to the effects observed. A private environment that is conducive to self-examination may be all that is required.

Additional research is required to elaborate these issues and to answer the many important questions they pose.

REFERENCES

Fine, T. H., & Turner, J. W., Jr. (1982). The effect of brief restricted environmental stimulation therapy in the treatment of essential hypertension. *Behavior Research and Therapy, 20,* 567–570.

Forgays, D. G. (1987). Flotation REST as a smoking intervention. *Addictive Behavior, 12,* 85–90.

Forgays, D. G. (1989). Behavioral and physiological responses of stayers and quitters in underwater isolation. *Aviation, Space, and Environmental Medicine, 60,* 937–942.

Forgays, D. G., & Belinson, M. J. (1986). Is flotation isolation a relaxing environment? *Journal of Environmental Psychology, 6,* 19–34.

Forgays, D. G. & Forgays, D. K. (1992a). The use of flotation isolation to modify anger/hostility and anxiety in Type A and Type B young adults. Submitted for publication.

Forgays, D. G. & Forgays, D. K. (1992b). Creativity enhancement through flotation isolation. Submitted for publication.

Forgays, D. G., Forgays, D. K., Pudvah, M., & Wright, D. (1991). A direct comparison of the wet and dry flotation environments. *Journal of Environmental Psychology, 11,* 179–187.

Forgays, D. G., & McClure, G. (1974). A direct comparison of the effects of the quiet room and water immersion isolation techniques. *Psychophysiology, 11,* 346–349.

Forgays, D. G., Rzewnicki, R., & Pudvah, M. (1991). Habitation effects in repeated flotation isolation trials. Unpublished manuscript. University of Vermont, Burlington, Vermont.

Jacobs, G. D., Heilbronner, R. L., & Stanley, J. M. (1984). The effects of short-term flotation REST on relaxation: A controlled study. *Health Psychology, 3,* 99–111.

Lilly, J. C. (1977). *The deep self.* New York: Simon & Schuster.

Rzewnicki, R. (1991). The effects of isolation and relaxation interventions for chronic tension headache sufferers. Master's thesis, University of Vermont, Burlington, Vermont.

Stanley, J. M., & Francis, W. D. (1984, September). The effects of REST and REST enhanced self-regulation on essential hypertension. Presented at the XXIII International Congress of Psychology, Acapulco, Mexico.

Suedfeld, P. (1980). *Restricted environmental stimulation: Research and clinical applications.* New York: Wiley.

Suedfeld, P., & Bruno, T. (1990). Flotation REST and imagery in the improvement of athletic performance. *Journal of Sports & Exercise Psychology, 12,* 82–85.

Suedfeld, P., & Coren, S. (1989). Perceptual isolation, sensory deprivation, and REST: Moving introductory psychology texts out of the 1950s. *Canadian Psychology, 30,* 17–29.

Suedfeld, P., Metcalfe, J., & Bluck, S. (1987). Enhancement of scientific creativity by flotation REST (Restricted Environmental Stimulation Technique). *Journal of Environmental Psychology, 7,* 219–231.

Taylor, T. (1985). The effects of flotation Restricted Environmental Stimulation Therapy on learning: Subjective evaluation and EEG measurements. In T. H. Fine & J. W. Turner, Jr., (Eds.), *Proceedings of the First International Conference on REST and Self-Regulation* (pp. 76–85). Toledo: IRIS.

Thackray, R. I. (1981). The stress of boredom and monotony: A consideration of the evidence. *Psychosomatic Medicine, 43,* 165–176.

Turner, J. W., Jr., & Fine, T. H. (1984a, September). REST-assisted relaxation and chronic pain. Presented at the XXIII International Congress of Psychology, Acapulco, Mexico.

Turner, J. W., Jr., & Fine, T. H. (1984b, September). Effects of restricted environmental stimulation therapy (REST) on self-control of heart rate. Presented at the XXIII International Congress of Psychology, Acapulco, Mexico.

Wrzesniewski, K., Forgays, D. G., & Bonaiuto, P. (1990). Measurement of the type A behavior pattern in adolescents and young adults: Cross-cultural development of AATAB. *Journal of Behavioral Medicine, 13,* 111–135.

Zubek, J. P. (Ed.). (1969). *Sensory deprivation: Fifteen years of research.* New York: Appleton-Century-Crofts.

Zubek, J. P. (1973). Behavioral and physiological effects of prolonged sensory and perceptual deprivation: A review. In J. E. Rasmussen (Ed.), *Man in isolation and confinement* (pp. 9–83). Chicago: Aldine.

18

Perceived Costs and Benefits of Cigarette Smoking Among Adolescents: Need Instrumentality, Self-Anger, and Anxiety Factors

Martin V. Covington and Carol L. Omelich
University of California, Berkeley

There is general agreement among health educators that the perceived consequences of a decision to smoke cigarettes are influential factors in the process of smoking initiation, resistance, and cessation. This view has been explicated most fully in the Fishbein model of behavioral intentions as applied to the dynamics of cigarette use (Ajzen & Fishbein, 1970; Fishbein, 1977). According to Fishbein and others (e.g., Ajzen & Madden, 1986), the intention to perform specific behaviors in a given situation is the best predictor of actual behavior. Behavioral intentions in turn are considered to be a function of both the personal and social–normative beliefs held by the individual regarding the positive and negative consequences of alternative actions. In the case of cigarette use, other things being equal, the fewer the perceived negative consequences and the more the positive benefits attributed to smoking, the stronger will be the intention to smoke. Conversely, if the balance of perceived costs and benefits of smoking is unfavorable, individuals will be less likely to smoke.

If perceived consequences do, in fact, influence health decisions, then making more salient the costs of smoking and, conversely, dismantling beliefs about the benefits of smoking should represent major intervention strategies for both smoking cessation and prevention goals. Although researchers generally acknowledge the importance of such cost/benefit analysis, many antismoking programs view the problem of prevention largely, if not exclusively, in terms of building resistance to peer pressure (for a review, see D'Onofrio, 1983; Covington & D'Onofrio, 1983). Few programs deal extensively with the motives to smoke that are implied in a cost/benefit analysis, such as the child's belief that smoking is instrumental in achieving a sense of maturity, autonomy, or affiliation. One likely reason for this situation is that researchers lack a comprehensive understanding of the consequences of smoking as perceived by youngsters in the age ranges generally tar-

Preparation of this article was supported in part by a National Cancer Institute grant to the first author as co-principal investigator with Professor Carol N. D'Onofrio, and in part by a California Division American Cancer Society grant awarded to the second author.

geted for intervention and of how such perceptions enter into the dynamics of decisionmaking.

The overall purpose of the present study was to investigate the perceived costs and benefits of cigarette use and their relationship to future intentions to smoke. More specifically, we were interested in determining which source of consequences—either costs or benefits—is the more salient in influencing a decision to smoke or not. This question holds considerable practical implications. For example, if the perceived benefits of smoking prove to be the more influential, then instructional strategies aimed at dismantling beliefs about alleged benefits should be accorded a more prominent role than is presently the case. Moreover, to extend this example, it may be that not all perceived benefits will influence intentions to the same degree or in the same way.

Three sets of consequences were selected for study: one representing the alleged benefits and two reflecting the potential costs of cigarette use. The source of benefits was related to need instrumentality, specifically the degree to which smoking is seen by children as an effective means for attaining a sense of (a) maturity, (b) autonomy, and (c) belonging. One of the two sources of perceived costs pertained to health consequences, namely, the perceived likelihood of becoming addicted to cigarettes and the potential health dangers of smoking, including lung cancer. The other cost was reflected in the affective consequences of smoking. Smoking can unleash a host of negative emotions. First, there are feelings of anxiety over parental reactions to one's smoking, including fear of possible punishment. Second, there is fear of peer displeasure and the possibilities of ostracism from the group. Third, there is a potential for self-upset at having smoked, reactions that are typically portrayed as self-blame and anger turned inward for falling short of one's idealized self-image (e.g., Averill, 1982).

The proposed analysis as well as the heuristic value of the larger cost/benefit model (Fishbein, 1977) rests squarely on the assumption that anticipated consequences actively influence smoking decisions in predictable ways. Given the centrality of this assumption, it is surprising to find that, with few exceptions (see Covington & Omelich, 1987, 1988), little empirical evidence on such causal dynamics is available, especially regarding the question of which of the consequence domains is most salient.

An additional focus of this study concerns the fact that most previous data on perceived consequences has been collected without reference to important situational factors. Two situational dimensions were explored in the present study: the nature of the group composition and the presence/absence of circumstances that deflect personal responsibility for smoking. In the first instance, perceived consequences are likely to vary depending on whether the context in which smoking decisions are made involves a few close friends or a large number of casual acquaintances and strangers. Another related but heretofore understudied situational variation involves smoking temptation in a solitary setting where the individual smokes alone.

As to the second dimension, it is well known that the perceived consequences of one's actions also depend on the individual's sense of culpability, as when, for example, a person who harms another without intending to do so is usually held less accountable than the individual who acts with malice. Analogously, parents who believe that their child was pressured to smoke by peers are likely to react less harshly than if the child had smoked of his or her own free choice. In this connection, research on the need to establish and maintain a sense of intellectual competency in school indicates that creating plausible explanations that externalize the causes of one's poor performance offsets the negative consequences of academic failure such as lowered self-estimates of ability, shame, and the threat to one's sense of worth (Covington, 1984, 1992; Covington & Omelich, 1979, 1981; Covington, Spratt, & Omelich, 1980). It is very likely that such self-aggrandizing tactics extend to any situation where the need to establish a positive self-image and a valued reputation is a prime goal. For example, in a health context, children's self-recriminations for violating parental rules about smoking may be minimized by convincing themselves and others that smoking was not a characteristic action, and consequently does not reflect on their reputation because they did not intend doing it. In effect, it is the difference between having smoked and being a smoker, with all the attendant negative personal characteristics that are associated with this label (Bland, Bewley, & Day, 1975; Borland & Rudolph, 1975; Horn, 1963; Jessor & Jessor, 1977).

It is even possible that perceived physical risk (e.g., becoming addicted) depends on the degree to which the individual can avoid accepting personal responsibility for his or her actions. According to this analysis, peer group pressure may operate not only to increase the temptation to smoke (Covington & Omelich, 1988) but also simultaneously to provide a plausible reason for disavowing personal responsibility, a condition that, in the process, releases one's inhibitions against smoking.

Finally, the present study considered the possibility that the causal impact of perceived consequences on a smoking decision may also depend on individual difference factors such as the child's smoking history as well as his or her age. Previous cost/benefit research typically has not preserved the distinction between smokers and nonsmokers. Nor are other relevant aspects of the individual's smoking history usually considered, such as the length of time a person has been smoking or age at smoking onset. Although we know enough to assert with some confidence that nonsmokers perceived greater risks and fewer benefits to smoking than do smokers, we remain essentially ignorant regarding more subtle, but potentially significant aspects of the smoking dynamic. For example, Leventhal and Cleary (1980) suggest that the process of smoking uptake is best understood as a staged progression, beginning with a preparatory stage followed by initiation and experimentation stages, and finally, culminating in a period of long-term maintenance. If their contention is correct, it is reasonable to expect that the perceived costs and benefits of smoking, and their relative causal importance to smoking decisions, may vary across these stages. For example, the young child's decision whether or not to try a cigarette for the first time is probably heavily influenced by peer considerations (Bergen & Olesen, 1963; Gorsuch & Butler, 1976; Hill, 1971), whereas a decision to continue smoking, to quit, or even to cut down may depend more on beliefs about personal inconvenience or stress, including the physiological repercussion of withdrawal. Any successful antismoking program must acknowledge the fact that there are, in reality, a number of potential smoking decisions, not just one, and that each decision is likely to be influenced by a somewhat different set of beliefs about consequences (Fishbein, 1977; Thompkins, 1966). Moreover, not only do smokers face different decisions than do nonsmokers, but so do children and teenagers as contrasted to adults. If smoking dynamics have a developmental history, then the age of the at-risk youngster may also contribute to and possibly interact in unexpected ways with a stagewise progression. For example, it is unlikely that a 16-year-old youngster who had smoked for 5 years will hold the same views of smoking as will a 12-year-old child who began smoking only recently.

In summary, the purpose of the present study was to investigate the relative causal roles of various perceived costs and benefits in a decision to smoke cigarettes, and to determine whether or not these dynamics depend on (a) the individual's smoking history, (b) age, and (c) situations that differ in degree of implied personal responsibility.

METHODS

Subjects and Procedures

The data reported in the present study were gathered in connection with the development of a theory-based antismoking intervention program by the Risk and Youth: Smoking Project (RAY:S) at the University of California, Berkeley (Covington, 1981; Covington & D'Onofrio, 1983). As part of the program of basic research, the RAY:S Smoking Risk Profile questionnaire (Covington, Omelich, & Schnur, 1982; D'Onofrio, Thier, Schnur, Buchanan, & Omelich, 1982; Omelich, 1985) was administered to 6,494 students in 51 schools in 12 cities in the greater San Francisco Bay area. Of these students, 49.2% (3,198) were sixth-graders, 31.2% (2,025) were eighth-graders, and 19.6% (1,271) were in the tenth grade, a sampling distribution across grade level that allowed for adequate numbers of youngsters with smoking experience in the lower grades. The total sample was composed of 8.7% Asians, 32.0% blacks, 8.6% Hispanics, 48.6% whites, and 2.1% who classified themselves as "other." This distribution roughly approximated the ethnic mix of the San Francisco Bay area. Boys and girls were represented in equal proportions across the three grade levels and the five ethnic group designations.

Current smoking status was measured by a single, self-report item as follows: "Check the *one* sentence below that best tells about you": "I have never smoked a cigarette (not even a few puffs)"; "I tried one or two cigarettes and never smoked again"; "I smoked for a while, but do not smoke any more"; or "I smoke cigarettes regularly." The incidence of cigarette use in the final sample of 5,249 students having a complete data file closely paralleled that found in national self-report surveys of adolescents (National Institute of Education, 1979). Some 2,390 subjects had *never smoked* (NS) ($N = 1,526$, $N = 581$, and $N = 283$ at grades 6, 8, and 10, respectively). Among the remaining subjects, three additional groups were differentiated: that group that had smoked only one or two cigarettes (*Experimental Smokers;* ES); that group that had smoked for a while and then quit (*Ex-smokers;* XS); and that group that smoked regularly at the time of assessment (*Regular Smokers;* RS). There were 1,631 ES subjects ($N = 676$, $N = 550$, $N = 405$, at grades 6, 8, and 10, respectively); 578 XS subjects ($N = 174$, $N = 229$, and $N = 175$, respectively); and 650 RS subjects ($N = 122$, $N = 310$, $N = 218$, respectively).

Although sex, ethnic, and socioeconomic group differences in smoking behavior have been demonstrated previously (Covington, Omelich, & Schnur, 1982; D'Onofrio, 1983), preliminary analyses of the present data set indicated that these sources of difference contributed only negligibly to variations in the dependent variables under consideration. Moreover, these individual difference variables did not interact with either grade level or smoking status to influence the dependent variables of primary interest to the present study. Thus these sources of individual difference were not considered as factors in the major analyses.

In addition to the index of self-reported smoking described above, predictor variables included distal antecedents (e.g., family characteristics), beliefs regarding the instrumental value of cigarettes, and the quality of prosocial decisionmaking skills.

One section of the questionnaire presented several brief, lifelike scenarios in which youngsters might be tempted to smoke. Four of these tempting situations represented group situations that varied along two dimensions: (a) the composition of the group setting involving either a few best friends (Intimate), or a number of casual acquaintances and strangers (Casual); and (b) the presence or absence of a reason that might deflect personal responsibility for smoking. In one version of the story line, justification for smoking was provided by the fact that peers had already begun to smoke (excuse), whereas in the other condition, no one was smoking, therefore leaving it up to the subject to initiate cigarette use (no excuse). The scenario for the Intimate/no excuse condition was presented as follows: You are alone with two good friends; some cigarettes are around, but no one is smoking yet. A fifth situation unrelated to variations in group composition depicted smoking temptation in a solitary setting as follows: You are all alone and find some cigarettes. These five situations formed one factor in the between-group analyses reported in this study, with approximately 1,050 subjects assigned randomly to each situation.

Measures

Irrespective of the particular smoking scenario presented, all subjects responded to the same Likert-type rating questions as follows:

Self-responsibility. "In this situation, how much would you feel you are to *blame* if you smoke?" (1 = not at all; 5 = very much).

Behavioral intentions. "Do you think you would actually smoke in this situation?" (1 = definitely no; 5 = definitely yes).

Smoking consequences. Eight theoretically derived items represented the basic smoking consequences thought to mediate smoking intentions (Covington, 1981, 1983; Covington, Omelich & Schnur, 1982). Three items measured specific affective costs: The expected degree of parental ($M = 4.18$), peer ($M = 2.84$), and self upset ($M = 3.81$) should the subject decide to smoke. Two additional items formed a health costs cluster: the degree to which subjects anticipated physical problems ($M = 4.11$) and becoming addicted ($M = 3.29$) as a result of smoking. The remaining three items were associated with need fulfillment and indicated whether or not smoking would be beneficial by promoting a sense of group cohesion ($M = 2.39$), autonomy ($M = 3.03$), or maturity ($M = 1.82$).

Statistical Analysis

Between-group differences for each smoking consequence were assessed by separate 4 (Smoking Status) × 3 (Grade) × 5 (Tempting Situation) analyses of variance. The appropriate F values were incorporated into the text for the sake of brevity. Determination of the specific source of any significant group differences involved the use of Dunn's multiple-comparison procedures (d) (Kirk, 1968), which permit testing a specific number of a priori contrasts at a predetermined level of significance ($\alpha = .05$). The postulated causal roles of self-responsibility and the anticipated consequences of smoking in determining smoking intentions were evaluated by a path analytic interpretation of multiple regression. Path analysis (Anderson & Evans, 1974; Duncan, 1966, 1975; Heise, 1975; Kerlinger & Pedhazur, 1973; Pedhazur, 1982) allows for all determining factors as specified by a causal model to be incorporated into an overall predictive analysis, thereby permitting an estimation of the relative contribution (both direct and indirect) of each determinant to variations in dependent variables of interest. Hypotheses regarding the similarity of these causal relationships across the five tempting situations, for the three age groups, and for those subjects with varying smoking histories were assessed by comparing the differences in magnitude of regression slopes for the relevant groups.

RESULTS AND DISCUSSION

Table 1 provides the mean values and standard deviations for eight smoking consequences by smoking status and grade.

Smoking Status

The smoking status effect proved significant for all eight consequences, indicating that the expected results of a decision to smoke varied as a function of the

Table 1 Mean values and standard deviations for eight anticipated smoking consequences by current smoking status and grade level

		Smoking status				Grade		
Depedent variable		NS	ES	XS	RS	6	8	10
Costs	(N)	(2,390)	(1,631)	(578)	(650)	(2,498)	(1,670)	(1,081)
Parent upset	M	4.41	4.14	3.99	3.57	4.35	4.17	3.78
	sd	1.08	1.14	1.21	1.37	1.11	1.15	1.30
Peer upset	M	3.18	2.77	2.47	2.06	3.05	2.67[a]	2.60[a]
	sd	1.43	1.42	1.36	1.28	1.46	1.41	1.44
Self upset	M	4.20	3.84	3.43	2.55	4.05	3.59[a]	3.56[a]
	sd	1.29	1.37	1.48	1.46	1.36	1.48	1.54
Physical	M	4.31	4.06	3.94	3.59	4.23	3.97[a]	4.10[a]
	sd	1.15	1.25	1.26	1.36	1.20	1.27	1.27
Addiction	M	1.36[a]	3.28[a,b,c]	3.17[c,d]	3.15[b,d]	3.18	3.33	3.46
	sd	1.73	1.62	1.61	1.55	1.73	1.60	1.58
Benefits								
Affiliation	M	2.26	2.43[a]	2.42[a]	2.67	2.36[a]	2.48	2.28[a]
	sd	1.40	1.37	1.36	1.34	1.40	1.37	1.34
Autonomy	M	2.96[a]	2.99[a,b]	3.12[b]	3.29	3.04[a]	3.04[a]	3.00[a]
	sd	1.65	1.55	1.52	1.51	1.62	1.55	1.60
Maturity	M	1.72	1.83[a]	1.93 [a,b]	2.02[b]	1.89[a]	1.84[a]	1.63
	sd	1.21	1.19	1.21	1.28	1.29	1.18	1.06

Note. Values with the same superscript (e.g., *a, a*) are not significantly different ($p > .05$).

individual's previous smoking history, all Fs $(3,5189) > 9.23$, $p < .05$, $\omega^2 = .003 - .137$. A series of pairwise contrasts between all smoking status categories for each consequence indicated that in all cases regular smokers (RS) perceived the consequences of smoking differently than did members of the NS group, $p < .05$. The mean values for exsmokers (XS) and experimental smokers (ES), typically fell between these two extremes. The significance of all pairwise contrasts is indicated by superscripts in Table 1.

Costs

First, consider the three affective costs of a decision to smoke. The RS group anticipated far less parental upset than did NS students ($d = .84$, $p < .05$). Similarly, the RS group expected their peer group to react less negatively to their smoking than did the NS group ($d = 1.12$, $p < .05$). Correlatively, smokers expressed less self-blame as a consequence of smoking ($d = 1.65$, $p < .05$). Taken in the aggregate, these results corroborate previous research. Disproportionately large numbers of parents of smoking children are themselves smokers (Borland & Rudolph, 1975; Covington & Omelich, 1987) and, for this reason, would probably be less inclined to treat their children's infractions harshly. Moreover, because disproportionately large numbers of the close friends of smokers also smoke (Kelson, Pullella, & Otterland, 1975), it is hardly surprising that these youngsters would take each other's smoking behavior in stride. Finally, given such peer and parental acceptance of smoking, and sometimes even its active encouragement by older brothers and sisters (Gorsuch & Butler, 1976), a decision to smoke among already confirmed smokers would scarcely violate their own developing personal norms or sources of self-definition.

Now consider the perceived health costs of cigarette use as a function of smoking status. A series of pairwise contrasts between smoking status groups indicated that the NS group perceived greater health risks in smoking and estimated a greater likelihood of addiction than did the RS group ($d = .72$ and $.21$, respectively, $p < .05$). Although there was a rank-order progression of differences in anticipated health costs between the four smoking status groups (NS > ES > XS > RS), addiction consequences were less reliably differentiated among subjects with some history of cigarette involvement (RS, XS, ES), $p > .05$.

Benefits

Next, consider the three perceived benefits of a decision to smoke listed in Table 1. Pairwise contrasts by smoking status within each of the consequence categories indicated that regular smokers believed that cigarettes were more instrumental in achieving a sense of group cohesion and a personal reputation for autonomy and for maturity than did the NS group ($d = .41$, $.33$ and $.30$, respectively, $p < .05$). However, compared to the anticipated affective costs of smoking discussed above, perceptions of smoking instrumentality were less reliably differentiated among nonsmokers, experimental smokers, and exsmokers (see Table 1).

Grade

Costs

Each of the three affective costs also varied with age. Irrespective of smoking status, the older the subjects, the less they expressed upset with themselves for smoking, $F(2,5189) > 9.03, p < .05, \omega^2 = .026$; the less they expected negative peer-group reactions, $F(2,5189) = 10.74, p < .05, \omega^2 = .019$), and the less they anticipated parental sanctions, $F(2,5189) = 50.20, p < .05; \omega^2 = .033$. The progressive suspension of such inhibitory factors as parental displeasure and internalized self-punishment would appear to be a natural consequence of an emerging preoccupation with wider peer group affiliation, and a quickening of the exploration of other life-style options as children grow older (Covington & Omelich, 1987; Krosnick & Judd, 1982). Moreover, as seen by the general absence of Smoking Status × Grade interactions, all children appeared subject to these same disinhibiting dynamics to an equal degree, irrespective of the individual's history of smoking. The only exception to this uniformity was a significant Smoking Status × Grade interaction for parental upset, $F(6,5189) = 2.09, p < .05$. Eighth-grade exsmokers expected their parents to be disproportionately more upset at their smoking. Although this effect was negligible for all practical purposes ($\omega^2 = .001$), it suggests one of the reasons why some adolescents become exsmokers: severe parental displeasure.

Perceived health costs also varied by age, both $Fs(2,5189) > 5.68, p < .05$. Sixth-grade students were more sensitive to the general health risks of smoking than were either eighth-grade or tenth-grade students ($d = .26, .13$, respectively). Also, tenth graders were more aware of the possibility of becoming addicted than were either of the other two age groups ($d = .28, .13$, respectively).

Benefits

Perceptions of the potential benefits of smoking also differed by grade but only for affiliation $F(2,5189) = 8.61, p < .05; \omega^2 = .003$, and maturity, $F(2,5189) = 33.90, p < .05; \omega^2 = .006$. Irrespective of smoking group membership, eighth graders appeared more accepting of the view that smoking helps maintain group cohesion than either sixth- or tenth-graders. Moreover, tenth-graders no longer adhered as strongly as younger adolescents to the view that smoking would secure them an appearance of maturity. This is only one of the many reasons why youngsters in the earlier adolescent years are particularly vulnerable to smoking uptake (see Covington & Omelich, 1987, 1992).

Tempting Situations

Table 2 displays the mean values and standard deviations for each of the eight consequences of smoking under a solitary smoking condition and under the four group conditions: Intimate group/casual group × Excuse/no excuse. The overall main effect for situations was significant for seven of the eight consequences, all F values $(4,5189) > 2.99, p < .05, .002 > \omega^2 < .048$. Only self-upset proved nonsignificant, $F(4,5560) = 1.28$, (n.s.), suggesting that degree of self-recrimination experience is independent of particular situations, at least those investigated here. A planned complex contrast for each of the remaining consequences between the two small group (intimate) and two large group (casual)

Table 2 Mean values and standard deviations for eight smoking consequences by tempting situation

		Tempting situation				
		Intimate friends		Casual friends		
Depedent variable		Excuse	No excuse	Excuse	No excuse	Alone
Costs	(N)	(1,054)	(1,043)	(1,058)	(1,018)	(1,076)
Parent upset	M	4.06	4.19^b	4.06	4.20^b	4.38
	sd	1.21	1.18	1.21	1.21	1.08
Peer upset	M	2.84^a	2.94^{a,b}	2.71^c	2.96^b	2.73^c
	sd	1.42	1.47	1.41	1.45	1.50
Self upset	M	3.83^a	3.76^a	3.79^a	3.74^a	3.86^a
	sd	1.42	1.46	1.45	1.49	1.46
Physical	M	4.02^a	4.18^b	3.94^a	4.11^b	4.26
	sd	1.25	1.18	1.29	1.28	1.18
Addiction	M	3.16^a	3.34^{b,c}	3.22^{a,d}	3.31^{b,c,d}	3.40^c
	sd	1.64	1.69	1.65	1.65	1.67
Benefits						
Affiliation	M	2.55^a	2.24^{b,c}	2.56^a	2.20^b	2.38^c
	sd	1.34	1.43	1.33	1.38	1.38
Autonomy	M	2.62^a	3.37^b	2.58^a	3.33^b	3.26^b
	sd	1.52	1.56	1.54	1.56	1.57
Maturity	M	1.80^a	1.85^{a,b}	1.77^a	1.91^b	1.78^a
	sd	1.19	1.26	1.18	1.24	1.23

Note. Values with the same superscript (e.g., *a, a*) are not significantly different ($p > .05$).

conditions, regardless of excuses, indicated that group composition has little, if any, impact on the perceived consequences on smoking, (all *d* values < .07). In no case did these *d* values approach the $\alpha = .05$ significance level. For this reason, group composition as a factor was not pursued further.

Similar complex contrasts were computed for each consequence between the excuse/no excuse conditions, irrespective of group composition. All contrasts proved significant, $p < .05$, with the exception of self-upset and maturity.

Costs

As to affective costs, the presence of an excuse led to a reduction in the perceived magnitude of negative reactions for two of the three factors. When youngsters perceived themselves as being pressed into smoking (excuse condition), they believed their parents would be less displeased than if they had made a free choice to smoke ($d = .13$), and also that their peer group would be less critical of their decision ($d = .18$, $p < .05$). The failure of the excuse condition to mitigate feelings of self-punishment is puzzling ($d = .06$, $p = >.05$). The lack of a significant Smoking Status × Situation interaction confirms that this outcome is not simply due to combining subjects across smoking status categories. Neither smokers nor nonsmokers differed in their negative self-reactions as a function of the availability of excuses even though, as was just demonstrated, nonsmokers had more reason to be upset with themselves. The distinction between public and private disclosure may be useful in interpreting this null finding (Covington, 1984; Miller, 1978; Schlenker, 1975). Excuses may prove more helpful in maintaining a public image of praiseworthiness than in convincing oneself privately that such a reputation is deserved.

The anticipated affective costs of solitary smoking deserves special mention. Because a sense of personal responsibility is likely to be maximal in solitary smoking, affective reactions were expected to be more severe here than under any of the group conditions. Indeed, this appeared to be the case. With regard to degree of perceived parent upset, solitary smoking was differentiated from ratings gathered under both the combined no-excuse group conditions ($d = .18$) and the combined excuse group conditions ($d = .32, p < .05$).

As to health costs, subjects tended to perceive fewer negative consequences of smoking if they followed the group lead (excuse) than if they initiated smoking on their own (no excuse). Regardless of group composition (intimate or casual), subjects in the excuse condition perceived themselves to be less at risk physically ($d = .17, p < .05$). Moreover, within the small group setting, those following the lead of close friends rather than initiating smoking themselves, also believed that they were less likely to become addicted ($d = .18, p < .05$). Similarly, a complex contrast between the combined excuse conditions and the solitary condition indicated that lower perceived health risks ($d = .28$) and lower estimates of "getting hooked" ($d = .21$) followed from smoking in a group than when smoking alone ($p < .05$). At the same time, once again the psychological equivalency of solitary and group situations where the individual initiated smoking himself or herself (no excuse) was further supported. Specifically, the physical ($d = .12$) and the additive ($d = .08$) consequences of smoking under these two circumstances were judged equally likely ($p > .05$).

These findings regarding health consequences are noteworthy for two reasons. They provide evidence of reality distortion in matters of health maintenance and, as a consequence, they indicate something of the complexity of the task of developing effective antismoking intervention programs. It is possible, of course, that no psychological distortion is involved in estimating the probabilities of addiction. Perceptions of fault and blame may, indeed, moderate the likelihood of becoming psychologically dependent. For example, the person who smokes casually, as a matter of situationally induced compliance, may be less addictive-prone than the individual who smokes irrespective of the social circumstances. However, such arguments are difficult to sustain with the findings of perceived physical risk. There is little reason to believe that the negative physiological effects of cigarettes on the body, especially regarding disease mechanisms (Jarvik, 1970, 1973), depend on situationally induced reasons for smoking. Moreover, it is unlikely that ignorance of health facts per se is the primary cause of such a self-serving distortion. The available evidence is clear in suggesting that virtually all adolescents, smokers and nonsmokers alike, understand that smoking may be harmful to their health (Covington & D'Onofrio, 1983). Rather, what appears to be happening is a minimizing or denial of what is already known and widely acknowledged (Covington, Omelich, & Schnur, 1982; Omelich, 1985). Obviously, antismoking programs must deliver more than facts to be effective against such rationalization. They must also attempt to personalize health knowledge (Fishbein, 1977). How this is accomplished, and its programmatic effectiveness, depends in turn on the causes of distortion. For example, it is by no means certain that the cause of the distortion implied in the current data is the result of an active denial or avoidance of facts as contrasted to the product of a developmentally immature view of cause-

and-effect relationships that is dominated by magical thinking. In the latter case, youngsters may process the correct information regarding health facts and cigarettes, but the meaning and relevance of such facts to rational, self-interested decision making may be distorted through the imperfect filter of childhood perceptions. More specifically, we know that when children maintain that negatively sanctioned behavior (such as hitting others) is not their fault, or at least not intended, they believe that things will turn out for the best (Whitman, 1972). The same reasoning may well be operating here with regard to health issues. The distinction between self-justified avoidance behavior and immature cognitions holds considerable implications for intervention strategies. If on the one hand the cause is a self-serving suspension of beliefs, then educational planners should explicate and expose mechanisms of rationalization and denial. If on the other hand the fault rests with a limited view of reality foreclosed by immature magical thinking, then questions regarding the developmental timing of instruction become paramount.

Benefits

Next, consider the situational determinants of the perceived benefits of smoking. Complex contrasts between the excuse/no excuse conditions proved significant for feelings of group affiliation ($d = .34, p < .05$). Naturally, whenever the individual joins others who are already smoking (excuse), a sense of group cohesion is more likely to be greater than when the individual himself or herself initiates the smoking (no excuse). In effect, waiting for others to start smoking reaps a double benefit for youngsters. First, it strengthens feelings of cohesion per se, and, second, it acts to suspend one's inhibitions against smoking by offsetting various negative consequences such as perceived parental displeasure. However, although joining others who are already smoking may heighten a sense of group solidarity, it is unlikely to enhance a reputation for personal autonomy and independence. Indeed, the excuse conditions lead to a reduced sense of autonomy compared to the no excuse conditions ($d = .75$). Thus it would appear that the goals of affiliation and autonomy may be somewhat antagonistic and offsetting; depending on circumstances, smoking may either add to a sense of social cohesion or provide evidence of personal independence, but not both simultaneously.

Solitary smoking elicited a level of felt autonomy and independence that was undifferentiated from the combined no-excuse group conditions ($d = .09, p > .05$). In short, solitary smoking maximizes responsibility for one's actions, and therefore represents an unambiguous source of evidence for independent decision making. However, solitary smoking appeared less evocative of feelings of affiliation as compared with those elicited under group circumstances where other peers are already smoking (excuse condition) ($d = -.18, p < .05$). Once again it appears that the situational cues for autonomy may be incompatible with perceptions of group cohesion and affiliation.

Two situation $\times$ grade interactions further illuminated these findings on need fulfillment. Eighth-graders appeared particularly sensitive to the affiliation benefits afforded by joining in with others who are already smoking (excuse condition), $F (8,5189) = 2.50, p < .05, \omega^2 = .003$, a result that underscores previously reported evidence of the heightened susceptibility of these middle adolescents to peer group pressure (Covington & Omelich, 1987, in press). On the other hand, tenth-graders perceived greater benefits to a sense of autonomy than did other groups in the two no-excuse group conditions in which they, rather than others, initiated smoking, F (8,5189) = 5.76, p < .05, ω^2 = .008, perhaps suggesting why these older adolescents were more likely to initiate group smoking.

Finally, consider the level of anticipated maturity elicited in the various tempting situations. Although the overall situational effect reached significance, F (4,5189) = 2.61, p < .05, none of the planned pairwise or complex contrasts was significant, p > .05. The presence of a Situation × Grade interaction likely accounts for this null result, F (8,5189) = 2.61, p < .05, ω^2 = .004. Only older subjects (tenth-graders) differentiated between the five situations regarding their potential to enhance a sense of maturity, with sixth-graders and eighth-graders perceiving all situations as equivalent for demonstrating maturity. This pattern of results may explain why smoking in a social context holds such appeal for many older adolescents who are struggling to establish independence at a time in their development when they are relatively unhampered by concern for parent reactions and by their own self-displeasure should they smoke.

Causal Dynamics

We can now address the question of the causal role, if any, of the perceived costs and benefits of cigarette use in the decisionmaking processes that underlie smoking intentions. The responsibility variable and the eight smoking consequence variables were entered into a hierarchical multiple regression analysis as predictors of intentions to smoke. This analysis accounted for some 19.8% (R^2) of the variation in smoking intentions.

By employing a path-analytic interpretation of these data, we can assess the direct effects of the linkage between self-responsibility and intention and that between consequences and intention, as well as the moderated indirect effects of self-responsibility via each of the eight anticipated consequences (e.g., self-responsibility, parental upset, smoking intentions). No assumptions are made in this analysis regarding the causal reciprocity between same-level variables (e.g., affiliation needs, parental upset). Any observed residual covariation between these same-level variables is assumed to be noncausal and originates from a common dependence on self-responsibility or on variables outside the model. To simplify the presentation, the full path analysis reported is based on the total sample collapsed across smoking situation, grade level, and smoking status. Comparison of the various dynamics occurring as a function of age, situation, and smoking group membership will be reported later.

Inspection of the first column of Table 3 indicates a significant zero-order correlation between self-responsibility and intentions to smoke of .137, p < .05, that decomposes into an insignificant direct effect of self-responsibility on intentions (ρ = .013, p > .05) and a total indirect effect as mediated through perceived consequences of − .150. The source of these various indirect effects can be seen in the eight direct linkages between self-responsibility and consequence linkages (not shown in the table). The degree to which individuals accepted personal responsibility for their actions, or conversely, abdicated responsibility, altered their sensitivity to these consequences, a condition that in turn had a causal impact forward on intentions. Specifically, to the extent that subjects felt responsible for a smoking decision, their anticipation of potential parental upset (ρ = .207), peer upset (ρ = .166), and anticipated self-recrimination (ρ = .311) was magnified, as was their

Table 3   Path coefficients $(\rho)^a$, R^2 increments, and percentage of causal effect (%C) for smoking intentions associated with self-responsibility and eight anticipated consequences of smoking

Causal source	Causal effect[a]	Percent of effect (%C)	R_1^{2b}
Self responsibility ($r = -.137$)			
Direct effect (ρ)	.013	1.3	
Indirect effect via:			
Parent upset	−.023	2.4	
Peer upset	−.014	1.4	
Self upset	−.081	8.2	
Physical	−.020	2.0	
Addiction	.006	0.6	
Affiliation	−.010	1.0	
Autonomy	.001	0.1	
Maturity	−.009	0.9	
Self-responsibility total		17.9	.019
Direct consequences effects (ρ)			
Parent upset	.110[c]	11.1	.048
Peer upset	−.086[c]	8.7	.027
Self upset	−.260[c]	26.3	.057
Physical	−.081[c]	8.2	.004
Addiction	.028[c]	2.8	.001
Affiliation	.143[c]	14.5	.032
Autonomy	.025	2.5	.001
Maturity	.079[c]	8.0	.009
Direct consequences total		82.1	
R^2 total		100.0	.198

[a]Standardized regression coefficients.
[b]All $Fs > 4.58$, $p < .05$.
[c]$p < .05$.

sense of autonomy ($\rho = .047$), $p < .05$. Also, recognition of a general health risk ($\rho = .249$) and possible addiction ($\rho = .197$) increased as individuals accepted personal responsibility, $p < .05$. Contrariwise, the likelihood of enhanced feelings of affiliation ($\rho = -.070$) and maturity ($\rho = -.111$) was decreased to the extent that subjects took responsibility for their actions. Each of these anticipated consequences had a direct impact forward on intentions, thereby indirectly transmitting the effect of self-responsibility (see Table 3).

Overall virtually all the modest impact of self-responsibility on intentions was mediated through the perceived consequences of smoking. Self-responsibility as such made little direct contribution of its own ($\rho = .013$). Of these mediating sources, feelings of self-recrimination were the most substantial transmitters, accounting for almost half ($-.081$) of the total indirect influence of personal responsibility on intentions (self-responsibility, self-upset, intentions).

Next, consider the direct influence of the various perceived consequences on intentions to smoke and their relative causal saliency. Table 3 indicates that all consequences, with the exception of autonomy, made significant direct contributions to variations in intentions to smoke ($p < .05$). For example, in the affective costs domain, to the extent that subjects anticipated negative parental, peer, and self-reactions to their smoking, intentions were decreased ($\rho = -.110, -.086, -.260$, respectively, $p < .05$). Also, in the health costs domain, perceptions of physical health risk as a consequence of smoking exerted an inhibitory influence on intentions ($\rho = -.081$). The only unexpected finding—a slight but positive correlation between concerns for addiction and intentions—appears to be the product of a statistical artifact. Because of the substantial shared variance between general health and addiction issues ($r = .241$), and because of the dominant hierarchical position of the former concern, addiction as a variable added little additional unique variance to reduced intentions. With respect to the benefits of smoking, to the degree that subjects perceived smoking as resulting in greater peer affiliation ($\rho = .143$) and maturity ($\rho = .079$), intentions were increased.

An assessment of the relative causal importance of these various consequences to smoking intentions is provided by a series of incremental F-tests shown in Table 3. As reported earlier, the multiple regression analysis employed the entire model and accounted for 19.8% (R^2) of the variations in smoking intentions. As an aid to interpretation and to provide a common metric for comparison, we have totaled over all direct and indirect pathways associated with each of the nine predictor variables in the model and have reported these aggregated values as a percentage of causal effect (%C) in Table 3. As the first predictor variable entered, self-responsibility accounted for 17.9% of the explained causal effect in intentions, of which the vast majority (%C = 16.6) was mediated indirectly by the combined consequences. As to the additional independent contributions to explained variance made by anticipated consequences, self-upset accounted directly for most of the causal effect (%C = 26.3), with the next most salient contributors being parental upset with 11.1% of the total causal effect and affiliation (%C = 14.5). Peer upset (%C = 8.7), maturity (%C = 8.0), physical health (%C = 8.2), autonomy (%C = 2.5), and, finally, addiction consequences (%C = 2.8) also made significant yet modest contributions to the variations in smoking intentions.

In summary, we conclude that anticipated consequences—both costs and benefits—do exert a considerable influence on smoking intentions, a finding that corroborates a longstanding assumption previously based largely on scattered, unsystematic, and anecdotal evidence. Moreover, as a group, those costs associated with affective consequences were the most salient causal source, both directly ($C = 46.1$) and indirectly as a mediator of self-responsibility ($C = 12.0$). In addition, anticipated negative consequences for health accounted directly for 2.6% and indirectly for 11% of the total causal effect, making the overall impact of perceived costs on intentions substantial (%C = 71.7). By contrast, need fulfillment, or the perceived benefits of smoking, in its combined direct (%C = 25.0) and indirect (%C = 2.0) influence played a somewhat diminished role (%C = 27.0). Finally, as discussed above, the direct effect of feelings of self-responsibility (%C = 1.3) accounted for a negligible amount of the total causal effect under the assumptions of the proposed model.

Finally, consider the evidence on whether or not the perceived consequences of smoking contributed equally to smoking intentions across the age range under investigation, and irrespective of the smoking history of the individual. As to the question of grade-level variations, pairwise comparisons of each of the nine direct regression slopes across the three grade levels revealed essentially identical regression weights, all ts ∞ < 1.96, p > .05. Thus, while the three age groups varied in degree of anticipated consequences, the causal mechanisms involved in these variations—whether associated with affective, need fulfillment, or health issues—were identical for all ages. One exception can be noted. Anticipated guilt for smoking (self upset) among eighth-graders and tenth-graders was a greater deterrent to intentions ($\rho = -.280$, $-.228$, respectively) than among sixth-graders ($\rho = -.146$), $t \infty = 6.04$, 3.84, respectively, $p < .05$. Whereas self-upset over a smoking decision may be more severe among the youngest students (see Table 1), such feelings appear to exert relatively less influence on their intentions.

Pairwise contrasts between the regression slopes of the four smoking-status groups for each direct linkage revealed several additional sources of difference. First, the intention to smoke among RS subjects ($\rho = .199$) and XS subjects ($\rho = .192$) appeared particularly dependent on affiliative needs as compared to the dynamics to which NS subjects are subjected $t \infty = 3.71$, 3.10, respectively, $p < .05$. This suggests that the RS and XS groups suffer a double jeopardy: Not only do adolescent smokers and exsmokers adhere more strongly to the belief that smoking is instrumental to group cohesion, but this belief also has a greater causal salience in determining their subsequent intentions than it does among nonsmokers. A second difference in regression slopes is of equal concern. Whereas the fear of addiction appears irrelevant to smoking intentions among NS ($\rho = .011$), ES ($\rho = -.007$), and XS ($\rho = -.034$) subjects ($p > .05$), awareness of the addictive consequences of smoking actually increases intentions among regular, current smokers ($\rho = .093$), $p < .05$, all $ts \infty > 2.31$, $p < .05$. Here one is reminded of a kind of learned helplessness syndrome (Abramson, Seligman, & Teasdale, 1978) in which young smokers—for whom smoking is already likely under the control of addiction mechanisms and psychological habituation—may be resigned to their fate despite recognition of the negative physiological consequences of continued smoking. On the other hand, fortunately, self-recrimination for smoking, to the extent that these feelings occur among RS subjects, is a more powerful deterrent of smoking intentions ($\rho = -.276$, $p < .05$) compared to its significant but less powerful influence among NS subjects ($\rho = -.086$) and ES subjects ($\rho = -.136$), $t \infty = 5.14$, 3.44, respectively, $p < .05$. Overall, these findings suggest that cessation instruction that focuses on bolstering a view of smoking as antithetical to one's self-integrity would be especially effective among confirmed smokers.

GENERAL DISCUSSION

The larger implications of the present study can be summarized along the following lines. First, the perceived costs of smoking accounted for a considerably greater portion of the explained variance in smoking intentions than did the perceived benefits as a whole (75% vs. 25%, respectively). This implies that the longstanding emphasis on the costs of smoking as an intervention strategy is not only appropriate, but now has empirical justification. Moreover, these data further suggest that among the potential sources of perceived costs, it is those affective costs associated with self- and other-upset that are the most important components. Of special interest here is the theme of self-anger that, as a single variable, accounts for more variance in smoking intentions than do all others. An overall organizing principle for antismoking education is suggested by these data: informed self-interest. By contrast, health risks (costs), which often dominate health curricula, are relatively modest contributors to intentions. This is not to suggest that health facts are unimportant, but only that they are but one of several contributing factors, and are probably not the most important. Knowledge of health facts is clearly a significant precursor to healthy smoking decisions. But such facts must be understood by youngsters in the context of being in their own best interests in order to be fully effective as inhibitors of cigarette use. Otherwise it is all too easy—and only too human—to dismiss or minimize health facts as unrelated to the individual. When this happens, there occurs a self-serving suspension of beliefs and values of the kind reflected in portions of the present data.

Second, the importance of perceived costs as inhibitors of cigarette use, especially those emotions associated with the violation of one's own self-standards (guilt and chagrin), appears to be quite universal. With only slight variations, the strong causal pattern of self-upset leading to inhibition is maintained among all smoking groups, whether of regular smokers or nonsmokers, and irrespective of age level. This parallelism in dynamics across different kinds of youngsters indicates the broad applicability of an instructional focus based on cost factors, especially those concerning self-integrity—whether the educational goal is smoking prevention or cessation. Also noteworthy is the power of the appeal to self-integrity among eighth-graders, the group that is most vulnerable to smoking uptake compared with the other ages investigated here.

REFERENCES

Abramson, L. Y., Seligman, M. E. P., & Teasdale, J. D. (1978). Learned helplessness in humans: Critique and reformulation. *Journal of Abnormal Psychology, 87*, 49–74.

Ajzen, I., & Fishbein, M. (1970). The prediction of behavior from attitudinal and normative variables. *Journal of Experimental Social Psychology, 6*, 446–487.

Ajzen, I., & Madden, J. T. (1986). Prediction of goal-directed behavior: Attitudes, intentions, and perceived behavioral control. *Journal of Experimental Social Psychology, 22*, 453–474.

Anderson, J. G., & Evans, F. B. (1974). Causal models in educational research: Recursive models. *American Education Research Journal, 11*, 29–39.

Averill, J. R. (1982). *Anger and aggression: An essay on emotion.* New York: Springer-Verlag.

Bergen, B. J., & Olesen, E. (1963). Some evidence for a peer group hypothesis about adolescent smoking. *Health Education Journal, 21*, 113–119.

Bland, J. M., Bewley, B. R., & Day, I. (1975). Primary schoolboys: Image of self and smoker. *British Journal of Preventive and Social Medicine, 29*, 262–266.

Borland, B. L., & Rudolph, J. P. (1975). Relative effects of low socioeconomic status, parental smoking and poor scholastic performance on smoking among high school students. *Social Science and Medicine, 9*, 27–30.

Covington, M. V. (1981). Strategies for smoking prevention and resistance among young adolescents. *Journal of Early Adolescence, 1*, 349–356.

Covington, M. V. (1983, April). *The development of an empirical model of cigarette smoking behavior in young adolescents.* Paper presented at the Annual Convention of the Western Psychological Association, San Francisco.

Covington, M. V. (1984). The motive for self-worth. In R. Ames & C. Ames (Eds.), *Research on motivation in education.* New York: Academic Press.

Covington, M. V., & D'Onofrio, C. N. (1983). *Smoking prevention and youth: Motivational strategies* (Final report No. 1-R18-CA-29558-01, National Cancer Institute). Berkeley: University of California.

Covington, M. V., & Omelich, C. L. (1979). Effect: The double-edged sword in school achievement. *Journal of Educational Psychology, 71*, 169–182.

Covington, M. V., & Omelich, C. L. (1981). When defenses fail: Affective and cognitive consequences of repeated failure in the classroom. *Journal of Educational Psychology, 73*, 796–808.

Covington, M. V., & Omelich, C. L. (1987). *Family vs. peer influences on adolescent smoking decisions: A developmental approach.* Unpublished manuscript, Department of Psychology, University of California, Berkeley.

Covington, M. V., & Omelich, C. L. (1988). I can resist anything but temptation: Adolescent expectations for smoking cigarettes. *Journal of Applied Social Psychology, 18*, 203–227.

Covington, M. V., & Omelich, C. L. (1992). The influence of expectancies and problem-solving strategies on smoking intentions. In R. Schwarzer (Ed.), *Self-efficacy: Thought control of action.* New York: Hemisphere.

Covington, M. V. (1992). *Making the grade: A self-worth perspective on motivation and school reform.* New York: Cambridge University Press.

Covington, M. V., Omelich, C. L., & Schnur, A. E. (1982, November). *Exploring the dynamic of adolescent smoking behavior: The inception of a theory-driven, research-based prevention program.* Paper presented at the 110th Annual Meeting of the American Public Health Association, Montreal, Canada.

Covington, M. V., Spratt, M. F., & Omelich, C. L. (1980). Is effort enough, or does diligence count too? Student and teacher reactions to effort stability in failure. *Journal of Educational Psychology, 72,* 717–729.

D'Onofrio, C. N. (1983, April). *Smoking among children: The nature of the problem.* Paper presented at the Annual Convention of the Western Psychological Association, San Francisco.

D'Onofrio, C. N., Thier, H. D., Schnur, A. E., Buchanan, D. R., & Omelich, C. L. (1982). The dynamics of adolescent smoking behavior. *World Smoking and Health, 7,* 18–24.

Duncan, O. D. (1966). Path analysis: Sociological examples. *American Journal of Sociology, 72,* 1–16.

Duncan, O. D. (1975). *Introduction to structural equation models.* New York: Academic Press.

Fishbein, M. (1977). *Consumer beliefs and behavior with respect to cigarette smoking: A critical analysis of the public literature.* A report prepared for the staff of the Federal Trade Commission.

Gorsuch, R. L., & Butler, M. C. (1976). Initial drug abuse: A review of predisposing social psychological factors. *Psychological Bulletin, 83,* 120–137.

Heise, D. R. (1975). *Causal analysis.* New York: Wiley.

Hill, D. (1971). Peer group conformity in adolescent smoking and its relationship to affiliation and autonomy needs. *Australian Journal of Psychology, 23,* 189–199.

Horn, D. (1963). Behavioral aspects of cigarette smoking. *Journal of Chronic Disease, 16,* 383–395.

Jarvik, M. E. (1970). The role of nicotine in the smoking habit. In W. A. Hunt (Ed.), *Learning mechanisms and smoking.* Chicago: Aldine.

Jarvik, M. E. (1973). Further observations on nicotine as the reinforcing agent in smoking. In W. L. Dunn, Jr. (Ed.), *Smoking behavior: Motives and incentives.* Washington, DC: V. H. Winston.

Jessor, R., & Jessor, S. L. (1977). *Problem behavior and psychosocial development: A longitudinal study of youth.* New York: Academic Press.

Kelson, S. R., Pullella, J. L., & Otterland, A. (1975). The growing epidemic. A survey of smoking habits and attitudes toward smoking among students in grades 7 through 12 in Toledo and Lucas County (Ohio) Public Schools—1964 and 1971. *American Journal of Public Health, 65*(9), 923–938.

Kerlinger, F. N., & Pedhazur, E. (1973). *Multiple regression in behavioral research.* New York: Holt, Rinehart, & Winston.

Kirk, R. E. (1968). *Experimental design: Procedures for the behavioral sciences.* Belmont, CA: Brooks/Cole.

Krosnick, J. A., & Judd, C. M. (1982). Transitions in social influence at adolescence: Who induces cigarette smoking? *Developmental Psychology, 18,* 359–368.

Leventhal, H., & Cleary, P. D. (1980). The smoking problem: A review of the research and theory in behavioral risk modification. *Psychological Bulletin, 88,* 370–405.

Miller, D. T. (1978). What constitutes a self-serving attributional bias? A reply to Bradley. *Journal of Personality and Social Psychology, 36,* 1221–1223.

National Institute of Education. (1979, November). *Teenage smoking: Immediate and long-term patterns.* U.S. Department of Health, Education, and Welfare, Contract No. 400-79-0010.

Omelich, C. L. (1985). *Adolescent smoking: Model validation, risk profile development and intervention assessment.* Final report submitted to the American Cancer Society.

Pedhazur, E. J. (1982). *Multiple regression in behavioral research: Explanation and prediction* (2nd ed.). New York: Holt, Rinehart, & Winston.

Schlenker, B. (1975). Self-presentation: Managing the impression of consistency when reality interferes with self-enhancement. *Journal of Personality and Social Psychology, 32,* 1030–1037.

Thompkins, S. S. (1966). Psychological model for smoking behavior. *American Journal of Public Health, 56,* (Suppl. 2), 17–20.

Whitman, T. L. (1972). Aversive control of smoking behavior in a group context. *Behavior Research and Therapy, 10,* 97–104.

19

Anxiety Research: Present and Future

Donald G. Forgays
University of Vermont

Tytus Sosnowski
University of Warsaw, Poland

Kazimierz Wrzesniewski
Warsaw Medical Academy, Poland

INTRODUCTION

The Nieborow meeting was convened to permit a number of active researchers in the area to discuss important issues in the field of anxiety and, more specifically, to focus on possible integrations of various approaches to anxiety research. What have we learned about this topic as elaborated in the preceding chapters?

We have learned that anxiety can be studied from theoretical or empirical points of view. In the first case, the researcher constructs a model, whether simple or complex, and specifies the relationship of anxiety to other important variables, for example, performance, and indicates the nature of the particular measure(s) of anxiety to be taken. In the second case, the researcher is empirically oriented, defines an area of relationship to be investigated, for example, anxiety decrease associated with relaxation, and employs a measure of anxiety that can be operationally defined, such as a self-report questionnaire. Within either of these broad approaches, the subfocus may be oriented to cognitive, psychophysiological, or behavioral process, or to a combination of these foci, and corresponding measures of anxiety will be indicated and made.

Thus in reviewing the preceding chapters close attention should be paid to the broad and specific approaches that each takes to the study of anxiety, the definition that may be provided of this term, and the specific measures that are made of this variable. When we do so, we find that there are many vagaries concerning the definition of anxiety. Several cognitively oriented contributors to this volume build the idea of expectancy into their definitions. Thus anxiety occurs when there is an expectation of negative events or the perception of threat to the self. Others in this group do not define anxiety or else sidestep the issue by suggesting that anxiety can be viewed in many ways, for example, as an emotion, a motive, a personality trait, and so forth.

The physiologically oriented contributors avoid defining anxiety altogether. However, because their measures commonly involve the autonomic nervous system, by implication, at least, anxiety is related to the functioning of this system.

One of this group does distinguish between cognitive anxiety (again, the expectation of something bad happening) and somatic anxiety (global uneasiness and feelings of alarm). This differentiation serves to remind us that there may be several different types of anxiety. It may well be erroneous to view different anxiety measures as reflecting different aspects of the same entity. Indeed, they may be measuring different entities that, in themselves, may be related or unrelated. We will continue to face this kind of dilemma until we have better developed theory and measurement within this area.

The health section of this book is also lacking in definitions of anxiety. One author, however, does suggest that the Behavioral Inhibition System (BIS) is the neurophysiological substrate for anxiety. This was also implied in one of the physiological chapters. Another health chapter suggests that anxiety occurs when an important response is called for and success of that response is far from guaranteed.

In some senses there are implied operational definitions of anxiety in many of the chapters, as indicated by the measures used in the research described. Thus anxiety is what is measured by a test anxiety scale, a state or trait anxiety scale, the Manifest Anxiety Scale or a subscale of the Profile of Mood States, or by DSM-III-R. Alternatively, anxiety is defined by measures of BIS, by heart rate changes, electrodermal activity changes, or by other autonomic nervous system changes.

We can see that the very reason for the meeting at Nieborow, to stimulate some rapprochement among the various approaches to anxiety, has not been served well at least in terms of the definitional and measurement properties of the term *anxiety*. However, we have come away with reasonably good agreement with respect to two aspects of anxiety: that anxiety involves unpleasant feelings of apprehension and tension, and that anxiety causes activation of the autonomic nervous system. These two aspects of anxiety do appear to be core dimensions of this concept (cf. Spielberger & Rickman, 1990).

In the rest of this chapter, we will attempt to do two things. First, we will summarize and integrate each of the three principal sections of this book in turn. Second, we will discuss the most urgent issues and research requirements in the anxiety area in the near and more distant future. These will have been suggested by our colleagues in their individual chapters or else are based on our own interests and speculations.

SUMMARY AND INTEGRATION

Cognition

For a number of years, studies of the relationship of anxiety and cognition have frequently used test anxiety as the index of anxiety. Selection of this measure appears sound and seems valid because most people face repeated evaluations in school and related settings and they report these events as sources of anxiety. Use of the test anxiety index occurs in several of the cognitive chapters of this book, not in a simple correlative manner, but rather in conjunction with other interesting variables or in theory testing.

For example, Carver and Scheier (Chapter 2) were concerned with how people respond to the experience of anxiety, which they say occurs when a person per-

ceives a threat to the attainment of a desired goal. Reaction to this negative experience is dependent on generalized expectancies about reaching the goal. Confident
persons continue working on goal attainment while doubtful persons discontinue
such efforts and may also disengage from the goal itself. Carver and Scheier assess
these notions in test anxiety and speech anxiety situations and find generally supportive results. The principal contribution of anxiety is *worry,* a cognitive preoccupation with failure, and not emotional reactivity.

These authors label these generalized expectancies "optimism" and "pessimism." The optimist is, of course, the person who copes in a focused manner
with the problem situation while the pessimist is more likely to vent emotion
and to disengage from the threatened goals when matters get too difficult.
These cognitive processes involve continuous monitoring and adjustment, with
feedback loops.

Carver and Scheier report very interesting findings on the optimism/pessimism
dimension with aftercare alcoholics (the relapse rate is greater for pessimists) and
for postpartum depression (pessimists are more likely to experience it). Based on
such promising relationships, future research should expand the practical application of this scale. It is possible, for example, that various intervention and prevention programs might be designed specifically for optimists or for pessimists.

A second expectancy theoretical approach to anxiety was provided by Pekrun
(Chapter 3) with his expectancy value theory of anxiety (EVTA). Defining anxiety,
as had Carver and Scheier, as that which occurs because one anticipates negative
events, EVTA seeks to be a more precise cognitive approach to anxiety than others
presently available. However, it also shares the limitations of other cognitive theories in terms of narrowness of scope and lack of physiological process information.
To test this model, which emphasizes both one's expectations of the outcome of a
threatening situation and the value of various outcomes, Pekrun studied the relationship of test anxiety to academic achievement and its social–educational determinants in Bavarian school children. His evidence suggests that this relationship
exists and that feedback loops operate to link expectancy/value appraisals, anxiety,
and the effects of anxiety. Anxiety influences achievement and achievement influences the development of anxiety. The social/educational anxiety determinants include pressure for achievement, competition, and punishment; family cohesion
correlates negatively with anxiety and appears to operate as a buffer. He concludes
that negative expectancies and values are likely to be primary determinants of
human anxiety by mediating relations between anxiety and achievement and the
influence of social factors on anxiety.

Pekrun's suggestions on the utility of EVTA in therapy and prevention
programs are provocative. He proposes that therapy may be directed to subjective
appraisal systems of clients or to situational variables. Much current therapy is
directed to the modification of subjective appraisal systems but the notion that we
might modify some environmental situations in therapy has appeared in the
literature only recently. His idea that EVTA might be useful in the prevention of
the development of negative beliefs is very interesting, but he does not describe
how this might be done. It will be no easy task. However, his notion of producing
safe environments as a prevention effort fits in well with much of the primary
prevention literature (Forgays, 1983, 1991), and aspects of this goal should be
attainable.

The work of Comunian (Chapter 4) also makes use of test anxiety as the index of anxiety. Her focus, however, is on the self and the role of anxiety in producing disorganization of the self. Her theoretical approach is basically Lewinian but she operationalizes her concern for self/anxiety relationships with the Spielberger scale as an anxiety measure and a Q-sort technique (MIPG) to measure self beliefs, beliefs about how the self is perceived by others, and beliefs about the ideal self.

She found five profiles among the older adolescent subjects on the 22 items of the MIPG scale. The "perfect harmony" profile was associated with the lowest level of anxiety, on both *worry* and *emotionality*. The "fear of being unmasked" and "openness–dependence" profiles were significantly higher on *emotionality*, and the "total rejection" and "accusing others" profiles were significantly higher on the *worry* than the "perfect harmony" profile. Interestingly, there were no profile differences associated with gender. These results suggest different organizational unities of the self for these various profile groups. It will be interesting to see if future research will demonstrate meaningful differences among these profile groups on a variety of other measures, both behavioral and physiological, representing various theoretical positions. In addition, as Comunian has suggested, study should be made of the organizational unity of persons varying widely in anxiety levels, as measured in several different ways.

These studies have all used test anxiety as the anxiety index. However, because test anxiety accounts for only a relatively small amount of the variance in school performance and in cognitive performance generally (Schwartzer, Seipp, & Schwartzer, 1989), it is clear that additional approaches must be developed and used if we are to understand the interrelationships of anxiety and cognition better. It is reassuring that such developments are already occurring, as indicated in the remaining chapters of the cognitive section of this book.

For example, Schönpflug (Chapter 5) examined relationships among anxiety, ability, and performance on mental tasks. Past literature has indicated that high-anxious individuals show higher levels of arousal and expend more effort in achievement situations than do low-anxious subjects (e.g., Eysenck, 1979). This older bottom-up view of arousal starts with external stimulation and proceeds to the central nervous system. Schönpflug seems to prefer the more recent top-down view of arousal in which individuals regulate their own arousal; such intentional activation starts in the central nervous system and goes from there to the relevant muscles. Effort is a self-regulatory process designed to improve performance, and it is clearly a top-down process.

The question Schönpflug sought to answer was whether the arousal systems of anxious persons are also top-down. Are they centrally initiated and controlled by the self, and intentional rather than reactive? Do anxious people perceive more demands in performance situations and intentionally increase their arousal in response to these demands, or do they increase their effort instead? In this conceptualization, performance can vary with both anxiety and effort. His results indicated that an increase in effort produced an emotional and a mental load; higher intelligence helped out with the mental demands while low anxiety contributed to coping with the emotional demands. Only the subject group that was high in ability (intelligence) and low in anxiety improved in all measured aspects of performance with increased effort. Thus, arousal matters only if one has high ability. Persons who are only highly anxious are not more aroused, they are not more active, and they do not demonstrate more effort in performance situations.

These results and conclusions are intriguing indeed, but one has to keep in mind that only a limited measure of anxiety was used. It would be interesting to repeat this paradigm using a variety of anxiety indices, including physiological measures taken throughout the performance sessions. Such measures might prove to be more adequate indices of effort and arousal than those available in this first study.

A very integrated approach to the examination of the interrelationships among anxiety, ability, and motivation is seen in the work of Hagtvet and Min (Chapter 6). These researchers suggest that the fact that test anxiety explains only a limited amount of variance in the very measures of cognitive and school performance that relevant studies seek to understand may be because of the use of simple bivariate correlations between anxiety and performance measures that may even disguise interesting relationships. In addition, past studies have tested performance as a single global measure rather than as a process, which itself may be a better index of performance, especially as related to anxiety. These authors respond to these shortcomings by presenting a model combining anxiety, motivation, and ability, and by using a series of five equivalent tasks to measure performance as a process (Raakeim, 1984).

They believe that intelligence is only involved in performance when there is a midlevel of familiarity with the situation; if there is no familiarity or too much familiarity, intelligence will not be involved. They apply this inverted U notion to ability, problem solving, and anxiety relationships, and incorporate the McClelland-Atkinson motivation theory. Thus a novel situation will produce more uncertainty and a higher level of fear of failure whereas more familiar situations will be associated with less uncertainty and a weaker avoidance tendency. Perceived threat to one's self-concept will elicit state anxiety. As familiarity with the situation increases, threat will vary with the success or failure experiences one has. Success should enhance one's feelings of control; repeated failure will continue the threat and state anxiety while weakening the motive to avoid failure.

They found an important change in the problem-solving process from the first two problems to the remaining three. Fear of failure and intelligence affected only the first problem, state anxiety had no effect on any problem, and there were gender and school differences in state anxiety, implying that one should be careful about subject selection.

They conclude that cognitive performance is not just a function of ability, anxiety, or negative motivation. All three of these factors contribute to performance, but at different times during the problem-solving process, depending on one's familiarity with the situation.

Examining the data of their study, it appears that the tasks used were not really equivalent. Problem 3 had only 20% of subjects solving it, in contrast to over 30% for all other problems, and the problem-solving process is stable after the third problem. This could be because of the separation of subjects into two groups at Problem 3, those continuing to work hard and those who had experienced more failure becoming disengaged. Such a separation would increase the stability of results for later problems. Although the authors believe that disengagement is maximal at the first and fifth problems, it is possible that it is maximal at the third problem, because according to their model, one would have to build up the failure and threat factors through the earlier experiences.

Bonaiuto and colleagues (Chapter 7) raise the issue of the definition of anxiety in their chapter, suggesting that anxiety can be viewed as an emotion, a motivating state, a self-perception, or a trait. They proposed a research paradigm in which measures are made on subjects whose anxiety level is induced from relaxed to very anxious, and in which anxiety is studied in conjunction with other affective and cognitive components. The dependent variables in these several studies concerned emotional and cognitive changes attendant to the stress and relaxation inductions. They included various measures of cause-and-effect attributions, perception of incongruities, and expectations of adequate explanations of the perceived material.

They found that their manipulations were effective, and they did lead to the predicted emotional, motivational, and cognitive changes. In three experiments in which they varied perceptual measures, including subjective clarity of causality and cognitive-based illusory contours, concretely portrayed visual events, and events that were verbally described, they found strong evidence for their predictions. Stress did increase the clarity of these illusory contours and perception of cause-and-effect relationships whereas relaxation decreased these relationships. Differences between the stress and relaxation conditions were statistically significant and there were interesting time effects as well.

They attribute these changes in emotional state and perceptual/cognitive performance to the conflict increase or decrease engendered by their instructional sets and provide evidence that they are not the result of a modification of visual attention that might also have resulted from their induction techniques.

These authors propose measuring these kinds of relationships in "real-life" situations and to use subjects who at experiment onset already measure high or low on anxiety/stress scales. They also propose a number of applied projects suggested by their results, relating the influence of stress and/or relaxation on important attributions of managers, police, judges, juries, clinicians, and patients. These prospects are very exciting and we look forward to seeing some of these observations appearing in future publications.

We can see from these cognitive studies that there has been concern about the definitional properties of anxiety. It is not strange that these authors define anxiety as that which occurs when internal or external signals cause a person to have trepidation about future events. Although this definitional approach may be adequate for the research of these authors, we can see how limited it is. This limitation determines, to a considerable extent, the measurement approach they take to anxiety. Thus, again, it is no surprise that several of them use a single and reasonably uncomplicated index of anxiety, in most cases, a measure of test anxiety.

It is clear that the concept of anxiety is not as uncomplicated as these authors have implied in their selection of measures and procedures. That this self-imposed restriction of focus has resulted in a substantial handicap in the utility of their results is certainly attested to by the fact that test anxiety does not relate well even to cognitive performance, much less to more general performance.

Thus researchers of the relationship of anxiety and cognition will have to expand their paradigms to reflect the various measurement approaches to anxiety. Test anxiety scales may continue to be used, among other self-report measures, but there should be strong consideration of the addition of behavioral and physiological indices of anxiety as well.

Psychophysiology

Psychophysiological research on anxiety and stress has a history as long as psychophysiology itself. Despite this fact, specific relations between anxiety and psychophysiological activity are not yet known, and relevant investigations have generated much controversy concerning the conceptualization of the problem itself.

Up to the middle of the 1960s, the weight of opinion seemed to be that the physiological activity observed in stressful situations may be effectively explained as a nonspecific, energetic component of emotional reaction. Examples of such an approach include sympathetic–adrenal excitation (Cannon, 1929) or activation (Duffy, 1962; Hebb, 1955). Continuing research, however, did not support these univariate conceptualizations. Results of much research suggest that psychophysiological activity can be better explained as a set of separate response patterns having somewhat different functional meanings (Lacey, 1967).

A good example of the pattern approach to psychophysiological activity is the research of Fahrenberg and his co-workers (1986, 1987). Their studies use a multivariate approach (repeated measures of the activity of different physiological systems in different situations) and they indicate the existence of relatively stable situational, individual, and motivational response patterns. Accepting the assumption of the existence of distinct response patterns leads to the issue of their functional and psychological meanings. Researchers working on this problem usually assume that mechanisms of physiological reaction to emotional and stressful stimuli have adaptive value. In particular, one could suggest that the function of psychophysiological mechanisms is to tune the organism to facilitate the best cognitive and behavioral control possible over the environment and, simultaneously, to maintain homeostasis. Of course, the assumption of the adaptive value of psychophysiological change does not necessarily hold for all conditions. For example, it is hard to believe that the massive increase of cardiovascular activity associated with many academic examinations really has a positive adaptive value. However, even if we disregard these relationship vagaries, the issue of the functional meaning of physiological change still remains very complex indeed.

One of the most important problems of behavioral–physiological interrelationships is the question of which level of behavior regulation corresponds to the activity of any particular physiological system. Although many have searched for the psychophysiological correlates of molar behavior, recent research indicates that physiological activity is often associated with psychological processes on a more elementary level. This point of view is emphasized by contemporary systemic approaches (cf. Schwartz, 1986).

An example of this type of interrelationship problem can be found in the research of Stern (Chapter 8). His chapter addresses the relationship between anxiety and eye blinking. His review of the literature and his own research indicate that the eye blink can hardly be regarded as a good index of anxiety, assessed either by psychometric methods or by between-group comparison (as, e.g., between psychiatric patients and healthy subjects). On the other hand, his results indicate that some parameters of the eye blink are related to task demands in vigilance and recognition tests. This suggests that eye blinking may be an index of some elementary cognitive process, such as information acquisition or information retention, rather than an index of a general construct such as anxiety.

A psychophysiological variable that is very frequently used as an index of anxiety is electrodermal activity (EDA). In the opinion of many researchers, both state and trait anxiety should be positively related to phasic or tonic parameters of EDA. This opinion is probably based on the high sensitivity of the electrodermal system to aversive and orienting stimuli (cf. Fowles, 1980; Ohman, 1983). However, results of empirical studies in this area are very far from being unequivocal (cf. Naveteur & Freixa i Baqué, 1987; Stern & Janes, 1973).

The chapters by Sosnowski (Chapter 9) and Naveteur and Freixa i Baqué (Chapter 10) demonstrate particularly well the complexity of the issue of the relationship of physiological activity to anxiety. The aim of Sosnowski's research was to test several hypotheses derived from the theoretical conceptions of Gray and Fowles. According to Fowles (1980), phasic skin conductance and tonic heart rate changes may be regarded as indices of two conceptual, mutually inhibitory systems, proposed by Gray—the Behavioral Inhibition System (BIS) and the Behavioral Approach System (BAS), respectively. According to Gray, BIS and BAS form the physiological bases of anxiety and impulsivity, dimensions regarded as alternatives to Eysenck's extraversion/neuroticism model. Sosnowski's results suggest that under special conditions a negative relationship between these two psychophysiological variables exists, which may be explained as an index of imbalance between the two regulatory systems, BIS and BAS. These data can be viewed as support for Fowles' theory, and, in particular, for the point that activation of BIS results in an increase in electrodermal activity.

On the other hand, the results of the studies of Naveteur and Freixa i Baqué lead to an opposite conclusion. Their two experiments indicate that subjects with higher trait anxiety, assessed by questionnaire, demonstrate lower electrodermal activity in aversive task situations than subjects with lower trait anxiety. They explain these provocative results on the basis of Gray's model. Assuming that BIS should be more highly activated in high- than in low-anxious subjects, they suggest that activation of BIS may lead to the inhibition of electrodermal activity, just as it inhibits programs of overt behavior. Thus the relationship between BIS and electrodermal activity suggested by Naveteur and Freixa i Baqué is opposite to that proposed by Fowles.

The lack of congruence between the studies of Sosnowski and Naveteur and Freixa i Baqué reflects quite well the general controversy concerning electrodermal research on anxiety. One possible explanation of the lack of correspondence is that different electrodermal reactions are, in fact, evoked by different situational demands. This raises the issue of the operationalization of theoretical variables in anxiety research, particularly that with human subjects. Gray (1982), for example, defines very clearly three classes of stimuli that should activate BIS: signals of punishment, signals of nonreward, and orienting (novel) stimuli. However, in experiments with human subjects, and even more so with observations of everyday behavior, the situations are usually much more complex than standard conditioning procedures, and their emotional–motivational meanings may be very difficult to recognize and control. A good example of the difficulty of the operationalization of Gray's theory in relation to human behavior includes problems with the questionnaire measurement of basic personality dimensions proposed by Gray himself (cf. Wilson, Barrett, & Gray, 1989).

Another important issue concerns the relationship between physiological and self-report data. Many studies show that psychophysiological and subjective response patterns to stressful or anxious stimuli need not correspond to each other (cf. Fahrenberg, 1987; Strelau, in press; Wrzesniewski & Sosnowski, 1987). In addition, we know that the validity of self-perception, even in the case of relatively easy-to-detect physiological changes like heart rate, is usually very far from perfect (cf. Katkin, 1985; Schandry & Bestler, in press). Thus it seems unrealistic at this time to expect to find strong, direct relationships between physiological and psychological variables. On the other hand, it is very difficult to accept the thesis that these two kinds of processes are unrelated. The correspondence between physiological and psychological processes remains one of the most difficult problems in our understanding of the mechanisms of human behavior.

In this same context, the chapter by Sokolov (Chapter 11) is especially interesting. Well known for his classical theory of the orienting reflex and later for his theory of sensory information detection, Sokolov proposes here an extension of his sensory detection model to the problem of emotion detection. His data indicates that a three-dimensional model of color space developed on the basis of an analysis of neuronal excitation corresponds well with three-dimensional emotional space developed on the basis of multidimensional scaling of subjective differences among emotional terms. The seeming isomorphism of both spaces opens new perspectives in researching the relationships between physiological and conscious processes, a very exciting prospect indeed.

Any analysis of physiological reactions to emotional stimuli raises the issue of the contribution of genetic and environmental factors to these behaviors. Despite their many obvious limitations, animal studies are among the few available approaches for investigating this problem. Manipulation and control of the genetic factor is, of course, much easier with animals than with humans. The chapter by Matysiak, Ostraszewski, Pisula, and Watras (Chapter 12) addresses the contribution of genetic and environmental (impoverished, enriched, or standard conditions) factors to the need for sensory (light and tactile–kinesthetic) stimulation and to emotional reactivity in rats. Their data seem to support their hypothesis that simpler forms of behavior, such as stimulus seeking, which requires no special training, are under the additive influence of environmental and genetic factors, whereas more complex behavior, such as emotional responses and avoidance learning, is influenced by the interactions of both of these factors. Such findings must, of course, be tested at the human level and this is no small task. Thus the relative contribution of genetic and environmental factors to anxiety behavior largely remains an open question. The results of Matysiak et al. suggest that these relative contributions may vary depending on the complexity of the anxiety response in question.

Health

There are at least four relationships between anxiety and health that are noteworthy. First, anxiety may be regarded as a psychological risk factor because numerous studies indicate that the probability of becoming ill may be increased by frequent exposure to stress situations. More complete analyses of such data, in terms of emotions experienced by the individual, may reveal the role of anxiety in the onset of various diseases. Second, anxiety may be regarded as a symptom of illness, for example, in neurotic disorders. Third, anxiety may be considered a psychological consequence of illness, or as a response to the biological and psychological threat inherent in ill health. Fourth, anxiety can be studied in terms of the intervention techniques that may be used in its reduction. Contributions included in the third section of this book deal with the three latter issues.

Fowles (Chapter 13) presents an analysis of anxiety as a symptom in three important psychopathological syndromes of anxiety disorders described in the DSM-III-R system. The analysis is based on the theoretical concepts of Gray and Barlow, and similarities and differences between these two approaches to anxiety symptoms are outlined by Fowles. This analysis has led him to formulate motivational concepts of anxiety disorders, and to integrate the views of Barlow and Gray. He distinguishes two motivational systems important for understanding anxiety disorders: (a) Barlow's fear or alarm reaction and Gray's fight/flight system, and (b) Barlow's anxiety response and Gray's behavioral system. These two systems differ from each other in the temporal dimension, effects on behavior, and also in terms of the presence or absence of vigilance and worry. This approach permits a better understanding of anxiety disorders because it provides an integration of a psychological approach with a biopharmacological one.

The next two contributions deal with anxiety and other affective states associated with somatic illnesses. Ostrowski (Chapter 14) studied anxiety in patients with myocardial infarction (MI) and factors related to the anxiety level of such patients. This topic is of considerable clinical importance because intense anxiety may have an adverse effect on the course of treatment and recovery from MI. Vegetative and somatic components of anxiety may result in complications during hospitalization and, later, the recovering patient may not participate normally in the activities of daily life because of the motivational components of these changes in affect. The data presented by Ostrowski suggest that level of anxiety and related emotional states depend both on the course of the illness and the amount of time since the heart attack. MI patients who underwent cardiac arrest and clinical death, as compared with those whose MI was uncomplicated, are characterized by higher levels of anxiety and other negative emotional states. Ostrowski's findings also suggest that anxiety level may increase with time, but only in patients whose MI has been complicated by clinical death. This was true not only for state anxiety, but also for trait anxiety as measured by the Spielberger Test. This latter finding is particularly interesting because it corroborates clinical impressions of personality changes in patients suffering from a long-term and dangerous illness.

Emotional consequences of somatic diseases regarded as a special kind of stress situation were studied by Wrzesniewski (Chapter 15). In his research, two types of determinants of the intensity of experienced emotions were considered: situational variables and individual differences. The former include varying levels of risk to life from various diseases, whereas an individual predisposition to specific types of responses in stress situations consisted of a measure of the Type A behavior pattern (TABP). In illnesses involving a high risk to life, TA patients showed more positive emotions and fewer and less intense negative emotions than TB patients. This pattern was reversed in the low-risk patient group, with TA patients displaying stronger negative emotions than TB patients. A more detailed analysis indicated that this seemingly paradoxical result is due to situational characteristics associated with illness other than the degree of risk to life. For TA patients, the psychosocial threat involved in the illness is probably more important than the physical threat.

The next two contributions to this section deal with interventions to reduce anxiety. An attempt was made by Depreeuw and De Neve (Chapter 16) to integrate theoretical, research, and clinical approaches to test anxiety. They propose their own model to explain test anxiety occurrence. The model, based on theories of

Lazarus and Heckhausen and on concepts developed by Gray and Fowles, led them to design a therapeutic program for highly test-anxious students. Two groups of students were identified, those having an active test anxiety profile and those with passive test anxiety. A questionnaire for assessment of the two types of test anxiety was developed, as were two different therapeutic programs, one for each group. This preliminary research program has confirmed the validity of their theoretical concepts and the resulting therapeutic programs.

Reduction of anxiety was one of the objectives of the use of flotation isolation by Forgays and Forgays (Chapter 17). In their first study, a relaxation effect was found in the majority of the float subjects, but there were important individual differences in the intensity of effect. On the basis of their early studies, they believed that if flotation isolation is associated with a reduction in stress, the technique should be helpful in the therapy of persons whose problems are caused by or exacerbated by emotional tension. Stress/tension was hypothesized to enhance tobacco use as well as the occurrence of chronic headaches. This hypothesis was investigated in two independent follow-up studies. In a group of heavy cigarette smokers, a significant reduction in the number of cigarettes smoked as well as several cases of smokers quitting smoking were found at a follow-up 2 years after a series of floats. For people suffering muscle contraction headaches, other interventions were used in addition to flotation isolation. Outcome was measured at 6 months' follow-up. The best outcome was found in the group in which floating was supplemented with progressive muscle relaxation training. The last study carried out by Forgays and Forgays examined whether the relaxation effect obtained by means of flotation isolation would be modified in Type A people. In comparison to TB subjects, TA subjects showed more emotional tension reduction, as assessed by questionnaire.

The research of Covington and Omelich (Chapter 18) does not deal directly with the topic of anxiety. However, it is quite likely that stress/anxiety is a component of the decisionmaking process regarding cigarette smoking by the young. Their findings constitute an important contribution to knowledge about this health hazard.

The focus of the study was the intention of young adolescents to smoke in the future based on a costs/benefits analysis. Their principal finding was that the costs and benefits of a decision to smoke varied significantly with the smoking classification of the respondent (never, experimental, ex-smoker, and regular smoker). Importantly, the perceived costs and benefits of smoking operate largely as mediators of self-responsibility, and costs were more salient than benefits in this regard. The feeling of a youngster of upset and guilt because parents and friends would be disturbed by his/her decision to smoke was related negatively to smoking category, with the regular smoker perceiving less upset than the never-smoker, and so on.

Based on these results, interventional strategies, whether for primary prevention or for cutback or cessation, would emphasize self-involvement and self-responsibility. The fact that self-upset is so involved in this decisionmaking process indicates a role of stress/anxiety in these relationships. This was especially so for the group most vulnerable to smoking initiation, the 14-year-olds. Thus future interventions for cigarette smoking for 11- to 16-year-olds might well emphasize self-involvement and self-integrity and focus less on the health risks of smoking. Although health risks may be a part of an information campaign, these students are either aware of these risks or deal with them by denial or by indulging in magical thinking. Therefore the knowledge of health risks alone plays little role in the decision to smoke.

These studies represent three of the four approaches to research on the relationship of anxiety to health. The research findings indicate that this relationship is very complex. Various theoretical concepts may serve as a rationale for the description of particular aspects of this relationship. However, selection of a single theory is associated with the risk of narrowing one's field of research, which may then have adverse clinical implications with respect to both the diagnosis and treatment of illness. Clinicians accepting a single narrow approach in their search for causes of anxiety will be limited to those that correspond with their theoretical assumptions. This, in turn, will determine the therapeutic interventions that they use. On the other hand, a general theoretical rationale is necessary for conducting research, which will then be useful in clinical work. A possible solution to this dilemma is to attempt to integrate various theoretical approaches, which will provide the basis for a more comprehensive description of the complex relationship between anxiety and health. It will also provide an opportunity for more efficient clinical interventions. Keys to such an approach can be found in the various chapters of the health section of this book. This approach may also be helpful to the development of future relevant research, which should begin with the consideration of a variety of problems concerning the relationship between anxiety and health or illness. Data presented here may be useful to such development by highlighting the already known aspects of the problem, pointing out those that require empirical verification, and outlining an appropriate sequence of issues to be investigated.

FUTURE RESEARCH

We have summarized what appears to be a reasonable representation of current research in anxiety, at least in the three areas defined: cognition, psychophysiology, and health. The panorama has been broad, much more so than that of other available books on anxiety, which usually focus on a single theoretical position, a single measure of anxiety, or on a single dependent variable, such as heart rate. On the basis of the present material, what appear to be the most important issues and promising research directions in future anxiety research?

It seems clear that anxiety research has burgeoned without a great deal of concern for theory. Anxiety theory that does exist is relatively undeveloped. One objective of science, of course, is to construct theories to explain facts and in just this way anxiety theories should attempt to explain anxious behavior. We identify the most urgent need in the anxiety area to be the development of more sophisticated theoretical positions. Relationships should be carefully thought out and relevant mechanisms should be identified. Only then should there be an attempt to describe the role of anxiety with respect to relationships with other variables and the kind of measure(s) to be made. Rather than to use anxiety measures that are already available, especially if they do not match the needs of the theoretical formulation well, researchers would then be under pressure to develop new measures or perhaps to use multiple existing measures. Both these resolutions would have a beneficial effect on the field. Those who are less theoretically inclined would be free to continue to do empirical anxiety research but we would ask them to attend to the additional points that follow.

A second important issue has been identified earlier in this chapter and it concerns the definition of anxiety. Just what is anxious behavior? The answer to this question is varied. The clinician may view a set of symptoms as an acceptable answer. Some researchers may prefer to describe specific procedures used to produce anxiety as the answer. Physiologically oriented researchers may define anxiety in terms of the action of certain anxiolytic drugs. Other psychologists accept anxiety as what is measured by self-report questionnaires.

Many researchers in the anxiety field do not offer a definition of this construct even though it is central to their investigations. It is true that one can proceed in such research with implied definitions, based on the measures of independent and dependent variables of the study, but it is prudent to pay more attention to definitional aspects of the anxiety concept as it is employed in the study. Doing so would also serve to bridge the gap between theoretical and empirical orientations.

Of those included in this book, the cognitive researchers have been most diligent in defining anxiety and there has been good agreement among them with respect to the properties of anxiety delineated. The definition usually includes expectations of future events with attendant varying levels of intensity. The definition is operationalized usually in terms of a relatively simple self-report measure. The definitional commonality observed may be illusory in the sense that the various vagaries in the definition have been dealt with expeditiously, that is, not directly, but through the selection of a compromise anxiety measure and a limited research paradigm. These latter adjustments may reflect a kind of social contagion in anxiety research and especially in test anxiety research. Future cognition/anxiety researchers should attempt to provide direct measures of the components of their definition and to operationalize them in appropriate measures.

Definitional issues of anxiety show no improvement in the psychophysiological and health chapters of this book. Psychophysiologists seem content with one or another indices of autonomic nervous system activity as an anxiety indicator, whereas health researchers pay more attention to the health issue than to the adequate measurement of the anxiety process that has led to or exacerbated the illness. We hope that future relevant research will attempt to specify more exactly the role of anxiety in physiological and illness processes and to respond to the measurement requirements so identified. Health research in anxiety should not be viewed as orthogonal to the cognitive, psychophysiological, and behavioral approaches in this area. Rather, it is an applied orientation and it may make use of one or more of these approaches and the inherent measures of anxiety implied.

We have been concerned in the past at not having found meaningful relationships among various measures of anxiety, especially those resulting from research reflecting these different approaches. This has led some to suggest the possibility of different kinds of anxiety. This may be so. But it may also be that our definitions and measures are at fault and we should try to improve these, at least until theory is better developed in the area.

An offshoot of the definitional problem just described is the precision of measurement of whatever definition of anxiety one finds appropriate. If the definition has a number of subterms, each subterm must be described so as to permit direct measurement of all properties in an operational manner. Precise operational measurement is only a beginning, for it does not guarantee the goodness of the measure. The goodness of the measure must be determined as usual in terms of its predictive utility as well as its contribution to theory development.

As we continue to be unclear about an acceptable general definition of anxiety and of the theoretical underpinnings of this construct, early future research should consider the use of multiple anxiety measures within a single focused area of research, such as the relationship of anxiety to cognition or to illness. Thus those who use self-report indices could use several such measures, psychophysiological researchers could use several measures of autonomic nervous system functioning, and so on. In the selection of multiple measures, care should be taken that the measures do not reflect disparate theoretical development or conflicting intended purposes.

Use of carefully selected multiple measures will have at least two benefits. It should expand the likelihood of finding new relationships in the area of concern because presumably the additional measures will add to knowledge about measure interrelationship. Moreover, this approach might permit the development of somewhat more sophisticated theory in this important area.

Finally, the most apparent gap in anxiety research is the lack of research designs that cut across the various areas of measurement concerned. This clearly includes the cognitive, physiological, and health research areas described above, and the measures of anxiety that these projects have used. It is critical that future research designs include the anxiety variables, measured in more than one way, and across focus areas. Thus future research should be directed to the understanding of the relationship of cognitive, psychophysiological, and behavioral variables to anxiety measures. This may not be as difficult as it seems. For example, early studies could simply expand the number of anxiety measures that are obtained. A cognitively oriented study might well include a measure of heart rate as well as one of test anxiety. A psychophysiologically oriented study could include a measure such as STAI as well as EDA, and so on.

These are small and feasible steps. Ultimately, however, we should develop paradigms that will include several anxiety measures that should reflect the three principal measurement areas: cognitive, psychophysiological, and behavioral.

The procedures that we have outlined here will define the kinds of facts that are relevant to the study of anxiety, those that must be explained by a "theory" of anxiety. To date, in anxiety research we have seen different sets of facts, different methodological approaches, and different classes of theory. There is a critical question as to whether all these observations have something in common. Is there something holding these disparate data together, similar to a factor "g" in intelligence? Correlational analyses seem to suggest that this is not the case. Much research indicates that high correlation coefficients are not found between different anxiety indices such as questionnaire responses, performance scores, and physiological measures. This being the case, we are again reminded of the need to define operationally what the term *anxiety* means in any piece of research and what kinds of facts a particular theory "explains."

Thus our future roles in anxiety research will be to collect many relevant facts and to focus on the regulatory mechanisms responsible for the various behavioral changes observed. Instead of investigating a simple relationship, such as that between anxiety and behavior, we should examine the various regulatory mechanisms involved in the control of anxious behavior and the interaction of these mechanisms. We should be concerned about how the subject processes information about physiological change, how and to what degree physiological processes are mediated by conscious mechanisms, and so on. There is little doubt that we should emphasize the development of better theories of anxiety to explain how different regulatory mechanisms are integrated in the mediation of anxious behavior.

REFERENCES

Cannon, W. B. (1929). *Bodily changes in pain, hunger, fear, and rage* (2nd ed.). New York: Appleton-Century-Crofts.

Duffy, E. (1962). *Activation and behavior.* New York: Wiley.

Eysenck, H. J. (1967). *The biological basis of personality.* Springfield, IL: Charles C Thomas.

Eysenck, M. W. (1979). Anxiety, learning and memory: A reconceptualization. *Journal of Research in Personality, 13,* 363–385.

Fahrenberg, J. (1986). Psychological individuality: A pattern approach to personality research and psychosomatic medicine. *Advances in Behaviour Research and Therapy, 8,* 43–100.

Farhenberg, J. (1987). Concepts of activation and arousal in theory of emotionality (neuroticism): A multivariate conceptualization. In J. Strelau & H. Eysenck (Eds.), *Personality dimensions of arousal* (pp. 99–120). New York: Plenum.

Forgays, D. G. (1983). Primary prevention of psychopathology. In M. Hersen, A. E. Kazdin & A. S. Bellack (Eds.), *The clinical psychology handbook.* New York: Pergamon Press.

Forgays, D. G. (1991). Primary prevention of psychopathology. In M. Hersen, A. E. Kazdin & A. S. Bellack (Eds.), *The clinical psychology handbook.* New York: Pergamon Press.

Fowles, D. C. (1980). The three arousal model: Implications of Gray's two-factor learning theory for heart rate, electrodermal activity, and psychopathy. *Psychophysiology, 17,* 87–104.

Gray, J. A. (1982). *The neuropsychology of anxiety: An enquiry into the functions of the septo-hippocampal system.* New York: Oxford University Press.

Hebb, D. O. (1955). Drives and the C.N.S. (conceptual nervous system). *Psychological Review, 62,* 243–254.

Katkin, E. S. (1985). Blood, sweat, and tears: Individual differences in autonomic self-perception. *Psychophysiology, 22,* 125–137.

Lacey, J. I. (1967). Somatic response patterning and stress: Some revisions of activation theory. In M. H. Appley & R. Trumbull (Eds.), *Psychological stress: Issues in research* (pp. 14–44). New York: Appleton-Century-Crofts.

Navctcur, J., & Freixa i Baqué, F. (1987). Individual differences in electrodermal activity as a function of subjects anxiety. *Personality and Individual Differences, 8,* 615–626.

Ohman, A. (1983). The orienting response during Pavlovian conditioning. In D. A. T. Siddle (Ed.), *Orienting and habituation: Perspectives in human research* (pp. 315–369). Chichester: Wiley.

Raakeim, K. (1984). *Why intelligence is not enough.* Bergen, Norway: Sigma.

Schandry, R., & Bestler, M. (in press). On the relationship between cardiodynamics and heartbeat perception. *Psychophysiology.*

Schwartz, G. E. (1986). Emotion and psychophysiological organization. In M. G. H. Coles, E. Donchin & S. W. Porges (Eds.), *Psychophysiology: Systems, processes, and applications* (pp. 354–377). Amsterdam: Elsevier.

Schwarzer, R., Seipp, B., & Schwarzer, C. (1989). Mathematics performance and anxiety: A meta-analysis. In R. Schwarzer, H. M. Van der Ploeg & C. D. Spielberger (Eds.), *Advances in test anxiety research* (Vol. 6, pp. 105–119). Lisse, The Netherlands: Swets & Zeitlinger.

Spielberger, C. D., & Rickman, R. L. (1990). Assessment of state and trait anxiety in cardiovascular disorders. In D. G. Byrne & R. H. Rosenman (Eds.), *Anxiety and the heart* (pp. 73–92). Washington, DC: Hemisphere.

Stern, J. A., & Janes, C. L. (1990). Personality and psychopathy. In W. F. Prokasy & D. C. Raskin (Eds.), *Electrodermal activity in psychosocial research* (pp. 283–346). New York: Academic Press.

Strelau, J. (1991). Are psycho-physiological/physical scores good candidates for diagnosing temperament/personality traits and for a demonstration of the construct validity of psychometrically measured traits? *European Journal of Personality, 5,* 323–342.

Wilson, G. D., Barrett, P. T., & Gray, J. A. (1989). Human reactions to reward and punishment: A questionnaire examination of Gray's personality theory. *British Journal of Psychology, 80,* 509–515.

Wrzesniewski, K., & Sosnowski, T. (1987). Anxiety and perception of real and imagined stress situations. *Polish Psychological Bulletin, 3,* 149–158.

Index